On Soul and Earth

On Soul and Earth offers an original perspective on the relationship between the environment and the human psyche. Physical spaces contribute to the building of identity through personal experience and memory. Places evoke emotions and carry their own special meanings.

Elena Liotta and her contributors also explore the neglected topics of migration and travel. The author has extensive clinical experience of working with patients from a wide variety of national and cultural backgrounds. Globalization is present in the clinical office as well as in the wider world and the transformations currently being wrought in the areas of cultural and national identity also impact on clinical work.

This book will be of interest to Jungian analysts as well as psychotherapists and mental health professionals, especially those who are addressing transcultural and multicultural issues including voluntary or enforced migration. It will also appeal to urban planners, architects and those interested in environmental issues.

Elena Liotta is a Jungian analyst with an international background. She has a private practice in Italy and works as a consultant for the public sector, teaching, supervising, and creating projects in the fields of education and social policy, including refugee and migrant services. She is a member of APA Div 34 Environmental and Population Psychology.

On Soul and Earth

The psychic value of place

Elena Liotta

With contributions by
Elena Angelini, Massimo Buttarini,
Flavia D'Andreamatteo, Marcella Fragapane,
Riccardo Mondo, David Peat, Luciano Perez,
Ursula Prameshuber, Ali Rashid,
Massimiliano Scarpelli, Silvia Tomasi

Translated from the Italian by Erika Pauli

Routledge
Taylor & Francis Group

LONDON AND NEW YORK

First published as *Su anima e terra* by Edizioni Magi

This translation first published 2009
by Routledge
27 Church Road, Hove, East Sussex BN3 2FA

Simultaneously published in the USA and Canada
by Routledge
270 Madison Ave, New York, NY 10016

*Routledge is an imprint of the Taylor & Francis Group, an Informa
business*

Typeset in Times by
RefineCatch Limited, Bungay, Suffolk
Printed and bound in Great Britain by
TJ International Ltd, Padstow, Cornwall
Paperback cover design by Lisa Dynan
Paperback cover image by Alessandro Bee

This publication has been produced with paper manufactured to
strict environmental standards and with pulp derived from
sustainable forests.

British Library Cataloguing in Publication Data
A catalogue record for this book is available from the British Library

Library of Congress Cataloging-in-Publication Data
Liotta, Elena.
    [Su anima e terra. English]
    On soul and earth : the psychic value of place / Elena Liotta.
        p. cm.
    Includes bibliographical references and index.
    1. Geographical perception. 2. Place (Philosophy) 3. Human
beings – Effect of environment on.   4. Human territoriality.
5. Emigration and immigration – Psychological aspects. 6. Voyages
and travels – Psychological aspects.   I. Title.
    G71.5.L5613 2009
    304.2′3 – dc22

                                                    2008022602

ISBN: 978–0–415–46148–1 (hbk)
ISBN: 978–0–415–46149–8 (pbk)

Dedicated to my mother, my father and my brother,
to Piercarlo and Monona,
to Fabio, Pablo and Alejandro,
to Michelina and Agatino,
to Amelia and Tina,
to my friends,
to my patients,
to all those
who have experienced migration

Contents

List of contributors

Elena Angelini is an architect, PhD in architectural and urban planning and was professor under contract in Architectural Planning in the "Ludovico Quaroni" Department of Architecture of the Università degli Studi "La Sapienza" in Rome between 1999 and 2004. She has written various articles on the relationship between contemporary and popular architecture (*Edilizia Popolare e Metamorfosi*). She was a researcher at the Dipartimento di Progettazione Architettonica e Urbana del Paesaggio at the same university, and is working on a monograph on the idea of space and its representation in illustration. She lives and works in Rome.

Alessandro Bee (photographer) has a degree in natural sciences and is specialized in teaching. He is a traveler and photographer. In addition to one-man shows and a book on Africa (*Africa. Deserti e savane – Deserts and savannah*, Abecwin, Moncalieri, 2003), his articles (text and photos) have appeared in the journal *Piemonte Parchi*.

Massimo Buttarini is a Jungian analyst. He also works with forensic psychology and clinical criminology, psychology of development and education, as a consulting psychologist for parents and teachers, and in the field of the psychology of work and organizations. He is the president and founder of the CESCRIV (Centro Studi sul Crimine Violento – Study Center on Violent Crime) and is the author of *Serial Killer: un approccio psicologico giuridico*, Edizioni Experta, Forli.

Flavia D'Andreamatteo is a Jungian analyst and sandplay therapist and has a private practice. She is a member of CIPA (Italian Center of Analytical Psychology) and IAAP (International Association of Analytical Psychology), AISPT (Italian Association for Sand Play Therapy) and ISST. She is collaborator in a research project with the Chair of Special Pedagogy – Department of Educational Science, Università RomaTre. From 1983 to 2006 she was in charge of the workshops of psychiatric rehabilitation at various ASL (Italian Public Health System) centers. She has planned and directed social–cultural interventions in favor of the physically disabled in

Italy and elsewhere in Europe and has various articles, documentaries and educational audiovisual materials to her name.

Marcella Fragapane[1] teaches art education. She is a painter (having studied at the Brera Fine Arts Academy), narrator of myths and fables, passionately interested in child creativity and art. She gives training seminars for teachers and parents, workshops on artistic languages and expression and on the educational value of the fable, and oversees stage installations in schools. Fascinated by the "shadow" since she was a child, she has made it the object of expressive studies in the theater and in psychopedagogic areas. She founded the International Festival of the Shadow Theater in Staggia Senese in 1996, and took over the artistic direction in 2001. She has collaborated with the CRT of Milan, the Teatro La Scala in Milan for "La Scala nelle Scuole", RAI (Italian television), UNICEF, town councils, libraries, schools and education authorities in various Italian regions. Publications, interviews, articles and videos on her work are available.

Riccardo Mondo is a psychologist and psychotherapist, and a member of the AIPA (Italian Association of Analytical Psychology) and of the IAAP (International Association of Analytical Psychology). He has been active clinically, didactically and culturally in the field of dynamic psychology for several years. He has written on psychoanalytical subjects, primary prevention and psychosocial rehabilitation. He is the author of *L'Arco e la freccia. Prospettive per una genitorialità consapevole* (Edizione Magi, Rome, 2003) and editor (with Luigi Turinese) of *Caro Hillman . . . venticinque scambi epistolari con James Hillman* (Bollati Boringhieri, Turin, 2004).

David Peat is a theoretical physicist. He studied with D. Bohm and has done research in England and in Canada with the National Research Council. His fields are quantistic theory and the theories of chaos and complexity. His scientific interests subsequently included humanistic studies, with meetings and interdisciplinary publications ranging from the Native Americans to Jung's work (on synchronicity and other themes), creativity and art. Since 1996 he has been living in Pari, in Tuscany, where he created the Pari Center for New Learning. His book *Pathways of Chance* (Pari Publishing, Pari) has also appeared in Italian as *Sentieri del Caso* (Di Renzo Editore, Rome, 2003).

Luciano Perez, MD, psychotherapist, is a trainer, teacher and supervisor of CIPA (Centro Italiano di Psicologia Analitica), a member of IAAP (International Association for Analytical Psychology), of the Società Italiana di Storia delle Religioni, and of the Associazione Amici di Eranos

---

1 Marcella Fragapane's contribution appears in Chapter 7.

(Ascona, Switzerland), and honorary president of the association "Amici della Collina" (Catania) for the study of archetypal and imaginal psychology. As a clinical psychologist, he works with dreams, religions and mythology, images and archetypal psychology. His essays and articles have been published in various journals and books. He has also translated and edited many books, including *Analisi dei sogni* [*Dream Analysis*], *La psicologia del kundalini yoga* [*The Psychology of Kundalini Yoga*] (Bollati Boringhieri) and *Visioni* [*Visions*] (2 vols, Edizioni Magi) by C.G. Jung, *L'alchimia delle parole* [*The Alchemy of Discourse*] by P. Kugler (Moretti & Vitali, Bergamo), *Animali guida* [*Animal Guides*] by N. Russack (Moretti & Vitali), and *Jung e la creazione della psicologia moderna* [*Jung and the Making of Modern Psychology*] by Sonu Shamdasani (Edizioni Magi).

Ursula Prameshuber is a psychologist, a psychotherapist, and a member of CIPA (Centro Italiano di Psicologia Analitica), of IAAP (International Association of Analytical Psychology) and of IARPP (International Association of Relational Psychotherapy and Psychoanalysis). Born in Austria, she lives in Rome where she maintains a private practice.

Ali Rashid[2] was First Secretary of the General Palestinian Delegation in Italy. He is among the founders of the Palestinian Movement for Culture and Democracy and was a member of the Chamber of Deputies in the Italian Parliament. He has published *Con I Palestinesi* (Massari, Bolsena, 2002) and *Orgogli e Pregiudizi* (edited by M. Gambino, Manni, Lecce, 2001) and has given many interviews for the press and television media.

Massimiliano Scarpelli is a psychologist and psychotherapist, a member of the AIPA (Associazione Italiana di Psicologia Analitica), and health manager of the ASL 1 (State Medicare Organization) of Naples, the city where he also maintains a private practice. He has done research in the Jungian field on the role of the symbolic function and the theme of individuation, and has published in journals including *Il giornale storico di psicologia dinamica* and *Studi Junghiani*.

Silvia Tomasi is a psychologist whose dissertation was on L. Binswanger. A member of the Comitato per il Telefono Azzurro in Rome, she works to make adults aware of the rights of children and for the prevention of abuse of minors. She is interested in the mother–child relationship, beginning with the emotional experiences of pregnancy and birth. She practices Qi Gong Taoist medicine.

---

2   Ali Rashid's contribution appears in Chapter 7.

Acknowledgments

I wish to thank Alessandro Bee for the cover photo and Bruno Liotta, Fausto Ferrara, Francesco Galli, Alberto Tessore, Daniele Vita, for their photographs. Cinzia Catena for her sculpture, Attilio Pierelli for his sculptures, Paola Maestroni for her etchings. Marcella Fragapane and Ali Rashid for their contribution to Chapter 7. My gratitude goes also to Paola Coppola Pignatelli, Paolo Aite, Sergio Mellina, Nino Di Paolo, David Peat and Maureen Doolan, Carla Zickfeld and Stephan Karkow. A special loving thought in memory of Mark Braun, architect, with whom I discussed key issues of soul and earth.

Special thanks to Cristina Boserman, who contributed to the retrieval of quotations and references in English, as did Matelda Talarico.

For the English translation I deeply thank Erika Bizzarri Pauli, migrant herself, with whom we started and concluded this long, intense and sometimes difficult journey.

My thanks, as always, to Paolo, my companion, for his support.

Introduction

Beginning with one's self

In a sense the theme of migration, and of the relationship with places, has accompanied me since I was born. For I too am a migrant. Unfortunately, yet also luckily, I belong to a sub-group of persons rarely recognized as migrants, since they are those fortunate few who apparently suffered no serious trauma as a result of their experience. For a long time I felt privileged. All the benefits I received because I was born in a foreign country and had traveled as a child were always being pointed out to me: knowing several languages; having seen, touched, eaten, enjoyed different things; being a bearer of something new wherever I happened to be. I was something special here, because I had been there. And vice versa.

Adults have no idea how much what they believe to be an advantage turns out to be an affliction for children, embarrasses them, makes them suffer. In the 1950s and 1960s my experience was not nearly as common as it is today. I almost felt guilty because being special gave me no pleasure.

When I was asked to say something in Spanish or English, to sing a song, to describe the places I had seen, to say what people in other countries, known first-hand, were like, or to describe what it felt like to travel by air, or whatever else, I always felt as if I was being quizzed, or somehow pressurized into sharing something intimate that I might not want to share.

It was not until I was an adult that I came into contact with the other aspect of migration, which brought me closer to those less fortunate than me. Even now, after years of clinical work with foreign patients and years of reflection on my personal itinerary, seen in the light of my knowledge of depth psychology, I still ask myself if, as one of the "fortunate," the irremediable breaks in the continuity of my life left a permanent mark, what must the exile, the displaced person, the political refugee, the emigrant escaping poverty, feel. They risk their lives on ramshackle boats or in dangerous hiding places, and for what? Paradoxically, migration in the global society is even more hazardous now than before, despite the fact that transportation on the whole is safer and more comfortable. Reception of the migrant in the foreign country has also become more ambiguous and the reality less promising. But I will discuss this later.

Actually my life as migrant was not initially of my choosing – and this is something I can share with those forced to migrate – nor did it depend on my parents, for I was born where they were at the time, in the city of Buenos Aires in South America. They too had been born elsewhere, my father in Tripoli in North Africa (once again in a land different from that of his parents, who were born in Sicily), while my mother's native land was Northern Italy. A maternal uncle had already gone to Argentina in the first wave of migration in the 1900s, and he stayed there the rest of his life. Together with the determining encounter of my parents, which took place on the ship to Buenos Aires, this unknown relative was one of the reasons why I was born where I was.

The more recent family, on both sides, also migrated. Some returned to Europe but not to the place of origin. There are not many of us and we are scattered, although bonds of affection exist.

The psychological and psychopathological themes that pass from one generation to the next, and with which they eventually come to terms, are known in psychological jargon as family "transgenerationality." I don't know if this hypothesis also applies to migrant families. Surely, though, some family migrations can be transmitted, like an echo, leaving an indelible mark on the itinerary of the individual lives and, sooner or later, someone will pay the price for the initial separation. I followed many patients, always among the fortunate ones, who returned to Italy at times as third or fourth generation, with scraps of collective memory, no longer knowing the language (already lost in the second generation), to seek their roots, to fall in love with an Italian, marry an Italian, study Italian art, attempting to capture something lost but which seemed to be indispensable in going on with their lives.

When I was beginning to work as a psychotherapist, receiving foreign patients and reflecting on their unique situations, *Psychoanalytic Perspectives on Migration and Exile* by Leòn and Rebeca Grinberg had just come out in Spanish. These two Argentinian psychoanalysts concluded their introduction by saying: "naturally our own migratory experience is not extraneous to the subject" (Grinberg and Grinberg 1989). The book became a classic for those who wanted to delve more deeply into the question and I always kept this in mind, with regard to both my work and my personal story.

The Grinbergs devote two chapters to "Those who cannot return" and "Those who return." I never went back to the city where I was born or to the places I lived in as a child. Yet I could have. I traveled elsewhere, in places that were geographically close, but never the same. I didn't consciously avoid them. It just didn't happen and the years passed, but perhaps sooner or later I will return. It is as if, in the meanwhile, the past has become a poem, a painting, an experience intuitively alive and available, but concretely out of reach. A perennial and subtle nostalgia for places that in any case would no longer be the same and that I wouldn't have seen changing. Or in which parallel stories of life would have taken place. It is all quite complex. For example, I am often saddened by the thought that if I had remained in Argentina, for age and idealism, I would have ended up among the *desaparecidos*. Actually I had disappeared from a land, but to be alive in another.

Subsequently, during my years in Venezuela, I became acquainted with the local history, that of the colonized Indios, the geography, the heroes, the folk traditions. This left in me a mosaic of sensations – colors, odors, atmospheres – and also of emotional and spiritual values, which I never encountered again in my subsequent and more intellectual European education. Yet I realize that my foundations and my cultural instruments belong to the Italian and European culture, consolidated by classical studies and mediated by an open democratic family. Despite this, however, when I had the chance to choose, I continued to look elsewhere, always feeling the call of the "rest of the world."

At the university I turned to Asia, a part of the mysterious world I had not yet explored, fascinated by its history, art, religions and philosophies. Here too, the emotional and spiritual values, the indigenous peoples and their traditions gave me more than the European culture where I sought out the highest moments, above all in the past. While the Italian university ambience in the 1970s was multicultural, it was different from what it is today. At the time there were Argentinians, Chileans, other South Americans, Greeks, who were all escaping from difficult political situations, and were in a sense "political refugees." India at the time appeared as the goal for initiation journeys, London as an obligatory stopover, the United States as a country to travel "on the road."

In its geography and in the meanings it takes on, the collective imaginary of places, above all for young people, varies from generation to generation. At a certain point, my landing in the field of analytical psychology gave me a sort of framework for this wandering and also provided me with a key to interpreting the diversity of the human experience from inside and in its universal foundations.

The land where I chose to live, where I have my home and where I welcome my dear ones, has nothing to do with the various scattered roots of my family and my personal past. Yet I feel at home here, in Orvieto, an Etruscan and medieval town in Central Italy. On one hand I could say, as the Grinbergs observe, that "I don't belong to any place and that I am a citizen of the world." On the other, I live in a specific place of my own choosing, and I am a citizen here in every sense and with all my senses. I belong, but there is no actual identification. Yet my love for the places, the daily living, the relationship with the community, is all very alive and present.

I must add that I don't consider this landfall as the exclusive fruit of a successful migration story. It has become clear to me that one never returns, one always goes away, as the Grinbergs say in a sort of epilogue to their book. And this does not depend on concrete goings and comings, but involves one's personal "process of individuation," in the words of the founder of analytical psychology, Carl Gustav Jung, who was never personally subjected to the trauma of migration. Yet, aside from his journeys for work and for love of knowledge, he too undertook a long inner journey, even though he remained anchored to his land where, towards the end, he built his most intimate refuge, the Tower of Bollingen.

The point is that, in various modes and measures, the psychological dynamics and the attachments set in motion by migration and exile are basically like those the non-emigrant feels in situations of change or loss, personal or relative to his community. For those who are born and grow up in the same place, sharing culture, values and traditions, there are no particular incongruities in the way the territory and the social context are mutually reflected, forming what is defined as "cultural identity." If, however, historical events interfere with the natural development of the life of the group – as is so often the case today – the pattern will change. We cannot yet say what will happen to stable cultural identities in the face of the changes brought on by economic globalization.

For the migrant, development has its ups and downs. He has already been subjected in the first person to a trauma and each time must find solutions that enable him to survive physically and psychologically.

Above all there is the problem of language, the most powerful cultural intermediary, vehicle for thought and symbol, principal entrance portal to social relations. Language is also the cultural foundation of the community, written in the Book, the sacred text which is Law, the inner place for many migrants. In his constant search for equilibrium the migrant must constantly modulate his relationship between the concrete and the symbolic levels of existence. Deprived of the concreteness of his own land, as it has been internalized, he is forced to turn to an inner level, which I define here as soul. The "roots of the soul," which ideally permit survival everywhere in the world throughout one's life, are also subject to development, as are the geographical roots of birth and the subsequent space–time locations in the world.

My work as psychoanalyst has given me an understanding of the subtleties of this relationship between earth and soul, between inside and outside, between symbol and concrete reality. This psychological understanding differs from the descriptions, representations, stories told by writers and artists in general, many of whom have first-hand experience of migration and have expressed themselves profoundly and exquisitely on the various subjects I will deal with.

There is a "land of the soul" that can make the real earth itself less demanding and less powerful. This place of the soul is not that of the rational and intellectual mind, of so-called linear thought on which Western culture has been prevalently founded in the past few centuries and which is currently in thrall to scientific and technological aspects and unable to satisfy fully the complex psychological needs of human beings. Nor can it constitute a solid group bond, for it often neglects all those aspects that are channeled, in a massive and harmful form, into the subcultures of superstition, commercial spiritualism, the emotional television ranting, racism and exasperated localism. Linear thinking continues to ignore what the psychoanalysts call, in an all-inclusive term, the Unconscious: that part of the human mind that projects its shadow onto reality, but whose violence is such that expert political analysts would do well to be more humble and less sure of their interpretations of human, social and historical matters.

The exponents of globalization treat the phenomenon of migration as if it were a game of chess with human beings as chessmen, manipulated in groups, large or small, by the economic requirements of the few. On the collective psychological level it is like playing with a time bomb.

The idea of a uniform, homogeneous planetary population, where everyone has the same needs and aspirations which our consumer and welfare society naively thinks it can satisfy, is anti-psychological. It is literally *out of place* on a concrete level where things are the other way round, marked by a fierce territorialism, not only with respect to one's own country but even one's own district, street or tiny village, competing with another equally remote village just up the way. As has always been the case.

In the following chapters I will attempt to deal with many of the themes mentioned here in the perspective of Jungian depth psychology, upon which I chose to base my profession, at the same time acknowledging the contributions of other authors who have enriched my study.

Contributions by a few colleagues follow the principal body of this text, an encounter with different experiences and interests, in the world of writing, where we all met, and where we would now like to welcome the reader in the same spirit.

The meaning of the book as a whole is well represented by the cover picture: a traveler, North African, walking in the desert, in an open space, a land where there is no hindrance to the journey, where the elements are essential and where belonging to a culture asks very little of the earth. The image is poetic and not political. Nowadays this cannot be taken for granted.

In Jung's words:

> The deeper we penetrated into the Sahara the more time slowed down for me; it even threatened to move backwards. The shimmering heat waves rising up contributed a good deal to my dreamy state, and when we reached the first palms and dwelling of the oasis, it seemed to me that everything here was exactly the way it should be and the way it had always been.
>
> (Jung 1963:268)

It was, for him, the profound impression of an infinite duration.

The title, *On Soul and Earth*, is in homage to Jung. The phrase also stresses the urgent need for reconsideration, already under way in Western culture, of the relationship between human beings and the planet that hosts them.

Chapter 1

Soul, earth and migration in contemporary society

Elena Liotta

> In the years of exile
> a handful of earth
> accompanied me
> in my wanderings
> and it was without weight
> for an hour or two each day
> it eclipsed my exile.
> Far from my homeland
> I brought with me my earth.
> It was there with me
> and I jested with it
> as one does with one's beloved
> and I toyed with it
> as one does with a rosary.
> It protected me,
> it gave me strength;
> bond with my homeland,
> it taught my feet the way of return . . .
> > Tawfiq Sayigh 2002 (translated
> > from the Italian by transl.)

This book is concerned with the relationship between people and their surroundings: that exterior space into which the individual is born, where he grows and lives throughout his life, by choice or by force; a natural environment or one constructed by his fellow human beings.

A place takes on meaning as a result of the sensations and emotions elicited and the consequent attachments formed. This depends both on the individual's intrinsic cultural conditioning and his personal psychological projection. The sum of what happens, important relations, other situations, confer a psychically relevant importance to the place that remains in the individual or group memory. External space becomes interior space, a subjective space and time, for it is experience, memory, and emotions. It is in this sense that we will be dealing with "soul and earth."

Yet this book is also – and above all – a reflection on the theme of migration, since, as explained in the introduction, it was inspired by the psychological phenomena connected to the migratory experience in the course of psychotherapy sessions with foreign patients. Together with my own personal story as well as other sources they coalesce in a sort of ongoing open-ended study.

Knowledge regarding the psychological relationship between human beings and their environment is augmented by observing the dysfunctions and ordeals of individuals and listening to their stories, transferring the centrality of this subject – long more or less ignored or sidestepped – into depth psychology. As will become evident in the course of the book, migration served as a point of reference for other less obvious transitions that are more difficult to identify but that produce similar effects on a psychological level: moving to another city or from one district to another, changing school or jobs, or even taking a tourist trip: a common experience in advanced societies.

This book is therefore addressed not only to migrants or therapists, but to all those who know what it means to leave their environment and familiar places for an unknown space. It is addressed to those who are aware of the sacred nature of certain environments or of other feelings associated with place, ranging from a reassuring familiarity to excruciating fear – see-sawing between agoraphobia and claustrophobia, panic crises and other common symptoms that are connected to space. It is addressed to those who wonder about esthetic and contemplative experiences, in other words all those who consider the relationship with the external environment worthy of greater psychological attention and awareness. I also hope to stimulate curiosity, if nothing else, in those who are not particularly interested in the environment, giving them an idea of how much it can enrich their individual personality and story.

My intentions are not specifically of an environmentalist nature involving the safeguarding, tutelage and maintenance of natural resources, but will be focused on the psychological premises: that first step in beginning a journey, the indispensable predisposition in developing an awareness of everything that contributes to our existence. The environment as nature, as planet earth, is always there in my analysis in the form of an indispensable substratum, compromised by its increasing exploitation by human beings.

The overtones and contours of the psychological relationship with the environment/place are of course much stronger for the migrant or the exile. Current social and political conditions all over the world, the great migratory movements of recent decades, the new demands on the public services that deal with psychological well-being, have all focused greater attention on the figure of the immigrant and foreigner.

Literature on migration varies greatly, ranging from statistical surveys to studies on different aspects of the experience – economic, political, sociological, anthropological, philosophical – and from a general comprehensive view regarding large groups to elements that are closest to the experiences of the individual or of the small group. Psychology, psychiatry and the social sciences have subjected them to scrutiny, especially with regard to concrete interventions of support and reception.

In addition to this specialized literature there are countless articles in the daily press and magazines, some of which edited by groups of immigrants in their own language, as well as information via the Internet: in other words, a broad and multiform coverage that can provide answers to questions raised by the general public. Perhaps even too much.

When one attempts to put all this material into some kind of order, contradictory elements inevitably come to the fore. They are not easy to understand and give one the feeling that everything and the opposite of everything can be said on this theme.

It should be specified that what is generically defined as migration is basically men or women who leave their land and attempt, not always successfully, to adapt themselves to life elsewhere, in an unknown land. In a sense it is a starting all over, rather like being reborn, with all the risks and fragility this condition implies. All human beings on this planet, in this same condition, share the same basic constitutionality.

Some of the places, moments, scenarios of the experience of migration will be discussed in this book. From departure to return, if and when there is a return.

The word "soul"

An explanation for my ever more frequent use of the word "soul" is in order. I have adopted the term here with reference to one of Jung's writings, *Mind and Earth*, which I will deal with at greater length in the next chapter.

I have asked myself how I can differentiate my approach, which remains psychological, in view of the evocative halo of multiple meanings that today surrounds the word "soul." The collective desire for a soul is not, as naively and rather superstitiously might seem to be the case, that of finding a soul in things, revitalizing and therefore making them worthy of attention and care. Although this wouldn't be such a bad idea. However, since we are dealing with a cultural phenomenon found in advanced and acculturated societies, I believe that this search for soul is a counter-tendency, a compensation for excessive intellectualism, for the threat of an alienating automatism inherent in technology, for disorientation resulting from globalization, for the loss of humanism implicit in monetary economics. I believe that what is being sought is an inner spirituality, in the sense of a new presence, turning an ear, an eye, an attention to different values, not always to be identified with those of traditional religions.

Women in Tamil Nadu village, India. Every morning a propitiatory Kolam pattern is made with rice flower. Photo © Alberto Tessore.

This perspective is what I hope to offer the reader: an attitude, a style, something that is in the eye of the observer and not necessarily in the thing observed.

Just as we take it for granted that an esthetic vision of reality exists, we could also imagine a vision of the soul: not to be confused, however, with the animistic vision. The difficulty lies in considering the spiritual and the animal aspects together, yet differentiating between them.

Jung, even though he was a doctor, psychiatrist and psychologist, in times in which psychology was already scientific, had no scruples in using the term "soul" in a general sense of internal dimension. Jung also spoke of the paradoxical "instincts of the spirit" as constitutional, archetypal, universal aspects of human nature, addressing that which was not concrete and tangible but mysteriously active. Both terms, soul and spirit, therefore belong to the language of the psychological, as differentiated from the religious, experience. As, on the other hand, does the term "archetype" which Jung defines as the primordial image, which is always collective, a mnemonic deposit; a typical basic form of recurring psychic experiences, of physiological and anatomical disposition; the precursor of the "idea," a necessary counterpart of instinct (Jung 1921).

Subsequently James Hillman and the entire current of archetypal psychology of Jungian inspiration reintroduced the soul as a mediating element between body and spirit, and proposed a symbolic approach for psychotherapy centered on the inner image defined, to quote John Keats, as "soul making." It is not by chance that many of Hillman's writings use the word "soul" in the title. The mark he left on clinical language and activity, as well as the cultural and sociological approach of his most recent works, has reinforced the autonomy of the interior world and highlighted the peculiarities of the form of fantastic or more specifically "imaginal" thinking as previously defined by Henri Corbin (Corbin 1973, 1983, 1989).

Indeed Freud was the first to adopt this concept, in particular with his use of the German word *Seele* (soul) to signify the internal world. Subsequently however, as noted by Bettelheim in *Freud and the soul of man*, when Freud was translated into English, *Seele* became "mind," shifting the meaning and aura of *Seele* to the mental processes that characterize the rational, linear and directed type of thought.

With regard to what happens to ideas and texts when they migrate from one place and time to another, this more scientific and modern interpretation of Freudian thought left many of Freud's successors with a concept of theoretical colonization and linguistic control of the Unconscious, rather than its "imaginal" or symbolic vision.

The political factor

A few introductory words need to be said regarding the political factor. It plays an important part in migration and the phenomenon of racism, two unusual subjects for the analytical psychologist, but charged with psychological valences for individuals and social groups.

Due to the importance today of the phenomenon of migration, in drawing up relevant laws the world of politics has taken varied stands. In a situation as complex as this, confusion is inevitable and disagreement tends to arise even among those who generally have similar ideas.

The crucial points discussed in various European and non-European countries mainly regard:

- favoring or opposing immigration
- considering attachment to one's own land or territory or country politically right-wing or left-wing

- whether words weighted with historical meaning, such as "race" and "nation," should be used and in what way
- whether cultural roots exist, and what part they play
- how local and global, similar and diverse, one's own and the other's, can be brought together.

Psychology can help elucidate a few points on the collective level, including the facts that:

- migration is a universal human phenomenon, whatever the underlying specific historical reasons may be
- loving one's own land, that piece of concrete where one is born and raised or is in some way rooted, loving one's own culture, language, traditions, is neither right-wing nor left-wing but simply something that characterizes most human beings
- true nomadism, formerly more widespread, is now a circumscribed phenomenon in the generalized tendency towards staying put, which leads any immigrant to put down new roots whenever possible in the hope of integrating with his new environment.

On the level of individual psychology, nothing authorizes one to think that it is healthier or more desirable to lose one's origins in favor of a (no better identified) recently introduced common value, in virtue of which we remain where work or interests of some other kind have brought us as long as the conditions of life remain constant, meaning those of the consumer society: "the new common land," fruit of an induced and inevitable globalization.

Arrival in Italy of 10,000 Albanians on the ship *Vlora*, 6 August 1991. From N. Di Paolo, with permission.

Conservative or liberal, native or immigrant, the inhabitant of the advanced society lives in the bubble of his material privileges, suspended in a disembodied, degenerated, inhuman environment, in which neither soul nor earth seems to be of particular importance.

Being a citizen of the world, in its literal sense, should imply respect and sensitivity for the conditions of life in the rest of the world, in addition to the awareness that we are not absolute lords of the earth and share responsibilities for its survival with others. Being citizens of the world should not be limited to equality of mandatory fashions, of commercial values, of common laws or regulations of coexistence, always imposed by a few on the many.

It is not by chance that the strongest resistance to the expansion of Western society comes from peoples with a strong territorial identity and deeply rooted traditions. The fact that all or some of their traditions do not correspond to Western ideas multiplies attempts at conversion, the equivalent of commercial and political colonization. With an ethnocentric spirit that is still very alive, the cultures and policies of Western societies, even the so-called democratic ones, launch periodic campaigns to modify social, economic and cultural phenomena in the rest of the world. They attempt to regulate relations between the sexes, educate the children, dictate working and living conditions, tell the others what to wear, what to produce, what to believe in. And this includes their individual and collective psychology. The Western model of life has been propagated for several centuries now under the aegis of progress and economic welfare. There is little respect for local traditions, and the future development of these delicate equilibriums remains a moot question.

Yet paradoxically in the West there are movements for the recovery and safeguarding of the environment, of resources and specific, local, even minority cultures. On the one hand, in the large European cities the culture of the various groups of immigrants survives as an ethnic fashion, in intercultural projects, in the urban fantasies of multicultural societies. On the other, the identical culture is systematically disrupted *in loco*, in the country of origin, surrendering to Western culture. It is like sending our out-of-date medicines to the Third World while research is being carried out on their old and primitive medicines in an attempt to recover natural pharmacology.

On racism

If I had published this book fifteen years ago in its original psychological frame, I would not have felt obliged to touch on the themes to be dealt with on the following pages. The changes in the contemporary scenario and their widespread psychological value make it impossible for me to ignore them. Racism, a phenomenon of varying intensity that accompanies the migratory processes, is one of these.

The official declarations of human rights stress the fact that we are all members of a single human family. Yet separatism, nationalism and colonialism are rearing their heads in the world of a market economy and control of resources, of growing environmental deterioration, of poverty associated with an increase in population. Today the immigrant and the foreigner are present everywhere and recognized by the laws of all countries. The presence of the foreigner, however, does not automatically trigger racism, just as not all racism involves the foreigner.

From a psychological point of view the foreigner is seen as "different," a difference seen as something alien, in turn seen as a potential danger, because what does not belong to the known, to the familiar, cannot be controlled. A lack of control puts the individual on the defensive and from there the step to refusal is short. The sequence, often entirely unconscious, can spread from the individual to the small and to the large group. As it becomes more important, it can come to a head within the group in a leader or be taken over and manipulated by one or more external leaders. The leader and the group will create a scapegoat with which to celebrate the collective perversion of the sacrifice, the concrete or psychological destruction of the other.

The human being is undoubtedly born with a predisposition for self-defense and is endowed with survival instincts. In specific periods of childhood, as explained by developmental psychology, the child will refuse what is foreign and seek protection in the familiar. This period, however, is short-lived and is normally replaced by the desire for socialization. Moreover, for the child the concept of "diversity" has no specific racial connotations. In adolescence the forming of groups, discrimination between males and females,

Refugees, Viterbo, Italy. Photo © Daniele Vita, 2006.

social classes, quarters, fashions, is a transitory process that normally ends up by facilitating socialization and the construction of identity.

Famous studies and experiments of the 1960s have shown that when faced with a common danger that threatens the group, internal conflicts, as well as antagonism and competition for resources, die out. Aggressiveness between groups of children and young people, which often includes the scapegoat phenomenon, also takes place among relatives and for a wide variety of reasons. All this is part of the human being, of his biopsychological nature, spontaneous and established throughout our history. Only education and the formative processes transmitted from one generation to the next can accentuate, or circumscribe, some aspects with regard to others.

Racism is the most distorted and perverse result of a process that "can" be interrupted in its initial stages, which "can" be prevented and circumscribed by means of the collective memory and conscience, by means of laws, with culture and education.

Unless this is not deliberately overridden for other purposes.

Racism is an adult phenomenon. It is the abuse of childhood, as well as an abuse of human rights. Characterized by contempt and exclusion, by that superior–inferior polarity that produces actions of discrimination and refusal of specific individuals and groups, racism of any kind whatsoever is not necessarily caused by enmity. There is something else, an incomprehensible element, which lies at the basis of its absurdity and irrationality. This is why psychologists and psychoanalysts have worked so hard to try to understand it.

On the other hand, the origins of psychoanalysis also lie in Freud's Jewish cultural matrix, considered by some a determining aspect in his discoveries of the psyche. Freud's life, which ended in exile in London as result of Nazi racial persecution, unquestionably influenced some of his theories (Bakan 1969, Gay 1987, Meghnagi 1993, Rubenstein 1985).

Subsequent psychoanalytical practice, including Jung's analytical psychology which encompassed many analysts of Jewish origin, studied the unconscious psychological mechanisms that lead to the scapegoat phenomenon and other defensive procedures (Adams 1996, Christopher and McFarland Solomon 1999, Samuels 1993a, 2001). These include the transferral of our weaknesses and inadequacies to the other, who is then scorned and attacked – defined by Jung as "projections of the shadow." Other theories stress destructive envy (since I cannot be like you or have your gifts, I will destroy you); and then paranoia, in which what is bad is always something alien and elsewhere, a constant threat.

In each of these cases we are unable to achieve the "otherness," i.e. to consider the "other than me" for what it is, hoping that the fact that we are alike yet different will be mutually respected. Otherness, then, is the final step with respect to extraneousness and diversity. It is obvious that the adult racist has severed all ties with otherness or perhaps he never even got there. In order to negate even that elementary solidarity among like that is shared by natural groups, including animals, he is forced to discover pretexts to eliminate, like an inert object, the disturbing presence. It is the same psychopathic mechanism as in the serial killer who kills only women with red hair.

Racism is an adult social disease of the group that practices it, a serious disease that can become a political weapon, a means of psychological manipulation of the abovementioned aspects.

The problem today in a society that considers itself multicultural lies not in the growing coexistence of different ethnic groups – this already happened in the past, in Imperial Rome and Renaissance Florence and in the Middle East (Goitein 1999), without leading to the conflicts noted today – but in the distortion of collective relationships, carried out by groups, corporatism, various kinds of terrorism, with other purposes and animated by the dynamics of power.

Aside from race, the threat to the cultural identity of a group that identifies with its territory is a threat to the life, to the survival of the group that paradoxically is willing to die so as not to disappear, as is the case today in Palestine. It happened in the past and it is still happening today with minority groups such as the Basques, the Chechnyans, Armenians, Kurds, and others.

The answer might lie in the existence of a more spacious territorial container, large enough to hold the various minorities peaceably. The aggregating power of the land, above and beyond ethnic and linguistic origins, is clearly shown by what happened in the United States. Despite episodes of racial

Kurdish refugees, Rome. Photo © Daniele Vita, 2005.

discrimination within, compared to other national groups the inhabitants now form a strongly cohesive group, identified by a common land and lifestyle. I believe that the *ius soli*, that right to citizenship based on being born on American soil, also played a part in uniting the inhabitants and making them powerful.

Land, territory, traditions, belonging and identification come together in a bond that shows its strength above all when it is threatened. It is easy for external observers to ask why this attachment is so tenacious: after all, it is only land. Logically it would appear that the greater value should be life, considering the problem from the point of view of both the invaders and of the defenders. But evidently the sense, the psychological and cultural aspects, that is the soul of this land acquires a role for the group that is more vital than life itself.

As with migration, I believe that those who have not personally been subjected to expropriation of their territory, their home and everything in it, must express themselves cautiously. In therapy sessions involving theft in the home, or the more usual car theft, unexpected levels of imbalance and anxiety, quite unlike those caused by simply losing objects – even truly cherished objects – were encountered.

The cultural unconscious

In the age of globalization, localism continues to lay claim to the unconscious and consciousness of the group, whether we are dealing with villages or countries. This must be taken into account if we hope to alleviate the consequences of an overly urgent economic and political demand for general standardization.

For Jung there is an intermediate link between the "personal unconscious" – that is, the history and potentialities of each individual – and the "collective unconscious," which unites all human beings in various universal aspects and attitudes, considered as primary and which he defines as archetypal.

This link, henceforth defined as "cultural unconscious," is based on group relations and on the needs for stability and protection that led ancient civilizations to form settlements and then to the birth of agriculture, of the city and of the house: that is of a place, created by man, to which one could return. A place in this sense is inseparable from the culture; an object of affection, full of memories, endowed with a sense of belonging (Adams 1996, Byington 1986, Christopher and McFarland Solomon 1999, Henderson 1984, Singer and Kimbles 2004).

It is this cultural unconscious that appears indirectly when we speak of soul and earth, and it can be considered a specification of the broader collective unconscious or as an enlargement of the personal and family unconscious. Aside from the perplexities that this concept can raise, I believe that, like other socio-cultural aspects, a hypothetical cultural unconscious can be part of individual existence without necessarily preceding or following it. In other words, it subsides and takes shape as external conditions and events change. While by the collective unconscious Jung meant the human constitutionality, the cultural unconscious is formed throughout the individual's life as a result of education and permanence in a determined social and cultural group, with its language, its traditions, its territory. And this includes the changing fortunes of the group.

Psychoanalysis affirms that everything that is unconscious exerts a powerful influence on the life of persons and groups. Identifying the aspects of the unconscious regarding groups, ethnic and geographical provenience, cultural inheritance and values that form and regulate the different societies and the lives of members is one way of enriching psychology and contributing to the desired educative and formative processes.

The suffering and nostalgia of the immigrant, of the exile, of the unwilling nomad, of the foreigner who finds himself unwelcome or persecuted, is an ordeal of denied identity, of a common and group identity: an offence to the right of a psychological, and at times even biological, existence.

In conclusion, if we wish to get to the psychological roots of the phenomenon, the racial aspect of the offense, or of the defense, is only one of many variables, as is being a foreigner. Its core is the fear or anxiety experienced when one is faced with whoever or whatever appears as foreign, a momentary embarrassment that can initially be expressed as perplexity or refusal, but which, as children teach us, can also be swiftly overcome. Hope is provided by the fact that some situations of racial conflict have gradually been toned down, that there are social groups that never even developed them, that even though they existed in the past they have then been absorbed by a new cultural identity that included both parties.

A fine illustration of this process is shown by H.M. Enzensberger in his *The Great Migration* (1992), when he describes both moments: the arrival of the foreigner and his integration into the group.

The scene takes place in the compartment of a train. Two passengers have settled themselves comfortably in, have taken possession of the space. The door opens and two new travelers enter. Their arrival is not well received, one can feel the reluctance of those already there to move over, to share the available space. Even though the former don't know each other, a sense of solidarity is created between them with regard to the new arrivals. The territory at their disposal belongs to them, and they consider the new arrivals intruders, as do the autochthonous inhabitants. There is nothing rational in this vision, but it is a deeply rooted feeling. The regulations of the railroads and of courtesy prevent open clashes, the new passengers are tolerated and one becomes used to them. Despite the "passing" situation, the persons defend their precarious dwelling with silent tenacity. Time passes and two other passengers open the door of the compartment. At this point the status of those who came in earlier changes. Only a moment before they were foreigners, intruders, and now they have already become the autochthons, claiming their rights, with a total lack of empathy for the new arrivals, who must face the same resistance and submit to the initiation of their predecessors.

It is peculiar, observes Enzensberger, how fast one can forget origins that are hidden and denied.

New words

In recent decades it has been said that words make things and that therefore changing them, letting them go, renewing them if necessary, is a way of changing and at the same time acting on things. The word "racism" is super-annuated and has now been replaced, rather feebly, or counterbalanced by "equality," in turn obsolescent, enervated by the impossibility of its realization. In the meanwhile more realistic attempts have appeared on the scene, such as "difference" and "diversity," and a series of prefixes that allude to the complexity and the relation, such as *pluri-*, *multi-*, *inter-*, as well as the need to visibly mark, through the prefix *post-*, the passage from the era of modernity to the current postmodern, post-industrial, post-colonial and whatever else society.

This so-called global society should, logically, also be characterized as "post-racial" and "post-racist." Other more specific proposals such as, for example, the establishment of a "logos of the stranger" by the philosopher Merleau-Ponty, represent an attempt to create a way of thinking that can overcome anxiety caused by the stranger, source of many discriminatory modes of behavior, including racism. In this approach, however, the factors that diversify can easily be transformed back into discriminating factors. The word "diversity" becomes synonymous with distance and a basic irreconcilability, which can be avoided only by embracing that tepid "respect" so frequently advocated. If we can't all be equal, then we are all diverse, and so on with all the possible imaginable differences.

I believe that what is missing is an aperture of a psychological nature and an attempt at integration on the level of human relations, definable in a positive form by the word "otherness," in other words a way of thinking and a culture of otherness, an education to otherness which by itself includes the diverse, the foreigner and also his fellow. Without the other, who is not only to be respected but also, in a non-rhetorical sense, loved, there are none of the relationships on which social life is based.

At this point, with regard to racism, the only obstacle would seem to be political groups that foment violence and ride the wave of migration and the phenomena connected to it, or the various types of cultural and religious integralism, whose interests and purposes can be manipulated.

Is it really true that anti-Semitism is re-emerging or, for one reason or another, are things being done to make it re-emerge? To what extent are some of the episodes of cultural intolerance real with regard to the way the media handles them? How much does the web of alliances and politics count in the scenario of wars and guerrilla warfare between countries and blocs? For example, in Israel and throughout the world the number of Jews opposed to the occupation of Palestine has been and is still growing. But one hears little about this. Governments are the ones that choose whether to adopt war or more or less violent, more or less legal, occupation. The serious mistake of confusing the people with the government nourishes that obtuseness that in other times and places produced the collective racist phenomenon. The fact that many of these governments were democratically elected and are therefore formally representative of their population is no reason to forget that often almost half of this same population has diametrically opposed opinions.

In this historical period the traditional political–cultural dichotomies are being reshuffled together with the borders between countries, the migration phenomenon, the reasons for wars and alliances, the struggles for rights of autonomy and political, cultural, and religious independence. Integralism is as much a characteristic of one side as it is of the other; conservatives and progressives are no longer identified by their old programs and their former battles, and at times have even crossed over.

The earth

All of this cannot help but influence and condition the relationship the citizens of every country have with their land, their sense of national and cultural identity, their vision of the foreigner in general and of the immigrant in particular, and therefore also all the ensuing social and psychological phenomena. Emblematic of the twentieth century is the story of the American dream and its role in the collective consciousness. It begins with the dream of the European emigrant landing in a happy, rich, fertile, vast land, which the native inhabitants do little to defend. It continues with the dream of the pioneer who conquers the frontier lands foot by foot. The dreams of all the other migrants from the rest of the world – liberation from poverty, from their humble origins, from discrimination; the possibility of success – are inexorably being shattered.

The earth, Jung would say, or the lands, we might add, are beginning to take their revenge. As early as the 1920s Jung presented a far-sighted vision, which can be reinterpreted in view of the contemporary panorama.

Jung's picture of the average American was as follows:

> Thus the American presents a strange picture: a European with Negro behavior and an Indian soul. He shares the fate of all usurpers of foreign soil. Certain Australian primitives assert that one cannot conquer foreign soil, because in it there dwell strange ancestor-spirits who reincarnate

Grand Canyon, Colorado, USA. Photo © Bruno Liotta.

themselves in the new-born. There is a great psychological truth in this. The foreign land assimilates its conqueror ... Everywhere the virgin earth causes at least the unconscious of the conqueror to sink to the level of its indigenous inhabitants.

(Jung 1927:49)

Jung maintains that this unconscious process of integration creates a great psychic potential, unknown to those who, like the European compared to the American, are historically conditioned and possessed by the spirit of their ancestors. They are held in thrall by their land and the lack of a dynamic contact makes for a static and conservative relationship. On the other hand, when historical and cultural conditioning is absent, so is memory and identity, with the risk of regressing to a state of primitive instincts or of being absorbed by the spirit of the place.

The Earth, the Land, therefore, can represent the vital humus of the origins and the flow of life, as well as a rigidly identifiable place, which holds back or repels. Belonging can be heart-warming, in memory and the continuity of generations, or it can become conflictual and freighted with destructiveness.

In any case – and it is from here that I will begin my exploration – the human being is not by nature insensitive to the place and environment in which he dwells. Throughout his life the human being maintains, unconsciously perhaps, a psychological bond with place, beginning with that of his own origins.

The dynamics of this relationship between soul and earth, observed in its various facets, will be dealt with in the following pages.

Chapter 2

On Carl Gustav Jung's "Mind and Earth"

Just as the tree does not end
with the tips of its roots
or of its branches
and the bird does not end
with its feathers and its flight
and the Earth does not end with its highest mountains:
so I too do not end
and I stretch up high towards the sky
and I am tree
and sun and house of the rain and of the wind.
The clouds, the dawn and sunsets
stars and moon cover my head
accompany me through my days
because my soul is the world.

Cherokee song

I want to begin this chapter with a discussion of the "process of individuation." Jung used this expression to describe an experience that was initially personal but which he then extended to his psychological theories of human existence as a journey, as a sequence of changes that lead somewhere, headed towards an apparently mysterious destination. For Jung the psychological goal is the realization of one's uniqueness, of one's authentic Self, becoming what is innate in one's nature, to be achieved by means of one's specific life experiences. Without going further into the matter, I shall simply refer to a peculiar mood that takes hold of us at some time or other when we become aware of an inner impulse, a sort of force that leads us, almost of its own accord; that makes us choose to go to unthought-of places, or remain where we don't want to remain; or even suddenly find ourselves face to face with new realities. It is a feeling that there is something within us that is following its own laws and dynamics, which have nothing to do with our conscious will. Attempts to make sense of this phenomenon include calling it, depending on the case, destiny, vocation, my road, the will of God, the configuration of the stars, the Unconscious, social conditioning, etc. And also (why not?) the process of individuation, stressing the formative aspect of life, in that constant alchemy between within and without, between the things that happen and what we do with them as we gradually become what we are.

The analogy between the process of individuation and journey and the metaphorical use of the words journey, way, path, road, itinerary and others has by now become part of everyday language. Life/journey moves concurrently on the physical land and in the inner world. At times it is the exterior journey that leaves its mark on the story of a life; at other times it is the inner journey, in persons who have never left their place of origin. And then it may be the inner and the exterior journeys that support or replace each other. I will devote a chapter to this theme further on.

In the story of ancient philosophy and the spirituality of all times, the idea of a soul that travels, that descends to Earth and then leaves to return to God, appears and disappears fairly regularly. This journey, which continues throughout life, is full of suffering and nostalgia caused by a body thought of as a cage, as a trap, as something that ties us down. Existence is seen as perpetual migration, the earth as a provisory dwelling, the soul as mutilated and aspiring to be reintegrated.

These cursory considerations simply mean that for depth psychology consideration of the human experience always includes the inner, invisible, subjective side with its symbols. Earth, then, is never simply the concrete earth. But let me add that neither is soul ever only soul, as long as one lives in a physical body and in space–time.

Jung made this key of interpretation the basis of his epistemology. He also brought this vision of the physical aspect integrated with its attributed psychological significance into his study of alchemy. Meaning is therefore not to be found in things and processes, but in the vision the human being has of them.

Once this is clear, soul, earth and process of individuation as journey will be the three fundamental poles to which I will frequently return.

Soul, earth and culture

Some of the keys for interpretation used in this book hark back to a text by Jung originally titled "Die Erdbedingtheit der Psyche" ("The Dependence of the Psyche on the Earth"). It was published in a collection of essays edited by H. Keyserling entitled *Mensch und Erde* (*Man and Earth*) and subsequently divided into two texts – one of which is the present *Seele und Erde* (*Mind and Earth*). Translated as "Mind and the Earth" in English in 1927, the paper is the basis of the present version, the final "Mind and Earth," by R.F.C. Hull, contained in Jung's *Collected Works*. These are all details that make it easier to understand the historically conditioned and dated parts of the text.

Reading it in the 1980s made me want to go deeper into the subject. At the time I was working a great deal with foreign patients, was married to an American, and, as I said, was beginning to reinterpret my own experience as a foreigner from the point of view of a psychoanalyst.

Jung's paper begins with an analysis of the idea of soul in Western culture. On one hand:

> mind would then be understood as a system of adaptation determined by the conditions of an earthly environment.
>
> (Jung 1927:29)

However, Jung immediately observed that this was not enough, because it would seem to make one think of a soul that was identified with the rational and conscious side, while the existence of unconscious, profound, archetypal aspects has been ascertained, that is:

> They are thus, essentially, the chthonic portion of the psyche, if we may use such an expression – that portion through which the psyche is attached to nature, or in which its link with the earth and the world appears at its most tangible.
>
> (Jung 1927:31)

Jung then launched into a detailed explanation of the nature of the archetype, of its proximity to the primordial instincts, of the close relationship that exists between the child and the primitive, who share a magic way of thinking, and that "religion of the night" which takes form in fairy tales, myths, fears and anxieties present even in the civilized human being.

> The psychic influence of the earth and its laws is seen most clearly in these primordial images.
>
> (Jung 1927:31)

In his attempt to depict the universal force and all-pervading aspect of the archetype, Jung compares it to the figure of the mother, initially an unconscious archetypal experience which gradually, as the child moves into adulthood, is transformed into a more limited and conscious, individual and personal sense, into that of the specific: one's mother. The powerful primordial image, however, remains in the unconscious and in the course of life tinges or even determines interpersonal relationships with society and with the world of feelings and with matter. For Jung it is more than a metaphor: it is a psychological reality active in the life of all human beings. Everywhere in the world, the earth and the mother are symbolically set together. And not only the concrete earth, but also the politically constituted territory.

Mother Germania is for the Germans, like *la douce France* for the

French, a figure of utmost importance behind the political scene, who could be overlooked only by blinkered intellectuals. The all-embracing womb of Mother Church is anything but a metaphor, and the same is true of Mother Earth, Mother Nature, and "matter" in general.

(Jung 1927:35)

Thanks to the subsequent contribution of Ernst Bernhard, the German psychiatrist of Jewish origin who introduced Jung's analytical psychology into Italy, we can include this country in our vision. In an essay titled "Il complesso della Grande Madre, problemi e possibilità della psicologia analitica in Italia" published in the review *Tempo presente* in 1961 and now to be found in *Mitobiografia*, Bernhard (1977) analyzes the permeability of the Italian to psychological elaboration, the mixture of foreign elements stratified

Mater Materia, terracotta sculpture by Cinzia Catena.
Photo © Paolo Pelliccia.

in history that constitute the Italian identity, the stereotypes and the shadow that surround it, finding the key to unlock the enigma of the Italian soul in the archetype of the Mediterranean Great Mother.

He believes that this unconscious collective image acts not only in inter-personal relationships between men and women, but also in a broader social structure, in law, in art, customs, morals, philosophy, religion, and politics. Bernhard illustrates the positive and negative aspects of this maternal and affective tendency, stressing the dominant centrality of the mother and the dependency that derives from it for the psyche of the Italian male in particular.

To return to Jung, he continues his presentation explaining that for the child, mother and father are the entire universe and, in a confused and magical form of identity, they end up by incarnating the forces of nature, the habitual places, the primary feelings, the horizon itself of the infant's life.

> The archetype of the mother is the most immediate one for the child. But with the development of consciousness the father also enters his field of vision, and activates an archetype whose nature is in many respects opposed to that of the mother ... "Fatherland" implies boundaries, a definite localization in space, whereas the land itself is Mother Earth, quiescent and fruitful ... The mother who gives warmth, protection, and nourishment is also the hearth, the sheltering cave or hut, and the surrounding vegetation. She is the provident field, and her son is the godlike grain, the brother and friend of man. She is the milk-giving cow and the herd. The father goes about, talks with other men, hunts, travels, makes war, lets his bad moods loose like thunderstorms ... He is the war and the weapon, the cause of all changes; he is the bull provoked to violence or prone to apathetic laziness.
>
> (Jung 1927:35–36)

All these things soon come to the fore in the life of the child. In the course of his normal development he will gradually move from an unconscious identity with his parents and their imagined attributes to separating the real parent from the archetypal force attributed in infancy. This unconscious identifica-tion is shifted to society, the lineage, the church, the nation.

In the second part of his essay Jung illustrates, at closer range, the theme of the soul related to its bond with the earth.

As I noted at the end of the preceding chapter, his hypothesis, formulated through his personal experiences in a sojourn in the United States in 1909, is that the earth and its autochthonous inhabitants in some way absorb the newcomer and colonize him on an unconscious level, both psychological and corporeal. In the formation of the Yankee type, Jung found extraordinary similarities with the Native American type, even though there had never been enough genetic mixtures to justify this concept.

What Jung called "the Indianization of the American peoples," the "going red," is a phenomenon that was to be revealed more in detail later, through depth psychoanalysis of numerous American patients. It must be remembered that Jung was writing these first reflections in the late 1920s, in an America that was unquestionably very different from what it is today, more or less idealized by the European culture. Even though he was a European solidly anchored to his culture, Jung managed to sense what was different, with the calm eye of the naturalist not involved in particular personal needs or projections.

In addition to the Native American component, Jung was also aware of a black component, that "going black" or the assimilation of the Black Culture by the white man – at the time more marked in Africa – that was more subtly expressed in America as a contagion on a psychological level. Jung gives a few examples: the American's laugh, the relatively shambling gait, the music and dance influenced by jazz and blues, the religious feeling, a certain dose of naïveté and childishness, the lively and loquacious temperament, the sociability of the group and the masses and the consequent lack of privacy which reminded Jung of primitive life in an open village, in which the identity itself was collective and participative. All of this was of course compared to the existence and culture of the European ancestors of the Yankees, in particular Germanic and Anglo-Saxon.

For Jung, the still pioneering situation of America in those years was not enough to explain this evident change in the psychological attitude of the immigrant. On the other hand I would like to add that the presence of the blacks, compared to the Native Americans, was actually much more recent and therefore, in line with Jung's hypothesis, would in turn have been subject to the same fate. Indeed, after being in America for such a long time the American Blacks, now called Afro-Americans, are clearly different from the African Blacks.

But what Jung was trying to say is subtler. If the Blacks contaminated the European Whites on a behavioral and social level, influencing the birth of the Yankee, how did the deeper core of American psyche evolve – that part we call soul – and what conditioning was it subject to?

Or, turning the question around, what happened to the original Native American? Not certainly the one who now, eighty years after Jung's comments, survives in the reservation as a sort of war trophy or who has been inserted and camouflaged in contemporary American society. In the 1920s Jung was already aware of the repression on a conscious level of the invader, of the population of an entire continent. Even so, following the idea of psychic contagion and going into the analysis of the unconscious, thanks to his work with American patients Jung succeeded in explaining many aspects of the collective American identity.

The myth of the hero, still strong in American culture, appeared to Jung as the deepest place of the encounter between the Native American and the

Afro-American musicians, Berkeley, California, USA. Photo © Bruno Liotta.

European. Resistance to colonization, the warlike characteristics, loyalties, strength, intelligence, the relationship with nature, the shaman religion: all this and more flowed into the American culture, subsequently shaping some of the fundamental aspects that still define the nature of an entire nation. Jung, in his essay, cites as an example the American concept of sport, which, compared with the European, seemed at the time similar only to the American Indian initiation rites – rough, rigorous, even cruel, concentrating on the outcome, the tenacity in achieving it, endurance in the face of difficulties – all legendary American Indian virtues. There is also the religious factor, the figure of the shaman and exorcist, which Jung associates with what he defines as early 20th-century American inventions: spiritism and Christian Science, founding principles of all the groups, sects and analogous forms of mental healing. In line with this type of sensibility, there was a certain magical concept in which the word assumed a power disturbing even then: for example, the use of slogans, which at the time made the Europeans smile and which were enormously effective in America.

Another essay of interest here that appears in the same book as "Mind and Earth" is "The Complications of American Psychology," dating to the same period (Jung 1930a). Here Jung, with regard to resemblances, contagions, influences, is even more precise when he says that:

It is not so much in the anatomical features as in the general behaviour, physical and mental. One finds it in the language, the gestures, the mentality, in the movements of the body and in certain things even more subtle than that. I only knew that a subtle difference existed between the American and the European just as it does between the Australian and the South African.

(Jung 1930a:503)

Further on, in view of the most evident differences, Jung expresses a judgment that is understandable in consideration of the times and the European mentality and tradition. He praises the Americans for their freedom, freshness, spontaneity, slang, nonchalance, and relaxed approach, which he found in the way they spoke, their intonation, comparable to their swinging gait. On other points Jung was more skeptical, such as on what appeared to him a lack of discretion compared with emotions and the overwhelming presence of collective emotions, or the excessive faith in a popular and intrusive press.

You are simply reduced to a particle in the mass, with no other hope or expectation than the illusory goals of an eager and excited collectivity. You just swim for life, that's all.

(Jung 1930a:505)

The leveling of the psychology of the people particularly bothered him. In its collective enthusiasm there was the risk that the individuals would be pushed into situations that they would probably never have chosen if left to their own devices.

With regard to earth and place, Jung also noted how everyone in America seemed to live as if they were city dwellers and how the tendency towards city life permeated the style of life in the country as well as the city. Even the smallest settlement refused to call itself a village. It was as if everything were collective and reduced to a common denominator.

Comparing the relationship with the earth of the American city dwellers with that of the Navaho, Jung observes:

The country is wonderful, nay, just divine still with a faint perfume of an historical eternity in the air, and those lovely crickets not yet shy of man. They don't know yet that they are living in America, like some Navahos. And the bullfrog talks in the night and days blessed with sunshine. There is real country and nobody seems to be up to it, certainly not that hustling noisily chattering motoring town folk. They're not even down to it, as the Red Indians are, with whom one feels peculiarly at ease because they are obviously under the spell of their country and not on top of it. So there at last is the peace of God.

(Jung 1930a:507)

Indian totem, Wichita, Kansas, USA. Photo © Bruno Liotta.

Once more clarifying his initial intuition, Jung noted that:

> It may seem mysterious and unbelievable yet it is a fact that can
> be observed in other countries just as well. Man can be assimilated
> by a country. There is an x and a y in the air and in the soil of a
> country, which slowly permeate and assimilate him to the type of the
> aboriginal inhabitant, even to the point of slightly remodelling his
> physical features.
>
> (Jung 1930a:510)

All this is difficult to demonstrate scientifically, adds Jung, just like so many
other obvious elements that cannot be scientifically verified – the expressive
nuances of looks, gestures, tone of the voice.

In effect, taking the linguistic aspect as an example, subsequent studies by the French otolaryngologist Alfred Tomatis investigated the way in which these physical characteristics influenced both the human mind and body, in relationship to place and climate. I shall speak of the work of Tomatis in the next chapter.

Somehow, Jung affirmed, the land gets under the skin, leaving a telltale sign on the spirit and mind as well as on the body.

> It is just as though the mind were an infinitely more sensitive and suggestible medium than the body. It is probable that long before the body reacts the mind has already undergone considerable changes, changes that are not obvious to the individual himself or to his immediate circle, but only to an outsider.
>
> (Jung 1930a:511)

Likewise, unless one knows the conditions underlying many of the characteristic aspects of a country they may seem bizarre or ridiculous. Immersion in the atmosphere of the place to which they appertain reveals their fundamental logic.

> Almost every great country has its collective attitude which one might call its genius or *spiritus loci*. Sometimes you catch it in a formula, sometimes it is more elusive, yet nonetheless it is indescribably present as a sort of an atmosphere that permeates everything, the look of the people, their speech, behaviour, clothing, smell, their interests, ideas, politics, philosophy, art and even their religion.
>
> (Jung 1930a:511)

With the examples provided by Jung, and following up what he says in "Mind and Earth," the basic tone of the French *esprit* would be *la gloire*, a marked mental attitude concerning prestige, in both its noble and its ridiculous forms. In Germany everyone would be impersonating an idea: no one is ever a common mortal but is elevated by the position held and the idea it incarnates. Sometimes the idea is part of a more sublime philosophy, at other times it is a harebrained prejudice, but always tending to the ideal. As for England, its contribution is the gentleman, retrieved from the dusty knighthood of the early Middle Ages: the shining armor of the spotless knight and the pious tomb of humble spontaneous sentiments.

Jung finds it harder to synthesize the *spiritus loci* of other countries, such as Italy, Austria, Spain, the Low Countries or Switzerland. One would need, he says, at least several phrases. As for Italy, we have seen how, decades later, Bernhard came up with the idea of the Great Mediterranean Mother.

With regard to America, the subject of this essay, Jung reviews the key ideas: money, first in the scale of values, followed by the heroic ideal, the spasmodic demand for excellence, for the utmost in performance, ambition leading to success and triumph, at times followed or immediately preceded by collapse due to excessive tension.

It is the heroic attitude, part of a competitive and primitive society, that brings out the true historical spirit of the Native Americans.

> The old European inheritance looks rather pale beside these vigorous primitive influences. Have you ever compared the skyline of New York or any great American city with that of a Pueblo like Taos? And did you see how the houses pile up to towers toward the centre? Without conscious imitation the American unconsciously fills out the spectral outline of the Red Man's mind and temperament.
>
> (Jung 1930a:514)

Jung's conclusion regarding what we might call "the return of the repressed" also turns to ancient Rome, when it was in a condition similar to that of the modern metropolis.

> It has always been so: the conqueror overcomes the old inhabitant in the body but succumbs to his spirit. Rome at the zenith of her power contained within her walls all of the mystery cults of the East; yet the

Roman Forum, Rome, Italy. Photo © Bruno Liotta.

spirit of the humblest among them, a Jewish mystery society, transformed the greatest of all cities from top to bottom.

(Jung 1930a:514)

And with regard to America he adds:

Thus a nation in the making is naturally a big risk, to itself as well as
others. It is certainly not my task to play the role of the prophet or of a
ridiculous advisor of nations, and moreover there is nothing to give
advice about. Facts are neither favorable nor unfavorable; they are merely
interesting. And the most interesting of all is that this childlike impetuous "naïve" America has probably the most complicated psychology of
all nations.

(Jung 1930a:514)

Other observations by Jung on this topic are found in two reviews of books
by Hermann Keyserling: *The Rise of a New World*, 1930, and *La Révolution
Mondiale*, 1934.

It would be of interest to compare Jung's observations in the light of the
recent tension between localism and globalization, the disruptive effects of
migration and the current economic policies of the advanced countries. Does
what Jung affirms still hold? Or is it simplistic and dated? Does the spirit of
place continue to permeate the latest arrivals, or has it withdrawn into the
more conservative parts of society, or is it disappearing under the excessive
weight of new modes of behavior and styles of life made common not so
much by the gradual migration of individuals or groups, but by accelerated
economic and commercial colonization?

The Swiss Jung and the Jewish problem

In discussing Jung's essay and other related writings I have purposely not
introduced comments and questions that might have referred, even indirectly,
to the critical debate that has long been going on in the field of psychoanalysis regarding the supposedly anti-Semitic aspects in Jung's theories (of
the 1930s). Tones that might be interpreted as discriminatory have been identified in various essays that deal with the psychology of the peoples and the
relationship between Jews and Christians. These polemics have been nurtured
by the fact that Jung, as president of the International Association of
Psychotherapy, did not at the time openly side with opponents of Nazism. All
this is quite true.

It is also true that, given the quantity and diversity of writings that have
dealt with this question, it has become difficult to synthesize. They sometimes appear as a juridical defense, a *mea culpa*, an exaggerated analysis of
the texts searching for explanations, for elements for the prosecution or the

defense, including a biographic and psychological analysis of Jung himself (Maidenbaum and Berwick 2002, Maidenbaum and Martin 1991, Ryce-Menuhin 1993, Samuels 1993b). Both sides – detractors and defenders – have, I believe, over-emphasized the question.

Perhaps, as Luigi Aurigemma observes in the introduction to the Italian translation of Jung's writings, even now exploitation involves antagonistic schools of thought, therefore preconceived ideologies with superficial inter-pretations destined to fail because of the strange but common psychological phenomenon that one finds only what one is looking for in any author. And therefore, one can also find the anti-Semite Jung.

A second point for reflection is the explicit question: why, concerning this particular argument, are there so few contextualizations of Jung's thought during his life (Gallard 1993) which reveal that in a matter of only a few years those ambiguous notes upon which the criticism was based disappeared, and that he took a clear stand marked by self-criticism? In going over the incriminating years, among Jung's many affirmations, let me propose two. In "After the Catastrophe" (1945), he says:

> our eyes are fascinated by the conditions around us instead of examining our own heart and conscience. Every demagogue exploits this human weakness when he points with the greatest possible outcry to all the things that are wrong in the outside world. But the principal and indeed the only thing that is wrong with the world is man.
>
> (Jung 1945:216)

In "The Undiscovered Self (Present and Future)" of 1957, Jung wrote:

> The horror which the dictator States have of late brought upon mankind is nothing less than the culmination of all those atrocities of which our ancestors made themselves guilty in the not so distant past. Quite apart from the barbarities and blood baths perpetrated by the Christian nations among themselves throughout European history, the European has also to answer for all the crimes he has committed against the colored races during the process of colonization. In this respect the white man carries a very heavy burden indeed. It shows us a picture of the common human shadow that could hardly be painted in blacker colours.
>
> (Jung 1957:296)

Despite this terrible lesson, the abovementioned horrors seem to continue to be perpetrated. On the contemporary scene where protest, unlike the past, has the means and force to express itself, a collective stupefying indifference still predominates, permitting the new demagogues to manipulate not only the masses but also many brilliant minds.

For me, a reader of Jung and many other twentieth-century thinkers, removed in time from his writings and the events involved, it appears obvious that some of what they had to say belongs to their times and we can profit from what is still relevant and useful for the present. Jung was an acknowledged pioneer with his theories of the collective unconscious and archetypes – of particular interest to us here. It must have been difficult for him to interpret the collective reality of his time in a psychological and not political key. He tried to investigate not only the German Unconscious in relation to the Jewish presence in Germany and Europe, but the general psychology of race, nation, group identity, and the psychology of historical and geographical roots. His views were always in relation to progress, to the accelerating scientific and technological development, including the increasing predominance of the North American continent. They were all touchy arguments, which not even the many illustrious representatives of European politics and culture of the time were able to deal with then and there. And the debate is still going on today.

Why, in Jung's generalized, perhaps ingenuous and a bit simplistic, observations on the different psychological makeup of the peoples, have scholars neglected to capture the larger theoretical paradigm of the moment, that of the types formulated in *Psychological Types* – an initial form of "thinking about difference" and a clear invitation to respect diversity rather than a rigid pigeonholing of stereotypes? His "national psychology" should be seen as a typology rather than an ideology.

The third point regards a fact that is often ignored or, rather, forgotten. Jung was Swiss, even if his language was German. He was Swiss and Protestant. His formation, both cultural and religious – his father was a Protestant pastor – and his identity as a citizen reflect, as so often the case with thinkers, the ambience of his country and family of origin, for which he cannot be blamed. He himself affirms, with regards to the chthonic character of the Swiss, that:

> From the earth-boundness of the Swiss come all their bad as well as their good qualities: their down-to-earthness, their limited outlook, their non-spirituality, their parsimony, stolidity, stubbornness, dislike for foreigners, mistrustfulness, as well as that awful Schwizerdütsch and their refusal to be bothered, or to put it in political terms, their neutrality. Switzerland consists of numerous valleys, depressions in the earth's crust, in which the settlements of man are embedded. Nowhere are there measureless plains, where it is a matter of indifference where a man lives; nowhere is there a coast against which the ocean beats with its lore of distant lands. Buried deep in the backbone of the continent, sunk in the earth, the Alpine dweller lives like a troglodyte, surrounded by more powerful nations that are linked with the wide world, that expand into colonies or can grow rich on the treasures of their soil. The Swiss cling to

what they have, for the others, the more powerful ones, have grabbed everything else. Under no circumstances will the Swiss be robbed of their own. Their country is small, their possessions limited. If they lose what they have, what is going to replace it?

(Jung 1928:484)

With these psychological premises, we believe that the enormous cultural broadmindedness inaugurated by Jung anticipated the awareness of differences, pluralities and complexities that characterizes post-modern culture (Hauke 2000).

A fourth point. The intellectual debates, limited to psychoanalytical, philosophical, political, etc. circles on account of their cultural consistency and elite wording, were relatively unimportant with regard to the culture of the masses, which has a rhythm of its own and adopts whatever is deemed useful, wherever and whenever it pleases. Even so, some of the tag ends of comments or cultural dialogues taken up by the mass media and employed in other contexts and with other meanings end up by leveling or, worse, branding an author on the basis of one or more elements of evaluation.

Everything, and the opposite of everything, has naturally been written about Jung, as of other thinkers non-ideological on principle but receptive to change, in the course of his long life and prodigious works involving experiences and elaborations that are occasionally contradictory. Once these authors, often prophetic heralds – an unpardonable sin for their contemporaries – have died, portions of their works may be rejected or revived, with the capricious see-sawing of cultural fashions or needs. An outstanding example is Nietzsche, used more or less by everyone for various purposes.

Finally, a few words on the Jewish question and Jung's place in my own cultural formation. My generation, in confirmation of the enormous importance of education in the formation of the individual, grew up weeping over Anne Frank's diary, on films devoted to the Holocaust, shuddering when the word "Nazi" or Hitler's name was mentioned. For a certain period there was an ambivalence with regard to Germany in general, to the Germans, their language, evocative of the cruelty of the SS uniforms. It was all to the advantage of the American liberator, hero, savior and bringer of good things, enjoyable and desirable, such as American cinema, music, the language, food, literature and fashions. Then at a certain point there was something new to worry about: the Soviet Union, with its Communism and the dilemma of how the two new blocs, the USSR and the USA, would distribute the Good and Evil in the world. The Berlin Wall and the concentration camps certainly did nothing to make the Eastern bloc model more acceptable, even though health and education for all were now available. Meanwhile, for those who were not as tied to the recent past and the war and were looking to the future, the Western model was beginning to reveal its less pleasant aspects. Self-criticism came from the United States on policies at home – criticism of the consumer model and the American way of life – as well as its policies abroad, culminating in the protest against the war in Vietnam.

This capacity for self-criticism on the part of America permitted the European who sided with Communism or was left-wing in general not to take his own preceding images to heart. It could be said, and still is, that there are different types of Americans.

In the meantime the fact that the Jews had finally been given a homeland after the dramas of the Nazi Holocaust seemed only just. And it is. Not only because all peoples have a right to a homeland, but because it had been denied them for too long.

For those who are not Jewish or for those outside the Jewish culture, this is more or less a picture that the mass media and the general culture in the post-Second World War democracies have provided.

Over sixty years have passed since the end of the Second World War and the

Empire State Building, New York, USA. Photo © Bruno Liotta.

international, as well as the political, situation has become extremely complicated, at least in the eyes of my generation. The problem is not the past as such, but rather the past that does not leave people free to analyze the present. It is not to be confounded with the memory of the historical event, which should remain unforgettable as a universal warning, in its educational value.

Today the question of a possible collective anti-Semitism is quite unlike the one that led to the Nazi Holocaust, because the world has changed as never before in the history of humanity. The horrors of the past are still there, but racism and territorial conflicts have multiplied and spread throughout the world to such an extent – and above all we are aware of them – that European and Mediterranean events must be seen in planetary dimensions. How many peoples in the 20th century were subjected to massacres and genocides? Can we think – in the light of the democratic values that we wish to make universal – that some peoples merit more attention or have more voice than others in seeing their territorial rights, or their traditions, culture, language recognized? That there are nations endowed with greater value, with a more significant history because of the strength, intelligence and illustrious personages that characterized them while the fate of other, less important nations is of minor interest, is less significant? That a conflict or war undertaken for racial motives is worse than one motivated by religion, economy, territorial disputes or whatever?

Some may say yes, but those who are concerned with the health of human beings, like doctors who have sworn on oath to carry out their duties, must not discriminate or exclude anyone on the basis of ethnic, cultural, religious or political provenience.

This vision, so to speak, of equal opportunities, rights and duties does not cancel any legitimate difference and uniqueness, original or temporary or acquired, but puts them in different logical orders.

Seen from this point of view, not all conflicts regarding the Jews are racial and it would be a serious error, as unfortunately happens, to transform them into racial conflicts. A territorial conflict, for example, is not a religious or racial conflict.

What does all this have to do with Jung and with analytical psychology?

A great deal, for if I do not take it upon myself to offer answers of some kind to these questions, in view of my personal approach to Jung and the subject of this book, I would risk being accused of anti-Semitism when I cite the Palestinian people as an example of their bond with the earth and suffering for its loss, for the destruction of their homes, their enclosure in camps and the exile of the refugees, in a war of occupation that seems to have no end.

Back to words and earth

In the first chapter discussing migration and racism I referred to the contradictions and ambivalences that surround words such as race, homeland, nation, earth, blood, people, and the like. Each of them can be interpreted, felt, treated with conflicting reactions, in the sense of the diversity, variety and otherness I have already indicated, or in the sense of the discrimination typical of ideological–political interpretations. But this does not depend on the words. "Race," for example, which I will not attempt to use, brings to my mind the geographical atlases of my childhood in which, in addition to the continents, their physical and political geography, the races of the world were represented. I would leaf through the book, entranced by the different faces, the colors, the clothing, as in the postcards of the Italian regions represented by traditional costumes. It all seemed an enormous wealth and I wanted to get to know them all, these men and women of different races, and visit their lands.

Words can of course be changed if they appear outdated or threatening because they have been misused. But biodiversity, to use a modern term, is an undeniable fact of life on the planet Earth.

What I have tried to do in this book when dealing with complicated concepts and found myself on thin ice, with words and meanings that were ambivalent, with cultural changes referring to both the past and the present, was to treat the human being and his complement of basic functions for adaptation and survival in the surrounding environment from a naturalistic point of view, being as honest psychologically as possible. All human beings know what nostalgia is. That's basically all there is to it.

Even so, my turning to the earth, as the original dimension, is neither naïve nor acultural, much less anti-cultural. For this is a particular moment, of great importance to me; a historical moment in which nature is really threatened and culture is struggling to impose its symbolic strength, the synthesis of critical intelligence and ethical values, the continuous search for knowledge. It is a culture supported ambiguously by other, often quite overt, powers.

In my use of the concept of earth, aside from nature that supports us all, I am also thinking of earth–house–culture, of a symbolic people such as the Native Americans and those who, like them, have lost their land forever, the indigenous peoples or natives of South America and of other continents, who barely survive when confronted with the economy of the advanced society. I am thinking of the Kurds, the Armenians, the recent events in former Yugoslavia, as well as the Palestinians; of all those oppressed groups, driven from their homes and subjected to various forms of extermination, forced to migrate or live segregated. I am thinking of their suffering and I don't believe that any of them are greater or more just than any others.

The phenomenon of uprooting and its effect on the psychological level, whatever the scale, is basically what I wish to deal with more in depth in this book. With this in mind, Jung's thought and work, even when accused of being ambiguous, have been useful in analyzing the problems raised here and to which I shall return. With regard to clinical observations, for instance, I

Grand Canyon, Colorado, USA. Photo © Bruno Liotta.

can only confirm many of Jung's hypotheses: even the more naïve ones, which are communicated with just as much naïveté by the foreign patients, who often have no particular knowledge or interest in psychological theories. Lastly, I believe that the current socio-political world, interpreted through Jung's own intuitions, or "comments" as he defines them, could enrich us not only in the depth and profundity of the analysis of the happening, but also in a comprehensive perspective of the current tendencies and movements towards the future.

Chapter 3

The place of origins

My mother groan'd! my father wept,
Into the dangerous world I leapt:
Helpless, naked, piping loud:
Like a fiend hid in a cloud.

Struggling in my father's hands:
Striving against my swaddling bands:
Bound and weary I thought best
To sulk upon my mother's breast.
          (William Blake, *Infant Sorrow*)

The purpose of this chapter is to demonstrate that from a geographic and social point of view the place of origin is a fundamental factor in the psychology of the individual and a force that accompanies the person, perhaps unconsciously, for the rest of his life. If one knows how to look, the beginnings hold everything. Moreover, a place of origin, where one is born, is also a place where a new form is created, original and unique, which takes us back to a discussion of the process of individuation.

I will close the chapter with a few considerations on the concept of "roots," often used as a synonym for "origins," and one that is nowadays also charged with rather vague valences.

Naturally, when thinking of migration, it is comprehensible that the place of origin, lost on a concrete level, can be reinforced on a symbolic level and take on different meanings within every personal story. Having been driven out, legally deprived of the right to live on one's land and speak one's own tongue, can be considered as a violence and an abuse on a psychological level, above and beyond the historical and political conditions in which the departure takes place. On the other hand, choosing to leave or flee from one's own place, whatever the reason, can make the event even more difficult to elaborate, for the pain remains but there is no one to blame. The emotion that accompanies their first return home in so many stories of emigrants is a powerful mixture of joy and pain, a rediscovery mixed with novelties and memories, a state of inner turmoil in which loss has to take rediscovery into account.

What could be more archetypal than origins? Their universality comes to the fore in man's eternal question: "where" do we come from, "where" does everything that exists come from? The answer always, in an imaginative or realistic way, begins with place. It is like recounting a dream, a fairy story, a true story.

The place where we were born is something that nowadays is impossible to forget or not know if only because every time we fill in a questionnaire with our personal data, "born in" appears as an identifying element, following our name and before another place, the changeable place of our residence. Surnames too occasionally incorporate the memory of the family place of origin through the centuries.

In childhood

In psychology, the place of origin, of the roots of the adult personality, is actually also a time, that of early childhood, and a relationship, the primary one with whoever takes care of the child, usually the mother.

Place and time are merged and connected in intrauterine life, in that original environment where the body of the mother and that of the child share the same material, separated only by the placenta, in a process of development with a well-defined end.

With regard to this primary condition, D.W. Winnicott wrote in *Human Nature*:

> After the baby is born this substance that joins and also separates becomes represented by objects and phenomena of which it can be said once again that while they are part of the infant they are also part of the environment. Only gradually do we demand of the developing individual that there shall be a fully acknowledged distinction between external reality and inner psychic reality; indeed there is a relic of the intermediate substance in the cultural life of grown men and women, in fact in that which most clearly distinguishes human beings from the animals (religion, art, philosophy).
>
> (Winnicott 1988:157–158)

It must however be remembered that the early stages are never truly abandoned, so that in studying an individual of whatever age all the environmental requisites, from before and from after, can be found.

In the individual life the place of origin is therefore a shared space of mutual hospitality. The child too holds within itself parts of the mother.

Recently a great deal has been written in psychological literature regarding origins, and a specific field of study, prenatal psychology, has now found a

DNA sculpture, Valencia, Spain. Photo © Bruno Liotta.

place in academic institutes and courses. Favored by the technological development of endoscopic studies, this discipline shows to what extent the period and place of gestation are already in relation with and influenced by the external world.

In the maternal womb, a place common to all as well as different for all, an obscure proto-mental representation of life is formed, a preconception of stimuli that arrive to the senses through the initial functioning of the body. Man's first home is a place of fervid activity. Is this place really as protected as we think when we look at it from outside? Is it as safe and warm as had always been romantically imagined? And to what extent is the embryo aware?

The myth of the expulsion from the terrestrial Paradise is sometimes interpreted as an obscure recollection of the event of birth. Today – and this does not mean a dissolution or a changing of the myth – what in the collective imagination has always been the blessed place *par excellence* and for which there is always a certain nostalgia, is the object of scientific and biotechnological studies that are transforming it into a field for experimentation and medical involvement, not without commercial implications.

Between myth and reality, the place of origin of life remains a special place in the collective imagination, a place that goes beyond the mother's womb. For there is more to birth than the actual delivery.

D.W. Winnicott once again highlights the importance of the environment right after birth:

> In an examination of the factors leading to integration and to the indwelling of the psyche in the body, one of these concerns the environment and general physical care as an expression of love.
>
> (Winnicott 1988:156)

"Environment" is a term D.W. Winnicott uses interchangeably with "place" to define what surrounds the child. It is characterized by both material and affective aspects.

Whether psychological birth – i.e. the perception of oneself as a unit, and therefore also of an environment perceived as exterior – is really out of phase with respect to the physical environment that precedes it, is a moot question among scholars. Unquestionably, the infant and the very small child lack the means to let us understand this clearly. We also know that there is no conscious memory of these first phases of life. Moreover, the "birth of the mother," as Stern and Bruschweiler-Stern (1998) note, that is the awareness in the mother of her new state and role, also takes time to shape up. In other words in the environment surrounding the child in the first months of life, the sequence of meals, changing diapers and sleep proceeds in a particular state of consciousness that encloses the mother–child pair, guided by instinct or tradition, rather than in relation to the concrete places that the adults prepare so carefully. The place, the environment, in the beginning is above all the body of the mother and her actions.

Even so, in this phase direct observation of the infant already shows that the child reacts to multiple stimuli as it passes from the mother's breast to her arms, or to others, to the cradle, the bed, the stroller, the chair in the car, and then all around, the room, the house, and its sounds, the voices, everything that populates the initial environment of life. All these places soon become recognizable and differentiated from each other.

How origins, space and time intersect is a subject of a philosophical nature, which psychology can deal with only up to a certain point. I would simply like to mention here that the coordinates in which we normally place our experiences, such as time and space, are categories that develop in the mind of the child as its brain matures and on the basis of the first experiences of life in concrete spaces and times prearranged by the adults. At the same time, from the beginning, the creative and imaginative capacity is developed in that same mind/brain, and is subsequently capable of overcoming the space/time limits, and imagining non-existent places and trips through time.

In continuing let me note that the place of origin is not only the object of individual curiosity, expressed by the inevitable question of the child: "where was I before?"

In myth

The same question characterizes collective symbolism, mythology and the specific "cult of origins," diffused in ancient and primitive cultures throughout the world, a confirmation of the fact that, as mentioned, it is an archetypal motif that has always accompanied humanity.

A few examples of the multiplicity of the places of origin follow: in Ancient Egypt, the waters of Nun, a sort of liquid in the darkness of non-existence which contains the spark of life; in Ancient Greece, Chaos; in the Near Eastern cultures the Breath, in China the Tao, the Tai chi, the main beam, the door of all things, the origin of Yin and Yang, the primordial cosmic egg. In Aboriginal Australia the place, the song and myth are closely connected in a sort of collective map of the territory; in the oral cultures of Africa, the place of origin of the world is the white, cloudless, empty sky with a suspended tree (Tanzania) or a drop of milk (Mali), the Nothing where death, creator of an immense sea of mud, lived (Guinea), or the lotus flower, and so on.

For the Hebrew and then the Christian culture, the breath, the Word – of God – together become a place of creation through naming. As is also the case for the Veda, the sacred books of India where the places of origin and nature of the Earth spring forth from the actions of a primordial mythical figure, a demiurge, of which, however, the origins remain obscure, set in a sort of uncreated, of infinite, of absolute, that subsequently and for a long time was to become a universal place of philosophical reasoning.

Today, the infinite and the uncreated are identified with the celestial universe, the cosmic space, through which space probes and other means of exploration built by human technology travel. But also with the infinitely small level of microphysics, those empty invisible spaces of probability, of quantistic uncertainty. In contemporary advanced society the myth of the origins is the scientific Big Bang, the great explosion from which everything began, a place that is also an event. Still today, however, there is a clear difference, already found in myth, between the origins of the world and the origins of man, the former an indispensable premise for the latter.

Jung is known for having dealt with the history of religions, of mythology, anthropology and ethnology, and for introducing the psychological study of symbolism, in particular with his innovative study on alchemy. Actually, behind what appears as a broad and detailed collective fresco, there was always, in Jung's mind, the single individual journey. It was through the eyes of the individual and his faculty for creating symbols that Jung set out to study the phenomena of the collective unconscious that appear in the form of images, rituals, artistic products, dreams and fantasies in the course of the history of culture. A central theme in Jung's work, which interests us here, is that of the origin of consciousness, i.e. of the ego that emerges from the Unconscious. In particular, Jung was extremely interested in the theme of

Atomic structure, Valencia, Spain. Photo © Bruno Liotta.

inner rebirth, since it was a transforming event at the zenith of that journey which, in the representation of the myth, was undertaken by the founding hero. The journey, initially symbolized by the *uroboros* image – literally "tail eater," the serpent that coils up on itself, constituting a first closed place – then takes the hero through various trials, up to liberation, to that birth–rebirth of the Self, identified with respect to its original matrix (Jung 1952).

This psychological journey, noted by Jung in other forms and images, as well as in historical texts of alchemy, is a model of the inner transformation, seen therefore as a passage from the *unio confusa* of all things, or the *prima materia*, to *separatio* and discrimination, up to the birth of the new form and new relationships, the *coniunctio*. As a hypothetical model, the scheme becomes applicable both on an individual and on various collective levels, and in all phases of life. There is not one single beginning, one single origin, but a repetition of transforming passages.

The place of origin, in this sense, is the one where the transformation takes place, a sort of alchemical crucible. The analyst's room can therefore also be a place of origin, that of the rebirth or new birth of the self, of new psychological awareness, to which the dreams, fantasies, scenarios of the sandplay bear witness when they present the image of the newborn or the *puer*.

Sandplay, invented by Dora Kalff, is a method I will often refer to, of an expressive–creative type (Kalff 1980). It is used by some Jungian psychoanalysts during psychotherapy with their patients. The play consists of a tray containing sand that serves as a base-container for the construction of a scene using miniature figurines and other materials (Aite 2003, Ammann 1991).

The Great Mother

Erich Neumann's studies then followed those of Jung. In his *The Origins and History of Consciousness* and *The Great Mother* he fully develops the theme that interests us here, above all from the point of view of the collective psyche and its cultural productions, although reference to the inner transpersonal dimension is maintained. In the first book, in the chapter dedicated to the *uroboros* and the creation myths, Neumann describes the place of origin as a symbol of the perfection of the beginnings, a place of containment of opposites and forebears, figuratively represented by the circle, by the *rotundum* of alchemy, with which concrete objects such as the ball, the egg, the womb and many others, including natural places, are associated.

Every depth, abyss, valley, sea and bottom of the sea, lake and marsh, as well as earth and lower world, cave or house and city are parts of this archetype. Every large object that embraces and contains and nourishes a small one belongs to the primitive maternal dominion.

Neumann also presents the regressive and destructive aspects of the uroboric condition, particularly pertinent for those, like the psychotherapist, who deal with psychological imbalances or mental illness. The Great Mother welcomes and takes into herself the small child and uroboric incest is always seen as a sign of death, of the final dissolution of the union with the mother. Symbols of this rite of reunion are the cavern, earth, sepulcher, coffin. It begins with burial in a fetal position in the Stone Age to the contemporary cinerary urn. The underlying meaning of many forms of desire and nostalgia, ranging from the mystical union of the saint up to the drinker's desire to lose consciousness and the Teutonic "romanticism of death" is this return to uroboric incest and self-dissolution. What we call uroboric incest is a turning back, a renouncing of oneself.

In *The Great Mother*, Neumann analyzes not only the maternal archetype, in its positive, negative and transformative characteristics, but also its universal symbolism, accompanied by illustrations that indicate as a primary and central symbol the vase, in its equation woman = body = vase, the point of departure in ancient art for all the other symbols, natural and cultural. In its negative aspect, that of the terrible, devouring mother, all those disturbing places that characterize initiation myths and stories appear, those in which life and death are set side by side, as in the case of the adventures of the hero: the vase-belly of Jonah's whale, the earth that buries and dissolves, the door that leads to the Underworld, the toothed vagina, water that submerges, and still others, taken from the vast mythological repertory of mankind. Neumann has this to say of the transforming character of the Great Mother:

> But nearly all the early and primitive documents trace the origin of the world and of man to the darkness, the Great Round, the goddess. Whether, as in countless myths, the source of all life is the primordial ocean or whether it is earth or heaven, the sources have one thing in common: *darkness*. It is this primordial darkness which bears the light as moon, stars, and sun, and almost everywhere these luminaries are looked upon as the offspring of the Nocturnal Mother.
>
> (Neumann 1955:212)

I must include a quote from Winnicott here, which enriches this concept.

> The idea of a wonderful time in the womb (the oceanic feeling, etc.) is a complex organisation of denial of dependence. Any pleasure that comes with regression belongs to the idea of a perfect environment, and against this has to be weighted the idea, just as real for the regressed child or adult, of an environment so bad that there can be no hope of a personal existence.
>
> (Winnicott 1988:159)

It is clear therefore that the place of origin presents itself to the human being in an ambivalent form: as a trustworthy safe place, that furnishes force and propulsion towards the exterior, or as a place that holds in and that threateningly attempts to reabsorb the new creative energies.

J. Pearson proposes a Jungian vision, which identifies the Great Mother Earth with the natural environment, today desacralized and in need of protection, as another key (in Christopher and McFarland Solomon 1999).

At this point, returning to the figure of the migrant, let me propose a psychodynamic hypothesis. Perhaps, after the separation from his land, the archetype of the nourishing and positive mother remains in the place of origin, while for those who have never left, the same place continues to host the archetype of the mother who holds back as well. Actual separation can correspond to an inner scission. Myth, however, tells us that the hero, wherever he is, must loosen his ties of dependency with the mother. That is just the point: wherever he is. The place of origin, like the mother, requires an inner confrontation, which, according to the subsequent movements of life, will be different for every individual.

In the case of psychotherapy, one must be careful not to underestimate or overestimate the concrete elements in a broader context that sees the human being as able to transcend, through psychological awareness, the historical

Madonna delle Rose, 16th century (copy after Raphael) Church of St. Agostino), Rome, Italy. Photo © Elena Liotta.

conditions of his own existence. I mean that through the memory and consciousness of the past, migrants and non-migrants can, in the present, be freer from the conditioning of the concrete earth/mother.

From birth on

The world is my womb,
and my mother's womb
was my first world.
R.D. Laing 1977: 43

Moving on from the figure of the great archetypal mother to the real mother, or the mother in a context, I shall now deal with the origins of man and woman on a personal level. We have already said that our own birth is never consciously remembered but is sedimented in our memory both through the primary experiences and the fantasies and through the stories of others, in the end constituting a personal myth of the origins.

Conception–birth is a process of manifestation, a literal coming into the world – first hidden by the body of the mother, and then made explicit – both from the point of view of the subject and from that of the other objects/subjects pre-existent in space. In this sense it resembles the creation of a work of art.

What interests me is the reception and the container, more than what is created, with regard above all to the qualities of the real mother of every child. The mother is the one who translates and filters the relation with life, is a sort of enveloping aura of the child's experience, providing the child with an initial disposition towards spaces and things, creating and presenting him with the spaces that surround him.

Let us try to imagine how this environment that surrounds a new life can at a certain point become the child's "own" space, its "own" place, its "own" origins.

Catapulted into the world endowed with senses – but not with sense – the child begins to know the world around him through his body and the body as it moves in space, adapting himself to a space that is already there.

Then, still in space, the child accustoms his eyes and calibrates his other senses, seeking there the persons on whom he is dependent and whom he loves, stimulated by the sounds of the mother tongue. He gradually acquires an awareness of near, far, above and below, and begins to structure and define, psychologically as well as physically, the environment, the places connected to his attachments, pleasant and unpleasant, the places permitted and those forbidden, eventually creating personal associations in an independent way.

When held in her mother's arms my two-month-old niece attentively observed the black stovepipe of the kitchen stove. What interested her most was not the fire but the stovepipe, that black band against the white wall. After that, every time that she came back into the room she would immediately look for the stovepipe, even from a different angle. It had become a point of reference, of recognition and of reassurance. She had chosen it among other things, and had created her personal place to refer to. Who knows how many shapes and adult choices for spaces and places have far-distant forgotten roots?

With regard to the "places of origin" everyone creates a personal *anima loci*, the soul of the place, made of colors, climate, sounds, habits, traditions of each specific family and the affects that weave all this together every day with the passage of time. It is the beginning of a "love for my places."

Language itself, the factor of culturalization *par excellence*, is also very

Chinese child, China. Photo © Bruno Liotta.

materially earth, geography. And what about music and the dances that characterize the different peoples and their countries? Or those creations so
immediately evocative of the places, such as blues in the United States or the
tango in Argentina, fruit of migration and nostalgia?

Alfred Tomatis supports the thesis of the "impedance of air," i.e. the profound influence, in learning a language, of the physical characteristics of the
sound, of its composition and the air that transports the sounds, beginning
with each geographical place and its specific climate. For study and treatment
Tomatis built a machine called "electronic ear" that sent stimuli to the ear
through an earphone and was initially used for persons who had hearing
problems and subsequently with other categories such as singers, musicians
in general, language teachers. He discovered the close bonds between body,
position, ear, hearing, way of listening, silence, psychological states, mood,

illness and geographical ambience. He discovered also that every language, every dialect, every place in which a language is spoken produced a specific "ear," in the sense of a form of listening, described in the envelope curve drawn on the spectrogram, endowed with precise frequency bands visible to audiological examination. There is an Italian ear, a French ear, an English ear. Every ethnic ear can be defined by its spectrum of receptivity, an ethnogram. For example, the French ear has a selective range from 1,000 to 2,000 Hz, the English ear from 2,000 to 12,000. The sound crosses the air, is carried by the air, which varies as a result of many factors, above all climatic, that constitute the impedance of air; factors to which the ear adapts, filtering determined frequencies, orienting the body and the posture. In humid places there is a greater fluidity of language – and this is not an ingenuous observation – of archaic metaphysical interdependencies. Which is why there are as many languages and dialects as there are places in which human beings live.

Unaware, as far as I know, of Jung's observations in "Mind and Earth," Tomatis observed that specific phenomena such as nasalization distinguish not the languages, but the places where they are spoken: strong in the English spoken in America; absent in that spoken in England; present in the English of Italian immigrants to America, for whom nasalization is not an original element; very strong in the Native Americans.

Returning to the process of individuation, it can be interpreted as the formation, moment by moment, of one's own individual uniqueness, the result of repeated daily experiences, of one's own constitutional background, of the new discoveries and acquisitions made in the course of life, and also of the imprint of the places where we were born and where we lived and live, of their culture and their language (Piaget and Inhelder 1967, Reagan 2000, Tobin et al. 1989).

There is always, albeit perhaps unconsciously, a geographic background to memory, to feelings, to the sense of continuity of one's identity; there is always an *I am, I was, we were, I will be, I would like to be, I would like to go . . . there*, in *that place*.

The place of birth, as is becoming evident, is never only the body of the mother, a collective myth or a geographical notation, the name of a city or a village, a nation. One can start from one aspect or another but then all the rest will be encountered, like a chain. And everyone when asked "where do you come from?" will begin the story in his own way, defining his own origins depending on the psychological importance of one element or another and the first conscious memories. I always recall the atmosphere, the landscapes, the light, the colors, the odors, the flavors and sounds, the feeling of air on my skin. Being in the body so fully is a gift of childhood. And then who and what is around, close by. The moods of the persons, their voices. And gradually, in life, the map is enlarged to include new places and new ambiences. They are very concrete aspects.

I'll let R.D. Laing say it in more detail. On the cover of the Italian edition of Laing's book, *The Facts of Life: An Essay in Feelings, Facts and Fantasy* is the picture of a child looking out perplexed from a large cabbage. But the author was not born under a cabbage (in Italy children are born in two different ways: under a cabbage or being brought by the stork). Here is his story:

> I was born at 17.15 hours on 7 October 1927, into a family that consisted of my mother and father, living in a small three-room flat on the south side of Glasgow. My father could not admit to anyone for several days that I was born.

> My mother and I slept in one room in separate beds, and my father slept in another room . . . my mother and father still swear they do not know how I was conceived.
>   But there is a birthmark on his right knee and one on mine. A fact against immaculate conception.

Elsewhere in the same book, Laing asks himself various legitimate questions.

> When did "I" begin? . . . Did I come from anywhere? Am I going to anywhere? Are there people who know more about these matters than I? . . . Is there any sense in wondering who or what I am and why I am here?

> This collection of cells has the impression that it is I . . . Or maybe we are footprints.

> I take it on the authority of biologists that, biologically speaking, we all have begun in the same way. Namely, as one cell, somewhere in one of the uterine tubes, or in the womb of one's mother.

> We are physical systems who, by our own experience, are *sentient*. We feel . . . We flourish under certain circumstances, and we wilt under others. It seems then that a healthy human being possessed of motility has a tropism for its optimizing environment. It seems that we have a tendency in the *opposite* direction.
>
>   (emphasis in original)

On others and the environment:

> That is, whatever, whoever I may be is not to be confused with the names people give *to* me, or how they *describe* me, or what they *call* me. I am not my name.

I am presumably *what* they are describing, but not their description. I am the territory, what they say I am is their map of me . . . What, or where, is the territory?

No *unfertilized ovum* ever implants. Implantation is to be *adopted*. The earth is my mother. My mother was my earth.

How many conceptions are desired? How many of us are desired *only* for conception, but not to be adopted by implantation?

The difference between being welcome and unwelcome, between a welcoming environment and an unwelcoming environment, is all the difference in the world. Even to enter a room. The difference between being welcomed or not welcomed! We cannot take the life cycle of the *wanted* as the statistical norm . . . *We* only know whether or not the environment influences us by noticing we are influenced . . . e.g., a toxic environment may render us insensible to its toxicity. Are we re-creating around us an artificial environment which has a tendency to induce in us an unawareness of its noxious characteristics: an anaesthetizing noxious sublethal environment?

(emphasis in original)

On mythology:

Mythology may be a key to our embryological experience . . . It is at least *conceivable* to me that myths, legends, stories, dreams, fantasies, and conduct *may* contain strong reverberations of our uterine experience . . . Some myths fit better than others but enough do to make me consider seriously the possibility that conception to implantation, and subsequent prenatal adventures, are represented mythologically in postnatal imagery.

(Laing 1977:13–43 *passim*; emphasis in original)

Place and creation of form

In the original place, in the place of birth, something miraculous happens: the beginning of something new, of a form that was inexistent and that gradually comes into being, opens, becomes more complex, or in common language, grows, develops. From the DNA helix to the human body. Everything that comes forth, nourished by the relationship with the environment and its resources, was implicit in the original form, in its model, in the predisposing possibilities. Every form is a limited whole, within which infinite configurations are possible.

Today, thanks to the ecograph, medical technology allows us to observe directly the invisible places of the conception of life and intrauterine development, absolutely inaccessible to our ancestors, who had to intuit and imagine them, creating their stories. As life continues, other places will host new beginnings, new origins, and new symbols will also appear as self-awareness gradually develops and meanings are built on new experiences.

The model of symbolic, mental creation follows the same course as natural creation, with similar elements, and it keeps the same language. Give birth, being born, growing, developing and so on are words that are also used for abstract concepts, such as a project; an idea; a theory; a scientific, philosophic system; a work of art. The model they share is as follows: there is an origin, a process, a container, a network of relationships, a code, an energy, a dynamic, a result, a product, a final manifestation. The cyclic process moves from the undifferentiated and from chaos to design, to order: a cyclic process well represented, as previously mentioned, by the alchemic model that Jung introduced to symbolically understand the evolution of consciousness, from the raw material to its sublimation, from lead to gold.

It is as if matter, the earth, were to take on life and soul, to remain in the theme of the book. *Animated* matter was a term used to distinguish plants and animals – endowed with movement and a span of time between life and death – from the static *inanimate* and apparently immortal material. The discoveries of contemporary science regarding the constitution of matter, the neurosciences and, in particular, the recent convergences between quantum physics and analytical psychology try to explain the interface between concrete, tangible and visible levels of reality and those implied, non-visible, but still intuitable and put to the test by subjectivity.

The concepts of movement, of form and information are central in this striving for knowledge. Matter is not at all as solid, dense and concrete as we perceive it. The earth is not a dimension as contrary and irreconcilable with the soul as many philosophical–religious visions had sensed. Form, rhythm, movement, dynamics have laws that are halfway between what matter is and what matter is not (Corbin 1989, Peat 1987).

With regard to human beings and their psychology, this new point of view gives us further insights into the idea of individuation: a journey towards one's own form, which is self-constructed in one's experience with the environment. It might be said that individuating one's self is recognizing, is delineating, this specific, inimitable form of "controlled origins," so to speak. A form that is also a personal style: the sign, the token, the signature, the interpretation of one's DNA.

At this point the dimension "earth" begins, so to speak, to become lighter.

The manifestation of the form, whether perceived as exterior to the human being or within the mind, needs space to unfold in its dynamic, changeable, animated nature. The form appears from that intermediate place of being and not being, or of being who knows where, before appearing.

Sensorial Space, interior. © 2006 Fausto Ferrara, Pino Barillà.

A natural example might be the rainbow. What is the place where the rainbow takes form? Suddenly the colors appear, an arch, a brief miracle. It wasn't there before and will soon disappear. Where does it go? the child asks. And reflections on water, the glittering of the sea? A scientific description of the phenomenon is never completely satisfactory.

It is the dynamics between implicit and explicit, visible and hidden, exposed and protected, that determines reality more than the fact of whether it is or is not concrete. Capturing a form fully is in fact the result of a collaboration between the individual and the world, an act of attention to the world. The rainbow depends on the position of the viewer, intercepting light, in that place and at that moment. It is a co-creation. An encounter.

If the earth really contained a soul, like the alchemic gold in matter, it would still be up to us to find it.

With respect to the relationship between soul and earth, it is clear that I am now destabilizing the earth and shifting the emphasis onto the formation of subjectivity, which in order to be creatively free must in part free itself from the concrete. In this case, the places change, become more indefinite, even if not necessarily symbolic or metaphorical. Some concrete places are less concrete than others, such as frontiers, or those that today are defined as non-places.

Emptiness or the void

Thus we reach another point I believe to be fundamental. There is always a void in the places of creation, including artistic creation. It might even be said that the place of creation, the original place, is "a" void. Not "the void." A particular void: the empty space of the white sheet of paper, the immaculate canvas, the empty room, the intact stone, the formless clay, the calm mind. All voids, apertures waiting to be filled.

Normally one tends to imagine places as containers of things that can be counted and described, as if the space had been made to be filled and classified by man. It makes me think of the adult together with the small child when faced with a new environment. He points to things, giving them names and qualities, calling attention to the objects rather than giving the child time to observe, contemplate, organize the experience on its own. We, humans as well as animals, have a specific innate predisposition for perceiving a void: the sense of depth, which helps us survive. In classic experiments, kittens and children put over a protected empty space are afraid to move for fear of falling, even if they don't know yet what it means to fall. Is it this instinctive fear of emptiness, the *horror vacui*, that makes us feel we must fill in the spaces?

Life needs an empty space, for a void is not simply something dangerous for those who cannot fly. Like all fundamental dimensions, it becomes in the course of life an ambiguous place, charged with negative or positive attachments accumulated according to preceding experiences. In the final part of one of my previous books, *Educare al Sé*, I propose various points of view from which to approach this emptiness: listening, silence, waiting, abstention, withdrawal. Elsewhere I speak of non-relation, non-action, non-thought, non-attachment. I speak of it as a mental state, in which what takes place is contemplation, an interior space that can be facilitated or even introduced by a concrete space.

There are physical places, natural or man-made, that spontaneously activate this state of emptiness, even though they are not concretely empty. Cathedrals, mosques, some landscapes, other enclosed or open places, put space in an order of a kind that produces access to places of the mind that would otherwise seem to be precluded. They give space a form that harmonizes emptiness and fullness, relieving anxiety and permitting a spiritually creative experience. Unfortunately these encounters between exterior place and interior world are becoming ever rarer in advanced societies. They may be artificially produced but this does not guarantee that they are truly experienced.

The relationship with emptiness reacquires all its threatening aspect in the field of psychopathology, in its extreme forms of withdrawal, of isolation, of solitude and loss. Few authors are sufficiently skillful to speak of psychosis or mental states without using psychiatric terms. Jung of course can, as can the phenomenologist in general, as well as Laing, previously mentioned. There is another creative psychiatrist who had a great deal to say on emptiness, in the sense of a place of origin:

Jean Oury. Tuned in to Lacan, some of whose central themes he elaborated on, Oury worked in the fields of institutional psychiatry and psychoanalysis, as well as psychosis, art and pedagogy.

For Oury schizophrenia is a disturbance of rhythm, in relation to the creative processes and the normal and pathological psychological states. Rhythm is a category halfway between space and time, and not by chance is associated with music, with the dance, with art in general. What interests us here is that in his analysis, always on a symbolic level, Oury sets particular importance on the idea of space: the site, the place that accompanies the psychic processes.

In *Creazione e schizofrenia*:

> A place of gathering, not necessarily of existing things, which make existence possible . . . something pre-intentional, pre-representative . . . Beginning with rhythm there is space and there will be time.
> (Oury 1992:39; translated from the Italian by trans.)

Giving form to rythm – *Gestaltung* – is what actually allows for psychic survival.

> *Gestaltung* (formation) constructs a space, a site. What interests us is this site, this absolutely specific space where something on the order of the random can manifest itself, but not in a non-psychotic dimension; that is not to be something closed on itself, but that there be something open . . . *Gestaltung* is dynamic, not static! It is the "informing," it is not the path that leads to, but the path that forms itself . . . It is a world that is permanently in the making, the making of the pre- . . . in order for an object to exist, there has first to be a construction. It is not a matter of time or of space or of protospace or of prototime; it is a matter of rhythm.
> (Oury 1992:31 and *passim*; translated from the Italian by trans.)

For Oury, rhythm is based on the unconscious interaction between figure and ground, and it is the power of the ground that acts on the motif. Form, rhythm, ground, all refer to a receiving place, the *kora*, a place where there is no absolute distinction between colors, between hot and cold, a place of a sort of effervescence.

Once more the uroboros. This place from which, at a certain point, movement and rhythm arise is also a place that conceals and keeps secret. Oury captures the connection between secretiveness and opening into another interior place/state: the atrium/retreat, the space in the monasteries where the monks stroll, a place of conversation and exchange, or the space in

What Is This (the Circle)? Calligraphy by Yamada
Mumon Roshi (1900–1988), Zen master.

front of the church, again atrium, the *sagrato*. From here desire and the word
can emerge.

Oury, with his liminal eye, stresses the element of the *pre-*, the space for
building and delimiting that which will be the self also in relation to the social
dimension. Like R.D. Laing and David Cooper, Oury's position is based on
anti-psychiatry or the sociogenesis of psychopathology and the relationship
between the individual and society, opening up new horizons. Although there
is an idiopathic dimension in mental disturbance, there can also be a margin
of freedom that can be recovered in a liberating praxis, through the group as a
subject. Thus we have a new container, womb, place; that *temenos*, sacred
place, in which, as Jung says, the archetypes of the collective unconscious –
the forms – live.

From emptiness to the form, to the other, to the others, to the group.

All psychoanalysis has at a certain point asked what the relationship was
between subject and environment, although by "environment" is meant the
social environment. First of all the family. Freud too talked of a complex of
the *Nebenmensch*, the neighbor, the social environment that already exists.
Actually nobody is born into a vacuum, into emptiness; we are born into a
structured world, full of things, customs and laws, incarnated in other human
beings.

In the West the "negative way" moved above all in the philosophical and
mystical spiritual terrain until Freud, through his theories on removal,
on denial, on the non-consciousness, introduced the *non* in the century of

positivism, when whatever was not full didn't count. The psychodynamic vision of mental pathology and the modern psychotherapeutic approach arose from this attention to deficiency, absence. Oury tells us once more that the emptiness, the non, to be edifying and functional must be representable in relation to a limit; must be, that is, an "enclosed void."

In other words, a place and not an unlimited space. And in the place, a form. The structure of the personality can keep itself as such only if there is no central flight, only if there is enclosure – a formal enclosure. It is necessary to know/be able to maintain/contain the emptiness.

In the East the Taoist philosophy is based directly on the formative power of emptiness:

> Thirty spokes share the wheel's hub;
> It is the center hole that makes it useful.
> Shape clay into a vessel;
> It is the space within that makes it useful.
> Cut doors and windows for a room;
> It is the holes which make it useful.
> Therefore benefit comes from what is there;
> Usefulness from what is not there.
>
> (Lao Tzu)

In moving from these intimations of the void to the migrant experience and rebirth in a new place, the void is found in the moments of the pre-, of waiting, of listening, of reception, an enclosed void that can, if necessary, also be the analyst's room. Without the void, there is no birth but only dispersion. Someone, something must receive the new arrival, as the earth receives the seed. One must go beyond the places of the mind and the above-mentioned towards the concrete places in which the arrival takes place. It can be the deserted beach where the shipwrecked person lands; the pier upon which the migrant first steps; the first pallet of the first night elsewhere, or the temple, or a house of friends, full of good wishes for the guest, the garden with its formal enclosure; all the architectural spaces in which the emptiness becomes an enclosed place, a special place.

Roots

Etymology is a discipline of the roots, that is of the origin and ramification of words. Etymologically "root" comes from the Old English *rōt*, from Old Norse, akin to Old English *wyrt*, root, Latin *radix*, Greek *rhiza*, and is now used in both a figurative and a concrete sense. "Origin" is also a generic word with both concrete and symbolic levels. Root was originally part of a specific language, that of botany, and was subsequently extended elsewhere. Roots and putting down roots refer to a level subsequent to that of origin – that is the seed, in the case of plants – which is the taking hold or anchoring to the earth, so that the plant can begin to nourish itself and grow. Metaphorically it is easy to establish a parallel with the rooting of a human life in the mother's womb. There is also the linguistic parallel, where the word "root" has been adopted to define the complex of sounds common to various significantly connected words. In everyday language the term takes on an affective meaning, indicating the force of attachment: a form of vital, primary dependency, identified with the place in which the roots grew.

The point of departure is of course the seed. First there is the earth, the *pre-* that is there and that man can make even more receptive by plowing. Then there is the seed, from a plant that has concluded its seasonal cycle. It is the memory of the plant. Then there is the meeting, the incubation, during which nothing seems to happen and at a certain point, never certain, a new life begins to sprout from the earth. Below, invisible, an equivalent growth is growing downwards, the root. So, while the plant visibly grows towards the light, something is growing invisibly in the opposite direction, in the dark, forming not only an apparatus for nourishment, but also an anchor for the plant itself. If we pull up the plant with its roots it will briefly continue to live and then die. If we maladroitly take it from the earth with its roots, it will have a hard time surviving. In attempting more delicate operations such as transplanting or grafting, the skill required is derived from specific knowledge.

There is also a temporary "putting down roots," in the sense of being attached to an umbilical cord that takes vital substance from the earth/placenta/body/*mater*/matter.

This brief *excursus* around the word "roots," ideally connected to the other words dealt with in this book – place, space, origin, earth – continues to keep us on the borderline between concrete and symbolic, even though only some aspects of the life of plants are applicable to the life of human beings. Indeed, the latter do not need to be anchored to the ground for survival, although they do need to use earth substances to nourish themselves.

Aside from their original meanings, words have a long life. They go through periods of particular popularity and others when they almost disappear, whether in the common current usage or the more selective cultural usage.

Nowadays in Western culture a certain ambiguity is attached to the word "roots." On one hand, as a result of the tendency to globalization, the concept of roots is negatively charged, since roots refer to something local, anchored to the earth as mentioned above. On the other, the political interpretation of the universal attachment to one's land is currently a regressive, conservative, protectionist phenomenon and therefore moving in the direction of racism. In other contexts, instead, the call of the earth means attention to local resources, to biodiversity, to environmental and social sustainability, in contrast to the deplorable aspects of industrial and post-industrial progress.

Although I have my ideas on the points at issue, what interests me here insofar as I am an analytical psychologist is that, beyond what we can imagine or hope for, the human adult still today feels the need to belong, a need for roots and concrete landfalls, with suffering and illness the alternative. When this need is not directly apparent it is because human beings, especially in the advanced societies, have simply shifted it elsewhere: into ideology instead of religion, laws instead of traditions, the state instead of the nation, critical reason rather than symbol. But it is defended with no less passion, attachment and violence.

Pertinent to my discussion is that the question of roots remains a psychic and cultural need to which those of the body and the senses must be added. The average Westerner lives his life in environments that are often standardized, independent of their geographical context, in that new transversal continent called consumer society, where habits, products, rituals remain the same no matter where one moves. Privileged individuals, including intellectuals, journalists, writers, politicians who dictate what culture is, can comment on the same film, speak the same language, meet the same type of persons, eat the same food, buy the same merchandise in New York, Paris, Tokyo, Sydney, Rio, Bombay, Johannesburg. They feel themselves to be citizens of the world, see the positive aspects of globalization, consider attachment to the land, to the cultural identity, to their own roots as conservative rhetorical residues, somehow primitive in a negative sense. Yet, seen from another point of view, these travelers are living in environments they themselves have produced. The earth is something else.

The questions I ask myself and that I ask those who denigrate roots are: how is one to consider the historical memory, the culture itself in its historical bases, and the belongings of various kinds, including ideal and political? Are they not all roots, albeit fleeting, waiting for the chance to attach themselves somewhere? If, as happens with the word "race," we don't like the word "roots," let's find a better one, but without forgetting that a psychological dynamics that corresponds to it universally exists: that of giving the mind a place where it can settle, where it cannot lose itself and where it can find itself again. In fact when thought loses its orientation, we speak of insanity.

The person without a country, the traveler, the wanderer, the individual who does not tolerate settling down, can rationalize and intellectualize his position in just as specious a way as he who exalts the motives of race and nationalism to reject the foreigner in his land. Those who flee are not necessarily better than those who dig themselves in. What was valid yesterday, for the generations oppressed by a totalitarian education, by 19th-century traditions, by limiting ideologies, by great destructive events, is no longer valid today for those who live the opposite condition of disorientation and a creeping daily loss of identity. Reproposing or imposing values that reinforce disorientation, such as a globalization that has not been elaborated, nor accepted as one's own, leads towards the entrenchment of localisms.

The salt of the earth: Collecting salt in a tiny lake, Borana, Ethiopia. Photo © Alberto Tessore.

It is a matter of times and contexts. If in the past the desire to leave, to cut all ties, to raise doubts, criticize, destabilize, demystify was the soul's answer to an excessive identification with the land, and with the religious and cultural traditions, today in a confused and destructured world, with its overwhelming stress on commercial values, mass media seduction and false identities, it is fairly obvious that the opposite reaction is created: a search for security, in other words for roots and clear landfalls. Faith in the omnipotence of progress and the metropolitan model of life, applied everywhere even mistakenly, is being eroded thanks to the disillusion of those, of the many, who now suffer the worst consequences.

The affective, cultural, geographical, linguistic roots are therefore, primarily, an affective reality based on the psychosomatic substrata of the human being, a psychological experience so common that there is no person who does not make continuous and even unconscious reference to it. Historical and political conditioning can then play as they wish on these realities, building new myths or alternatively reanimating the old myths, from nomadism to residence and vice versa. But one can disregard the authentic movement and true needs of persons only up to a certain extent: not against their nature, and even less in attempting to uproot them.

All patients, and not only foreigners, tell the psychotherapist today of their solitude, their feelings of being lost and disoriented and an innate feeling of insecurity.

In conclusion, the origins and the roots dealt with by psychology, whether general or developmental, whether psychodynamic or psychopathological, are those of the functioning of the mind and its contents. An awareness of these dynamics and their interweaving with geographic, economic, ideological, political and other factors can be used in different ways, depending on the intentions of those who govern. There are now also new disciplines of study, such as cultural psychology and environmental psychology, that take the relationship between individual and society beyond the psychology of the subject and the small group, towards an in-depth study of the spaces and places in which human beings pass their existence. From the perception of the infant to the movement in space of the child, from the individual to the group on a physical and on a social level, all levels of shared living require new forms to rebalance the excessive abstraction and solipsism that has dominated the discipline of space in the past century, beginning with architecture and town planning.

In this chapter I have tried to highlight the value of the internal continuity that begins with the origins and arrives at the point in which one is in the present. It is a non-rigid and non-exclusive continuity, aware of both the space and the surrounding places, as well as the time in which one lives there: not only in reference to oneself, but also, if possible, taking account of one's own group and the broader collective movements.

> Root of my root! I return,
> you can be sure, I return.
> And you are waiting for me in the hollow
> of the rocks, you are waiting for me in the thorns,
> in the olive groves and in the color
> of the butterflies, and in the echo and the shade,
> in the winter of mud and the dusty
> summer, in the tracks of the gazelle
> and the wings of all the birds.
> Nostalgia rages in my steps
> irresistible, the earth,
> calls me in my veins.
> I'll surely be back, keep
> voices and smells for me,
> and images and flowers,
> keep for me the voice and the timbre,
> and the features.
> (Tawfiq Zayyad, *The Voice, the Odor, the Aspect*;
> translated from the Italian by transl.)

Chapter 4

Space, *genius loci* and sacrality of place

After dealing with the places of origins, I shall now consider the idea of space in general, its various descriptions and determinations on the basis of human perception, and the theme of depth, which I feel is extremely pertinent to the psychological discourse.

I shall then deal with the *genius loci*, the spirit, the soul of the place; and then, in the next chapter, with charts of various kinds, geographic maps and imaginary places.

Even if not explicitly mentioned, the figure of the migrant and his relation with space and places will always be there, above all when concrete places are no longer directly experienced but remain alive in his memory, in his imagination, whether or not return is possible.

In order to make these aspects less abstract I am introducing a few definitions of space with reference to sandplay, the expressive–creative technique I use in my clinical and formative work. The scenarios created by the patients or other people involved in sandplay are, compared to language, more obviously connected to the concrete spatial dimension. It is a delimited space; a free and protected space always available in the analyst's room; a space that can be organized, destructured, filled with personages and stories, treated as if it were a miniature stage, an enclosed place in the analytical setting, observed in a psychodynamic key.

Definitions and operations

Space: extension of place, variously limited, empty or occupied by bodies (1350); extension of time (1310); place outside the terrestrial atmosphere (1819); interval, empty place in the pentagram, between one letter and the next in typography (1500); *spatium*, connected with the Latin *pat, patere*, to be open, exposed.

It is something that refers to infinity and omnipresence, a sort of connective fabric that binds everything together and keeps them separate, such as air, such as sand. A basic, neutral material that can assume, be the source of, various forms. It returns to itself after being modified.

This space, in its psychological version, becomes a mental category, a sort of "intimate immensity," also capable of being represented in a finite space (Bachelard 1969).

The empty sandtray is there to receive and the sand is like a carpet, a "pre-," the geological memory of the earth.

Place: portion of space ideally or materially determined; from Old French meaning open space, from Latin *platea*, broad street, from Greek *plateia (hodos)*, broad, flat, akin to Sanskrit *prthu*, broad. Physical environment, physical surroundings, house, dwelling, spot.

Place is therefore a more concrete and significant delimitation of the more general and indefinite space. It refers to geographical, topographic bodies or the characteristics of a room. Today the use of the word has been greatly broadened in a metaphorical sense to indicate any position of relevance, with regard to which it can also assume temporal value, close to "moment." The use of the adjective "local" is also becoming common to define a portion of a whole called "global." In the sandtray one uses the space available, and since it is presented as empty even though limited by the container, within this realm of play the patient feels free to create and construct a place, a scene in which to set a meaningful story. A portion-place is carved out of the infinite. Other places can also be represented within the scene. This is more evident when several people are playing together.

Site: of Indo-European origin, used as synonym of "place," it actually refers to the idea of positioning, placing, leaving (Latin *sinere*), from which "situate" and "situation" as circumstance, condition. There is also the prefix *sito-* that refers to food, from a Greek term of obscure origin, *sitos*, for grain, food. Grain placed, put in the earth? On the whole the particular nuance of the term "site" seems to refer to a human action, as in archeology, a place that bears witness to the cultural activities of human beings. Perhaps we should use this term – the action of siting, and the word "site" – to indicate the creation of the scene in the sandplay, since it seems to have all the characteristics described including the archeological one relative to a past to be discovered.

Territory: region, country (14th century), late derivation of the Latin *terra*, of a restricted Indo-European area; involving law; country over which various kinds of jurisdiction are extended; in social sciences: physical space organized according to juridical relationships and customs where a community lives and works. The meaning of the term is rather close to that of "zone" (band, strip, from the Greek *zone*, belt), and of *area* (Latin) in its conventional aspect although it can concern any situation and context.

In the sandtray it calls to mind the evidently significant places, endowed, so to speak, with their laws; often delimited, protected, separated from others; at times also in contrast to other places. The form of a band, of the belt – whether a river, a fence, an enclosure, a wall or other – is rather frequent.

Position (in Italian *posto*, spot = a small extent of space, a particular place, area, or part): space determined by the availability, choice and assignment (apportionment); from the Latin *positu, ponere* (15th century), circumscribed and reserved space; it has to do with order; place occupied by a person in a public space; place in which something happened; installation; social condition; job, task, assignment. Apparently the social, public, collective aspect is dominant.

During the sandplay it unquestionably has to do with the placing of the figures, of their overall organization, in particular when they are in some order, of the feeling often verbally declared that the objects have to be "in a certain position" (place), of a conscious presentation to external eyes and public. The play is always done with the analyst present looking on, and it is photographed at the end.

Dwelling: place where people live, or remain for a time; where they tarry, Old High German *twellen*, to tarry (13th century), therefore the place in a determined time and the verb "to dwell" for the action. A crossing between space and time. The word is not used much in everyday language, where it is replaced by the more concrete "house." In Italian the word *dimora* would be the equivalent. In English there is a distinction between "home" and "house" that does not exist in Italian: "home," from Middle English *hom*, from Old English *ham*, village, akin to Greek *dome*, village. One's place of residence, domicile, a familiar or usual setting, the focus of one's domestic attention, habitat, a place of origin.

I think of the sandtray itself as a dwelling, a temporary episodic stopover in a journey. The dwelling of the moment, unique, of every sand scene. Perhaps the last sand scene in a series is a more stable dwelling, a point of arrival. It is of course always a process that will later have other stopovers. In the sandtray the dwelling appears in the form of house, also considered a symbol of the Self. What interests me is which of the various types of houses available are chosen, how the form changes, if and why the house appears or disappears, in what part of the sandtray and when – especially when I am working with foreign patients.

"Environment" and "Earth," meaning planet and place where mankind lives, are two words scattered there and there throughout the book.

This sensitivity to the environment is also expressed in the sandtray, a possible conflict or, better, a coexistence of nature and culture, references to historical and contemporary events, where part of the "cultural unconscious" intermingles with the personal and collective unconscious.

Naturally in the sandplay signs of what the patients or others (whether foreigners or not) have suffered due to uprooting, nostalgia, a harsh environment, come to the fore. The sand world is peopled initially with exotic figures, travelers, grounded ships, crashed airplanes, scenes of war, geographic settings far from that of real life. Then the first elements of connection and synthesis appear, paths, bridges, figures of mediators, carriers of things, apertures in enclosures, protection of privacy, and gradually a new order of existence takes shape, integrating the past and the present with their respective places.

From definitions I would now like to pass to some of the questions pertinent to reflections on the theme.

The earth, in addition to being that space, place, territory, dwelling that concretely surrounds my body, has also become with the passing of time the object of many an *excursus* of the human mind, of projections of the soul, of various operations of evolutionary adaptation including those of science and technology by which it is now dominated.

For example, to begin with, *measurement*, inimitable instrument of control with which man seeks to compare to himself everything that does not correspond because it is too large or too small. The yardstick is a measure of the step of a man walking on the earth.

Space is the traditional object of a formal, objective and scientific discipline: geometry – which means measuring the earth – and which has constructed axioms and theorems to establish the behavior of space in terms of

Earth Cubic Globe. Photo © Bruno Liotta.

unvarying characteristics. Today with the new visualizing and measuring technologies, classic geometry has been flanked by non-linear geometry, known also as "fractal," a dynamic geometry of variations and of natural forms.

Observed by means of systematic disciplines, such as geometry and mathematics, space appears as an omnipresent real dimension. It is, however, untouchable, identified with air – in a way measurable, but only by experts. I mean that the small measuring instruments we have at hand, such as the ruler, are nothing compared to the medium and large extensions that at a certain point move into and are lost in infinity. To measure the volume of space, one has to know how to do calculations, and to associate volumes and quantities becomes even more complicated. Roughly estimating length, height and volume of a space becomes increasingly doubtful, approximate, trial-and-error.

On one hand then this space is vague, and on the other too abstract. Although physical geometry was created for practical purposes it immediately moved up into philosophy, towards pure geometry with Euclid, Pythagoras, Thales and other ancient philosophers, branching out in the course of the centuries into one form after another: analytical, algebraic, differential, projective, descriptive geometry, up to the non-linear geometry just mentioned that is also known as non-Euclidean geometry.

From the axioms to the hypotheses, geometry has always moved together with philosophy and we could add psychology, with its specific contribution to the theme of spatial perception.

Of the philosophies and epistemologies of space and of space/time, to remain on a theoretical level, some are more in keeping with depth psychology. One is the more transcendental current, on the ideal line that from Kant and space in the sense of pure intuition leads to Cassirer and the philosophy of symbolic forms, describing a multiplicity of possible spaces: the expressive mythical space, the representative space of language, pragmatic space, artistic space, expressed in the creation of works of art. Then there is the phenomenological–existential current, with Husserl, Heidegger and the psychiatrist Binswanger, where space is anthropological, centered on the existence of man and therefore a matter of planning, positioning, situational, dynamized and determined by man's body and his actions. The contribution of Merleau-Ponty, with regard to phenomenology, is particularly close because of his interest in the experience of perception and the ambiguities implied between subject and object, and his interest in the body, fundamental place of existence.

Various psychoanalysts, including Jacques Lacan, Ignacio Matte Blanco, Wilfred Bion and D.W. Winnicott, of whom I shall speak later, were fascinated by space, by geometry and the topological representations in relation to the structures of thought, of language, of dream and also the formalization of their theories.

Actually the original psychoanalytical theory also took its first steps in a spatial scheme. Gradually as the dreams, the symptoms, the fantasies, free associations and emotional experiences of the patients came together in the mind of the analyst, Freud succeeded in conceiving a place for their origin and provenience, as well as their subsequent preservation – a place that the analyst perceived as a theoretical container: the Unconscious. Discovery of a new mental continent or theoretical creation, the first Freudian "topic," as it was called, gives a spatial criterion and a geographic sense to the Unconscious. It is a place, an elsewhere that is underneath, below the conscious Self, a storeroom for things of the past, forgotten or repressed, of instinctual energies that push outwards, a mysterious and potentially dangerous place.

It can easily be asserted that the spatial metaphor and the imaginary of places has unconsciously also taken over the language of depth psychology. There is no escaping it now.

In Jung's work the unconscious has gone beyond the personal level, in a great subterranean reservoir, where treasures, energies, resources for the great creations of mankind are also hidden. All the places of myth and the spontaneous types of symbolism are there and represented. It is important to remember that Jung was also an advocate of the concrete relationship with the earth and the natural environment and, above all manual labor, which he considered psychologically healthful.

Then there are James Hillman and other analyst psychologists such as Robert Sardello, Ed Casey, Ruth Ammann, books like the one by Elena Caramazza, analytical psychologist, and Mino Vianello, sociologist, where space is analyzed in relation to the differences in gender and power (Vianello and Caramazza, 2005); various books by Paola Coppola Pignatelli, architect and university professor influenced by Jung's thought; publications halfway between art and psychoanalysis that partially touch on the subject, in other words substantial figures and works serving as cultural reference but which have not yet succeeded in inspiring an environmental sensitivity in analytical theory and practice. It is as if the so-called external world somehow remained extraneous, something for explorers, borderline interests.

The space/place that psychoanalysis has privileged, in addition to the Unconscious, has been and still is that of interpersonal and above all primary relationships. It is there that pathologies are created; it is there that cures are developed.

But relationships can be seen in different ways just by shifting one's point of view. By including the "capacity of relationship" it becomes clear that everything is relationship, from the mother to the environment.

The entire book could, if you like, also be seen in this key. In speaking of the relation between soul and earth and migration, I am concurrently dealing with the other relations, loss and mourning, including but not limiting myself to the original relation.

Space and self-organization

To return to space and the experience of the common man, the fact that space–air around things takes on the identity of place, of one's own place, or becomes even an abstract place, continues to be something mysterious. Is it, in other words, a matter of the mystery of words, or is it only a question of mental categories, or is space there, on its own, with its objects inside and its own particular laws? Surely to man's senses space also appears as a dynamic body that shows different facets and an interior organization of its own, perhaps simply dependent on natural physical processes, such as the force of gravity (up and down), that of the rotation of the earth (right and left), transformations caused by the elements (volumes, full and empty, aggregating and disaggregating), entropy and all the rest.

Place, unlike indefinite space, is omnipresent, represents a reserved body, sometimes closed, half open, or open, that however retains its sense of shelter and return. One can return to a place: to space would make no sense. Place is made. Even when it is natural, it is made in the mind of man who recognizes and names it. Space has always been there and one can imagine it afterwards as well. Place can be changed or lost, space cannot. Place can be remembered and be the source of nostalgia, space cannot. It is a question of scale and significance that takes shape in the human mind, which, as we know from Jean Piaget, begins to "construct reality," including spatial reality, during early infancy, accomplished through the senses and movement. Something similar happens to adults who create sandplay scenarios during psycho-therapy: a new reality arises following inner mysterious organizing patterns, in other words the individuation process (Liotta 1993, 1994, 1998a, 1998b).

Others define this construction as "organization," some as self-organization, to highlight the autonomous processes that are, in any case, triggered by the relations between the systems in space and in time.

In the preceding chapter I discussed the passage from the place of origins to the form. I shall now observe its development in the common space of natural processes that concern all living forms.

In biology Humberto Maturana and Francisco Varela have defined as "autopoiesis" the creative function that becomes evident in the interaction between organic structures and ecosystemic structures. The structural order is a real spatial architecture from which a unit is created. This is how the environments are formed: interior, cellular, organic, the species, the biosphere. Even when mutually compatible, environments constantly disturb each other, setting off mutual changes of state, interruptions, differences that make historical variations possible, revealing the variable time/story in counterpoint to that of structure/function/space.

Morphogenesis, in the natural sciences, is a form of autopoiesis, a self-organization, going back to original elements that contain the design of the interior three-dimensional structure; a kind of *logos*, intelligibility of space.

Mandala Bhavachakra, the Tibetan Wheel of Life. © Istituto Lama Tzong Khapa, Pisa, Italy.

Morphé indicates the qualitative properties, the constitutional type, the appearance; distinguished from *schema* that concerns the abstract, analytical figure, the geometric perception.

In the eighteenth and early twentieth centuries, Goethe's *Naturphilosophie* offers us examples of transcendental morphologies, that is ideas of forms–dynamic development, in which the form represents the hidden structure, the organizational plan, the code, the underlying design. Then we have the philosophic anatomies, studies of archetypes, attempts at transfer between plants, animals, crystals on the principle of analogy, of connection, of the principle of balancing of mass that compensates the forms in their organic totality. The *Urbildung* is the original form. *Urtier* for the animal, *Urplanze* for the vegetable world. It is all a flow of forms, structures, which are repeated, alternate and are reflected in the different kingdoms of nature, up to man, with his creative and artistic productions, from graffiti to modern art.

In *Poetics of Space*, G. Bachelard, advocate of a "material imagination" – as much of a paradox as it is spontaneously intuitive – speaks of the house, the house where one is born, from the cellar to garret, and of the house in relation to the universe, further specifying the essence of his space, a sheltering space. Then he broadens this space both through the images of the nest, the shell, the hut, and through the corners, the drawers, the chests, the closets. Poetry, literature and art in general, as well as dream and fantasy, bear witness to this twofold investment of a space seen on several registers: plant and animal world, human body and abstraction, language and form–color.

From natural forms to those of objects, natural or artificial, space is always present, as an enclosed volume and as an external volume, background and limit from which human perception draws the outlines of the things contained – in the visual field – changeable depending on the perspective.

In his book *Species of Spaces* Georges Perec describes the different points of view and nuances of daily life in a European country, France, in a spatial key, with a cultured and profound sense of humor. From the page – for the writer – to the bed, through the bedroom, the apartment, the building, the street, the quarter, the city, the countryside, the country, Europe, up to the world and cosmic space, a long procession of places stretches out. Confronted with the dizzying array of symbols that whoever wishes to busy himself with metaphorical and physiological meanings encounters, this interpretation of the relationship with space incarnated in the various idiosyncrasies, habits and neuroses of civilization brings back to earth what would otherwise run the risk of losing its specific weight and force.

Can every space, for example, be inhabited by the bizarre theories of psychoanalysis: can the tower house the phallus, the house the body of the mother, or of the Self? And the tree? Does it incarnate the male or female principle? For it also depends on who dreams this house, paints it, narrates it, plans it, in what culture and in what time.

At this point let me also add: but in what kind of a real house does this individual who dreams and speaks of places live? This is also depth psychology. I would like, in other words, to stress the importance of keeping at bay the seduction of symbolism and interpretation and not losing oneself in the mental space, at just the time in which the environment surrounding us is moving ever further away from our idealizing projections. So far away that it can be attacked, damaged, ignored in that interdependence that guarantees us survival. We might think that, on a par with the psychosomatic diseases through which the body tries to call the attention of a distracted mind to itself, the concrete terrestrial space is also "ill" and tries to divert to itself the attention we continue to pay to other abstract, cultural, self-referential worlds.

Space and psychology

Space has become the object of studies in the modern psychological disciplines, in branches such as the psychology of perception, Gestalt psychology and the so-called field theories, the most recent health psychology and the specific environmental psychology, to which I would add other fields such as proxemics and various theories by authors who are not all psychologists, who have studied the relationship between the body, space and movement (Berthoz 1997, Feldenkrais 1972, Pierantoni 1986, Rolf 1978). This wave of new information describes and explains the cognitive and emotional experiences prompted by the different experiences of space.

The disclosure of optical illusions, the discovery of the organizational principles within perception, of the principles of orientation, the greater awareness of field dynamics and the dynamics of interaction between persons in the field, clearly put the subjective aspects in touch with the objective aspects of the spatial experience. The background to the abovementioned disciplines is general psychology (the study of the functioning of the senses, of learning, of memory, of motivation, etc.), personality psychology (types and differences) and lastly psychodynamics. From a theoretical point of view various hypotheses regarding research, conceptualization and ideas crisscross in this general network. Their central interest is space and they are also inspired by philosophy, esthetics in particular, and physics.

In view of the mixture of psychological and material factors underlying its origins, a separate chapter would be required to deal with architecture: the art and technique of constructing buildings that determine the living spaces of human beings. Currently architecture is an area subject to interdisciplinary reconsiderations regarding the relationship between psyche and space in the light of the demands and limits imposed by the contemporary lifestyle.

This has been no more than an attempt to give an idea of the extension and complexity that the subject of space in general has acquired in the course of the 20th century – not without repetitions, asides and redundancies – in particular when one is aware of how it began in antiquity with the happy and essential union of geometry and philosophy.

With our feet on the ground

Insofar as I have no intention of providing the reader with a compendium of current ideas of space, I have simply indicated some of the areas and the relevant authors touched on in the pursuit of my specific concepts.

Since, owing to my profession as psychotherapist, I feel more at ease when faced with accomplished and narrative space, I will immediately put my feet back on the ground, or in the sandtray.

When my patients work with the sandplay – as I did in my personal and

Art Omi Museum, Ghent, New York. © Fausto Ferrara, 2007.

professional training – it comes naturally to identify with them and enter the space of the empty sandtray, looking at it from the inside.

A sort of fall, a voluntary descent, like Alice in Wonderland when she grew smaller. In my experience with the play it was as if, now small, I was passing through and estimating how much space was available and was then walking around at random or heading for somewhere specific, looking for the perspective from which to bring out that temporary world that had to be proportional with regard to the external spatial dimension as well. This was not all consciously done. It was a subtle sensation that percolated out with time and with practice together with the patients. Since it is play, as realistically defined as the spatial limits may be, within these limits everyone can accommodate the perspective to whatever he or she sees fit.

It is interesting to investigate, on the individual level, the size of the "spatial correspondence," to be thought of as a sort of cipher, a personal index. The final scene clearly shows how this index differs from one patient to the next. I have calculated that for me it is around 100 m. Seen from the inside, the sandtray, which I know is a rectangular box 72 × 50 × 7 cm, becomes 100 m long, open, without an edge, with one side slightly shorter. This is my index for a vital internal space projected outside, in which I feel myself proportioned to the environment and the objects contained therein. Probably it is also the portion of the world I feel I can manage and control. In some of my sand worlds, I put figures that alluded to further spaces, moving outwards or coming from outside, at the edges. It is as if I were in a territory with fluid boundaries that could be crossed and which was part of a larger whole.

Introducing the idea of a psychological measure of space – beyond the realistic evaluation of space that in any case remains a sign of maturity and psychological balance – each individual will manifest his own way of concretely

structuring space, as for example in the furnishing of the house, the place-
ment of the desk, in planning the garden, in writing, the movement inside,
setting up apertures and closures.

Finding things

In addition to being the object of specific professions, the reorganization of
space is an activity that periodically occupies the life of many persons and
families, motivated by psychological rather than concrete reasons. From the
renovation of the house to other changes that follow fashions or induced
requirements, inhabited spaces are continually subject to modification. Many
women have told me, and not only in analysis, of their periodic reorganization of the spaces in the home, the interiors of closets, drawers and other
containers. This activity may be a sign of anxiety and compulsion but it can
also be relaxing. When the emotions, fantasies, recollections involved in these
occupations are analyzed, they take us to important aspects of identity, as if
reorganizing space were working on one's self, even on one's own body,
putting things back in place, into a new place, more suitable than its former
place. It is at least an attempt to achieve a better form.

But there is more to it than that. Organizing space is a way to find one's
own things, or the things that are needed, whether it is a closet, a desk, or one's
mind. Remember that the function of memory itself, the mental continuity
that permits learning and survival, has from antiquity been based on the
relationship with space, more specifically on the transformation of space into
place. The art of memory used the "*loci* method" – that is, associating a
recollection to a place and constructing bridges that lead to it. The "theaters of
memory," together with the "trees" and the "wheels," are imaginary archives
of medieval and then Renaissance encyclopedic knowledge in which names,
places, images and words are standardized, as in hieroglyphic writing (Yates
1969). Here the reality of space dilates and shrinks depending on what is
required, up to the representation of the known world. In the 18th century
d'Alembert in his introduction compared the *Encyclopédie* directly to a globe,
on which to be shown were the principal countries, their position and mutual
dependency, the straight roads that joined them, often interrupted by a thousand obstacles. Those which can be known only to the inhabitants or travelers
of each country would be shown on detailed small-scale maps which would
then be the various articles of the *Encyclopedie*, and the tree, or figured
system, would be the globe.

Today these mental constructs of places are no longer necessary, replaced
by computer programs, with everything this entails ranging from the psychological and psychodynamic point of view with regard to the function of
memory, the sense of orientation, the relationship between space, cognition,
recollections and attachments.

It can be affirmed with regard to all these examples that the "sense of space" coincides with mental organization and with orientation, dependent on achieved knowledge and memory as well as on the archetypal formal principles. This is why the sense of space is an individuating, idiosyncratic factor. As with writing – another way of occupying space, that of the blank page – each of these has a corresponding way, one's own way, of setting up, containing space and living within that space, from posture to movement.

From cosmic space to the geographic space of the Earth, and then the private space of the home, up to the still more intimate space of our inner world, human beings establish, physically and mentally, their territories, their jurisdictions, their trajectories. Some are collective, others individual and highly personal.

We can at this point imagine how destabilizing, on the psychological level, it is to have to renounce, at times suddenly, the order of one's life, the sense of protective familiarity that habit creates with regard to places, spaces, their sounds and colors, especially when they are places one has chosen to live in or to remain, or where one was born.

Genius loci and sacrality of place

Back to the soul after discussing space and the various cultural perspectives from which it is observed and interpreted. The soul does not reason, does not observe, does not interpret. The soul intuits, feels, contemplates. If the soul speaks, I believe it speaks in dialect, with sounds as close as possible to the land of its origin. I see the *genius loci* as the incarnation of the spirit of the place, not a spiritualization of the land.

It is as if certain places had, or autonomously assumed, a special evocative quality. It is not an uncommon experience and gave rise to the idea, and as a result also the name, of the *genius loci*, that is of a particular presence of the place. Conceptually grouped together are the identity characterizing a place, consisting of historical values and previous existences, natural and artificial factors and symbolic meanings shared by the inhabitants – today on the verge of being lost – and personal experiences, solitary or shared, of the sacrality or speciality of a place, as represented by poets, artists, mystics.

The *genius loci* corresponds to an innate need to anthropomorphize the environment surrounding man, to create a sort of eco-psychological niche, a mirror of the human structure that is both body and matter, earth, as it is psyche, mind, anima or soul. We know that primitive peoples thought that every sensitive object was endowed with an anima, the source of the adjective "animistic." Jung frequently reminds us that the ethnologist Lévy-Bruhl coined the expression *participation mystique* for this feeling of communion that man has when faced with the surrounding environment.

From the point of view of depth psychology, the mechanism on which this phenomenon is based is the projection on the external world of the images, meanings, feelings that the human being carries within himself. More evident

Etruscan tomb, Necropolis of San Lorenzo, Montecchio, Terni, Italy.
Photo © Paolo Pelliccia.

in primitive peoples, in children, in some forms of psychopathologies, this projected participation, which makes little distinction between the "me" and the "other than me," can achieve the intensity of possession and take over the consciousness of the individual, or become part, with less intensity, of any artistic, poetic, spiritual, contemplative experience. In the latter case, when faced with a specific landscape, an experience of communion can be set in motion that carries within itself a sense of beneficial belonging, or containable feelings of restlessness, melancholy, solitude, anxiety or fear.

Other theoretical positions have been developed around this theme in the field of psychology. Among the many I will choose that of Gestalt psychology. In the search for perception, this school attributes emotions not only to the internal state of the individual, and therefore to projection, but also to the

Cacti worshipped as a sacred place, Shantiniketan, West Bengal, India, 2000. Photo © Francesco Galli.

formal qualities of the object, for example of a landscape. It is therefore the landscape, the place, that arouses emotions. This thesis is reinforced by further and more recent studies that demonstrate how much closer than imagined the psychological relations of human beings with their environment are, experienced today more unconsciously than in the past.

Gods, myths and names

Of old, our ancestors did not ask themselves all these questions: nature, space and place were simply alive, on a par with human beings. Among the many gods and genii that accompanied daily life, mention can be made of those of the rivers, woods, mountains, lakes, cities, countries and the entire sensible world. In particular every city, every social group, was attributed to a divinity, to a symbolic element of collective value.

With regard to the earth, the positive and joyous aspects connected with its prosperity and fertility were counterbalanced by the darker and more melancholy aspects localized underground, both divinized and then amalgamated in orgiastic rites such as the Mysteries of the Greek and Mediterranean area. The major divinities include Gea, Cybele, Dionysus, Demeter and Persephone, Hades and Hecate. Then there are the Nymphs, in particular the Oreadi, who lived in the valleys, mountains and gulleys, divided into families according to place – Echo is the most famous – and the Dryads, who merged

Shivaist sadhu, Shantiniketan, West Bengal, India, 2000. Photo © Francesco Galli.

with the trees, and Satyrs and Silenes, and the best known genii of the woods such as Pan and Sylvan, fauns, Priapus. Other Italic divinities of the country-side are Saturn, god of sowing and founder of agriculture and his wife Opi, goddess of abundance, both protectors of marriage and the family; Vertum-nus, who was in charge of the changes of the seasons; and Pomona, pro-tectress of gardens and fruit trees; Flora, goddess of flowering, of the bees, at the center of the Floralia fetes; Pale, protectress of the flocks; Termine, lord of the boundaries of private property but also of the boundaries of the State, and then many, many others.

These hosts of divinities appear in stories set in natural settings, with ani-mal and plant elements intermixed with human elements – goat's hoofs, horns, hairy bodies, floral ornaments and garments – evidence of a desire to represent a multiform extraordinary nature in a way that mirrored the way the men and women of the times related to their environment.

In Europe the patron saints and village festivals of today can also be thought of as a residue of this veneration of place, deprived of its contempla-tive aspect and its intense original value, but still evidence of a return to the roots, in the world of today. Eating, playing, gossiping, dancing take place in the piazzas, and not elsewhere, eschewing the discotheque, the dance floor, the private home. It is done in the name of the saint, a figure bound to the history of the place or in any case chosen as a tutelary deity, protector of the local community and religiously celebrated during the festival with processions, ceremonies and specific sites.

Place names too give us an idea of the relationship between human beings and places, which are characterized and recognized by means of identifying elements. Naming them is part of the relationship between man and environment. Naming to recognize, to share, to possess, to control.

Do we really know the origins and meanings of the names we so often pronounce, such as those of our place of birth and residence, of places we have loved or feared, of places where we would dearly love to go?

The name of a place originally mirrored the "spirit" of the place, incarnated in the patron saint or in an outstanding inhabitant, in the natural features, in other symbols or things. Among the names of Italian towns there are many that refer to mountains, hills, valleys, etc., or to buildings such as towers, castles, abbeys. In America the names of towns are more likely to reflect trees or plants, such as Oak Grove or Chestnut Hill. Water in its various forms is also important, as are any particular identifying characteristics.

On a conscious level the name of a place in its everyday usage has lost its original meaning. As the level of awareness and sensitivity gradually wanes we are generally no longer aware of its natural peculiarities, except in unusual cases.

Spirit and identity of place in global society

If we consider the origins of street names in most large cities, it becomes clear that all relationship between name and place has been lost. We live

Pilgrimage to San Vivenzio, Blera, Viterbo, Italy, 1995. Photo © Francesco Galli.

in dimensions where the fact that it is day or night is irrelevant and the phases of the moon or the weather are of minor relevance (unless a weekend is coming up).

At this point, when a phenomenon has exhausted its original force, new forms of "spirits of place" appear and the inhabitants of advanced societies find themselves involved in even more complex systems.

Any number of practices could be cited. One example is *Feng-shui*, the quest for the ideal orientation of the bed or other pieces of furniture in the city apartment. Others include "bio-watching," the last frontier of multiple appeals to observe rather than act on and disturb the natural environment, and "orienteering" in general – learning anew to orient oneself in space – and the choosing of farm holidays and adventurous vacations. The fad for the ecological house and the enhancing of natural materials is an attempt, using natural untreated wood, to restore a vitality, a relationship, with the tree and the earth that is apparently thought of as lost. Games made of natural materials or found objects such as pine cones or shells are proposed to small children, things in other words that once, depending on the place where they lived, they would have found by themselves right outside their door.

How else can one interpret this emphasis on nature and on a lifestyle that looks back in time, if not as a way of compensating for the degeneration and disorientation of an increasingly technological metropolitan lifestyle? One

Buildings in Hong Kong. Photo © Bruno Liotta.

could, of course, discuss at length the real advantages scientific progress has given in terms of health. This is not the place to bring up the question of pollution, nor do I intend to uncritically demonize well-being, hygiene, relief from fatigue and other benefits that advanced societies enjoy. I am only saying that evidently human beings need an added value to reality, something that is in the things themselves: the feeling that some are good or better, with respect to others that are bad, rather than simply neutral and cold, that it is possible to feel protected and for which security doors and disinfectants are not enough.

I am not referring to superstitions, which, in any case, continue to prosper and nourish the market, even in advanced societies, but to subtle insinuations of a thought that at this point I would no longer define as magic, but simply as emotionally charged. Evidently human beings, even those culturally evolved, still need to feel affections in the surrounding environment. Concern regarding places, objects, daily acts, food and clothing, based on the idea of health and respect for nature, seems to restore, at least to some, this affectivity.

As exemplified by the sacrality and importance of the pilgrim sites of the great religions in the world, as well as of the indigenous religions, both in the past and now, the *genii loci* are still very much with us.

The sacrality of certain places can be defined historically by a particular event (miracle, trial, apparition, birth, martyrdom or some other death) in the life of an outstanding figure as well as by factors that are foreign to the place, but have made it special, have sanctified it (a battle; a natural event, dramatic and exceptional; a discovery; a meeting). A symbolically and collectively vested place is subsequently visited in the hopes that physical contiguity will turn out to be salvific and enlightening, or as part of a precise religious program that includes the pilgrimage among its commandments.

The place itself can evoke a sacrality, depending not only on its apparent qualities but on the perception of the individual. While it seems obvious that places that are naturally serene and harmonious, esthetically pleasing, universally beautiful (the marvels of the world, the places that have become world heritage sites) correspond to an emotional experience, it is also true that threatening, gloomy and disturbing scenarios elicit an emotion of awe and marvel that testifies to the presence of beauty.

"Numinous" is the term used by Rudolf Otto, followed by Jung, to indicate the presence of the *numen*, the spirit of place. The numinous quality, as an indication and measure of the emotion aroused, is thought to go back to an original archetypal value of the object observed.

Mountains, woods and forests, seas, rivers and other bodies of water, islands, subterranean cavities, the desert, glaciers and so on are archetypes relative to natural places. Then, in more detail, come the elements that compose the scenarios and their inhabitants: for example, trees, stones, flowers, other determining aspects such as colors and quantity, the number of elements present, the variety of animals and human beings, male and female.

In addition to natural places, man-made places can also be the source of numinous experiences simply because they were built with the same logic, on the basis of archetypal architectural models such as the circle, the square, the triangle and the other geometric forms, following the universal laws of symmetry, proportions and harmony.

For example, building a temple, in its various historical–cultural expressions, is an attempt on the part of man to contain and to strengthen the numinous experience for his fellows, exalting the bond between god, the place and the group. However, the city, the house, the square, the garden, the theater, the arena, the necropolis, and other places devoted to social life can become, in their beauty and sense of meaning, archetypal associations for the inhabitants and for those who visit them.

Nor is the beauty of the present enough. The ruins of the past are so powerfully evocative that at a certain point in history they even produced a discipline to study them, archeology, and special places, the museums, to contain parts and objects. Archeology, like depth psychology to which it has

Romanesque church of San Pietro at Norchia, Viterbo, Italy, 2003. Photo © Francesco Galli.

often been compared, is based on passion, on the search for something unknown – the former concrete, the latter symbolic. It is subject to surprise and delusion, methodologically empirical, strongly bound to places, to the earth, more precisely to the site, which is already sacred on account of the many lives that lived there, as well as for its capacity to survive longer than those who built it.

A patient in analysis digs down into his own subterranean places, makes his way through the crowded lands of the collective unconscious, finds something, reconstructs, puts his own story back together and conserves it with greater awareness. While he works on his archeological site, he does so in another special place, made "sacred" by the analytical setting, by the rules governing time, space and use. The *genius loci* analyst, invested with the role of guardian, watches over the sacredness of the process of individuation. In analytical treatment, everything concerned with a sense of place, quarter, house or analyst's studio, furnishings of the room, atmosphere in general, is a good example of how even the most simple and anonymous of places can become, in particular situations and occasions, a special place. Patients who create places of their own with the sandplay, within a place for the session, sometimes have the numinous experience of having depicted a "sacred space," even though they are not architects, or artists, priests or analysts. Seen from outside, these sand scenes emit a particular esthetic quality that corresponds to the experience. It can be compared to the experience of understanding, both by the patient and the analyst, that the dream under discussion is "great," important.

From the historical and cultural point of view the universality of symbolism and forms and the evocative power exercised make the sacrality of places first psychological and then, depending on the case, religious. This explains why the symbolism of places in art is so widespread and appears in all the expressive and creative forms, beginning with childhood (Bachelard 1969, Durand 1972).

The word "site," now so frequently used on the Internet, the virtual network, also needs a few explanatory remarks. It is a place where the only concrete things are the magnetic material containing the memory that is introduced and the computer that houses it. The magic that inhabits modern technology has its *loci* and its *genii*. In this communicative space, the site represents a station where information is sorted out, a point of arrival, of passage, of new departures. The *genius* is represented by that intangible sensation of being together with, in contact with, virtually accompanied, seen, observed, even without our knowing it. Today, alone or in a group, it can participate in the memory, general place-soul, presenting and adding information of its own, or constructing it in its own site. It is interesting on a collective psychological level that the terminology of space and place immediately colonized a scenario that has very little that can be called local, in the conventional sense. The word "portal," infrequently found in common language, has also been recovered and brings to mind "portal" in the architectural and archeological, slightly esoteric, sense.

Metaphor, magic, affect, symbol, superstition, sacrality: whatever the psychological aura that hovers around it, the relationship between the human being and the place is not simply a physical or a cultural matter. The psychological levels and equilibriums, both unconscious and conscious, the personal constitutionality and typology, the moments and passages of life: all this, we might say, paraphrasing Hillman, "make place" as well as soul. Even in the contemporary global society.

Space, play and Self

I have never forgotten the observation made by a patient with regard to her city, the quarters, the peripheral zones and other areas she was initially unacquainted with, but of which she gradually became aware as the analysis proceeded. By chance, various encounters, having to do with work or other reasons independent of her will, took her to new territories. Here she discovered their identity, the inhabitants, what the places had to offer, adding them to her mental topography and feeling herself enriched, more in charge of herself and the space around her. While she was "making soul," i.e. discovering herself, at the same time her sense of space, of its extension and depth, was also growing, and her repertory of places became more varied and larger. Again for no good reason, her interest in traveling when on vacation, even to other continents, waned. Towards the end of the analysis she had a chance to buy a house, her first house, in one of the areas "discovered" during our work, an area in which she felt "in the right place."

To conclude this part I want to return to D.W. Winnicott, who was always interested in the inner places where the psychological phenomena take place. Once more his idea of "space, of object and of transitional phenomena" supports mine.

Unlike philosophers, and many psychologists, psychiatrists and psychoanalysts, Winnicott offers an interpretation of space which, even though it concentrates on the relation between mother and child, never forgets either the individual dimension of the true Self nor the real external place and environment. Through the mechanisms of progressive illusion and disillusion over reality that accompany the growth processes, he follows the transitionality of the places up to the adult ones of art, religion, culture.

> It is assumed here that the task of reality-acceptance is never completed, that no human being is free from the strain of relating inner and outer reality, and that relief from this strain is provided by an intermediate area of experience (cf. Riviere, 1936) which is not challenged (art, religion, etc.). This intermediate area is direct continuity with the play area of the small child, who is "lost" in play.

Saturno 3, 1966 Inox Sculpture, Washington, DC. © Attilio Pierelli.

In infancy this intermediate area is necessary for the initiation of a relationship between the child and the world, and is made possible by good-enough mothering.

(Winnicott 1985:15)

"The Location of Cultural Experience" dates to 1967, barely four years before his death, and is again contained in *Playing and Reality*, in which Winnicott clarifies and integrates preceding ideas. His thesis that:

The place where cultural experience is located is the *potential space* between the individual and the environment (originally the object). The same can be said of playing. Cultural experience begins with creative living, in the first place manifested in play . . . in the potential space between the subjective object and the object objectively perceived . . . The potential space happens only in relation to a feeling of confidence . . .

In order to study the play and then the cultural life of the individual one must study the fate of the potential space between any one baby and the human (and therefore fallible) mother-figure who is essentially adaptive because of love.

(Winnicott 1985:118)

Is it this trust, indispensable for the healthy growth of the Self, is it this warmth, this affection that human beings seek afterwards also in the environment?

The Jungian Alfred Plaut (1966), quoted by Winnicott, says that the capacity to form images and to use these constructively by recombination into new patterns is – unlike dreams or fantasies – dependent on the individual's ability to trust (Winnicott 1985:120).

I hope I have explained why the *genius loci* is part of the imaginary heritage, a constitutional part of the human being.

Chapter 5

Maps and geography
Reality and fantasy

The Earth as a whole has seven parts:
The head and the face, Paionia, seat of the largest souls.
The second the Isthmus, the cervical marrow.
The third part between viscera and diaphragm, Ionia.
The fourth, the thigh, Hellespont.
The fifth, the feet, the Thracian Bosphoros and Cimmeria.
The sixth the belly, Egypt and the Egyptian sea.
The seventh the interior stomach (the bladder) and the rectum.
The Euxinos Pontos and the Maeotian marshes.

> Pseudo-Hippocratic tract
> (translated from the Italian by transl.)

Another point of contact between the earth, places and the human soul appears in the universal impulse to create maps. Aside from the previously mentioned mnemonic technique of *loci*, other earlier ways of representing geographical sites have been suddenly superseded by modern technology, capable of memorizing and drawing maps for us. However, as noted, the mind of man moves on, nourishing both the new and the old and retaining aspects of the past on an unconscious level, above all the characteristics of his species.

His capacity to imagine has not stopped simply because machines can now think and calculate for him. On the other hand technology has reached a point where it needs skills above and beyond those the human mind is capable of, as in the field of calculus. It is a matter of mutual respect of limits.

Drawing a map, even of the simplest kind, is something small children love to do as soon as their motor and intellectual development permits: their room, their house, the path followed in going to school, a treasure map.

I remember that when I was in school in Venezuela we had to draw a map of the country. The most exciting part was edging the coast in blue, holding the point of the pencil and moving it in wavy lines to indicate the depth of the water. Even now, forty years later, I could still draw the shape of Venezuela with my eyes closed.

Maps, charts, diagrams of various types are all graphic representations of spaces of various kinds showing itineraries and points of arrival. They therefore range from conventional road maps, used in touring a country, to topographic, geological maps, city and land register maps, each with its own use, to the street plans of the city and the geographic atlas we delight in leafing through, searching for unknown places, imagining trips. They are all realistic representations, based on a physical reality despite the difference in scale. Today there are also photographic maps – aerial photo images – which give us the true view of the earth's surface but no longer excite our curiosity the way the irresistible creations, symbolic and approximate, of the mapmakers of the past aroused that of the travelers and explorers of their times. Today the spaces and places of the geographic atlas, no matter how remote and isolated, become alive for us with their ethnic groups, animals, vegetation, different traditions, thanks to the documentaries and other photographic materials so abundantly presented by the mass media that even a child can identify their location in the world. Do we really still need to travel?

What is really lacking, though, to counterbalance this mass of information that takes us meekly to places decided on by someone else, is "maps to get lost by:" deceptive maps that teach us how to rely on intuition, that restore the pleasure of a chance discovery, the surprise of encountering a place.

Fantasy and imaginary worlds

In the absence of priceless but inexistent maps of this sort, which you or I could draw up for ourselves if we wanted, the next best thing is the maps of the imagination. The sandplay and all the scenarios I have seen created during my clinical work are in effect real maps of the inner world that reconfirm the spontaneous creative aptitude of every individual (Liotta 1994). But there are also the imaginary geographies, which really belong to artistic invention, and the maps that represent them, in a broad sense.

The subject matter is immense, a confirmation of their psychological basis. Since imaginary journeys are dealt with in the next chapter, here I will discuss only representations of space.

The imagination, as previously observed, exists in parallel to rational thought. The cartography of the past, which we think of as fantastic today, should not therefore be seen exclusively as the fruit of an error in interpretation, due to ignorance and superstition. Our ancestors did what they could with the information on hand and with the intuitive and elucidatory capacities available. Their maps are rightly defined by scholars as "conjectural." It was a sort of imposed solution, midway between fantasy and reality, that D.W. Winnicott would place among the transitional solutions. The earth was shown flat and linear, not only because it corresponded to the Biblical version of a flat disk suspended between the waters of the sky and the subterranean waters, but also because it was confirmed by the direct experience of the human being who walked on the earth with the linearity of the horizon before him. After all, today we continue to see and speak of a sun that rises and sets, from and into the earth. It is a matter of cognitive, and at this point solely linguistic, egocentrism.

Up to the 14th century Roman geography and the Bible had determined the form and description of the earth in the West, designing universal cosmographies that illustrated all of creation, from the lands to the inhabitants, real or mythical, with customs, economy, historical facts, outstanding figures and others, as in Ebstorf's 13th-century *Mappa mundi*. The imaginary, unknown, marvelous places were drawn and accepted as real and nothing succeeded in canceling them for a long time, neither reliable travelers nor the discoveries of subsequent centuries. The terrestrial Paradise was always in the Far East, even if monsters and other imaginary creatures gradually began to disappear from the maps. This confusion remained after the appearance of America and other new lands. We have conjectural maps of the North Pole, of Tartaria, of the Americas and Africa, in addition to the planispheres, but also maps and illustrations of the places of memory, in the form of archipelagos and groups of islands. It was not until the 18th century, after Cook's voyages, that the southern hemisphere and the outlines of the continents began to be more precisely drawn (Calabrese et al. 1983). With regard to the interior of the continents, Livingstone's travels in Africa, not much more than a century ago, were still a mixture of realistic information and traditions of the past, some still of the classical world.

All these spaces and places represented in the maps were subject to the caprice of human fantasy. In the absence of other information, the unknown empty spaces were filled, adding archetypal motifs, cultural residues of the past, as well as projections of their own desires, to the tales of travelers and their knowledge of astronomy. The main purpose was to succeed in defining a map of the world and just where man was to be found on its surface.

Today, however, the question "where are we?" is no longer relevant: not in a geographic sense.

In classical antiquity geography, as was the case with geometry, moved along the same roads as philosophy, literature, geometry, astrology and myth. We also have information on cartographers: Anaximander, Democritus, Eudoxus of Cnidus, Hecateus, Homer himself. Beginning with Icarus, the theme of the aerial voyage – see the earth from on high to define its shape – continues up to the imaginary stories of Lucian, in the 2nd century and much later, putting geography and symbolic philosophy together in the same basket. Faced with the unknown, the impulse to know is increasingly characterized by taking distances, in space, to find a position from which to see oneself from outside. This meant that maps that faithfully mirrored a place and provided a recognizable measurable location, within everybody's reach,

Ptolemaic world from G. Reisch, "Margarita Philosophica," c.1503.

could now be drawn. The symbolic part is no longer in the forefront and gradually finds refuge elsewhere.

Today the goal of objectivity has finally been achieved, although, as in the past, we still cannot actually "see" all the spaces and places represented on a map or photograph. It remains a matter of trust.

In only a few centuries, geographical maps passed from extremely limited real information coupled with a wealth of intuition and imagination to a credibility and precision of immediate operative value, up to the present almost total coincidence between reality and its representation. A partial superimposition of reality and fantasy still exists, I believe, in that same horizon, the cosmic space, in which both scientific research and science fiction continue to search for other or new forms of life. I find it hard to believe that money and brains should be invested in a scientific approach to this illusion of what hypothetically exists, worthy if anything of a writer or artist.

Today when one thinks of purely imaginary geography, the most immediate association is that of science fiction, in other words a deliberate and explicit compromise between the imagination and science projected into the future. On close examination, however, much of science fiction mixes historical periods, past and future, around what we can define once more, together with Jung, as archetypal themes: the struggles between Good and Evil, the myth of the hero, love, loss, nostalgia, exile, return, the trials, the encounters with the masters, and so on.

The places in which the stories take place are also archetypal with updated variations: interstellar space has taken the place of the sea, and spaceships have replaced seafaring ships (Jung 1958).

In conclusion, provisionally, imaginary geography, as different as it may appear century after century, seems to keep its constants unchanged. Physical geography, with the passing of time, has come closer to the real object, thanks to special journeys, new means of transportation and particularly with the introduction of machines that see and measure much further than the human eye.

Were I to dwell any longer on imaginary geography, I would run the risk of losing myself in an enormous multiform number of representations that derive from a proportionately limited number of "spatial organizers." After reading about and looking at the illustrations of the various utopian islands and cities, the countless paradises, lands of Cockaigne, inexistent planets, halfway lands and dream lands, conceptual maps that depict the empire of poetry or the semantic fields of Vice and Virtue, the wedding map and lastly the cards of the geographic games, beginning with the traditional board games (Game of the Goose), I have become convinced that when faced with space and places human beings are obsessed with their definition and depiction, second only to that of the depictions in general of everything that exists in the world.

The more unreal the places are, the stronger is the need to make them real, localize them, as if the flow between imagination and reality were something constant and irrepressible. As an analyst I am supposed to know that linear and logical thinking can be used in the service of madness or to keep it within bounds.

I am comforted by a statement made by Italo Calvino that explains why I feel relatively uninterested in imaginary stories and settings but have a real passion for true stories, dreams and play. Calvino, with regard to dictionaries of imaginary places, has this to say:

> The first impression is that imaginary geography is much less appealing than the real thing: a methodic gray pall falls over the Utopian cities, from Francis Bacon's Bensalem to Cabet's Icaria, as well as the countless satirical–philosophical 18th-century journeys, not to mention the edifying allegorical–religious stages of Bunyan's *Pilgrim's Progress*. And a feeling of saturation, if not lack of air, accompanies the overcrowded topographies of the Wizard of Oz, or of Tolkien, or of C.S. Lewis. But sooner or later one meets up with worlds based on an evocative fantastic logic . . . the invention that continues to be the most elegant and ingenious is Abbott's geometric Flatland.
>
> (Calvino, quoted in Calabrese et al. 1983:30;
> translated from the Italian by transl.)

The Empire of Poetry from "Mercure de France," 1696.

With the exception of a few masterpieces, including the places imagined by Swift in his *Gulliver's Travels*, I believe that Calvino's impression, valid for much art of a purely imaginary type, depends on the fact that behind the fantastical effervescence, this art maintains a linear, almost flat or planimetric, thought structure, and a simple representation of space, even on the symbolic level: above, below, right and left, the cardinal points, division into quarters, the mandala and other archetypal forms, with regard both to space and places and to the objects and figures contained therein.

But without the sacred.

It is as if the forms and places had been emptied of their essence, disguised, camouflaged, in a pretence that can be defined as *falsa imaginatio*, reveries that then and there distract and titillate the mind, but have no impact on the psychological level.

Imagination with regard to space and places can also be something else. I too, like Calvino, who succeeded in constructing fantastic places and worlds with a powerful psychological impact in his *Invisible Cities* and in the *Cosmicomics*, am fascinated by a less common area of imaginary production where space is explored in what might be called its "torsions:" hyperspace, parallel universes, cyberspace or virtual space, topology, hypothetical model-making, as in *Flatland* of which I will speak further on, all those forms of space that disturb perception, make one doubt one's reason.

Take the sensations that accompany Escher's visions. Or the sense of disorientation, immobility, amazement, encountered in the paintings by De Chirico and Savinio. In Dali's paintings, on the other hand, the torsion becomes distortion, a deformation that is clearly legible because it concerns the outlines of the figures.

My choice here, for a more profitable psychological analysis, is that of the "point of view" and its, so to speak, Escherian reflections. Let's see things from the artist's point of view, looking in perspective from inside the spatial representation. Where is he looking? For example, applied to the subject being dealt with, the imagined creation can concern a spatial dimension, an inexistent land, or a geography that is the imagined depiction of an existing land. It depends on what your imagination is focused on. Another example: the imaginary map of an imaginary treasure, or the description of unlikely worlds, can in turn be part of a game – invention of a child or an adult, and this too makes a difference – of a cultural game, an artistic current, a psychological test, or it can be a way of disguising reality to leave one free to speak of that reality – as, together with other interesting observations, Luciano Perez maintains in his essay "Geografie e topografie reali, immaginarie e immaginali." A whirligig of reality and imagination.

The point of view can move backwards or forwards as one likes between reality and imagination, discovering in the various forms of play that it is almost always the archetype that dynamizes and gives meaning to the map. A treasure is hidden in the earth: alchemical pursuit, the revealing of the invisible, the spark in the darkness. It is the pursuit that designs space and classifies the places as archetypal, aside from whatever exterior form they assume. I remember a fascinating game we played when I was a child. We would dig a shallow hole in the earth and put precious objects into the hole, which was no larger than a hand. The objects if possible were to be brightly colored, shiny. A piece of glass was put over them and then it was covered up with earth. One had to leave some sign or be sure to remember where it was so we could find it again, like a treasure at our beck and call. I didn't know Jung at the time, or his story of that game nor its universal origin.

Archetypes, once more with a provisional conclusion, can also be presented in very realistic and plausible forms, as in dreams or the many folk tales in which geography, spaces, places and landscapes, and also the personages, are those of everyday life.

Thomas More's Island of Utopia, T. Martens, 1516.

Why then, one might ask, do we have to work so hard at inventing, manipulating, transforming forms and representing them in unconventional, out of the ordinary ways, as in the case of imagined geographies, of imagined places, science fiction and the like? One possible answer might be: pure delight in the form and pleasure of variations, the need to be free of pure functionality, or a defense against the fear of a vacuum and the feeling of helplessness in controlling space – attempting to miniaturize and contain it on paper or a screen – or an inner competition between the conscious and unconscious, as if we were thinking that since the unconscious was so good at creating dreams, we should let the conscious try it too, for technology today can construct whatever it wants, to the point of creating a whole, completely virtual, reality.

Representation and depth

Just what did I mean with the term "torsion of space"? In real or imaginary maps or topographical plans, the miniaturized space represented produces various psychological reactions depending on how it is presented. For example, when compared to two-dimensionality, the evocation or direct representation of three-dimensionality is somehow disturbing. Depicting depth has always been a problem in art, and still is for children learning to draw and for adult amateur artists.

The depth of the visual field and shadows, in other words what provides space, places, persons and objects in space with a physical body, brings the perception of reality too close to its representation. The birth of perspective in the Renaissance was an epochal event for art and the development of linear thought. Now both, perspective and thought, have been reappraised by modern and contemporary art in exploring new alternative depths by means of fantasy and imagination.

Speaking of places in dreams, memories or fantasies, as in psychoanalysis, is one thing, as is reading and writing of places and spaces, real or extraordinary. Designing, modeling or evoking with one's body a particular place is something else, and still different is photographing and filming places and details, framing them in what can be called a peculiar mobile form of perspective, so very real but so very intangible.

Photography was subject to the same amazement and suspicion some people have today when confronted with the techniques of so-called virtual reality. It was thought the photograph might steal the soul of the person photographed, and even before that perspective and other tricks to make things seem three-dimensional were suspect.

On the other hand, a sense of magic or transgression is also subtly at work in the person who produces the images: capturing or creating reality with one's own sign, stealing the secret of its forms from the earth. Art must have begun this way, in this tremor, in the secret space of the caves with their paintings, in the emotion of making a mask, a totem, in reproducing colors and painting one's body. Periodically the fashions of primitive cosmetics also return, which mirror the body and natural space, in a powerful need to go more in depth, into the flesh, in the relationship with space.

The innovation of virtual reality in many of the fields that deal with representation is that it stimulates three-dimensional perception, so that one moves visually within a place as if one were really there and not only imagining it.

I once wondered what the difference was, since basically a drawing, a story, a painting and then the photo, the film – in other words everything that is represented – is already a virtual reality. Yet it's not the same. It is depth, that third dimension, that catches one off guard and induces a sort of vertigo, leading to an alteration of the state of consciousness. We have no idea what this will eventually lead to.

Houses on the water, China. Photo © Bruno Liotta.

Perhaps as technological progress moves forward its leaps and bounds can be compared to mutations dependent on progressive and mutual feedback, between the perception of reality and its representation, moving towards depth. This is what happened in the sphere of psychology with the various types of psychoanalysis. Go ever deeper, in the earth, in the mind, in space, in water, in the past, in prehistory, in the future, everywhere.

Now, I wonder, returning to the concrete reality of the earth, what might a reference to depth, expressed on a spatial and perceptive plane, not limited to artistic and mass media representations, mean in an apparently superficial society such as that of the consumer West?

In the course of my thinking about perception, space and its representations, at a midpoint I encountered James Hillman, who in some way succeeded in answering my question, with regard to the soul.

In his *City and Soul* he shows us how and where, today, the soul of the city exists, listing various traditional ideas of soul – including depth – that concretely put architectural and urbanistic space in relation to each other.

> So we would have to imagine the creation of depth by means of levels, which can be experienced in different ways, such as levels of light, shadings of light which give the impressions of leveling and depth.

The Row Houses, San Martino, Italy, internal courtyard. © Fausto Ferrara, 2005.

Qualities of contrasting texture and materials also afford varieties of depth. Through narrowing as intensifying, going further into something, gives one a sense of deepening. The city alley as the place of depth, the heart, is the dark part of the city, the mystery of the city. I'm sure no one speaks in favor of alleys nowadays. I'm sure they all have to be lighted and opened but the alleyway and the narrow way, bending and twisting, is one of the modes of intensifying and adding a depth dimension.

(Hillman 1978:2)

Hillman reminds the city that neglects the soul that there is more than just the sense of depth, that the emotional memory and the dramas of the past, the importance of images and symbols, its crucial basis in human relationships, must be kept in mind.

There is still a great deal to be understood concerning space and the places of life in relation to the mind of the person who concretely creates them, and also concerning the value of depth as a category of thought which I associate immediately with the category of relation. If the space of the city is based on human relationships, every relation needs space and place – enough space and distance between persons and a place that collects and keeps the relation together. Depth is the awareness of that "between," of the otherness that fosters the relation.

In a city that neglects the soul, a community takes refuge in virtual spaces, meets online, looks for depth and intensity elsewhere. It needs to ensnare the body through images, in an attempt to remain attached so that even in make-believe the emotions of discovery can be experienced first-hand.

At this point it seems that the most recent frontier of the discourse on soul and earth can be identified with that of the relationship between human beings and technology. In other words: the theme of the overwhelming power of linear thought. This by itself would be enough to fill numerous books – as it has. But there is more, in confirmation of the indomitable vitality of imaginative thought.

Pluri-dimensional space

Here I am, talking about three-dimensionality – which on a psychological level and in particular concerning depth is not in the least to be taken for granted – and meanwhile science fiction and the logical–mathematical creative thinkers attempt to demonstrate the existence of the fourth, fifth, sixth, infinite and plural dimensions.

I can understand the amazement of Square, the protagonist of the flat, two-dimensional world that E.A. Abbott describes in his *Flatland* (1882),

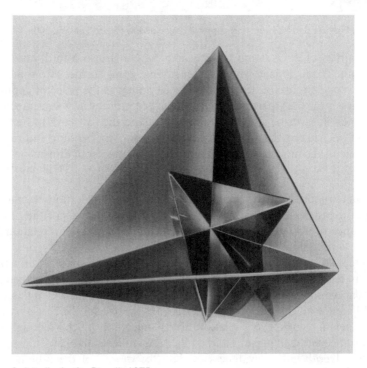

Sedicicella, Attilio Pierelli, 1975.

when rising up from his sheet of paper he finally discovers the third dimension, that is depth:

> Once more I felt myself rising through space. It was even as the Sphere had said.
> The further we receded from the object we beheld, the larger became the field of vision. My native city, with the interior of every house and every creature therein, lay open to my view in miniature. We mounted higher, and lo, the secrets of the earth, the depths of the mines and inmost caverns of the hills, were bared before me.
> (E-text version, transcribed by Aloysius West)

When, however, one attempts to describe and imagine the form, positions, perspectives of the fourth or more dimensions, I immediately think of the eternal desire of flight from the human condition, manifested here and there in myth, invention, play, pseudo-science-fiction and spirituality in the story of mankind.

Keeping prudently to the fourth dimension, first I shall cite science.

Einstein says that our physical space, as we conceive it through objects and their movements, possesses three dimensions and the positions are characterized by three numbers. The instant in which the event takes place is the fourth number.

With a sigh of relief I can accept the idea of time, the fourth dimension to add to the extended, Cartesian space. If this is really the fourth dimension of space, then it would seem to be another archetypal element deposited in the collective unconscious – the recurring theme of the journey in time – also to be traced in various spatial–temporal alterations, pathological or ecstatic, which can manifest themselves in states of consciousness or perception. Time is indeed a dimension to be added to the three with which we characterize space, a dimension that also becomes psychological, like the others, and that, as the phenomenologist psychiatrists Karl Jaspers, Ludwig Binswanger, and in particular Eugene Minkowski say, defines human existence in a constant union with space.

You may wonder what happened to time in my treatment of the subject, but here it is a question of a lack of space and not time.

I refer the reader to the chapter on the journey for that aspect of becoming, of change and loss, connected to the moving and alternation of space that makes the temporal experience more evident.

Even so, continuing with my explorations, I discovered that not everyone believes that the fourth dimension is to be identified with time.

R. Rucker, mathematician, essayist and science-fiction writer, devoted a book, entitled *The Fourth Dimension and How to Get There*, to the subject, in which he maintains that defining the fourth dimension as time, or as color in relation to light, does not satisfy the requirements of a further spatial dimension, difficult but not impossible to visualize mentally and to represent. Unless one turns to analogy of the following type: the fourth dimension is to three-dimensional space as the third is to two-dimensional space, that of *Flatland* in other words. But Rucker stresses the fact that nothing is to be accepted without leeway. In his idea of pluri-dimensional space, the fourth would be only one of the many spatial dimensions, superior to the three we know.

His book helps, graphically as well, to imagine them: directions and doors through which to leave space, directions in which space is curved, directions in which to meet other universes; the possible forms of space, flat, hyper-spherical and hyperbolic, and its global form, falling under the study of cosmological science. I am also reassured by the fact that in his formulation of the theme, Rucker sustains his reasoning in terms of degrees of freedom, beginning with the movement of human beings.

> The point I am making here is that in terms of degrees of freedom, motion on the Earth's bumpy surface is basically two-dimensional. The surface itself is a curved three-dimensional object, granted. But any motion that is confined to this surface is essentially a two-dimensional motion. It could be that mankind's perennial dream of flight is a hunger for more dimensions, for more degrees of freedom. The average person only experiences three-dimensional body motion when he or she swims underwater. Driving a car involves sacrificing yet another degree of freedom. One speeds up or slows down (possibly even reversing direction), but that's all. The road itself is a space curve in three-dimensional space, but motion that is confined to this particular curve is basically one-dimensional.
>
> (Rucker 1985:5–6)

For Rucker, as with Abbott, traveling between different dimensions is a way of enriching the imagination and its capacity to take different positions, avoiding rigidity and preconceptions and democratically tolerating the positions of others.

When, in *Flatland*, the Square tries to transfix the Sphere, it gets angry, takes him and raises him up in space. For him this is a traumatic experience, a change in perspective that interrupts the conflict and opens up to something new.

Forcing perception

Before returning to analytical psychology, my home turf, I would like to mention another door to imaginary spaces and worlds. The use of so-called psychedelic substances goes back to antiquity and has been with us ever since. In the 20th century it even became a socially widespread experience, espe-

Prayer before beginning to gather peyote. Photo © M. Benzi.

cially among young people. Aside from the ritual and religious use of the indigenous peoples of America, taking LSD or peyote was for many an initiation trial, a flight, a search for extreme experiences, a way of exploring new dimensions. Whatever the reason, in using similar substances there is an awareness at the beginning that "the trip" forces one's body and perceptive capacities to a limit that is more powerful, less playful and potentially dangerous compared to that of virtual reality. This is why the use of psychedelic substances is outlawed. By comparison, virtual reality is more like a highly refined sort of Disneyland, in which an average well-balanced person is always aware that it is a game, despite the reservations expressed by many psychologists on its use as entertainment.

The psychedelic trip does not take place in the world of fantasy, but in the perception of the real world. Among the reports by various researchers who experimented with the effects of LSD or mescaline on themselves, with differing results since it is a highly individualized experience, I shall cite a classic: Aldous Huxley's *The Doors of Perception*.

With regard to the spatial relations, the experiences described by Huxley fall into the field in question, that of the discovery of new dimensions within the only concrete reality in which we live. In the case of the use of substances or technology outside the body, this access is forced.

Even if only briefly, it should be remembered that there are also meditative practices and psychophysical exercises, used for thousands of years, within spiritual, religious or interior pathways in a broad sense, whose purpose is the same. Exceptional phenomena of the altering of awareness in a space–time sense, such as dislocation, journeys of the soul, the overcoming of the corporal and material limits, are referred to in literature on the subject as the concomitants of spiritual development and are considered as powers that can be abandoned without becoming addicted.

In describing his experience with mescaline and the answers he gave at the time to those who interviewed him, Huxley says:

> True, the perspective looked rather odd, and the walls of the room no longer seemed to meet in right angles. But these were not the really important facts. The really important facts were that spatial relationships had ceased to matter very much and that my mind was perceiving the world in terms of other than spatial categories. At ordinary times the eye concerns itself with such problems as *Where? – How far? – How situated in relation to what?* In the mescalin experience the implied questions to which the eye responds are of another order. Place and distance cease to be of much interest. The mind does its perceiving in terms of intensity of existence, profundity of significance, relationships within a pattern. I saw the books, but was not at all concerned with their positions in space. What I noticed, what impressed itself upon my mind was the fact that all of them glowed with living light and that in some the glory was more manifest than in others. In this context, position and the three dimensions were beside the point. Not, of course, that the category of space had been abolished. When I got up and walked about, I could do so quite normally, without misjudging the whereabouts of objects. Space was still there; but it had lost its predominance. The mind was primarily concerned, not with measures and locations, but with being and meaning.
>
> (Huxley 1954:14)

Through a perception that Huxley, together with Blake, defines as "clean" – that is, cleansed of the functional and utilitarian aspects rather like that of an innocent child – the vision of reality is something esthetic and "sacramental," spreading out to everything present, putting exterior and interior into an immediate marvelous communication.

The experience is not necessarily visionary and depends on other factors, including those of personality. Giving his experience as an example, Huxley tells us how he was conditioned by information he had previously received on the substance and its effects, expecting visions of all kinds: multicolor patterns, animated buildings, landscapes with heroic figures, revealing symbolic representations.

> But I had not reckoned, it was evident, with the idiosyncrasies of my mental make-up, the facts of my temperament, training and habits. I am and, for as long as I can remember I have always been a poor visualizer. Words, even the pregnant words of poets, do not evoke pictures in my mind. No hypnagogic visions greet me on the verge of sleep. When I recall something, the memory does not present itself to me as a vividly seen event or object . . . To those in whom the faculty of visualization is strong my inner world must seem curiously drab, limited and uninteresting. This was the world – a poor thing but my own – which I expected to see transformed into something completely unlike itself . . . The other world to which mescalin admitted me was not the world of visions; it existed out there, in what I could see with my eyes open. The great change was in the realm of objective fact . . . I was seeing what Adam had seen on the morning of his creation – the miracle, moment by moment, of naked existence.
>
> (Huxley 1954:10–11)

Mapmaking and psychoanalysis

I would like to end by citing Alfred Plaut's thoughts on imaginary maps and geographies. I have already quoted this Jungian analyst in the preceding chapter. Interviewed by Andrew Samuels, another Jungian analyst, Plaut discusses the subject referring to his own story as migrant and traveler, highlighting the way in which the geographic map combines functional and imaginary aspects.

> Yes, this is the precise intersection between what one might call sheer fantasy, exploration of that fantasy and actual discovery of outer reality. Prior to the middle ages, maps were already partly scientific, based on Ptolemy, and partly dictated by religious beliefs. It is the remnants of these beliefs which we see in what you have called fantasy. I would tend to refer to the search for the centre because of the psychological overtones.
>
> (Samuels 1989:160)

Establishing an analogy between the mapmaker and the psychoanalyst, Plaut affirms that:

> There is a region of the mind which we cannot reach by direct observation. That certainly is one parallel. I think the other is that we, like mapmakers throughout the centuries, are searching for the centre. Whether that centre was called Jerusalem in the mapmakers' mind, or whether it is

called the self in the mind of Jungian analysts, it is the search for *a* centre. But I also think the "centre" is quite ephemeral, it has only what Jung calls "heuristic value" – giving you an orientation. By the light of that orientation you can actually make discoveries.

(Samuels 1989:160–161; emphasis in original)

Analytical theories then adopt mapmaking and Plaut notes that the difference between a geographical and an analytical area is that the first is circumscribed, while the second is unlimited, more like the maps of Paradise – on which he had written an essay – since both will never be completed:

You see, many of my cartographical and geographical friends would call my map, which you have just drawn out of me, "mythical." All fantasy maps, whether deliberate fantasy or just unconscious fantasy, are of course mythical in the sense which I pointed out earlier on. The search for paradise is an outstanding example.

(Samuels 1989:181)

Plaut goes on to say that when one cannot succeed in considering Paradise as a symbol or myth, it has to be localized on the map, as many mapmakers seriously did in the past.

Maps and plans, whether based on reality or on what one considers to be reality, show, says Plaut, the transience of perception and of the sensorial impressions as well as the projection of desires.

So we once more have a paradox: the representation of space depends on where one starts. Objectively realistic, such as photographs of Earth from the satellites, the same for everyone; or imaginary, subjective, like the drawing of a child, the work of an artist, an aboriginal, or like the ravings of a madman: cosmographs of other worlds that are not antagonistic to the first but that can represent, depending on the case, an added value of creativity. If, as Winnicott affirms, creativity rests on illusion, the difference is only that of contextualizing illusion in play and leaving the latter free to remain what it is. Error and misconception belong to another category, that of right and wrong, useful elsewhere.

A third form of map can be added to these two, the map where real places never appear, a category of places particularly meaningful for the analyst. According to Plaut:

It is the one we really hold dear, to which we accord the maximum priority. It is our goal (destination), the aim of our life. That is the "real place."

(Samuels 1989:181)

Melville says in *Moby-Dick*: "It's not on any map – real places never are"; the emphasis is on the map that a man has in his mind, what is important to him, what is his priority, what is his goal, what is his life aimed at: *that* is the "real place."

(Samuels 1989:182; emphasis in original)

The category of truth, subjective, sums up and contains the two preceding categories, realistic and imaginary. The "real" place, as compared to the "false," aside from the metaphor, is the one in which one feels "right," where space, the great infinite space, at a certain point comes together in the place, one's own place, and everything seems to be in harmony even if, offhand, one can't really understand how or why. One may however have walked a long way before arriving.

Those who work with the sandplay at a certain point – and herein lies the mystery – say: "OK, that's it, it's done."

Chapter 6

The journey

The mobility that characterizes human beings more than any other species on the planet is an expression of the relationship between earth and soul. No one knows to what extent traveling is something man does naturally or whether it is the result of a cultural evolution. In the course of time the journey also developed an epistemology of its own, varying with the peoples and the historical periods.

The journey is, above all, a form of movement, more precisely a going from one place to another. For tens of thousands of years it meant walking. One step after another, like the child learning to walk. Man then discovered that he could go faster and cover greater distances by mounting on the back of an animal. Next came the invention of the wheel, and so on. Walking today is prescribed as therapy by doctors, but is otherwise eliminated as much as possible thanks to the increasingly varied and fast means of transportation and machines such as elevators and escalators. In advanced societies, walking is a hobby, a sport, tourism. In daily life contacts between one's feet and the ground are becoming an exception, even more so when it is a question of real earth.

To speak today of a journey and of traveling means dealing mainly with movements that take place on fast means of transportation, especially apart from daily life with its continuous routine journeys, short trips to the store, or somewhat longer itineraries, such as commuting to work or school. The journey, for it to be truly that, has to be an event, has to produce a detachment, some kind of break in the life of the person involved.

When traveling, the person automatically becomes a foreigner in those lands he considers foreign. For some reason, however, the foreign visitor behaves as if he were in a free zone, where he observes and takes what he needs as he passes through before returning home. He seems to be less interested in how others see him, in the foreign land, and what he leaves behind, aside from trash.

Reflecting on some of the unpleasant sensations, however momentary, that frequently arise during a journey in a foreign land – difficulty in adapting to the sensorial stimuli, irrational anxiety, problems connected to food and

In flight. Photo © Bruno Liotta.

sleep, language difficulties, feeling extraneous – helps us understand what happens to foreigners when they arrive in our land, whether passing through or as immigrants to stay.

Nomadism, migration, colonization

In the course of life, some individuals, like the animals, travel over various routes on the earth, varying in length and time, by choice or by an act of God. Alone or in a group.

In migratory animals the territories and relative distances are deposited in their genetic memory. Resident animals also move within their territory. Obviously this rigorously codified relationship with space is connected to adaptation.

Human beings, on the other hand, use space more casually, ideally exemplified by the space ship headed for the cosmic unknown. Human beings have always persistently been looking for something new, for some "elsewhere." It is not just food, not just power, not only wealth, nor reproduction, that guides the human in his wanderings on the earth, both great and small. An inhospitable territory, in itself, does not lie at the root of a migratory movement and the ensuing cultural developments, although a scholar such as Jared Diamond thinks otherwise. An evolutionary biologist, he interprets the story of mankind by observing cultural differences in the light of environmental, geographic and territorial conditioning, interwoven with technological progress and the effects of disease.

I agree with this point of view but would like to add the psychological aspect, without resorting to typologies or other interpretative paradigms that claim different attitudes towards life of the various populations. I wish simply to note that there are marked differences and that they also come to the fore in the relationship with the territory and in the reasons for moving. With the exception of the great calamities where the inhabitants are forced to leave a territory if they want to survive, there must be some other impulse, aside from rationalizing explanations, that makes one people – and not others – leave their land of origin to seek new places in which to settle, to fight even to the death to evict other groups and take possession of their land. I can find no rational explanation for the love the Eskimo bears to his world of ice, or that of the Bedouins for their desert, both emblematically harsh and unwelcoming lands. Yet both have been living there for centuries, for millennia.

Some places seem to exert a particular fascination, creating a powerful bond with the inhabitants. It is almost as if the desert, whether sand or ice, creates a resonance that mitigates the difficulties of adaptation. It may also be a matter of formal qualities: the essentiality, the absoluteness, the radicalness of its forms and colors, which, with regard to the desert, have always evoked intense and extreme psychological experiences. To Ernest Renan's aphorism that "the desert is monotheist," Bruce Chatwin answers that life in the desert consists of more than empty horizons and radiant skies that free the mind and let it concentrate on the divinity. If he wants to survive, the Bedouin must constantly adapt to the challenges offered by the desert. According to Chatwin the peoples of the desert, where the monotheist faiths arose, display a disdainful indifference for the Omnipotent.

Whether what keeps them on their land is a religion or something spiritual is a moot question. The power of the archetype is extremely earthbound. It is instinctive and may well be incarnated in the spirit of freedom that makes these peoples wander far and wide over their land and construct a collective imaginary, in which the sunny sky becomes Hell, the sun is a bony woman who dries up the pastures and the Moon, husband of the sun woman, is a slender vigorous youth who protects the sleep of the nomad, guiding him on his nocturnal travels and bringing rain. In his *The Songlines* Chatwin, in the wake of the anthropologist Fredrick Barth, also maintains that when confronted with certain nomads whose rituals are few and who lack any kind of deep-seated belief, it can be affirmed that:

> The journey in itself *was* the ritual, that the road to summer uplands *was* the Way, and that the pitching and dismantling of tents were prayers more meaningful than any in the mosque.
>
> (Chatwin 1988:224)

The approach of the 4th-century Christian hermit monks, who also lived in that same desert, the land of the Bedouins, was different. Of the maxims of the fathers of the desert, collected by Thomas Merton, I have chosen the following to serve as foil for the preceding:

> Just as a tree cannot bear fruit if it is often transplanted, so neither can a monk bear fruit if he frequently changes his abode.
>
> (Merton 1970)

The desert is seen both as an invitation for an intense earthly wandering, and as an immobile and silent place in which to encounter God.

Nomadism, the migrations of conquest, colonialism – I am not putting them in the same category, but simply listing them with regard to the general idea of movement – are movements that respond to a need, in their relationship with the land, that is never exclusively material. Indeed, their approach to the land differs.

The *nomad* experiences and, in his own way, dynamically possesses his land, through movement, by not settling in man-made places and by keeping himself free from the conditioning imposed by a sedentary lifestyle.

The need for dominion and for extending control of the land is stronger for peoples devoted to conquest and colonialism and finds expression in the material and formal possession of ever-broader territories. This is how the great conquerors of history expressed their superiority.

From the point of view of terminology, nomadism, from the Greek *nomàs*, defines the nomad as one who goes from one pasture to another, the shepherd in other words. This is why he could not have a fixed residence. Hunting and gathering Paleolithic man was also a nomad until the discovery of agriculture gave him new ways of obtaining food from nature and as a result a more sedentary life, tied to the land. Then came the city and all the rest. The fact that from then on the principal desire of human beings was that of not having to wander in search of food says a lot about how the land influenced the development of culture. The peoples who subsequently continued to live a wandering life, at this point by choice, developed as did the sedentary peoples, their traditions and customs turning their wandering into a precise place, with specific means and cadences, and a corresponding

Herd looking for water, Borana, Ethiopia. Photo © Alberto Tessore.

social and community context. Which is why they are also called traveling societies.

Migration on the other hand is a moving that might be called one-off. It is larger and intent on reaching new lands where the cultural identity is subject to various transformations depending on the peoples and the lands reached. Etymologically there seems to be an Indo-European significance regarding change. Many migrations of conquest, better known as invasions, were motivated by the need for survival, the search for new pastures. Unfortunately, this type of invasion has not yet stopped.

Colonization refers to the transfer of groups to occupy and exploit a territory, if necessary preparing it for settlement. From the Greek to the Roman colonies, to the European colonialism involving territories across the sea, and the recent strategy of the occupation of Palestine by Israel, this inexorable advance is defined by a word etymologically connected to the land: colonist, from the Latin *colere*, he who cultivates the land.

There is a risk in looking at the above-named phenomena from the point of view of movement and travel of putting widely different situations on the same level. The archaic migrations of *Homo erectus* and then *sapiens* – in point of fact simply their spread over the planet – have nothing to do with the subsequent waves of movements and intermingling involving groups of farmers and shepherds, both with new technologies and often fighting for the best territory. Nor should these first movements be confused with the better known historical migrations of predatory peoples from central Asia, invasions that reached as far as Europe and the Mediterranean. Another less dramatic type of migration consists of the gradual transfer of farmers and artisans to the city, again quite distinct from the forced migrations of slavery and trade in human beings. These too, unfortunately, are still going on.

What all these migrations have in common on a historical–economic level is the gap between countries that are technologically more advanced and those that lag behind. The former dominate the latter to appropriate the resources. The latter move towards the former in the hope of sharing the wealth. The great period of European migration took place between 1840 and 1930, coinciding with the process of industrialization. A fifth of the

Statue of Liberty and sailboat, New York, USA. Photo © Bruno Liotta.

population of Europe emigrated at the time to various parts of the world, particularly the Americas. By 1900, the New World countries were already able to compete economically with northwestern Europe. These movements increased the general birth rate by a factor of as much as 14 in less than two centuries in the immigration areas, with obvious changes in the preceding balances between races and peoples and a progressive increase in race conflicts. In subsequent decades up to the present, aside from the forced migrations of the two world wars, of other wars and political events in general, the phenomenon of so-called "free" migration seems to be coming to the fore: from the less developed countries to those technologically more advanced, such as European countries and the United States.

Analysis of current migration on an international level seems to indicate that it is fundamentally tied to the interests of employers looking for cheap labor. Every government, then, justifies opening its borders to immigration, regulated or illegal, depending on whether the population is growing or not and whether workers are needed for essential jobs.

In this and in the next chapter my itinerary will follow the themes of travel, exile and nostalgia, from an interior and subjective point of view as well as with regard to the collective psychological components. My path passes between Georges Perec's two "nostalgic and (false) alternatives" (see Perec 1997:71): either that humanity, constitutionally, has always tended to settle down, or that it has always been characterized by a need for movement, and the conquest of the land of others. I have of course found valid testimonials in the history and culture of all times and places for both positions, whether peoples, groups or individuals.

For the many who moved from one continent to the other in the course of the centuries, there were always just as many, or more, who remained where they were. What is notable is the capacity of the white European to succeed in achieving both of these at the same time: to have territories in which to settle, build his culture, prosper, and at the same time migrate, travel and conquer new lands.

With this in mind, it is interesting to note Jung's recount of a visit to the Pueblo Indians in 1924 and his conversation with the chief:

> "See," Ochiway Biano said, "how cruel the whites look. Their lips are thin, their noses sharp, their faces furrowed and distorted by folds. Their eyes have a staring expression; they are always seeking something. What are they seeking? The whites always want something; they are always uneasy and restless. We do not know what they want. We do not understand them. We think that they are mad."
>
> (Jung 1963:276)

When asked to be more specific about his impression, the chief observed that the white man says that he thinks with his head, while the Indians "think with their heart." And Jung, a white European, commented as follows:

> I fell into a long meditation. For the first time in my life, so it seemed to me, someone had drawn for me a picture of the real white man. It was as though until now I had seen nothing but sentimental, prettified colour prints. This Indian had struck our vulnerable spot, unveiled a truth to which we are blind.
>
> (Jung 1963:276)

Jung then began to reconsider the history of the West and its conquerors: Caesar, Scipio Africanus, Pompey, the Romans from the North Sea to the Nile, the Christians who went out to convert humanity, from Saint Augustine to Charlemagne, the Crusaders, Columbus and Cortez and all the others who with fire, sword and torture had come to the Pueblo, peacefully worshipping their celestial father in the sun. The white man had even reached the South Seas, bringing firewater, syphilis and scarlet fever that decimated the peoples on the islands.

> What we from our point of view call colonization, missions to the heathen, spread of civilization, etc., has another face – the face of a bird of prey seeking with cruel intentness for distant quarry – a face worthy of a race of pirates and highwaymen. All the eagles and other predatory creatures that adorn our coats of arms seem to me apt psychological representatives of our true nature.
>
> (Jung 1963:277)

Diamond's book, mentioned above, begins with an interesting question put to him by a young New Guinea native: how was it that his land – where 1,000 independent peoples had lived for 60,000 years – was conquered by the Europeans in two centuries. Diamond broadens the question to the history of the world, and adds other more specific questions such as: how come a Spanish captain with 168 soldiers succeeded in taking over the Inca empire, defended by an army of 80,000 men, rather than the other way round with an Inca prince landing at Cadiz and capturing the king of Spain? The title of his book, *Guns, Germs and Steel*, is sufficiently eloquent to provide an answer. Even so, if Diamond answers the first part of this question – how come the Spanish captain won? – with plenty of information and brilliant intuition, the second remains unanswered. I propose it again out of the context of war and make it mine: why did some peoples never feel the need to leave their regions, neither in the past nor today, and conquer others, or go and live there peacefully? Does there necessarily have to be a reason why the Inca prince should have conquered Spain? Or, in the case of the Pueblo, some country in Europe?

The journey is part of migration, of nomadism, of colonization, but also of infinite other movements undertaken by man throughout his life, qualified by the reason, by the occasion, by the means of transportation, by the destination and others still.

Many authors, in various spheres, have already dealt with this and on the whole I trust their reflections and conclusions.

But not always. Even though I will try to keep to the lines of my discourse, every so often I will be contesting a position. While traveling, listening, talking, reading, on a theme that seemed taken for granted, various aspects that were anything but obvious came to the fore, aspects that needed clarification, above all when reconsidering the meaning of the journey in the world of today.

Journeys, transits and non-places in contemporary society

In an attempt to answer his initial question – in what way does the journey act as a force that changes the course of human history? – E.J. Leed, in his *The Mind of the Traveler*, also considers the collective psychological aspects, evaluating the social effects of the journey.

The author maintains that the journey is no less than the central force in historical transformations, and that the creation of place, of the map, of the

Planes and buildings in Hong Kong. Photo © Bruno Liotta.

territory is to be attributed to mobility. Frontiers, says Leed, are made by those who cross them. He believes that place consists of the relations and interactions which form the ethnic group and that the ethnic group is not a localized entity. The book, full of interesting ideas, deals with the structure and history of the journey; of the philosophic, scientific journey; of the individual and identity transformations the journey produces; of traveling societies, both nomad and those of today; and of the modern traveler. In addition – and this is important – Leed admits to the historical, almost absolute, predominance of the male presence, with respect to the female, in all the contexts of the journey and of traveling.

Even though I accept the dynamic vision within the logic that animates Leed's study, there is another viewpoint that does not in the least take for granted the idea that moving and traveling are *tout court* universal dimensions and universally desirable. For Leed, looking at the world as if it were articulated in settled ethnic groups, societies bound to the earth and specific places, connected to each other by equally stable groups, is a "retrospective distortion."

Proposing to see society from the point of view of mobility would mean changing one's approach: society would then appear as a hodge-podge of semi-autonomous production and reproduction units connected by markets, structures of communication and of exchange. This different image of society would mean giving up the illusion of permanence, immutability (which is what we usually mean by "structures"), and thinking of societies as the result of transitory, never constant relationships, continuously broken and made anew by events of encounter and separation. In other words, as a system that is continuously subject to processes of scission and fusion, separation and aggregation.

Indeed there are any number of ways to look at mobility. The Italians walk, or rather move over, old Roman roads to visit even older cities that have been there for thousands of years, using new means of transportation. Are space, place and journey different for someone from America, from the United States? Jung might think they were. And this is just what I am saying in this book.

Leed also believes that ethnic identity is formed by encounters with the other, that it is "only" through mobility, contacts and relationships with others, the result of traveling, that an awareness of the collective identity is formed. Jung says so as well, and I too, as a person and analyst whose work is based on the relationship, on the construction of identity and otherness through personal contacts, believe this to be true. But I would eliminate that "only." On reading Leed's book I was afraid for a moment that I had been left behind, with my ambition to bypass the jumble of new mass ideologies that seemed inconsistent with my first-hand experiences.

Leed's vision is not dynamic but hyperkinetic and only partially corresponds to the real situation in which the peoples of the Earth find themselves today. We must ask ourselves who is really participating in this collective merry-go-round and reflect on the fact that there are still whole masses of people who believe in the permanence and immutability of their social structures, to be maintained at all costs.

It seems to me that this proposal of constant mobility, of the transitory state and social fragmentation, is leading humanity to a sort of permanent and global exile, which has already made so many victims in the advanced societies. It seems to me that children bear the brunt of this disorientation and unrelenting rhythm of life, that not all those who travel benefit from their experience, especially if they have to travel or do so from hidden persuasion, and that, thinking of otherness, the Inca respected the diversity of the Europeans even though they had never met them before. But I may be wrong.

I'm not wrong, however, with regard to the testimony of all my patients and students, Italian and others, who spoke to me of a pleasure in traveling that is never as great as that of returning; of the joy in remaining, possibly quietly, somewhere, with one's own things, one's dear ones and, above all, at one's own leisure. In the course of his book Leed introduces critical notes and also counter-tendency observations, but the choice of his theme – interpreting the history of mankind through the journey – ties him to presenting primarily the positive aspects that influenced the formation of mankind as we know it today. In the epilogue, recognizing that the situation of today would authorize nostalgia for traveling in the past, Leed still sides with all those who declare:

> We cannot escape the global civility that generations of travelers . . . have created.
> This world we cannot, as yet, leave. Travel as tourism has become like the activity of a prisoner pacing a cell much crossed and grooved by other equally mobile and "free" captives. What was once the agent of our liberty has become a means for the revelation of our containment.
>
> (Leed 1991:258–286)

My reference to the relationship between soul and earth is a way to begin escaping from a mobility that seems to be going round in circles and is moving in a vacuum. In traveling one should have an anchor and a place to return to, so one can stop when and for as long as necessary. If not concretely, there should at least be an interior stopping place where the soul can pause and give itself a chance to metabolize the experience.

For the journey depends on the mind of the traveler. And the mind has to be able to think.

In the face of economic and political arguments, proof exists that the influence exerted by the psychological aspects of travel, mobility and relation to the land is just as important for the individual as it is for the collectivity. Depending on the situation, it can be even greater. I do not believe that the

Boats and buildings in Hong Kong. Photo © Bruno Liotta.

tenacity with which some peoples resisted invasion and colonization, with or without war, can be explained by economic or political reasons alone.

In summarizing the above, talk today of journeys, migrations, etc. means talking above all of the white man and his far-flung influence, achieved not only through "arms, steel and disease" but also with the distribution of consumer goods, the economy based on money, the diffusion of mass media and mass tourism, and lastly, with the diplomacy of vested interests. All this has inevitably completely changed the meaning of the journey. The white man's way of traveling today means going straight and as fast as possible to the destination. The real journey, as a specific experience, is disappearing, watered down and merging with other experiences.

Globalization has become a sort of permanent journey, where what predominates, between real and telematic journeys, is the communication network. There seems to be a constant aspiration for a co-presence in time – everything in "real time" – undermining the idea of space and the traditional journey and its duration.

Even if the ways of traveling of the past still exist in many countries and in less advanced societies, they are curiously mixed with modern means of transportation, introduced in the most remote corners of the Earth by tourism.

Here is the description that Alessandro Bee, the photographer who took the cover photo of this book, gives in his travel notes on the roads of Nepal.

> I want to pause on the concept of road. Let's start by saying that here this concept doesn't exist! Here the "road" is a lane on which everything goes, in the real sense of the term, that is EVERYTHING. A cow, a rattle-trap pick-up, a goat with bleating young one, a bus that couldn't be more beaten up, a rickshaw, an old man pulling along his buffalo, serene as if he were in the rice paddy, orange trucks decked out as if it were Christmas, people selling oranges and peanuts . . . and all this in a road as wide as one lane with us. Fantastic! If one manages to catch "the poetry" (and it's not always easy, on the contrary . . .) of a Nepalese road, you truly realize that there's a whole people in a road. And here, goodbye to tranquility and the peace of the most isolated village. You don't honk your horn every so often, but use it more or less like the gas pedal. It is an incredible madhouse in which everybody manages to understand everyone else, as if there were one strange language between vehicles and men. And everything of course at a crawl – it took me more than two hours to cover 30 km. To be noted that the direction one should go in – here it's on the left – practically doesn't exist. In the sense that even the buses are continuously slaloming in that kaleidoscope of the Nepalese road. You're sure you're going to plough into or ram the back of someone at every curve, then paradoxically everything continues. You graze, you almost ram someone, gaily honk your horn and then everybody goes on. Not to speak of the buses. In Guatemala I had seen some wrecks, but these . . . the seat backs are never blocked, so every time the bus brakes you are catapulted ahead – and the road I was on today was a mountain road. The windows – windows? – if there are any they are broken, but this makes no difference because there aren't any anyway! The bus is not just drafty: today, at a certain point, I put a sweatshirt on my head that made me look like a Tuareg. Then obviously the bus doesn't stop at the bus stops, at the most it slows down, so that you throw yourself in, or better there's a guy at the door who throws you in. Luckily I caught the bus at the head of the line . . . On the bus I got to know a university student, he keeps me company for a bit and we begin to talk. At a certain point it turns to politics. I discover he is an advocate of the GREAT NEPAL, wants to annex Sikkim and Bhutan. I can't believe it! Even here?!
> (Bee, private communication, 2004; translated from the Italian by transl.)

Aside from these experiences of full immersion in the local world face to face with the different cultures, the route, the crossing, the street, are ever less perceptible in tourist traveling of today, above all in organized mass vacations. They become almost irrelevant, where what matters most is the comfort of the means of transportation, and the fastest way of getting there, keeping the travelers occupied with other activities, such as the cinema on the plane.

It's all to take your mind off something . . . but off what? The anxiety of the journey? The fear of losing your bearings, of dying along the way? If that's what it is, then there are a number of powerful and obscure elements in traveling that should probably be taken into consideration.

The existential journey

In the realm of psychology, but also in that of philosophy, art and religion, the valences assigned to the journey vary. As in space and place, movement is seen as a metaphor, symbol and element of the imagination.

Writers and artists, philosophers, wanderers and pilgrims in search of themselves, of God and of the truth traveled far and wide, leaving testimony of their experience. They are almost always individual journeys, in which the interior search and the journey itself seem to be one and the same.

In addition to the tourist journeys of the masses, today it is also seen as a trial, an undertaking, a personal commitment, in which the actual journey becomes a place and a time for reflection. "Having an experience" in the sense of taking a trip is well exemplified by the etymology of the word experience: *ex-per-iri*, in which the concepts of risk, fear, crossing and attainment are mixed. The idea that traveling can "improve," can have positive effects, is

House in Sidamo, Ethiopia. Photo © Alberto Tessore.

implied in the adventurous vacation trips, in those in the name of solidarity, in trips towards personally significant goals, to find or reach something dear, to realize a dream or an ideal.

Once more, when faced with these considerations, we find ourselves with various spurious alternatives: either the solitary search for oneself, like the hermit at the top of the mountain or the eternal traveler, the itinerant monk or pilgrim who is always on the move. Staying put or walking doesn't necessarily make one wiser or closer to God; it's not that simple, according to what those who know say.

An initial hypothetical scheme is that of a real concrete journey on land, on sea or by air, which psychologically affects the traveler. Then there is the existential journey, followed by the fantastic, imaginary journey, which I will deal with further on, and lastly the interior journey of the soul, in which physical moving may be irrelevant.

Sometimes, however, one dimension seems to need the other, and they intersect and are superposed. In what I call the existential journey, the real and the interior journeys are herewith submitted to closer examination.

Jung had this experience too. As previously mentioned, he traveled a great deal in the course of his life seeking to know and meet, as a European, with cultural diversities. There is at least one chapter devoted to his journeys in all his biographies, including his autobiography.

> We always require an outside point to stand on, in order to apply the lever of criticism. This is especially so in psychology, where by the nature of the material we are much more subjectively involved than in any other science. How, for example, can we become conscious of national peculiarities if we have never had the opportunity to regard our own nation from outside? Regarding it from outside means regarding it from the standpoint of another nation ... I understand Europe, our greatest problem, only when I see where I as a European do not fit into the world.
>
> (Jung 1963:274–75)

Jung went to Africa (Tunisia, Algeria and Egypt in the north, and Kenya, Uganda and the Sudan in the center); to America (the modern cities built by European immigrants and the native villages of New Mexico); and to the Orient. The descriptions of the places in his letters or elsewhere are full of color, of sensorial references to daily life, social and religious traditions, rites, the physical aspects of the inhabitants, the animals and the landscapes. His desire to communicate also led him to learn the local languages and talk with those he met, especially figures of importance in collective psychology such as priests, monks, witch-doctors, doctors and healers, tribal chiefs.

Deserts, gardens, indigenous villages, forests, savannas, rivers, lakes and waterfalls, temples, palaces, all aroused a deep emotion in Jung, seen as a return to the origins, to a free and full interior world, which he felt was buried by the stratification of the western culture of progress.

Around the end of the 1930s Jung went to India and visited all of it, from North to South and to Ceylon.

> India affected me like a dream, for I was and remained in search of myself, of the truth peculiar to myself . . . When I visited the stupas of Sanchi, where Buddha delivered his fire sermon, I was overcome by a strong emotion of the kind that frequently develops in me when I encounter a thing, person or idea of whose significance I am still unconscious . . . When you have completed one circumambulation, you enter a second higher circuit which runs in the same direction. The distant prospect over the plain, the stupas themselves, the temple ruins, and the solitary stillness of this holy site held me in a spell. I took leave of my companion and submerged myself in the overpowering mood of the place.
>
> . . . In India I was principally concerned with the question of the psychological nature of evil. I had been very much impressed by the way this problem is integrated in Indian spiritual life, and I saw it in a new light . . .
>
> In Christianity more is suffered, in Buddhism more is seen and done. Both paths are right but in the Indian sense Buddha is the more complete human being.
>
> (Jung 1963:304–310 *passim*)

Jung's trip to India had provided him with an opportunity to reconsider his position as a Christian, son of a Protestant pastor, and to reinforce his position as a psychotherapist who cannot avoid confronting suffering.

The personal significance of a journey is part of the psychological analysis of the experience, in addition to a host of other aspects that cannot be dealt with properly here. Guidelines can be imagined. Speaking about a journey and traveling means speaking above all of a corporeal experience, consisting of sensations, perceptions and movement with reference made to the motivations and choices that led to a departure and the feelings involved, pleasant or painful. The experiences that accompany the actual journey are followed by arrival and adjustment to new surroundings. The encounter with the new leads, ultimately, to a discussion of the return.

Some of these themes are dealt with in more depth in this book while others have been barely touched on.

What I hope to do here is analyze, through the relationship between soul and earth – and in this case the journey – various cultural paradigms in our society, still not touched by doubt, even among psychologists and other professionals in the field. Yet in meeting more or less the same persons I note a growing sense of anxiety and collective bewilderment that leads me to consider the shadow aspects of the journey.

Tamil Nadu farmer, India. Photo © Alberto Tessore.

The shadow of the journey

For most people their familiar everyday world is seen as one of habit, bore-dom and a desire to escape. Unaware though they may be, many people live in a perennial state of restlessness and seek distraction by a constant urge to go elsewhere, from which they will again go elsewhere – cinema, theater, con-certs, exhibitions, sociality in general. Going to a park, a garden, by definition a special place, different from the home, doesn't mean going there for a walk, to smell the flowers, look at the colors or stretch out on the lawn. Often it means sitting on a bench, generally uncomfortable, to watch a performance. This is not meant as a criticism of culture or cultural sharing, but rather the fact that culture has become a market for a perennial displacement of one's real self, for a search for stimuli that should also exist within, in one's daily life, if only one could stop and listen to oneself.

While a good deal of travel literature publicizes the transforming effects of a voyage on the individual, of its role in helping to construct social relation-ships, of its function in revealing differences and otherness, we cannot ignore the shadows of the journey that not only betray these vocations, but distort them in a utilitarian sense, including the knowledge of oneself. One can come back from a marvelous journey, laden with documentation, souvenirs, things to talk about, and feel enriched, much the way one does after a good meal or a day at the hypermarket: in other words, exhilarated by all the good things assimilated. Satisfied, but not necessarily transformed. Once the intoxication has passed, everything begins all over, up to the next trip. For some traveling is like a drug; for others a form of collecting. This gratifying element of the journey explains the therapeutic function attributed to it in the past, not only concerning various ailments for which a "change of air" was recommended, but almost always for psychological disorders, the ailments of the soul. "Why don't you take a trip?" is still being suggested to those who are depressed, or have recently divorced and should "stop thinking about it" or find themselves a new partner as soon as possible.

Personally I am not opposed to a temporary mitigation of psychological suffering by means of distraction, but I am not favorable to it when flight masquerades as therapy, for it just doesn't work. Getting away as a reprieve from suffering is one thing. Expecting it to magically disappear or be definitively resolved, simply because the source has been left behind or because unusual stimuli make us forget it for the moment, is something else.

The shadows of the journey, seen as flight, consumption, superficial tourism, the frauds of travel, the delusion of the journey, all fall into what I believe can be called a "pathology of travel," as if this antique and noble activity had fallen ill, like other things in our society, and was in need of therapy.

With regard to the persons, the hypothetical or real travelers, there are specific pathologies that involve space and movement, such as claustrophobia and claustrophilia, agoraphobia, the phobias concerning the airplane (much more common than generally thought) and other means of transportation, which necessarily influence the lives of the persons, especially in a society where traveling and moving about is often inevitable.

For some time now I have come to the realization that various psychological ailments considered on the increase in number and seriousness, such as phobias and anxiety syndromes with panic attacks, reveal the exacerbation of various characteristics in our society. In the past many people would not have manifested these ailments simply because they would never have had the chance to do so, since life was organized in times, places, means of transportation closer to the constitution and limits of the human being. The phobia of the plane, for example, is a recent introduction in the history of transportation. It shows its "intelligence" in refusing the irrational request of complete faith asked of the mind and body: that of entrusting oneself to the air (remember the experiments on visual depth where even kittens backed away from an empty space), the mechanics, the skill of the pilots, perfect strangers. In addition, without wings of our own.

I have traveled a great deal by plane, for long stretches and when technology was not what it is today, without developing phobias. I enjoyed the miracle of aerial vision, the sea of clouds, the colors of night and day; I slept and ate, even in stormy conditions, but I never thought it was a "normal" experience, it never became a habit, and I understand my patients – some of whom were pilots and flight assistants with temporary crises – and those who still feel awe when faced with what threatens our instinctive prudence of keeping our feet solidly on the ground.

There are also, contrary to the phobias, real fixations, travel obsessions, such as the *fugueur*, mad travelers, afflicted by that semi-hypnotic "ambulatory determinism," now forgotten, that in the nineteenth century became almost an epidemic of mad and compulsory travelers (Hacking 1998).

Wandertrieb, automatisme ambulatoire, dromomania and *poriomania* are some of the names of the psychiatric syndrome that made some individuals walk and travel unceasingly, without knowing why, alienated and followed by amnesia of the happening. Even today this shows up as a specific pathology, characterized by flights, sudden unexpected departures, in a state of diminished awareness. For those who have seen the film *Forrest Gump* it is that desperate running around the world, which the protagonist does whenever his mental suffering becomes unbearable.

I believe it is easy to identify in this extreme a feature that many normal people manifest, in addition to the abovementioned "traveling to forget." When the mind, the soul, are at their wits' end, the body sets itself in motion, in a sort of extreme attempt at life, acts, moves, discharges or recharges, walks, runs, outdistances. Jogging is something that has spread throughout the world as an anti-stress activity. But distances don't necessarily count, for one can run away from one room to another, from one building to another, or even just a few steps. That's the way we're made: what is a resource can also become an ailment. Which is why many truths about human nature can be drawn from the pathology.

The imaginary and archetypal journey

A type of "creative flight" – and I hope the lovers of the subject won't take me to task for my definition of "flight" – is that of the fantastic, imaginary journey, constructed by the mind to express something that goes beyond the real journey. Journeys through the air have been present in the collective psychology since antiquity and I don't think they ever produced phobias. Perhaps they were imagined, symbolized, ritualized simply because human beings would have liked to fly like birds. Now that they can, the imaginary journey continues to proliferate in new forms, in fantastic literature, in art, in the products of mass media and virtual technology. The terms "imaginary" and "fantastic," and sometimes also "symbolic," as used here, can all be considered counterpoints to the real.

The implausible in imaginary journeys – as seen in the discussion of fantastic places and their maps – may be the means of transportation, the destination, or the personages, or all these aspects taken together. The *Odyssey* and *Gulliver's Travels*, for example, are imaginary in the various stages of the journey and in the subsequent landfalls, even though the journey as such, the transit, its means and the final destination, are in both works relatively believable, particularly when compared to journeys on hippogriffs, flying carpets or cannon balls. Dante's *Divine Comedy* is a mixed journey, imaginary with regard to places and settings, partially real with regard to the principal personages and the other figures, realistic as a journey–visit on foot and with a guide, as shown in various illustrations. But it is above all an interior journey, both autobiographical and allegorical of life in general, if we agree with the explicit meaning Dante gave it.

Monsters, marvels, abductions and siren songs, traps and surprises, loves and battles, all these and more are presented during an imaginary journey. The exaggeration and the extraordinary forms that often characterize it are meant to astonish, attract the attention of the listener or reader with regard to the fate of the protagonist, always more or less the same, archetypally defined as "the way of the hero."

The protagonist leaves his land of origin, his family, encounters the unknown, goes through countless trials, discovers new realities, learns from experience and then, with his concrete or symbolic treasure, makes his way back home to tell the others what he saw and experienced, to reconstruct a new order, to establish his life and that of his group anew.

In the course of the centuries the collective consciousness with regard to the journey and its heroes has changed, leading to variations in this archetypal scheme, particularly after the great journeys of discovery. From Ariosto's Orlando to Cervantes' Don Quixote, Bacon's travelers towards the New Atlantis, Swift's Gulliver and Defoe's Robinson Crusoe, one can follow the crucial passages of sensibility, different types of wandering, displacement, restlessness, which move away from pure fantasy to approach satire and a progressive disenchantment with life.

Various fantastic elements also remain in the reports of the great journeys of discovery and the mythical halo that surrounds their protagonists: from Marco Polo to Christopher Columbus, Vasco da Gama, Magellan, Cook, Bunyan and many others.

The journey that appears in more recent Western literature – the romantic, sentimental or adventure journey – definitely privileges human vicissitudes, exemplified in the experience of the individual who travels for pleasure or choice and is not subject to dictates, whether religious or otherwise.

The psychological aspects increase while the imaginary aspects fall away, almost disappearing in this context, to flow together and re-emerge more expressly in a specific genre, that of fantastic literature and imaginary journeys – what is now science fiction – which reached its apex in the

Orlando Furioso, illustration by Gustave Doré.

eighteenth century, with hundreds of publications of this kind, mainly in English, German and French.

At this point, it is as if the possibility of fantasizing around the earth waned as it was gradually discovered and conquered, subdivided and confined by the dominant political and economic powers. The journey therefore became more real and at the same time more intimate and personal. The Grand Tour became fashionable, as did travel accounts by illustrious persons, from Goethe to Stendhal, Ruskin, Henry James, Proust and many others, including the travelers of today who continue to show us what surprises are to be found in the still unknown corners of the earth. At a certain point Jules Verne's novels represented a modern compromise between fantasy and reality, where the imagination anticipates, more than deforms, reality, on the terrain of verisimilitude.

Every epoch and every moment in the story of western culture had a journey of its own which is inscribed in the general concept of life and in the collective psychological sensibility. Here I want to discuss synthetically how the theme of journey lends itself to epitomizing the relationship between the human being and the earth – the earth as it was known in every historical period – and the need to imagine and invent what was not yet known, what was out of reach, what was desirable or to be feared.

This is why the journey is so rich in symbolism and is considered by depth psychology an archetypal theme that appears in the dreams and fantasies of the individual as well as in the collective accounts. The ultimate destination of this type of journey is always a center: the center of the world, symbol of truth and immortality, the true Self, the center of the mandala, that diagram that brings together place, map and journey at one and the same time. The center, in a dream or in myth, can be represented by a precious object to find, a sacred book, a stone or a cup like the Grail; or by a mountain to climb, a subterranean place in which to acquire the wisdom of the ancestors, by the promised land, an Eden or an original immortal garden.

The archetypal journey always takes on the meaning of knowledge; of initiation, formative or spiritual progression. This leads directly to the

Journey to the Underworld, Etruscan vase c. 320 BC, Museo Claudio Faina (by kind permission), Orvieto, Italy.

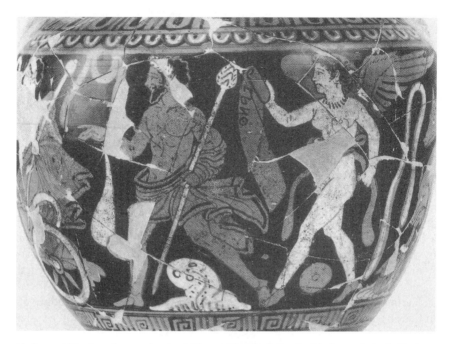

Hades and Vanth welcome the dead, Museo Claudio Faina (by kind permission), Orvieto, Italy.

interior journey, which is something more than and different from the imaginary journey.

The interior journey

This particular journey, not generally a universal experience, belongs to the soul of the individual, the only one who can bear witness to it to the end. It is a solitary journey, even when the person undertaking it does not isolate himself, and is unique, even if it can be represented in forms common to the cultural context. Basically it coincides with psychological development, the internal becoming of the soul in the course of life or of particular periods in life.

In preceding chapters I have dealt with place, space, the stable dimensions of existence. Taking on the theme of the journey is a way of reintroducing elements such as movement, as well as time and becoming; that process that Jung defined as "individuation," the becoming of oneself, mentioned at the beginning of the second chapter, introducing the essay "Mind and Earth."

This becoming is not an automatic occurrence but takes place as a result of the slow flow of time, favored by the crucial passages of life and the resulting changes in perspective.

Philosophy has long polemicized, and still does, on the relationship between being and becoming, and on the nature of both dimensions as well as their intersection.

Psychology too, especially the kind defined as psychodynamic and psychoanalytical, and in particular psychotherapy, must believe in the idea of becoming if it is to believe in healing, in the itinerary that leads from pathology to recovery, changing the patient's attitude towards life. This is why both the language of analytical psychotherapy and its imaginary are expressed in terms of journey when dealing with interior movement and processes. Ways, itineraries, walks, roads, paths; all journeys of many forms, depending on the moments and the people: flights, explorations, falling and sinking, incursions into the past and the future, migrations and exile, by sea and by land, in dream and in fantasy. Literature on the subject is abundant, to which the reader is referred (Widmann 1999).

The "psychoanalytical journey" therefore by right falls into the category of contemporary interior journeys.

In my training as an analyst and my experience with my patients, foreign or not, the idea of undertaking a journey together to discover the self – a journey which had a direction and a sense – was of help in overcoming inner difficulties, suffering in the past and present, and the various symptomatologies that may have been present. Using the sandplay, and review of the sand scenes in sequences at the end of the treatments, further convinced me that the places of departure and of arrival of any interior journey are related to the dynamism of the form: one's own form rather than an ideal form.

Frequently a patient stages an itinerary, with figures of travelers, of particular landscapes, unconsciously or semi-consciously imagined within an organization of space that is both personal and archetypal (Liotta 1994). The distribution of the objects in the sandbox and the presence or absence of personages in itself represents an allusion to an itinerary that is often also indicated with other materials, such as bridges, roads, means of transportation, colored powders, that join some places and leave others isolated. Journey and form penetrate each other.

Looking at the sand scenes of the patients in sequence at the end of the therapy is like leaving together for the journey of their story of analysis. The restlessness that marked their unease, their search, so like that of the wanderer, his losing himself and finding himself, his persisting in his search for particular concrete places – the desert, the forest, the exotic or wild environment, the sea, the island, the heights, mountain peaks, the heart of the city, the ancient or the modern city, the subterranean world – calms down in the end in the last sand scene. A pause, perhaps only temporary, but in any case the covering of an itinerary.

I should now like to express an impression and a doubt: it appears that the idea of the journey has permeated the various types of psychoanalysis. It should perhaps be thought of, like other metaphors, paradigms and basic assumptions, as a potential conditioning detrimental to other forms in which the interiority and its becoming could express themselves. Might not new metaphors open up; might not one "become" even standing still? I'll leave the question open.

So once the journey has been completed and the place has been found, what happens next?

Inevitably what appears next is "the return." "Going" at a certain point turns in on itself and takes a road, which can be new or the same as that of going, but which is "the way of return."

The return is another innate aspect of the journey, to be discussed in the next chapter. After having wandered around, experienced all sorts of things, hoped, been deluded or disenchanted, the traveler returns home, no longer the same person because he can now see with eyes that are different from when he left. It is a theme that is to be found everywhere and in all times.

It might be interesting to note that even incorrigible travelers sooner or later encounter the problem of return.

Bruce Chatwin refers to the legendary moleskin travel books – now cult objects for metropolitan travelers – in his *The Songlines*:

> I had a presentiment that the "traveling" phase of my life might be passing. I felt, before the malaise of settlement crept over me, that I should reopen those notebooks. I should set down on paper a résumé of the ideas and encounters which had amused and obsessed me; and which I hoped would shed light on what is, for me, the question of questions: the nature of human restlessness.
>
> Pascal, in one of his gloomier *pensées*, gave it as his opinion that all our miseries stemmed from a single cause: our inability to remain quietly in a room.
>
> (Chatwin 1988:180–181)

Pascal, like other philosophers and thinkers of Western culture – Montaigne, Rousseau, Thoreau – looked at the dimension of the withdrawn and solitary life – in his case, to be noted, with a goodly portion of divine Grace – as the basis for the knowledge of oneself, at the same time substantiating the fact that the human tendency was to go in the opposite direction: the flight from oneself in distraction, in worldly entertainment, in going somewhere else, in traveling.

For Pascal, and for Chatwin, who read him centuries later in a world that had decidedly changed, the anxiety of death is the natural and inconsolable unhappiness of the human being, and is held at bay by entertainment, by divertissement. For Pascal, however, entertainment was worse than the ailment because it stopped one from thinking of oneself and therefore led even more to ruin.

Chatwin observed, however:

Could it be, I wondered, that our need for distraction, our mania for the new, was, in essence, an instinctive migratory urge akin to that of birds in autumn?

(Chatwin 1988:181)

From what he believes he has learned in South Africa and Australia, Chatwin reinforces his hypothesis that natural selection has designed us – from the structure of our brain-cells to the structure of our big toe – for a career of seasonal journeys *on foot* through a blistering land of thorn-scrub or desert.

If this were so; if the desert were "home"; if our instincts were forged in the desert; to survive the rigours of the desert – then it is easier to understand why greener pastures pall on us; why possessions exhaust us, and why Pascal's imaginary man found his comfortable lodgings a prison.

(Chatwin 1988:181–182)

Naturally every thinker looks after his own interests, those of his own specific distinctive features – personality, choices of life and idiosyncrasies. It is as if he did not completely tolerate his own individuation and the solitude and isolation involved. Travel literature is no exception, and seems to reaffirm some of the positive values as opposed to others considered limiting. As if one could say, without specifying and without contextualizing, that the journey in itself were good or bad. This also holds true, in inverse form, when extolling sedentariness, contemplative states, the journey in a room, meditation on a single point, the detailed vision that gives a glimpse of the totality. In this case the conclusion would seem to be that moving someplace else is of absolutely no use.

Traveling, like so many other human activities, is subject to the "personal equation" as Jung called it, i.e. the psychological attitude that is more spontaneous, more in tune with some people than with others, and the same holds for sedentariness, contemplation, attachment to a specific place. Everyone will give the best of himself and to himself, bringing his own natural disposition to completion, to flowering, without surrendering completely to the inevitable cultural conditioning.

Lastly, the desire to stay put or to travel is also subject to change in the various phases of life, or as a result of experiences that seem to leave no room for more.

At the moment this is my own position. By acknowledging this, I hope to protect myself from accusations of partiality or of driving a hard bargain. By now I know quite well what it means to go and to stay put.

There really is a time for leaving and one for staying. Both are subject to a broader vision, which is beautifully expressed by the various authors mentioned below, in an imaginary dialogue in a virtual round table that might be titled "in praise of the interior journey." Addressed naturally to those who are currently in the time for staying.

In this sense I will take H.D. Thoreau's words as my own invitation:

> Direct your eye right inward, and you'll find
> A thousand regions in your mind
> Yet undiscovered. Travel them, and be
> Expert in home-cosmography.
> (Thoreau 1957: 559)

There's a mass of literature of varied provenience that sings the praises of the small world around us, the ordinary world at our fingertips, inviting us to discover the almost unnoticeable changes "simply" by paying more attention, increasing our capacities for observation and awareness. In other words, by turning daily life into a journey of discovery while remaining in the same places. This is extremely difficult, but certainly more economical, more ecological, more democratic since it is something anyone can do, and it is not as risky as traveling: especially nowadays.

For some in the past as well, this was the way towards oneself.

To those who address themselves to the going, an answer might come from various ironic authors of the turn of the 18th century for whom traveling was a fashion, the equivalent of the flight from oneself denounced by Pascal and many others before him. One is Laurence Sterne, the first of the writers of the modern "sentimental journey" or of the inner existential digression that keeps company with real traveling. Another is Xavier de Maistre with his more radical *Journey around my Room*, which the author undertook without moving from his room where he was kept prisoner after a duel. He explored every meter, every object in the room, letting his mind wander freely in all directions, associating: traveling, in other words. In his 42 days of wandering from bed to armchair, library and paintings on the walls, including an adventurous fall to the floor, he discovered the value of retreat, encountering his own duplicity – the soul and its shadow, defined as the beast, which was nothing but a literary anticipation of the unconscious – critically digressing on the vices and fashions of the society of his time, which was not after all so different from ours today. When he finally acquires his freedom again, he takes his leave of that "enchanting land of fantasy":

> This day, certain persons on whom I am dependent affect to restore me to liberty. As if they had ever deprived me of it! As if it were in their power to snatch it from me for a single moment, and to hinder me from traversing, at my own good pleasure, the vast space that ever lies open before me! They have forbidden me to go at large in a city, a mere speck, and have left open to me the whole universe, in which immensity and eternity obey me. I am now free, then; or rather, I must enter again into bondage.

The yoke of office is again to weigh me down, and every step I take must conform with the exigencies of politeness and duty. Fortunate shall I be if ... I escape from this new and dangerous captivity ... Was it as a punishment that I was exiled to my chamber, to that delightful country in which abound all the riches and enjoyments of the world? As well might they consign a mouse to a granary.

(de Maistre, 1908:127–128)

Undoubtedly not all inner journeys and exiles that take place in reclusion are as agreeable as this, but de Maistre hoped to call attention to a creating of space and time for the encounter with oneself, for the knowledge of oneself, for giving one's life meaning.

Other participants in this imaginary round table might come from the Orient, stating the same idea in different ways and styles:

Without going outside, you may know the whole world.
Without looking through the window, you may see the ways of heaven.
The farther you go, the less you know.

Thus the sage knows without traveling;
He sees without looking;
He works without doing.

(Lao Tzu)

Or:

Let go and be spontaneous
Try not going and not dwelling
(Seng Ts'a)

The aura that emanates from contemplative poetry, in particular the Japanese haiku, springs from seeing things with the eye of a "foreigner," as something special, as if they had just been discovered, even when they are simple and ordinary. A sense of wonderment of the known.

I still want to see
the face of god
wandering among the flowers of dawn
(Basho)

In my leaving,
in your remaining,
two autumns
(Shiki)

Farmer, China. Photo © Bruno Liotta.

My village:
though small,
the woods are mine
    (Issa; the above excerpts were all translated from the Italian by
    transl.)

Religious literature and poetry would also be represented at this meeting.
They often circle around going, coming, staying still, with as protagonist the
soul wandering in search of its center, of its God, on earth and in every other
place. Here too once again there is the alternative between the staying still of
the contemplative, the mystic, absorbed in his inner journeys, while he finds
himself the guest respectful of the place, and the wayfarer on the move, the
itinerant preacher, led by his God in the renunciation of all earthly bonds.
    The journey, together with others such as silence, ecstasy, light, love and

annihilation in God, is one of the key concepts in the Sufi tradition (Corbin 1973, 1989; Del Re McWeeny 2004; Perez 2001, 2003, 2004).

The Sufi journey takes on a circular mirror form, between the soul and God, separated and striving for an attainable union, along a meandering way from one place and stage to another, sometimes clearly predetermined and guided by the master.

> Your Self is a copy made in the image of God. Seek in yourself all that you desire to know.
>
> (Jalalud-din Rumi, in Happold 1975)

> . . . Pilgrim, Pilgrimage, and Road,
> was but Myself toward Myself; and Your
> Arrival but Myself at my own Door
> (Farid ud-Din Attar (*Bird Parliament*), in Happold 1975)

In Europe Saint John of the Cross would take us to his Mount of Perfection, of which he also drew a map where the peak, destination of the soul, symbolizes the dwelling of God. Only one of the three ways that begin at its base – the way of Nothing, of him who loves Nothing outside of God alone – can take the wayfarer to the peak, not "the way of him who loves the assets of the earth" and not the way of him who "loves the assets of heaven." The way of Nothing loses its boundaries and merges with the Mount.

> There is no road here, for there is no law for the man who loves God: he is law to himself
>
> (*Ascent of Mount Carmel*; John of the Cross 1991)

The way to God is defined by the author as Night, darkness, just as faith in the eyes of the intellect is dark, and God for the soul as long as it is bound to the world.

These last quotes are representative of how much ascension and stairs are part of the universal symbolism of the journey of the soul. Gilbert Durand explains their meaning from the anthropological point of view, on a par with the descent, the fall and the passage to the dark subterranean world.

Luciano Perez enlightens us on the psychological structure of the ecstatic journey of the soul, analyzing it as a theme present throughout the world, from Arctic shamanism to Western culture, in which it is characterized above all by the "spatialization" of the journey:

> Whether it is the descent of the oracle of Trophonius or the ascent to the third heaven of the Apocalypse of Saint Paul or Hildegarde of Bingen's visions, the ecstatic journey is strongly characterized by its verticality.
>
> (Perez 2004)

This verticality, also illustrated by philosophic and literary examples, entails interesting themes such as the separation of the soul from the body, the death and rebirth of the soul, luminosity and obscurity, colors, sounds and forms, which Perez interprets in the Jungian key of the process of the individuation of the Self, comparing the shaman to the analyst, in the role of companion in the journey of their patients. The same interest for the theme of journey is dealt with by Perez in another essay – *Homo viator, pellegrinaggio e devozione* (Perez 2003) – to which I refer the reader for the wealth and profundity of ideas regarding the theme of this book.

Enough, then. One can travel in all ways and with all means, on earth, and with the soul, staying still and moving. The theme of the journey has shown itself to be an exceptional lens through which to interpret the relationship between soul and earth. Because of this alternation between going and coming, leaving and meeting, losing and finding, of the absence and presence that continuously appears in existence, the soul must continuously seek a new virtual point in which to stop and pause, a point that cannot be solely concrete, nor solely earth, nor solely soul.

I have chosen only a few among the many authors I could have cited to help me reappraise the extreme positions regarding the value of traveling, with regard to the psychology of those who live in contemporary society. The extremes may be endowed with a certain romanticism, but they risk leading us into false positions, above all when they are exploited for other reasons and by other powers.

To be able to travel even staying in one place offers us a greater degree of freedom than having to depend on the real dimension of the journey and of the consumer inductions that surround it today. Simply that. This does not mean that one should not travel, or that traveling is not a constructive experience, or that staying in one place resolves all the problems and leads to happiness. The important thing is not to confuse the two levels, interior and exterior.

To take the subject matter treated in this last part back to a purely psychological level and close this chapter, I propose an eloquent cartoon by Altan.

I TRY TO GET AWAY FROM MYSELF,
BUT I'M ALWAYS THERE,
RIGHT ON MY HEELS.

Chapter 7

Exile, nostalgia, return

Exile

We are not always free to choose when or where to travel.

The pride of the nomad, the sober dignity of the wayfarer, the courage of the errant knight are alien to the exile, the emigrant, the vagabond, the homeless person and the vagrant, set apart by their human frailty aggrieved for the loss of their land or their social exclusion.

There is a type of wandering that society sees as failure, a sort of guilt. The emigrant or the outcast has to demonstrate his worth before being integrated or reintegrated into the community. The same thing happens for the foreigner, once welcomed as a "divine" bearer of news (from the Unknown), and today seen as a stranger, an intruder looked upon with reserve. The epithet "of no fixed abode" almost seems an insult.

A person without a country of his own is weak. In our welfare society he is less creditable than those who own any number of abodes, so-called real estate, collectibles. Paradoxically this same society promotes mobility and the enjoyment of mobile assets, consumer goods, as well as the occupation of non-places, and the territory of the planet on which we live is thought of as something virtual and global.

From the point of view of collective psychology, those who can afford it still consider ownership of land a guarantee of future survival. The more they have, the better they feel.

The same feelings come to the fore with regard to what we can call the land of birth – of which I wrote in the chapter dedicated to the place of origin – also known in some circumstances as "homeland." In Italian the expression *madre patria* covers aspects of both fatherland and motherland.

"Homeland" and "patriotism," together with "roots" and "race," are words whose meanings vary from place to place.

Aside from the fate and fashions of words, what I want to underscore, in the wide range of literature on exile, is the relationship between exile and the homeland, united by a feeling of nostalgia.

Exile is a particular form of migration and can be transformed into a sort

Colombian refugees, Bari, Italy. Photo © Daniele Vita, 2006.

of wandering, a perpetual journey, but can also mean the acquisition of a new citizenship and geographical belonging.

Driven from one's land

By "exile" I mean first of all the real condition, decreed by others, of expulsion from one's land, an unwanted separation accompanied by inner suffering. The exile, the political refugee, those who flee persecution or an invasion, other groups of refugees or entire peoples who are deported, the victims of chronic and lengthy wars or unbearable economic or natural conditions: all confront an exceptional event that leaves a permanent mark on their lives, even when they subsequently return to their homeland or constitute a new homeland.

The dimensions of the land shape the story of the exile, first as homeland and place of daily life, then as a new land to discover and in which to put down roots – although the memory of the places left behind and nostalgia for them remain – and lastly as the land of origins to which to return.

In their *Psychoanalytic Perspectives on Migration and Exile* the Grinbergs (1989) analyzed the psychological components of the different phases of exile, beginning with "leave-taking," a farewell characterized by hopes of return tinged with uncertainty. In dramatic conditions the absence of leave-taking creates a feeling of restlessness in the exile that has to be appeased by subsequent contacts in an effort to maintain the tie, even at a distance, with those who remained and with the place left behind. If, of course, all this is possible.

Many exiles, today as in the past, feel as if those left behind and they themselves had died, a result of a separation that is often sudden and traumatic and that cannot be resolved as it would be if the death were real. This interior scenario of perennial mourning is due more to the impossibility of return than to the imposition of departure.

The Grinbergs observe that many exiles also suffer the "syndrome of survival," feeling they have saved themselves, leaving their less fortunate relatives and friends to their fate, or they have a deep sense of guilt for the same reasons. Depression, desperation, disillusion frequently accompany these experiences.

As the exile gradually becomes integrated into the country where he came to rest, the break with the "sacredness of exile" can be felt as the loss of a preceding identity, as betrayal of one's cause, a feeling that one is out of place and unable in this new situation to reproduce the fundamental nucleus of one's life.

The traumatic displacement of context, in space, aggravates the temporal experience and distorts it. The future becomes synonymous with the illusion of returning home, and life before exile is turned into a myth. The present oscillates between hope and disillusion, between positive feelings for the welcome received and refusal of all that the new country can offer, rather like abandoned children who pour their anger and suffering for the lack of affection on their new adoptive parents, only because finally there is someone who will listen to them.

The state of regression and dependency that characterizes the exile at the beginning can also manifest itself in an overwhelming and urgent necessity to obtain what he needs: an oral avidity, according to the Grinbergs, with which he seeks to placate the anxiety that limits his capacity to give and interact with the new society as well as with any members of the family who are with him in exile. Life as a couple and as a family, in general, suffers from these shocks, added to the lack of stability and the continuous feeling of being transitory as its members wait to return home.

Lastly, the need to accept work that is sometimes far below the capacities, professional qualifications and roles the exile had at home leads to frustration, insecurity and depersonalization that make it difficult to constitute an identity other than that of exile.

The more gifted, stronger and better adjusted persons manage to deal with these negative and painful feelings, to wait for the changes, to continue in some way with their professions, to turn the painful experience into an enrichment of themselves, and in some cases also of the culture of their homeland or of the country that has taken them in. Artists, scientists, doctors, actors and other categories have frequently succeeded in transforming the suffering of exile into a new resource. But, as with migration, this is a privileged condition in which chance and fortune also play a part.

Frankfurt, Germany. Photo © Francesco Galli, 2002.

In a life of exile lived with dignity, even with the constant desire to return, the ever-present impossibility of return becomes a condemnation, a tragic destiny, an early death. The fantasy of return clashes with the anxiety of dying in a foreign land and not being able to join one's ancestors even after death. Not being received by one's own mother earth becomes the ultimate drama.

The moods of the exile can degenerate into real psychopathologies that require psychiatric help, even if, originally, they are the same moods present in less dramatic and definitive occasions of separation and displacement. In the following chapter I will deal in more depth with the psychotherapy of foreign patients.

The 20th century, as previously noted, was a time of great migratory upheaval that shows no signs of abating in the 21st. Exile has played a greater part than in the past in all these movements, both because geopolitics has become more complex and because international relations and alliances change rapidly, turning those who had occupied their own lands without fear of being turned out into new exiles.

In the testimonials of exile, the sense of place and its perceptible character-istics is very vivid, both in the memories and in the fantasies of return. Contrary to what one might think, neither communication technology nor the culture of the cosmopolitan man, citizen of the world, is enough to allay the physical need for a land that is one's own. We have seen handfuls of earth from one's homeland kept for years, significant objects brought away at the last moment becoming sacred, the desire for the food, the odors, the colors of one's own land, the emotions called forth by familiar sounds and music, the periodic impelling need to speak one's own language, perhaps even one's own dialect, fluently.

This is why the feeling of nostalgia becomes the pivotal point for my discussion of exile and the possibility of return.

Exile of exclusion

As this discussion becomes more psychological, the concept of exile, compulsory and suffered, will be broadened to include situations that differ from the official one of political exile.

Anyone who suffers from nostalgia seems to me to be absorbed, captured in a form of self-induced but undesired exile. An example is the analogy between exile and imprisonment, as also sensed by the Grinbergs:

> Some exiles have said that the vast world into which they escape is no more than a prison because they are deprived of the ability to be in the one place they wish to be: their own country. Others who are imprisoned for years at home feel that they, too, are in exile because they are condemned to remain disconnected from their country.
>
> (Grinberg and Grinberg 1989:160)

The relationship between prison and exile appears in all forms of punishment that make use of expulsion and exclusion. Anyone who disagrees on ideology becomes a political exile: the powers could eliminate him, but have decided only to banish him spatially.

In the past children were disciplined by sending them to their room, without supper, or standing them up alone behind the blackboard or in a corner.

Not being part of the social context of belonging, being segregated, produces such distress that it can be used as an instrument of blackmail in general and, in the case of children, as a way of teaching them discipline: you didn't behave according to the rules, so your society will marginalize you until you fall into line (Liotta 2003).

In adult life these strategies of conditioning continue to function in increasingly refined ways. The distinct separation of social classes in the bourgeois society found expression in a formal exclusion from various privileged places: rituals, proper dress, membership cards, qualifications, culture, formal aspects that clearly presented an environment where some were in and some were out. Exiles are those who have lost their rights of entry, of participation and of belonging.

In its full sense this would include other types of exile, being fired from a job because of excess personnel, incompatibility, or mobbing – an initially unnoticed exile that is kept up until the person has no choice but to leave,

Shopping Center. Photo © Bruno Liotta.

with feelings very like those of the exile. Or bullying, as happens in school and peer groups.

In these examples there is a manipulation of human feelings, an explicit forced interpretation or a subtle induction that insists on obedience to the power that governs the particular situation. Generally, it is not the physical life that is threatened, but the life of the soul.

Exclusion and dismissal decided by society – in line with the possible etymology of exile as dismissal from the land – are focused more on the space, the earth, the place, than on an affective subtraction. It is not so much "I won't talk to you because you've behaved badly" as "you can't stay here because you didn't obey the unspoken rules" or simply "we don't like you."

I believe that maintaining this spatial significance, together with that of the forced nature of the event, lets us maintain the unique meaning of the word "exile."

Exile in myth, symbol and spirituality

The theme of exile also appears in the phenomenology of the religious, spiritual, mythic – fantastic in general – experience, and as a temporary episode in many fairy tales, stories, legends and accounts.

The place of exile, in this case, is not only a country, but any place in which the protagonist of the story is imprisoned or held against his or her will, via a

Theseus and the Labyrinth (detail).

potion, seduction, a trial, distraction, amnesia willed by others. In the organization of the story, this capture and reclusion can become a crucial moment of passage of an initiatory nature, of interior elaboration, of meeting with oneself, a sort of "dark night of the soul" followed by liberation and the encounter with a new world. I won't spend more time on this aspect because it is superimposed on that of the journey, in particular the fantastic and imaginary journey.

A classic example, to which an important essay of a psychological nature has been dedicated, is the myth or fable of *Eros (Cupid) and Psyche*, in the version of Apuleius. Erich Neumann has interpreted it in the light of female psychology and in a key of analytical psychology. Psyche, so beautiful the gods envied her, was forced into a wandering exile after disobeying the order never to look at the face of her husband Eros. Punishment for disobedience was the loss of her beloved, separation from him and the paradise in which the couple lived, the entry into a destiny that Neumann interprets as "individuation." Seeing the face of her beloved, the heroine of the myth knows him and she places herself, separate, before him. This forces her to come out of the unconscious obscurity of the relationship and become aware of herself, with final reunion on a new level of love and full awareness. The psychological development hinted at in the myth involves facing up to various trials and tribulations, fearful and alone, despairing and distressed to the point of suicide. Although there is a happy ending, the central part of the story consists of the long and agonizing exile.

The same thing happens in the myth of Demeter and Persephone and in that of Orpheus and Eurydice. The circumstances and solutions are different, but the plot is the same, that of an immediate and painful separation and wandering through the world in search of what seems to be lost, to find something that one actually did not have to begin with.

And of course there is the myth of Eden, from which, punished for their disobedience, Adam and Eve were expelled, forced to wander through the world and suffer the trials of terrestrial existence.

These considerations lead me to another aspect of my discourse.

A more internal exclusion is that of the exile of the soul: the feeling of being marginalized, even though this is not the case, of lacking a relationship with others and with the world. This psychological state is sporadically found accompanied by various pathologies, but is always present in depression. Many patients describe it in these very terms as a feeling of remoteness, of detachment, of loss akin to mourning for something that was and that now seems inexorably gone, with no hope of return.

In addition to various mystical currents, some doctrines compare the universal condition of the human soul on earth to exile, defined as a state of perennial suffering for the remoteness of the divine homeland.

In Christianity and the other great religions there is an ultra-terrestrial life that precedes and follows the terrestrial, depicting, more or less explicitly, the temporaneity and end of the latter. Exile means something only if counter-posed to a condition of original belonging. This vision is, moreover, coherent with a dualist spirit that conceives of life as a journey between Evil and Good. After death the soul, tending more and more towards the Good, will conquer the Kingdom of Heaven, that Paradise from which it had been thrust with the exile of birth.

The predominant idea in the Gnostic doctrine, springing from the heart of early Christianity, is that the soul is something extraneous to the world and to one's body; a soul in flight, reaching out in an attempt to return to God. The terms "other," "extraneous," "foreign," "strange" are key words in the Gnostic texts guiding the spiritual process. It is surprising and strange to have come into the world; existence is presented in the beginning with a sense of discomfort or inadaptability, the *kosmos* itself is defined as *anoikeion*, non-familiar – psychoanalysts might remember Freud's definition of *unheimlich*. Gnosis defines itself as *xene*, a foreigner, and God is also a foreigner. "Extra-neous" and "foreigner" are connected in a continuity that starts from the negative meaning, passes through relativization, and finally becomes positive:

> Extraneousness is no longer relative to a situation, does not presuppose a relationship with something else, but defines a nature of and by itself independent from and superior to the world, an essential "self" known to come from the Beyond . . . insofar as its "homeland" and its true "place," the origin of its being . . . are beyond the kosmos . . .
> Thus, gradually, "foreigner" or "stranger" becomes a sort of synonym of "transcendent", more precisely of "transcosmic", of "hypercosmic" . . . just as "election" is "foreign to the world" and by nature "hypercosmic,"
> (Puech 1985:235; translated from the Italian by transl.)

Suffering–exile are frequently coupled in Gnostic literature, which is also marked by the explicit use of the term "exile." The Gnostic suffers and lam-ents his condition, expresses nostalgia for the distant homeland, of which the memory must always be maintained, with a constant awareness that he is extraneous to this exile, to this "sojourn in a foreign land," a world to be kept at a certain distance and of which he must not become a part, at the cost of losing all possibility of salvation.

> Come from the Light and the gods
> Here I am in exile and separated from them.
> My enemies, swooping down on me
> Led me among the dead.
> May he who frees my soul from anguish
> Be blessed and find liberation!
> (Fragment by an unknown author, from Puech 1985:275;
> translated from the Italian by transl.)

These are not merely obscure doctrines of antiquity, for in the course of centuries a certain continuity of this current of thought has been maintained. Christianity, Gnosticism and Neo-Platonism came together in Plotinus, unique in his synthesis and the way in which he reflected the turbulent milieu of his time. Via other authors Plotinus was to influence the Latin Middle Ages, leavening for the Renaissance and a current of inspiration, through new concepts and languages, for the more recent theological and philosophical culture. Spinoza, Leibniz, Schelling, Novalis, Hegel, and Bergson, to name just a few, reveal traces of "plotinism" in their systems of thought. The same can be said in more recent times of psychoanalytical thought, and Jung was no stranger to all of this.

In gnosis, the soul is constantly attempting to escape from an earth that is seen only as prison.

From the psychological point of view it is difficult to say whether true exile is the one on earth or the one towards the "hyper-cosmos." If then, on a psychological level, this pessimistic vision originated in the disquieting but unequivocal fact of human mortality, we must further question ourselves as to what the cultural paradigms that inspire "transcendences" of this type were, and still are.

Speaking of the forms of suffering in Western society, Salvatore Natoli in *L'esperienza del dolore* affirms:

> From the Greeks we learned loyalty to the "earth," from the Hebrew-Christian tradition the seduction of the "Kingdom." Loyalty to the earth means loving this earth for what it is, with all its suffering, in the conviction that life and suffering are inseparable, that nothing can be truly lived outside of the possibilities the present offers every man. This is why keeping oneself liege to the earth means adhering to the here and now of the world, attempting to draw the basis of one's possibilities from the situation we are in.

> Becoming infatuated with the unknown, projecting oneself into an indeterminate future, obscuring the cruelty of the present but also skipping over its occasions, is an empty dream, insipid and mad. Pindar's poem calls our attention to and reminds us of the tragic realism of the Greeks:

> There is
> a species among the hollow men
> that despises what it has, searches far
> in the footsteps of fantasy
> with inane hopes.
>
> > (translated from the Italian by transl.)

Rembrandt, *The Return of the Prodigal Son*, c. 1669.

The "Kingdom," Natoli continues, is not different from the "earth" but is the earth itself freed from suffering, death, and evil. The Kingdom is not necessarily a hereafter, but a world to come, a world in the future. And he cites Isaiah:

> For, behold, I create new heavens and a new earth: and the former shall not be remembered, nor come into mind.
> But be ye glad and rejoice forever in that which I create . . .

> And I will rejoice in Jerusalem, and joy in my people: and the voice of weeping shall be no more heard in her, nor the voice of crying.
>
> (Isaiah 65:17–19)

In this vision, salvation – Jerusalem – is promised, will be realized in the future, and is to be awaited and hoped for. The present becomes memory or expectation, the painful present is a passage, the earth is desolate: a "vale of tears."

Further on, Natoli draws his conclusions:

> The Hebrew-Christian tradition is certainly not nihilist, but generated a historical psychology receptive to nihilism, for it placed the significance of the present elsewhere.
>
> (Natoli 1986:251–274; translation from the Italian by transl.)

In Islam too, gnosis – the form of knowledge of the divine – goes beyond faith, uses spatial rather than temporal metaphors, and in particular uses the idea of a movement from the origin to return to the origin, in a vertical dimension.

In his *Storia della filosofia islamica*, Corbin, lumping together Jews, Christians and Muslims – the Peoples of the Book – stresses their hermeneutical vision of life: a journey in which the "true" meaning is revealed to the believer, which makes existence "real" compared with what is only appearance. Exile on earth and the return to God, even if not expressed in the historical incarnation of Christianity, are what underlie the circumspection shown by Islamic philosophy when faced with the dangers of secularization.

The same can be said for Early Buddhism when it proposed anew the same vision of an apparent existence, the wheel of rebirth – the *samsara* – a perpetual wandering from one life to another caused by painful enchainment to the law of *karma*, through the experiences of its founder, who discovered the reality of suffering, illness and death during his gilded, untroubled life. Unlike the Peoples of the Book, who have God at the beginning and at the end of their terrestrial exile, Buddhism remains within human limits: one can draw from the most true and deep reality along the way of non-attachment, which is also a path of liberation from suffering. The existence of God is one of the questions without an answer.

It cannot be denied that the journey of life – from the mother's womb to the earth which receives the body after death – can in some cases and for some periods take the form of exile and sufferings.

That all existence is compared to exile is, however, a feature of the great religions, with the exception of a few currents, and in contrast to native and primitive religions whose relationship with the earth is not as painful.

In modern and contemporary society, scientific progress, the dramatic increase in secularization, and a growing atheism have led to an increasingly critical relationship with religion. This is not true for spirituality in the broader sense, which has turned from the West to the East, and towards the rest of the world, in search of new languages and new forms with which to

express itself. At the same time and conversely, Buddhism and other Eastern religions, spurred on by political changes in the Orient, display that "going West" that had been prophesied of old.
Migrations of the collective soul towards new lands.

A new paradigm of the relationship between human beings and the earthly life might possibly consist of not seeking to flee the earth, but sanctifying it from inside, protecting and taking care of it without separating good and evil in the sense of up and down, conjugating immanence and transcendence.

Setting the figure of the exile in this broader vision seems to me a way of acknowledging his significance for western culture. At the same time it is a way of opening up a less gloomy prospect, showing that there are more ways than one of imagining the earthly journey and that the earth has a significance of its own.

Keeping one's feet on the ground also means sticking to the present: to a present that contains both suffering and joy.

If the exile, even though suffering for his loss, can manage to become aware of the new land in which he now lives and of its psychological potential, he may find a way out of his desolation and a possibility for inner growth.

The difference between political exile and the exile of the soul, trapped in earthly life, is great, but the profound psychological experiences of a soul that cannot find peace and asks to return to who knows where have united much of humanity over the centuries. Some can identify the external events that caused their suffering and seek to remedy their loss. If it is the land that has been lost, they will try to reconquer it. However, the same feeling can pursue and torment those who have never been subjected to exile decreed by others, those who have never lost their own land.

One of the main features of exile, whatever the circumstances and concurrent causes, is nostalgia defined as a characteristic feeling of that condition.

Nostalgia: feeling, sensation and intuition

> Oh longing for places that were not
> Cherished enough in that fleeting hour
> How I long to make good from far
> The forgotten gesture, the additional act.
> (Rainer Maria Rilke, *Vergers*, XLI)

Nostalgia is commonly considered a sentiment associated with displacement, whether in space or time. Let me begin with spatial displacement. Not being elsewhere, or being elsewhere, always calls up nostalgia. If we like, it is a latent mental and affective condition ready to appear at the slightest provocation.

The pluri-dimensionality of the feeling, and the fact that it has already been dealt with by various authors, psychoanalysts and not (Campolieti 1987, Carotenuto 1988, Daniels 1985, Frigessi Castelnuovo and Risso 1982,

Harper 1966, Lorenzi 2000, Prete 1992, Vecchio 1989), has induced me to look at all these dimensions in the hope of providing a more general view of nostalgia and not limiting it to the more commonly accepted "yearning for the past" or the psychoanalytical infant's suffering at being separated from its mother.

There is the nostalgia of the *nostos*, literally "the return," the return home to that "nest" with which it is etymologically related. Then there is nostalgia for whatever is absent, missing, a suspended mellow nuance that overrides reality, informing life both in time and space and defined by some as "false nostalgia."

In both, the components earth and soul are present in equal measure.

Nostalgia often appears during psychotherapist treatments, but is not limited to foreign patients. It can follow a real event, a dream, or an encounter that harks back to the past.

But is it really only a feeling? My guess is that it is something more, for in nostalgia, the cognitive, primarily intuitive, aspect precedes and is sometimes more determining than the emotional aspect. It is therefore a complex mood consisting of a mixture of various psychic elements that are hard to distinguish.

For example, let us imagine a sequence: recollections, which arrive autonomously and perhaps suddenly, reactivate the sensorial faculties, colors, flavors, places, concrete landscapes, people, and then also the feelings of previous experiences. Memory, in all the complexity of its psychobiological

Refugee camp in Saharawi, Algeria. Photo © Daniele Vita, 2002.

mechanisms, is unquestionably a dominant part of nostalgia. Therefore we already have: memory, sensorial faculties, intuition, feelings, enveloped in a cultural and social evaluation. There is something suspect about nostalgia, something associated with artists and vulnerable, dreamy, otherworldly personalities.

I don't know why, but I always end up with some "false alternative." There are those who maintain that one must always live in the here and now and not give in to the seduction of nostalgia, and then there are those who set great store on memory and the preservation of things dear, of important events, of common meanings, to transmit from one generation to the next. Both have convincing points in their favor. I believe that in this case too the various propensities evince culturally conditioned aspects and personality traits that can be regulated in the course of life by reflecting on one's own experiences.

Obviously the extreme in a pathological sense of either of these positions is something else. The nostalgic person can be a tragicomic figure, but those who conversely ignore their personal and collective story, attached to a massified anonymous reality, are no better off.

In some individuals attachment to the past, in particular to things rather than places and persons, can become an obsession or can border on fetishism. This does not, however, mean that the collector, the antiquarian, and the archeologist all have warped personalities. To feel nostalgia for a period of one's own life – or for periods of the past that have not been directly experienced but that belong in some way to the story of one's own family – is not pathologic. Thinking of what a place must have been like in the past and regretting the way it has now been disfigured is also a way of being aware of the damage that has been done, and is not simply an unseemly diehard type of nostalgia.

Nostalgia that focuses on the past can also become perpetual mourning for an idealized nucleus, which cannot delude because it is distant. This time we might say, yes, it is nostalgia for the realm of the Mother, a utopian place, a pre-verbal paradise, landscape of senses and emotions, that absorbs the soul and makes it impossible to live on the earth of the present.

But there are also other types of nostalgia.

There is the nostalgia for an inaccessible present. Nostalgia of what it should and could be, the languor of the unrealizable, like that of an impossible love.

And there is nostalgia for the future, that unconscious memory that jumbles up parallel universes, with a presentiment of the moment in which, perhaps, an undefined tension, not always connected to precise goals and objectives, will be resolved. A sense of waiting for the circle to close upon itself.

Nostalgia thus becomes a figure of time, thanks to the hint of return, but there is more. Ibsen's "woman of the sea" waits, day after day, for years, for the sailor with whom she is in love to arrive, but at the same time, day after day, for years, she scans the infinite space, beyond the great water, that different land that receives and contains a piece of her soul. Inner changes take place, in her long contemplation, in this space of waiting.

The paradox of "a-temporality of the unconscious," which the conscious mind futilely strains to capture, emerges from nostalgia. Everything has already happened and has not yet happened, everything has already died and still has to be born. Nostalgia concerns not only real past experiences but also an inner state of fullness, achieved only briefly but always pursued. Another paradox: archetypal images are collective memories, while their sudden and unexpected irruption makes them appear to the individual as new presences, creatures from the future and bearers of renewal.

In the course of psychoanalysis nostalgia can appear in the form of a sensibility that heralds the crucial moments that often precede profound changes.

To describe the complexity of this relationship between soul and earth, I will give the testimony of a patient I will call Sofia.

A woman of our times, Sofia struggled through a difficult life and an equally fatiguing analysis. She had everything but actually she felt as if she had nothing. At a certain point, after a few years of analysis, Sofia was struck by the "disease of nostalgia," but a strange nostalgia, without a precise object from her past, detached from the recollection and memory of her personal consciousness. She herself was perplexed in the face of a general mood that appeared once her attacks of panic had ceased: when, that is, she had stopped defending herself and worrying about her survival, and the possibility of finding a path of her own, of increasingly authentic choices, began to emerge.

I will add beforehand that I believe that this type of nostalgia is set in the collective unconscious and serves in the realization of the Self, an "individuative nostalgia." A nostalgia of individuation.

It had all begun with the sensorial and affective response to a "place." It was a landscape whose characteristics, the combinations of essential features, the sensorial stimuli and the inhabitants, recreated for Sofia a familiarity unknown to her in her real-life experience. It was of course a place she had never been to before nor was it connected to family traditions.

Sofia was to discover, only later, that centuries ago a maternal branch of her family lived not far from "her place" and that the paternal branch could be connected to it via migrations that had taken place probably a couple of thousand years earlier! Recollections too faint and impersonal to have an *a priori* psychological meaning. But, to keep with what we know, Sofia found no way to explain how natural it was for her to move in a land that was not that of her personal origins, particularly when faced with the feeling of non-belonging experienced up to then. And even stranger, in that place the symptoms of fluctuating anxiety that had always followed her, taking the form of aggressive fantasies and moments of panic due to the threat of an unexpected and uncontrollable event, had miraculously stopped. There it all disappeared. She had always liked to take long walks, but never by herself. Now, in these places, she went around alone; unknown rustlings and sounds no longer made her jump; she went to explore impervious zones; accompanied by a faith receptive to the unknown, she no longer feared invisible presences around herself. Amazed by such confidence, she said:

> It is as if I had already been here, perhaps in another life (and she laughed because she did not believe in these things), but it is not the classical *dejà vu*, it is as if I had never been aware that I had a tremendous "nostalgia" for all this and now the nostalgia has calmed down because I have found it anew. And what I have found is within me, not only in this place even if the place is important. But how can I say I have found it again if I haven't ever been there? And for what did I feel nostalgia?

This excerpt from a session of many years ago made me begin to wonder about this aspect of nostalgia and to see it in concomitance with important inner transformations, fundamental changes in existence, not only with my patients but also in other real contexts and in literature, drama, biographies.

All kinds of places can be emotionally charged. With all of them a sense of belonging fraught with Eros can be set in motion, turning them into places that are felt near by and familiar. What seems to be expressed here is a desire for belonging, of knowing where one is, finding one's boundaries, giving oneself a Land.

My studies then moved towards an exploration of the bonds with the psychological components revealed by nostalgia.

With reference to the clinical example, a "sensorial nostalgia" and an "intuitive nostalgia," both of a more cognitive than emotional nature, can be identified. There was no suffering here; there was the *nostos* but not the *algia*.

Once more it was Jung who furnished me with a few keys. In *Psychological Types*, in the part "Definitions," he defines more precisely the functions of sensation and intuition.

The "sensation": the place enters the mind through sensations. The sensations receive stimuli from both the external and the internal worlds, that is, from our own body (*coenaesthesis*, pain, well-being, various stimuli).

Sensation is one of the fundamental elementary psychic functions, a salient characteristic of the child and of the primitive, a given fact not subject to the laws of reason, even if subsequently its contents are rationalized. A distinction has to be made between "concrete sensation," dependent on the reaction of the classical sensorial organs with the environment, and "abstract sensation," a form of perception that in this sense can be called esthetic sensation, that is endowed with principles of its own. For example:

> The concrete sensation of a flower, on the other hand, conveys a perception not only of the flower as such, but also of the stem, leaves, habitat,

and so on. It is also instantly mingled with feelings of pleasure or dislike which the sight of the flower evokes, or with simultaneous olfactory perceptions, or with thoughts about its botanical classification, etc. But abstract sensation immediately picks out the most salient sensuous attribute of the flower, its brilliant redness, for instance and makes this the sole or at least the principal content of consciousness, entirely detached from all other admixtures. Abstract sensation is found chiefly among artists.

(Jung 1921/1971:462)

But immediately afterwards Jung states that the abstract, esthetic, artistic sensation is not as primary as the concrete sensation, but is already differentiated and in some way addressed to an "esthetic attitude."

Therefore at one extreme we have the relationship with concrete and external reality "through the senses" – the "sensation" – and at the other we have the relationship with the inner psychic reality, which can be attained only by means of a different function, "intuition." In order to capture that which is uncertain, or invisible, we need a suitable function that goes beyond sensation. It is not by chance that intuition is often defined as an "extrasensorial capacity" or as a "sixth sense."

Jung says:

I regard intuition as a basic psychological function (q.v.). It is the function that mediates perceptions in an *unconscious way*. Everything, whether outer or inner objects of their relationships, can be the focus of this perception. The peculiarity of intuition is that it is neither sense perception, nor feeling, nor intellectual inference, although it may also appear in these forms. In intuition a content presents itself whole and complete, without our being able to explain or discover how this content came into existence. Intuition is a kind of instinctive apprehension, no matter of what contents. Like sensation (q.v.), it is an irrational (q.v.) function of perception . . . Like sensation, intuition is a characteristic of infantile and primitive psychology.

(Jung 1921/1971:453–454 emphasis in original)

Jung sets sensation and intuition at the diametrically opposed extremes of the functional axis that intersects with the feeling–thinking axis, configuring a complete diagram of the psychological functions in his theory of the personality. I will not linger over the functions of thinking and feeling because they are more recognizable and clearly spelled out in our culture and our educational systems, while much less attention has been paid to the sensation/ intuition axis, which in some cases has even become atrophied.

Intuition, moreover, must be used with caution. Its etymology helps us identify the traps: *in-tueri* (Latin) "looking within" and, with a dual significance, "image reflected in the mirror" and "contemplation." Intuition is knowing the intimate essence of things without turning to reasoning or proof, known also as the eye of the intellect, in the sense of "interior intelligence," "spiritual seeing." It is also a capacity or habitual disposition to readily perceive reality.

The presence on the same axis of sensation and intuition tells us of their interdependence and how they balance each other. The presence of sensation places healthy limits on intuition, which by its nature has the tendency to overdo. For example, today a series of widespread phenomena that depend on anomalies of the sensation/intuition axis are induced by a culture that exalts speed and the overcoming of material limits thanks to technological development. Since intuition is characterized by speed and immediacy – this is also its strong point – it can concurrently become an obstacle for many achievements on a material level: daily actions in the sphere of work or maintenance, i.e. the normal life of the body and in daily space/time, but also of recreational or creative activities that in any case require adaptation to the inertia of matter, the weight of the earth.

Back to exile, return and nostalgia. Intuition is free to play around as it likes in the ebb and flow of thoughts, images and feelings in the period of waiting and separation. It becomes either the key to coming out into reality or the trap that keeps it in one's imagination. Foreseeing and working actively for the return is something else.

Intuition, the inner eye, also has its dysfunctions. We clearly see them when the psyche falls ill, in a maniacal delirium or in syndromes of a hypomaniacal or hysteric nature. Restlessness, inner anxiety, ideational acceleration, the impelling need to get rid of the uncontainable perceptions crowding an inner world by turning them into actions/symptoms, the inadequacy of healthy defenses, all seem to indicate a congestion that in order to sort itself out needs a "ground line," a "return" to the reality one sought to break away from through the "great ideas" and "brilliant intuitions," none of which will ever be realized.

On a collective level the deviation of the intuition/sensation axis has become dangerous for the individual and for humanity. The potentialities, the tendencies of others or of oneself can be intuited; the developments of situations can be glimpsed; but only their development in time and space, through the relation with what is opposed to intuition, can confirm or refute the vision of the mind. The development of self-awareness and the process of individuation therefore need sensation and intuition to be integrated in the same measure.

And nostalgia? Today it seems to be spreading as a general sentiment in all the directions that I have more or less touched on though not necessarily dealt with: nostalgia for the past, for old things, for once upon a time, but also for recent times; nostalgia for the future, that of a return to some "normality," once more a journey downwards and backwards, nostalgia for elsewhere, where there is less apprehension and more peace and serenity.

To get back to what I was saying: the word "nostalgia" originally meant "homesickness" and a return that was initially towards the homeland, eventually moving on to other symbolic and internal lands. I have attempted to analyze the "suffering" of nostalgia, surely a feeling, or better an awareness, of the fact that something is lacking. But this does not always imply a loss. It can be a yearning for something one needs and desires, still far away in space and time: nostalgia for things not experienced, or not yet had, but intuited. Nostalgia for things unappreciated and lost. Nostalgia for something that can still be done on a psychological level to "fulfill," to conclude an experience. Together with the feeling of loss in these cases, I also see the participation of intuitive and sensorial aspects, one on the part of the soul, the other of the earth, which is what I am trying to deal with.

> *Nostalgia*
> The mind divorced from the heart,
> living in a placenoplace,
> missing others,
> sleeping waking looking for
> safe walls,
> sounds out of place in the morning
> eternal regret for not
> living
> in any possible place.
> a life not yours,
> I want to get off the merry-go-round
> and change my hobbyhorse.
> a summer cry
> Arab lullaby sad and deep:
> "ceusa friscaaa"![1]
> that light is not yours,
> it is not yours
> it is not light.
> it does not glitter
> it does not burn
> it is not blinding
> carrying off your heart
> to distant Olympuses
>
> I lived among the gods
> in a place aggrieved

---

1   Fresh mulberry.

cascading jasmine
balconies and terraces
overflowing with chattering swallows
sharp tails
calling attention to a sky
bluer than cobalt
I miss you red land
of martyrs' oaks
I miss you
full moon
fragrant
under bowls of oranges
thirst slaked by strong arms
and coarse phrases

I miss
at my feet
amalgamated mud
wet soil
games
played by
full-blooded brothers
loaves of earth
to bake quickly
in fires of straw

bell-like laughter under pizzuta grapes
Villagecreche
crechevillage
set up with care
with tinfoil stars
small holes burst open
of honey and mulled wine
shaped by unskilled hands
into sweet "coddure"[2]
and scoldings to lively children
and an old woman
taking care of and nurturing
among flavors of blackened olives

---

2   Sicilian ring-shaped cookies with pinched holes from which the filling of mulled wine and
honey exudes.

crowded memories
hold your peace hold your peace
the mind refuses
a life divided torn apart
by a dull pain
of a return denied
>   (Marcella Fragapane; translated from the
>   Italian by transl.)

The return

With the attainment of maturity and at the zenith of biological existence, life's drive towards a goal in no wise halts. With the same intensity and irresistibility with which it strove upward before middle age, life now descends; for the goal no longer lies on the summit, but in the valley where the ascent began. The curve of life is like the parabola of a project-ile which, disturbed from its initial state of rest, rises and returns to a state of repose.

>   (Jung 1934a:406)

Nostalgia, like an arrow, indicates the direction and the place of return. For the exile, the return represents a fundamental aspect of his individuative process.

A vivid inner image of the place left behind remains with a person involved in a forced or chosen exile, a long or a short journey, or estrangement for various reasons. Whether it is the native place or some other place of residence, when he moves off, the place that gradually disappears from the traveler's sight is reproposed, projected towards the future, as the goal of the journey of return: especially if it contains home and family, his belongings.

We can begin by saying then that the return is "homewards" and then define the home, in the spirit of this book, as both a real and a symbolic element of human life. Home is the house that has a body – the earth on which it rests, its walls – and also an interior, a soul of its own, intimately personal.

I have already spoken of return, in a more or less explicit manner, in dealing with the journey, exile and nostalgia. But there are a few things I have not yet said and which I will deal with in this last part of the chapter.

Return – re-turn – is *turning* fortified. *Turning* from Old French *tourn*, tour lathe, circuit, partly from Middle English *turnen* to turn, the action of turning about a center or axis, rotation. What we have is the repetition of a move-ment, its circularity, and a point of arrival, point of reference. The most common meaning of the term remains the "return to the place of provenience (where it came from)," and then, figuratively, "the reacquiring of a lost quality, picking up an interrupted action" and also, finally the result of a transformation, of the "correctness, correspondence, restitution" of something (in Italian *mi torna* means to make sense). There are thus any number of possible interpretations of the return, to which less attention is generally paid than to the other subjects dealt with in precedence.

When one returns, it always seems that the journey is shorter, that the task is coming to an end, that the place is there waiting to receive the weary body and restore the soul. Finally home. But it is also true that the return, the initial enthusiasm for the novelty of the journey – whatever it is – has been consumed and one is back in the everyday world, which may be disappointing with respect to what one expected. That the return, in the sense of turning back, simply alludes to a "decreasing" cyclic nature, inverse: well illustrated by the voyage of the sun which, after the splendor of midday, gradually sinks until, to our terrestrial eyes, it disappears in darkness.

The return holds within it a time for reflection, autumn, and forebodings of death.

Jung maintained, with regard to the second half of life, that in this phase "those who learn to die remain alive." What happens, in this phase, is the inversion of the parabola, the "birth of death."

In Jung's vision it is a fundamental phase in the individuation process. In fact, I would add, enough distance has been covered, there have been occasions for experience and knowledge and there is still enough road left to cover, to invest, to distill a sense to the life that remains.

It is not possible, according to Jung, to live the evening of life the same way one lived the morning, since the truth of the morning can represent the error

Funeral monument of a livestock owner, Rift Valley, Kenya. Photo © Alberto Tessore.

of the evening. The afternoon of life should have its purpose and meaning and not be simply a degraded appendix to the morning. In other words, old age is not to be thought of in terms only of loss. Those who fail to see these psychological possibilities continue looking for new stimuli, purposes, future prospects – in the externally expanded, active, productive sense, as in the first part of life – and find it very difficult to accept both the revision of their past and the limits that the idea of death places on their life. Therefore, the idea of a life that continues after death, aside from the religious contexts in which it appears, is a universal psychic need of the collective unconscious. Life, observes Jung returning to the metaphor of journey, is as teleological as one can get, with a hard and fast orientation to a goal, up to the state of rest represented by death.

As in the metaphor of the seed that after resting in the earth germinates again, life after death is re-born, re-turns to life, takes us to the ancient mystery rites and to a whole world of symbols and images of an "eternal return" (Eliade 1954), that cyclical nature which is in the world itself.

> Life has always seemed to me like a plant that lives on its rhizome. Its true life is invisible, hidden in the rhizome. The part that appears above ground lasts only a single summer. Then it withers away – an ephemeral apparition. . . . What we see is the blossom, which passes. The rhizome remains.
>
> (Jung 1963:18)

In a vision of the existential journey, the return inexorably becomes the movement towards death, as the natural conclusion of the life of the flower, or towards an ultra-terrestrial passage, if one thinks of the rhizome or believes in reincarnation, in life in the hereafter, in the resurrection of the body.

Perhaps, thanks to this not always perceptible backdrop, returns of any kind are touched with a melancholy, depressive mood, close in its ambivalence to that of departure. If there is loss in going away, we also find it paradoxically in the return. Far from being a simple coming back home, unpacking the suitcases, looking at the souvenirs, the photographs, signs of the trip that gradually fade away, renewing contact with one's world and its inhabitants, all these make the return a specific kind of psychological moment: the euphoria has died down, the party is over, the unknown has been revealed, the mirror will give back the image of oneself more or less the same, now as well as then. There may however be rare exceptions in which the journey leads to a radical change in the orientation of one's life.

When on the other hand it is not a journey or a sojourn of one's own choosing, the return can acquire more intense and explicit features.

We spoke of exile, of migrations, of forced separations and therefore of a return charged with expectation and projections. It might seem that in this case the return would become the most beautiful and culminating moment of the journey. For many it was, when the situations that had led to the exile were definitively changed, permitting a return that became reintegration, compensation, reconquest of oneself, of one's places, of one's life.

But the exiles, the refugees, the displaced did not always have their expectations fulfilled when they returned home. Perhaps their expectations were too focused on the return? Time, the length they were away, is obviously determining in the relationship between the waiting and the psychological investment in a possible return.

In his *The Moon and the Bonfires* Cesare Pavese (2002) noted that a country meant you were not alone, knowing that in the people, in the plants of the earth there was something of yours: even when you weren't there, it was waiting for your return.

When one leaves behind parts of oneself – and one feels that there is something waiting – the need to return sooner or later comes imperatively to the fore: the return becomes a sort of trial, a heroic undertaking, in which one attempts to recover something precious, healing the wound that had remained open.

David Gerbi, born in Tripoli and then expelled by Gadaffi together with all the Libyan Jews in 1967, a refugee in exile in Rome, became a psychoanalyst. He is also committed to the movement for peace and defines as follows his "wound of the refugee":

> I spent thirty-five years of my life hoping I would see the land of my birth again one day. The desire was however also accompanied by a fear justified by history: to be persecuted again . . . thus my innocent enthusiasm and my desire for the places of my childhood slowly died . . . Yet despite the conscious suppression and the unconscious repression of my desires, the energy and motivation to return never vanished completely. I had to admit that this inner and exterior conflict accompanied me all these years, but what could I do?
>
> (Gerbi 2003:269–270; translated from the Italian by transl.)

The author defines the components of his identity: Jewish in religion, Sephardim in tradition, Italian in citizenship, Libyan in origins and other aspects characterized by the places in which he lived for his studies, work, journeys – Europe, America, Far East, Africa, Amazonia, South America – and he asks himself what will happen to this inner geography when the possibility of a return eventually becomes real:

> What do I expect from a return to my native land?
>
> I want the chance to return in full liberty and dignity and I want to reconcile my new image with that of the refugee that belongs to my past.

In other words I want to adapt my old image to my new identity . . . Who knows how it will change my relationship with the places after I have come face to face with my Land? I cannot exclude the possibility of renouncing something that by now belongs only to the past and, without a feeling of guilt or betrayal, I will perhaps feel closer to my Italian component. On the other hand I was born in Tripoli but am Roman by adoption and I hope this second identity will not make me feel guilty! There is also the possibility, less plausible, that I will discover in myself a true citizen of Tripoli. In any case I am sure that facing the past will change my relationship with the present.

(Gerbi 2003:275)

When finally, after long preparations for a journey that was more than personal in its significance – becoming an official act showing a willingness for a reconciliation between Arabs and Libyan Jews, and in a broader sense a proposal of tolerance and peace – Gerbi arrived by plane in Tripoli, in 2002, he was overcome by emotions that were manifested in his soul and body:

It is as if the waters of the Red Sea were opening . . . We go outside and suddenly I feel this familiar air, this freshness, this breeze that I remembered from when I was a child, I see the particular light of Tripoli, hot but not blinding . . . I am accompanied to the hotel. In the car I begin to hear people speaking Arab and I begin to remember where I am: the route, the palms with their round dates, orange and yellow . . . I want to ask the driver to stop so I can take a bunch, taste that sweet and forgotten flavor once more.

(Gerbi 2003:329)

The book continues narrating the experience of this long-awaited return and the first thoughts on its psychological effects.

Suddenly I feel that I have grown, become completely adult . . . I feel I am a new person and am happy that despite all the obstacles I did not let myself be discouraged. My old dream of returning to Tripoli had become reality.

(Gerbi 2003:356–357)

But there is more, for as in other similar cases of return from exile to the place of origin, there is then another return: that to the house of the present, in the place and in the country of adoption. Here the landscape, for Gerbi, changes from personal to collective and the author realizes that there was more to the journey than seeing the city of origin and his family's shop once again; it was also the discovery of a path to be shared in constructing peace.

In other situations the political events that led to exile unfortunately remained unsolved, and the return, when it did take place, was tormented and full of anxiety.

In the new country, even when the exile feels welcomed and has a family and work, what is happening in the country of origin is never far from his mind and the continuous threat to the people and places resulting from military occupation, wars, other calamities, or discrimination by governments on a racial or ideological level is ever present. Intense feelings of solidarity with his countrymen make him remain with one foot there, near them. The return, then, becomes a moment full of contrasting feelings: joy, tenderness, suffering, fear, anxiety, anger.

Overwhelming emotions, joined to an awareness of a collective tragedy still in progress, mark the description of Ali Rashid's first return to Palestine in 1995. Palestinian, a representative figure of his people and their rights, he has been very active in building peace in the Middle East. Many of his fellow countrymen are also exiles in foreign countries, but those who have remained are equally in exile, in the sense that they are a people deprived of their own country or driven out of their homes. Palestine today is an ensemble of territories, zones and refugee camps, decided theoretically by other governments, cut out of the land where the Palestinians have lived for millennia. The land and the places have not only changed but have disappeared, have been destroyed, reconverted, expropriated by the Israeli occupation, under the eyes of their preceding inhabitants.

Below is Ali Rashid's report describing his return, written for this book and based on a version he had previously published.

It was amazing. It took the plane only three and a half hours to cover the distance to the place from which I was expelled thirty years ago. Normal customs and passport controls before falling into or being catapulted back from the past into the living present, sweet and asphyxiating, a half-century of collective dreams, hopes and stories. I had prepared everything at the last moment, informing only a few friends just minutes before leaving, to avoid discussions for which I was not prepared, even to avoid thinking. It was difficult to think, or believe completely in what was about to happen.

I had just arrived at the airport of Tel Aviv and looked around disoriented. I filled my lungs with that humid summer air, about which Gassan Kanafani wrote in his novel *Return to Haifa*, and imprinted in the mind, in the testimony of the blind man with regard to the massacre and expulsion of the inhabitants of Ramla and Lydda, where there is now an airport, or in the other stories that make up our identity. A host of Israeli flags seemed to taunt me, rising up between what my eyes told me and the dreams of an entire life. The airport building is in English colonial style, like those one sees everywhere in the Middle East, but it is made of a familiar white stone. Many shadows move around me, but all of them, at first, including officials and police, look like tourists. The only things that are mine are the stones.

Having to speak English to make myself understood by the airport authorities in what I had always considered my country fills me with sadness. Once more that feeling of eternal impermanence and death I had momentarily lost, takes over again. Looking out the window of the plane as it was descending, the stretch of sea and coast of Palestine brought tears to my eyes and countless nostalgic and moving stories came back, told in the most varied places during my long wanderings. This plain of red and fertile land was once planted with sesame, according to Abuh Saleh, a notable of the former inhabitants of Gemso, in the refugee camp of Zarka in the desert of Jordan. Looking for the first time in my life at the sea of Palestine, which as a boy I said had been stolen by the Israelis, and the red lands of the plain, the idea of return materialized and I felt for the first time all of a piece. I was finally at the center of my vital space, at point zero of my Cartesian plane. Until my axes were cut when I entered the airport. What dirty tricks our sight plays on us exiles when every so often it is overcome by an intuition that springs from a memory told, elaborated by any number of fragments or dreams put together like a puzzle. Images that are at a lower level, in the depth of the unconscious, in that bond between earth and soul. We Palestinians, we exiles, don't have the earth underfoot; we have the earth in our souls.

In all these years, and in our various diasporas, all my people and myself have had no other country but this, that now seems to have changed management, like a bar. At the airport I already feel that again, after years, I will have to support disillusionment. All my life I have been searching for a place where I will not feel a foreigner and now, here, I feel like a zombie. The emptiness and the absence weigh on my head like a millstone. A foreign zombie in my own land.

And here was the pretty girl in charge of security. After welcoming me to Israel, she asked what my profession was. "I am a Palestinian diplomat," I told her.

"But don't you have a diplomatic passport?," she asked. "To have a diplomatic passport one has to have a government and to have a government one has to have a state and there is no state without territorial sovereignty. As you know, you have taken our country, you have expelled us, and you have settled here in our place," I said.

"You left: there's a lot of land in the Arab world, why didn't you take it?," she said. "Because it wasn't ours, in those lands we were foreigners, shut up in camps, this has always been our only land," I answered . . .

That tourist visa burned within me, it humiliated me and had already left me sleepless for many nights . . .

The three young men who are waiting for me, my twin brother's friends, welcome me to Palestine. During the short trip to Jerusalem I begin to look at a Palestine that is unrecognizable. They are young and don't know that I never returned, that I had never seen this part that was occupied in 1948, except transfigured in dream and story. On the other hand, I barely remember the occupation of 1967, but it has always been the subject of our debates and our work.

One of the young men accompanying me says, "You must be from our parts, from the province of Jerusalem, Der Yasin or Lifta, I can tell from the dialect." Reacquiring my dialect was like waking from a years-long sleep, like picking up a conversation interrupted before falling asleep. I was sixteen when I left my family and since then had had no chance to speak it. In the Arab world the language I used was the classic Arab, and elsewhere Italian and English.

"You're right," I told the boy. "I am from Lifta" . . .

We finally arrive in Lifta, but I can't see anything; it's dark and a heavy rain is starting to fall. They tell me that little is left. They will have built other houses, but something must be left, I know that this was where my country was and I was happy to shut an eye to reality, in case it was so different. In those forty square kilometers there are the names of places the tales and stories of childhood were filled with: those names were the only goal and anchor of our problematical existence.

After the mass expulsion of 1948, entire villages moved elsewhere and the refugees settled in new places of residence respecting and maintaining the same aggregations of provenience. In the refugee camps and in the various cities of the Diaspora the names of the new quarters that rose were the same as those of the original towns. As time passed surnames too were given according to the town from which one came, almost an attempt to keep an identity closely tied to the lost villages . . .

By now it is total silence, my face wet and my body hunched over in the front seat of a car that is entering the old city . . .

In the hotel I continued to speak in dialect; I felt at home. I hear someone calling me the "gentleman from Lifta" and finally I feel like someone who can sit down, after having been standing all his life, and the memories turn into a flow of cotton flocks that slowly get thicker and thicker and are transformed into a soft pallet.

The night passed between sleep and wakefulness. A sense of fear began to take over and at four in the morning I called my grandmother in America. She is the real repository of our memories, the witness of our continuous departures in all directions. A few years ago, and she was seventy at the time, she went to America to her children in the hope that with American citizenship she would be able to return here. Her voice, initially joyful, then broke down into sobs. She asked if I had seen the houses. For her they were not only a story, but the only piece of life that was worth living . . .

Yesterday I hadn't seen any signs indicating the names of those places: there were other names in Hebrew, but I didn't want to go into it so as not to open again and prematurely other wounds. I told my grandmother that I had just arrived and that I needed other indications, more specific coordinates to find our house.

"You can't mistake it," she said. "From the French hill up to the UN headquarters and then north, those are the lands of your grandfather, and all the olive groves up to the first houses of Lifta are ours, the house is in the middle of the Roman olives and on the right of the house is a large cave under the granary, you can't go wrong."

Fear gripped me from head to foot; I was trembling and confused: if my brother had still been alive he would have sustained me . . . I began to feel the gravity of my tragedy, intuit the irreversibility, I was in total panic. I was no longer sure if I could or wanted to face this trial, open another page of my story, never seen before now, confront nostalgia with reality, have the dream clash with hard reality. Lose the symmetry . . .

(translated from the Italian by transl.)

I wanted to keep the original form of this piece, including the ending which might seem suspended, but the silence that follows gives an idea of the intensity and complexity of the feelings that accompany what is perhaps the most painful return imaginable: that in which nothing of what was left is found and with nothing that might compensate for the loss.

I opened the first chapter of this book with the poem of a Palestinian poet, of which however I only cited the beginning. Here is the second part, which deals with the return. The handful of earth preserved in exile . . .

Launching it into the air,
suffocating, of my land,
without vegetation or life,
there I've scattered it:
offered in sacrifice
as soon as, back,
I fell prone
on the face of my earth.
My desolate earth,
the trees uprooted,
the earth mixed
with mire and dung;
in its cities silence:
the vultures flee.
This land is not mine:
never seen in the past;
my heart is far away
and, as for my feet
they are in a hurry to follow it.
Are they once more
going towards exile?
They are starting out
towards another exile.
That land to which
I returned yesterday is not mine.
A fistful of dust
that I lost is my homeland.
           (Tawfiq Sayigh 2002; translated from
                      the Italian by transl.)

There are still many human beings in the world who, for various reasons, cannot "return home" to their place of origin, not even for short visits as tourists.

For those who "can return" there are "temporary emigrations," in the words of Grinberg and Grinberg (1989). These include students, those who have grants, guest professors, commercial representatives, or the "visit journeys" to their land of origin. These revisitations are often marked by a need to check on things: returning to see if the reality left behind is still the same or if someone, something, has in the meantime modified it. Here there is an element of truth, of a registering of one's relationship with the experience of the past: seeing anew, feeling anew what it is like to be there again, in those places where one lived part of one's life, right there in the spaces, the panoramas, the homes where particular events took place, significant for our individual story. A verification that actually takes over more of the present than the past as such.

We know by now that in the mental space of nostalgia, places change shape with respect to their original concrete form and the distance between them becomes evident when, on our return, we barely recognize them. Not only because more often than not the places – like people – have really changed concretely, but also because they are being compared to inner images, with a relevance and a meaning they will take on now. There is no way of knowing what will happen, which is why the emotions on returning are so overwhelming, depending on how long ago the emigration took place.

Emigration for work, one of those involving choice, covers a broad range of experiences and individuals. These involve the conditions of departure, the length of time spent in the new country, and the return, when there is a return. In fact, included among "those who can return," there are those who never do, those who return for a visit, those who return for good, sometimes after many years of absence, resettling in their country of origin.

Pinturicchio, *The Return of Ulysses*, 1509.

In his book *La nostalgia nella valigia*, Sergio Mellina deals with the return of those who migrated for work and the psychological difficulties that occur even in apparently privileged situations.

> Often the emigrant who returns to the place where he was born, where he spent his childhood, does not come back only to build a house, his new house, a tangible sign of success, but he returns also and above all to seek an answer to his nostalgia . . . But even making up for absence with return, with revisitation, with repatriation, things have changed with time and memory finds itself in trouble. The temporal references are no longer as he remembers them: what is internal no longer corresponds to that which is external: "I came from too far away – says Pavese – I no longer belonged to that house . . . the world had changed me" . . . Rarely is the return compensated by what one finds.
>
> (Mellina 1987:169; translated from the Italian by transl.)

The delusion of return is not a sporadic fact. Often the sensorial and affective life with which these places were once throbbing has been extinguished. They have been emptied, and there is no way to bring them back to life.

Sometimes returning results in symptoms of malaise or a real psychiatric pathology. This may depend on the circumstances of return: on a negative reception or a lack of reception; or a return of the unsolved problems from which the emigrant had fled.

It may therefore depend on a difficult context or on an inability to cope with the impact, as described by Mellina.

In foreseeing both positive and negative aspects, the theme of return as found in literature from antiquity onwards seems quite realistic and impartial, even when the version with a positive outcome tends to prevail, as in the exemplary case of the *Odyssey* and of Ulysses. The word "odyssey" now refers to a long, devious and turbulent journey, not limited to return, consisting of stages, places, unexpected events and trials, through which at the end the desired goal is reached. But not all the Greeks returning from the Trojan War were as fortunate as Ulysses. Some had misadventures of various kinds after returning to their native land.

Since it is a return, one often thinks more of the position of the protagonist – the returnee – than the situation he will find on his return.

After the misfortunes of his journey, Agamemnon returned to find that his wife Clytemnestra had betrayed him, and death by the hand of his rival Aegistus was lying in wait. His son Orestes, who had fled from the tragedy, returned years later to avenge his father but had to flee again, returning only after regaining the favor of the gods. Other heroes, such as Ajax of Locri, were shipwrecked on the return homewards, or once home found situations that were unsustainable and had to go elsewhere, such as Diomedes, Philotetes, Idomeneus, or Teucrus, founding new cities in new countries. *Nostoi*, returns, was the official name given to this kind of tale in the Trojan cycle (Scarpi 1992).

The adventures of Aeneas, although they have been compared to those of Ulysses with regard to the journey, do not take place in the course of a return. Since he was a Trojan, he had not left the city, which he had defended to the end. Aeneas if anything represents the most famous example of a migration crowned by success, a pacific landing on an unknown land, starting a civilization. The founding hero of antiquity is never violent – never abuses the land and its inhabitants – unless he is forced to face mortal dangers.

But back to Ulysses. He finds a situation that is anything but tranquil when he returns from his odyssey. His Ithaca – kept intact by the nostalgic yearning, which is the heart of the myth, together with Penelope who is the vestal – will require further trials from him, through which, in the optimistic version, the definitive return home will be sanctioned. Post-Homeric traditions had him die by the hand of a son he had with Circe, who had sent him out in search of his father.

The return of Ulysses is actually an ideal point of departure for that movement westwards that was to take the Mediterranean civilization further and further, beyond the columns of Hercules, towards unknown lands beyond the sea. From which, after more than two millennia, the migrants continue to wish to return to the places of origin, to see, like Ulysses, "the smoke of the houses rise to the sky before closing their eyes for ever."

Things have not changed all that much, and many more recent emigrants have had their "bad returns."

In his long experience as a psychiatrist committed to public services, in his dealings with migration for work and the associated mental disturbances, Mellina refers above all to cases characterized by poverty, from underdeveloped areas and represented by workers or "lumpen proletarians." His attention is drawn to various aspects of migration for work, one of which, the result of the "marginality of failed migration," I wish to touch on here. The phenomenon concerns both foreign emigrants in Italy and Italians abroad who then return home. Compared with successful migration – the hagiography of the uncle in America – the author thinks it is more useful to study the motives of psychopathological manifestations in other contexts with a view to developing a clinical practice of reception and tutelage of migrants. Since from a scientific point of view the malaise of emigration remains an enigma, Mellina feels it his duty to deal above all with social, political and economic factors, before touching on the hidden frustrations that mark the life of the apparently normal emigrant.

With reference to the return home, the author stresses the various experiences that accompany returns motivated by external causes or a lack of integration: feeling that, as intruders, they are refused, ill-supported in their native country, with a consequent growing anger; having to face serious problems, critical and traumatic, of personal realignments to models of life and schemes of behavior that are no longer habitual and that in part have been repressed; in other words, the emergence of a return that becomes "double emigration." In his experience in psychiatric hospitals, Mellina identified a high percentage of patients who had at least one migratory experience in their personal history, from Southern to Northern Italy or abroad, that ended badly, in the mental hospital. Even if the nature of their symptoms, according to official diagnosis, did not indicate that they were related to the migratory experience, their stories proved otherwise.

Clearly then, the ambivalent feelings of return – the "shadows of return" – are there even when the return was something the emigrant never lost sight of during his stay elsewhere.

At a certain point those who decide to return are filled with doubts, because recrossing, inverting the route, the events of migration, still other separations, other losses, other changes, submitting their families to them, is not an easy choice. The sensation of being "strangers" in their own country, of nostalgia for the adopted land and retaining its language and customs, periodically returning to meet friends, is a familiar experience for many migrants who have returned, and who often end up, like other foreigners, in forming their own communities.

Yet this desire for home is stronger than the feelings of loss, of nostalgia, of exclusion from what was laboriously rebuilt elsewhere. We have to resign ourselves to the fact that the relation with the land and places of origin – that is, with the past – overshadows the relation with the persons and environment of the current life.

Like many of my patients, Ulysses was not poor, had not emigrated to find work, had not been politically exiled. On the contrary, he won the Trojan War with personal success; had his cultural identity, his homeland, his family, means and men at his disposal; yet he suffered long the pains of return. His exile was limited to a period of around ten years, marked by delays but also by discoveries, pleasures, formative encounters and conflicts. On a psychological level he gained patience, humility, acceptance, constancy, a sense of limits, all of which made him wiser and capable of managing his arrival home.

This aspect of return, which I also connect to the initial quotes from Jung in this chapter, could become a possible metaphor for individuation. Can we therefore say that individuation is also a "return home?" For now I shall leave the question unanswered.

There are other figures after Homer's Ulysses. In the 13th century another famous Ulysses, that of Dante, becomes not so much the wandering exile who tries to return home as the precursor of modern man, attracted by the unknown, interested in discovering, knowing, conquering reality.

The last of the famous Ulysses figures is that of James Joyce and takes us to the 20th century, the exile who tries to return home, who is looking for a "home of his own," if we interpret it symbolically. Dante and Joyce were two expatriates, and have frequently been compared. Joyce was inspired by Dante, and when he settled in the "cosmopolitan" Trieste, in voluntary exile from "narrow-minded" Dublin, he immersed himself in the Italian culture. There he wrote *Exiles*, *Dubliners* and conceived some of the chapters of *Ulysses*. In his major work, Joyce constructs an entire day of wandering – a mental pilgrimage – in the city of origin, with Leopold Bloom (Ulysses), Stephen Dedalus (Telemachus) and Molly (Penelope), Bloom's wife, as principal characters. Daily life for Leopold Bloom is what the Trojan War and the return from it were for Ulysses. Dublin is his Mediterranean sea and the persons met during the day correspond to the mythical and imaginary creatures in the Homeric poem. The myth is still there, but there is no hero. For Joyce, the wanderings of Ulysses are set in the events of everyday life, in a journey experienced internally and owing much to Freudian inspiration. It represents the *epos* of the wanderer, of him who is a foreigner in his own land. Joyce, an Irish Catholic, educated by the Jesuits, epitomizes himself in the Dublin Jew, explorer of the mind and of the city. All in a complex, when not chaotic, world, which is that of contemporary civilization. A voluntary exile, in all his works and in different ways, Joyce was always to speak of Dublin and of his exile. He thus consummates his return.

The return, however, is not only a matter of shadows. It can also be liberating, re-creative and can provoke sudden and sensational healings, at least according to doctors in the past centuries, when "nostalgia" was first officially recognized as an "illness." Up until 1800 nostalgia was considered a serious, at times mortal, illness, frequently diagnosed in soldiers or others who had left their native land. The lack of domestic walls and familiar landscapes became an obsession and when return home became impossible, the result was sometimes death. Undoubtedly today, with such greater ease in means of communication and transportation, nostalgia as an illness has become less evident. It is also possible that the development and acceleration of individual and mass movements have in other ways weakened the cultural and national identity, creating a sense of disorientation and a psychological weakness that can be sounded out when analyzing foreign patients, or those whose experiences of uprooting were abnormal.

Home and the nostalgia that motivates a return home assume greater psychological and symbolic significance. Homesickness is also superimposed on the search for an inner state of identity, a continuous and contained experience of self, received in a home of one's own. Because of this need, the home – the real home – is everywhere and traditionally considered a symbolic reflection of the identity, of the soul, of every individual. In much of the literature on nostalgia and the psychiatry of the migrant, the term "uprooting" often appears, involving the tree, another universal symbol. It is again a stable element, standing solidly on the ground, firmly anchored in its depths. When nostalgia becomes an illness, the tree does not grow because its roots do not penetrate the earth: they do not dare, it is not permitted, they haven't sufficient energy. Every tree needs its earth. Without roots somewhere, return, a journey, are out of the question and all that remains is flight, pursuit, wandering. After transplanting, roots take time to grow and these delicate processes require strength, good soil and favorable conditions outside, in addition to extra care for the first few years.

The question constantly reappears as to whether individuation can incarnate itself in the return home: a home that is as symbolic, interior, as it is real, exterior, which feels right to the individual. If only the symbolic aspect were taken into consideration, then once "individuated," one place would be as good as another and a concrete return, a need to wander here and there, would be unnecessary because the home, the place, the journey, everything would be inside.

It is a fascinating hypothesis, but what keeps my thesis on soul and earth in equilibrium is that the body, as long as it lives, has to live somewhere, get up in some dawn, in some landscape, eat something or other, communicate in some language: in other words, decide, if it can, where to live with its dear ones. The real house cannot be ignored.

In leaving discussion to some future time, I find the following passage particularly pertinent. It mixes nostalgia and desire for a return, which is impossible but not because it cannot be realized concretely. The human soul longs for eternity and immobility: something that no home, no land, no tree apparently succeeds in placating.

> I would like there to exist places that are stable, unmoving, intangible, untouched and almost untouchable, unchanging, deep rooted; places that might be points of reference, of departure, of origin:
> My birthplace, the cradle of my family, the house where I may have been born, the tree I may have seen grown (that my father may have planted the day I was born), the attic of my childhood filled with intact memories.
> (Perec 1997:90–91)

At this point I too will try to find my way of return, the conclusion to this chapter.

Once a child who was drawing his house asked me: "but where is the real house, now, and when I stop drawing it, where does it go?" He could understand, rationally, that concrete things were there where he had left them, since he had acquired the so-called "permanence of the object," but he was also aware that the image, in addition to being on the sheet of paper, took on a life of its own. The child, in other words, was questioning itself on the relationship between the concrete object, its image and our memory. At the time a few lines by Ariosto came to mind: wits, tears, the sighs of lovers, things, hopes, places . . . everything that on Earth "is lost," said the poet, a great traveler of the imaginary, ends up on the Moon.

The Moon, the space of dreams, of poetry, of art. The soul of things dissolves, the image is blurred, flies away and returns to the planet to which it originally belonged. I told the child that the images went to the Moon and, believe me, he understood the metaphor.

As for the return, inspired by the child's question, let me formulate a similar question: where did the places and their things go while we imagined them and remembered them from far off?

Far away, only inner traces, mental images or photographs, of the places that have been left remain. They can never literally replace the concrete things, like a reproduction, for their inner life would shrivel and die out. They must continue, so to speak, to breathe the atmosphere of the Moon. Then, upon return, disillusion will be less probable or less distressing, painful. The images will have changed within, they will have grown together with new experiences, they will be capable of dialoguing with their preceding form, they will accept the fact that the concrete place had a life of its own, beautiful or ugly as it may have been.

The traveler who returns has only to accept the fact that things have gone on without him, that they have dared to modify themselves without his permission, that he was unable to control them, that one cannot be physically in two places at the same time, that leaving is really a bit like dying, but only a bit. Like returning.

In an equally metaphorical language, the alchemist encounters Ariosto when he affirms that "the image comes back down from the Moon," like dew

Returning Home and Sitting Down Peacefully, calligraphy by Yamada Mumon Roshi (1900–1988), Zen master.

in the morning, to reanimate the earth that has been chilled by the night and to announce "the return of the soul."

The *Sublimatio*, a crucial phase in the alchemical process, is defined also as "the return of the soul," and illustrates the new union between Mother Earth (body) and the moon child (Soul). The text of *Aurora consurgens*, cited by Jung, says "Here the soul descends flying and restores the purified corpse." A creative phase follows this return, the generation of countless children – represented by the image of *Denarius* – that closes the description of the great alchemical work (Jung 1946). Alchemy, remember, was interpreted by Jung in a psychological key to illustrate the process of individuation and other aspects of his analytical psychology.

The return home, in this symbolic key, is the return of the soul that reconnects with its oldest and deepest roots, abandoned only on a concrete level, but still alive, above all in exile, thanks to the deprivation of the real place. The place remains alive in the soul: in the land within, as Ali Rashid said. Tolerating the incurable part of the loss and accepting the fact that places change, like everything else in life, including ourselves, is the premise for a creative return. For those lucky enough to have access to this vision.

Thus perhaps I have come closer to a satisfying answer to my question.

Chapter 8

The foreign patient

Premises

In the course of this book I have tried to keep to a minimum the psycho-analytical aspect of my profession, as well as everything that normally accompanies it when presented clinically and technically: diagnosis, key theo-retical concepts, specific language, interpretations and in-depth studies of clinical cases.

Moreover, I declared in the introduction to the book that choosing to be an analyst gave me an opportunity to interpret the human experience – including mine of course – from the inside and in its universal foundations, compared with the many diversities that came my way. In the meantime, though, as happened with the book – which began with the places of origin and moved through other places and spaces, during the journey, in exile, together with nostalgia – in the end it all came down to an unexpected return. This return was also an inversion, which Jung defined as *enantiodromia*: the passage from one pole to its opposite.

After years of clinical practice with foreign patients, an *enantiodromia* of my theoretical bearings took place: from the universal and internal founda-tions of the psyche towards the real determinants and characteristics of the individual forms.

Orthodox psychoanalytical learning as such and its language were broad-ened to include other types of knowledge and languages, without, it is hoped, losing either their meaning or their profundity. At least not in my mind, nor within my work.

In part it is the discourse itself that has taken me a bit off course, since my main interests are not psychopathology or the analytical technique but rather aspects of life that do not always become a mental illness. My interest in the subject, however, began in a clinical venue and fused with my personal experiences and those of colleagues who in turn have written in various ways and contexts.

Often during my clinical practice I had to admit honestly that there was no way in which the broad repertory of psychoanalytical interpretations could cover the fullness of such a vast human experience as migration, with its different aspects. At times thoughts or phrases that were theoretically correct and that I might have expressed in a session remained unsaid, for I felt they were out of place, uncalled for.

The importance of ethnic and cultural diversity in the constitution of identity and personality – as well as the possible dysfunctions of these processes – fades and moves into the background compared with the dominant image of a psyche that is universally represented as a "family in an interior" when one enters the field of depth psychology, above all in the theoretical paradigm of classic psychoanalysis. Both for orthodox psychoanalysis and for many psychotherapies of psychoanalytical inspiration, the mother and the triangular dynamics of early childhood remain the pulsating core of psychic functioning and therefore also of the psychological disorder. I have already dealt with the importance of the mother and the beginnings of life, mostly in the chapter devoted to the place of origin.

I would be satisfied if this book succeeded in giving more visibility to the other components and their relative interaction with the primary dynamics, especially in view of a type of psychotherapeutic treatment of foreign patients that takes the peculiarities of their situation into consideration.

In order to achieve this I must deal with a few ambiguous points, both in psychoanalytical theory and in literature on the subject, in which the foreigner does not seem to be specifically considered. In the form of questions, the recurring perplexities might be:

- is being a foreigner only a temporary condition, or is it a stable feature that affects the structure of the personality?
- or, stated differently: is the foreigner, basically, really someone "different," or is it all relative to the context in which he finds himself?
- doesn't what happens to the foreigner, on the psychological level, also happen to others, in different forms and circumstances?

My answer to all these questions begins with a "yes . . . but."

Certainly the definition of "foreigner" is relative, certainly it corresponds to an exterior, social condition – that depends on time, i.e. on its duration, and the particular context. Certainly the word should not take the form of a definitive label, nor refer to a permanent identification. Anyone can be or feel oneself a foreigner for a given period, and feeling oneself a foreigner is not always in line with the registry data. Here, however, discussion would include the metaphorical aspects that I have already dealt with in the preceding chapters.

As for the diversity of the foreigner: he is of course not diverse in that he is a human being – with two legs, two arms, two eyes, like all human beings. But with regard to the rest, yes, he is different as an individual among the others, all different, and also in his belonging to a group, among other diverse groups – and I'm not referring to race or ethnic group. I'll return to this later.

On the analogy of the experiences of the foreigner with those who are not foreigners, I will once more say "yes . . . but." The foreign patient can have one or more of the following recurrent behavioral problems: momentary psychological disorientation, anxiety or other symptoms that accompany a sudden uprooting, difficulty in adapting to a new environment, confusion or disharmonic stratification of identity, pluri-language dysfunctions, traumas of forced migration, reactivation of themes concerning the story of the family of origin, specific conflicts in mixed marriages, and others.

The psychological dynamics of these patients are in any case similar, in a qualitative sense, to those of so-called minor migrations within the same country, or even a temporary transfer for study or work, including at times vacations.

On an even smaller scale, some experience deep-seated feelings accompanied by symptoms and other manifestations of loss when abandoning a home of one's own, even if it is simply moving to a different house in a new area, or changing work. Almost everyone, without being officially a foreigner, has felt this at one time or another.

It might be said that in the subliminal continuity joining health and illness, it is ultimately the quantitative aspect that brings things to a head, so that if a move or restructuring of a house throws the family psychologically off balance, we can imagine what it must mean, even in psychologically stable individuals, to change not only their home but also continent, language, friends, food, climate, habits and everything else, all together.

However if we wish to go beyond the ambivalence of the "yes . . . but," I would take it upon myself to say that there is a basic irreconcilable diversity in the foreigner, which remains even after integration into the new environment: an indelible sign that reflects the elsewhere of his past.

I could in other words define this diversity as a "stratification of different experiences in the constants of daily life." And this is where the earth returns. Anyone born and raised in the same geographical and cultural area interweaves his life with the constants that characterize it, even though his personality and his story differ from those of others. The children of this land become men and women who speak the same language, eat more or less the same food, breathe the same air, in the same climate, surrounded by a specific light and dominant colors, and with that specific landscape, the faces of those people, those forms of animals and plants, listening to the sounds, the music, accustomed to the ways, gestures, rituals, the style of relating and communicating within the group; in other words they participate in everything of which everyday life, and that of special days, is made, in that common fabric that holds life together, unaware of when and how it was woven.

This is what unravels and must in some way be mended whether it involves those who experienced migration as young people in a developmental stage, those who crossed over as adults, or those who belong to the second and third generations of immigrant families.

How to deal with the rich complexity of the condition in which the foreign patient finds himself, aware of his various facets, is what I learned to do together with the many patients I met in my professional life and whom I here thank for their contribution.

Constructive criticism of psychoanalysis

After expounding my position, I shall now go on to deal with a few ambiguous points that I believe to be of particular note in the psychotherapy of foreign patients, and which I encountered in the psychoanalytical thought and literature of my training and my subsequent studies and explorations.

Let's go back to the role of the mother and the maternal figure. When the human being grows, for better or for worse, the original capacity for relating that is established with the mother broadens to other relationships with persons and places, things, the surrounding environment, up to the entire world. The subsequent psychophysical constitution of the human being will never more be that of the child, for the psychophysical terrain has changed irreversibly. This is why I believe that the psychoanalytical concept of "regression," apparently easy, is one of those to be handled with particular caution, because it can lead to forced and arbitrary interpretations. The personality does not regress. Particular modes of behavior can regress, a wound can be opened, the "abandoned child" or the "angry child" can emerge. It might be said that an individual does not escape from his own story, or something of the sort, but the adult part must always be kept in mind, because otherwise resources are detracted from the healing and the patient is kept in a "claustrophyliac" or "uroboric" environment, as Jung would say.

From when he is born the human being displays a precise interest in the surrounding environment, experienced not only as the extension of the mother, contrary to what many psychoanalysts who do not keep up with the most recent psychological studies presume. In the past too, before these studies, direct observation had already demonstrated the autonomy of the child in organizing his perception and learning with regard to space, to places and their forms and contents.

Although I acknowledge the centrality of the primary relations, I prefer to consider them as a point of departure for psychic development rather than a constant reference for every subsequent interpretation and theorization. I don't believe, for example, that the physical sensations, the memories and various attachments referring to places and abstract entities such as homeland, typical of nostalgia, are simply a transference of nostalgia for the mother, the maternal uterus, the house in which they lived together. This is however what many psychoanalytical works on the subject still maintain.

From the early months of their life – and not only the eighth month with its "separation anxiety" – children have a clear perception that distinguishes the mother from the context, exhibiting preferences and refusals for some places and objects, as well as a specific interest for the space where their explorations and maturing phases, such as learning to walk, take place. They find pleasure in constituting their personal habits and routines, occupying the space, in terms both of play and of eating and sleeping. They choose favorite foods, colors, objects, and people, aside from the mother, with whom they wish to stay. By the time a child is a year old it has already broadened its personal interests in the world and can do without the mother on various occasions, even happily, when peacefully absorbed in observing and experimenting with the surroundings. Of course the presence of a mother or her substitute mediates and favors this relationship with the world, protects it, but I do not believe in superimposing the relationship on the growth process and its subsequent passages in adult life.

If a mother has "used" her child for her own affective needs, keeping the child tied to her apron strings, conditioning it negatively with respect to its initiatives and freedom, transferring to the child her own neurosis; if she was unable to protect her children, when necessary, from traumas or other dysfunctions, that is another issue, often upstream from some of the psychological distrubances of childhood and the adult.

What I have been trying to do is to restore greater autonomy and psychological dignity to places, spaces, objects, nature, the environment, to everything that is "not only the mother," for I believe in what my patients have told me, in what I myself have experienced and also what I learned in over ten years of training, supervising and observing educators and teachers dealing with early infancy (children up to three years old).

There is a clear difference between nostalgia for the maternal embrace and nostalgia for the places of childhood. It might be, for example, a nostalgia for exciting experiences involving the body, such as the first adventures, the first social games, all things that in reality separate the child from the mother. Memories of that peculiar energy, a physical lightness, of that untiring energy of childhood, connected to that particular garden, those stairs, that square. Memories of the taste of a particular food, of the music of a carillon, and then in later childhood and adolescence of the sounds of a language which spoke words of love; landscapes seen from the window of the study, the lanes of the village through which we walked every day, appointments with friends, under a specific monument, or the market, the lakeside walk, the river, the beach where one first played and later fell in love. Nostalgia is always of beautiful moments, constructive experiences in one's identity. The mother does and does not play a part.

Finding oneself detached from the context of life is more traumatic on the psychological level for an adult than separation from the mother, a gradual process of autonomy that had presumably already taken place. But I'll return to the trauma theory later.

In dealing with the term "foreigner," etymology takes us from the Middle English *foreing* back to the Latin *foris*, outside. In significance it can be seen at times as synonymous with "stranger," etymology a generic *ex-tra*, "outside of," "outside of a relation with." A stranger, says the dictionary (*Webster's Ninth New Collegiate Dictionary*) is a "foreigner, a resident alien, one who does not belong." A foreigner is "a person belonging to a foreign country," "stranger."

The foreigner is then far from his country and his home and outside, at least at the beginning, of the new country and the new home. He is suspended. Without land. His part of suffering, the part subjected to psychotherapy, in line with these premises, should not disregard the concrete condition in which the patient finds himself, and it is legitimate to think that if he had stayed where he was his difficulty might never have become manifest.

In analytical psychotherapy, if the paradigm of early object relations is superimposed on his current situation, the foreigner runs the risk of losing the full significance of his present condition.

In a sense this was the case with the theme of nostalgia.

Nostalgia as an illness was a pre-psychoanalytical diagnosis. But Johannes Hofer, the doctor who had coined the term in 1678, ended up by interpreting every possible symptom as nostalgia; this was followed by others, one of whom was Karl Jaspers, who went so far as to connect it to criminal behavior, including pyromania and homicide.

Nostalgia for the home, which was the original meaning of the word, thus became nostalgia in a general sense, and was subsequently connected by psychoanalysis to the anxiety of separation and therefore to the relationship with the mother. In other words, the home, the place, the ambience would be secondarily significant because the mother or a mother substitute was or is inside, and the foreigner, therefore, was no longer one who had left his country, but one who had left his mother or his fundamental relationship.

As an analyst, I wouldn't be quite so sure. This is not what we find in the literature, in the poetry, the dreams, the stories of patients, except in particular cases or undertones. What we find are the places, nature, the things, sensations and many other persons. If, of course, we are able to give them a visibility and importance.

Foreigners, society and mental disorders

It is true that there are particular situations, serious pathologies of the psyche, in which mental and affective disorganization and destructuration do effectively seem to have taken the individual back to the primary levels of thought, behavior and dependency. In other situations these levels are latent and exist together with the better-organized levels of a mature ego, emerging only in particular occasions. In still others, they remain completely silent and occasionally come to the fore in dreams or other products of the fantasy.

It is interesting to note that the DSM-IV, the diagnostic manual used by all psychiatrists and psychotherapists in the world, periodically reviewed and adapted to the new medical, social and legislative requirements, has only recently included migration in the list of elements of psychopathology. There is no specific category – which I believe is fair since it avoids labels – but migration appears in *Adjustment Disorders*, code 309, characterized by depressed mood, anxiety, or both; behavioral disorders; and others not specified. They can be acute or chronic, if they last less than or more than six months. In the last chapter, with various updatings, still other conditions to which clinical attention can be paid appear, introducing the problem of acculturation, code Z60.3 with reference to migration, code V62.4 Acculturation Problem (American Psychiatric Association 2000).

The American Psychological Association has a committee that deals with the problems of ethnic minorities, and guidelines are worked out that take account of multicultural questions. In these contexts and the relative literature, subjects covered are acculturative stress, culture-bound syndromes, culturally responsive psychotherapy, cross cultural psychotherapy, mixed-races identity, and others.

The human psyche is a complex system in which everything can be alternately present and visible, past and hidden. This is why it is said that the line between normality and pathology is labile, that what makes the difference is the presence of a mature and functional ego and that "psychotic nuclei" can also emerge in the healthy person.

Insanity is what is shown to society without shame and without veils. It disturbs the conventional criteria of coexistence, the ideological certainties, forcing society to reconsider itself. This holds even when the insanity does not constitute threat or violence. One cannot be mad in peace. One has to be ill and be treated. This holds for all those who, with various diagnoses, become psychiatric patients, or clients for the psychotherapist, in its various forms. And also for those who today dose up on psychotropic drugs.

Today psychiatric malaise is also nominally included among the diversities to be respected. But that's not the way things really are, despite at least half a century of cultural pressure, initiated by the antipsychiatry movement. In the sociogenetic hypothesis of mental disease, the psychiatric patient is truly a foreigner, exiled in a society that raises barriers to keep out those who do not adapt to its values and goals. Both Freud, who denounced the unease and neurosis that accompany civilization, and Jung, with his theory of a collective unconscious and above all the tormented process of individuation, insisted on the centrality of the relationship between individual and collectivity. Their works represent a new level of awareness of the social environment and the acknowledgement of its fundamental influence on human existence.

All the disciplines that saw the light around the end of the 19th century and exploded in the 20th – anthropology, ethnology, sociology and obviously psychology – set great store on the part played by society in the formation of

Paola Maestroni, *Nobody Knows*, 2004.

the individual. More specifically these included the following psychological schools and currents: behavioral psychology, social psychology, the systemic and field theories, the subsequent developments of psychoanalysis in the French sphere with Jacques Lacan, Gilles Deleuze and Félix Guattari, and in particular Julia Kristeva; the theoreticians of object relations in England; the culturalist current – which included economic and political forces and cultural conditioning among the determinants of human nature – in the United States; up to hypothesizing, with Erich Fromm, the existence of a "social unconscious." Nor was there a lack of particular approaches and theories, such as Gérard Mendel's sociopsychoanalysis and J.L. Moreno's sociometry, or other admixtures that produced, among others, a "transcultural" branch both in psychology and in psychiatry.

The purpose of this synthetic excursus is to delineate a new field in which the figure of the foreigner, included among the diversities to be respected, cannot help but take on new meanings and positions (Ancis 2004, Fernando 2004, Kottler et al. 2004, Laungani 2004, Leff 1988, Mio and Iwamasa 2004, Papadopoulos 2002).

Even so, the experience of being foreign is no longer what it once was. One leaves one place to go to another, which often is not all that different in the case of the urban life of advanced societies, but where a different language is spoken. In that case one is a foreigner only because of the language and communication. One leaves behind a certain type of food, habits, a lifestyle, and if one wishes this too can be found at a great geographical distance, so that it is not necessary to adapt to something different, but one also loses the stimuli and advantages. Traveling is no longer fatiguing, a challenge, an adventure towards something new. Integrating oneself in a new country is no longer very different from adapting to one's own society, in which, in some passages, the individual can feel as excluded and marginalized as an immigrant who has just stepped off the boat. The experience of belonging to one's own community, the community itself, the customs and the relations that constitute it are no longer what they once were (Liotta 2003, 2006).

There is something ambivalent and disturbing underlying the general loosening of the bonds between man and the earth that is often advanced as a benefit and a sign of progress. The figure of the foreigner becomes the subject of commercial exaltation or social negation, becomes a literary and intellectual metaphor or the object of collective diffidence.

Apart from bureaucratic definitions, various sociologists and psychologists deal with the problem of defining what a foreigner is, together with the concepts of cultural or collective identity and integration, with a demystifying approach that reveals the conventionality and arbitrariness upon which discriminating paradigms and unjust laws are based (Kozakai 2002).

Actually, however, today the adult still tends to be suspicious of anyone who does not belong to his clan, tends to join those who resemble him, to constitute groups and homogeneous subgroups, for interests or other characteristics, up to the mafias and all the corporations that manage power, selecting and defining the enemy. The foreigner, extraneous or diverse, is the obvious choice. In the face of the irrepressible power of ethnic, racial and cultural conflicts, discussions regarding terminology, concepts and ideologies seem to be no more than erudite and academic disquisitions.

Moving ahead, with respect to the word and idea of "diversity," moving beyond the otherness – which I introduced in the first chapter to highlight the relational dimension – at this point I would also propose concepts such as: particularity; specificity, in the sense of what I called "its own form," neither the same nor different from others; together with the general ideas of coexistence, com-presence, pluralism, multiplicity, varieties of the "forms," which seem to correspond more closely, on the level of intentions, to what should come to a head in reality.

An approach of this sort would make it possible for everyone to bear witness to his own religious faith, with or without a veil, with or without a crucifix, dressed in one way or another, without giving offense to anyone. Why not leave them all instead of eliminating them all?

Ethnopsychoanalysis and psychotherapy

> Try as we may to concentrate on the most personal of personal problems,
> our therapy nevertheless stands or falls with the question: what sort of
> world does our patient come from and to what sort of world has he to
> adapt himself? The World is a supra-personal fact to which an essentially
> personalistic psychology can never do justice. Such a psychology only
> penetrates to the personal element in man. But insofar as he is also a part
> of the world, he carries the world in himself.
>
> (Jung 1942:95)

Supported by Jung's affirmations, I shall now attempt to deal with the specific
condition of the foreigner who for some reason asks the psychotherapist for
help, thus becoming what I have generically defined as the "foreign patient."

When psychopathology becomes manifest in an adult, the psychological
changes – which never stop in the course of life, because they move together
with the adaptation to the external and internal environment – have evidently
been arrested, faced with an adaptation the forces at his disposal cannot cope
with. This is what we call a crisis.

Immigration creates an objective crisis situation, a test. Just how serious it
is, and to what extent it can be dealt with, depends on the strengths available.
The migrant who doesn't make it will sooner or later need help from outside.
This is where psychotherapy steps in and seeks to understand, clarify, restruc-
ture, bear witness to the crisis and past psychological damage, if any, and
see why the capacity for adaptation is unable to cope with the present crisis.
The history of the damage is reconstructed and then an attempt is made to
heal it as much as possible through the corrective experience of the therapeutic relationship: individual or in a group, in a public service or a private
setting.

A word of clarification is in order with my criticism of the psychoanalytical
premises. For example, there could be a risk in therapy with a foreign patient
of attributing the origins of the anxiety or other symptoms to an "Oedipus
conflict," which may well be part of a more general picture of malaise with
regard to the crisis of adaptation. Some psychoanalysts believe that "letting
a multitude of cultural psychologies inherent in every ethnic group flourish
with the idea of a super-determination of culture over psychism" is "dangerous" and "in complete disagreement" with the vision, for example of Tobie
Nathan's ethnopsychoanalysis (Dahoun, in Algini and Lugones 1999). The
specialists might "go off track" theoretically in working with migrant
patients when faced with the cultural difference and this would influence their
disposition towards the patient. Or they might accept these differences in a
stereotyped and classificatory way.

As a Jungian psychoanalyst – is this the only difference? – I see the danger
of psychoanalytical ethnocentrism rather than that of cultural psychologies.

The destructuring of so-called normal or healthy mental functioning is not due only to psychogenic, internal, psychoanalytically important causes. It can also take place with the ingestion of chemical substances, the degeneration of cerebral tissues, great traumatic events such as wars, natural calamities, other serious episodes that involve individuals and groups. This is why the modalities of "crisis intervention" were created first, followed by a more in-depth psychology of the emergency.

One never knows what effects a difficult or unsuccessful migration, expulsion or other dramatic alienation will have on a given personality until it happens. Drawing conclusions about hypothetical and precedent mental illnesses is therefore not really legitimate.

In some situations it is too easy to say that the patient is now in a crisis because he was already fragile. Natural and human frailties can always become psychological symptoms if submitted to the pressure of a traumatic event – known as "culture shock" in literature on migration – and the event by right plays a part in the structural component of the nosographic picture. This happens in the case of mourning too, for example, which is considered an event that has its natural and physiological implications.

The "trauma theory" had been abandoned by psychoanalysts for quite some time, a result of periodic changes in paradigms, which includes psychological theories, when concepts basic to their work and the life of their patients disappear from one day to the next as a new theory appears on the horizon. Now though the trauma theory is making a comeback (Kalsched 1996) thanks to research, clinical experience and a variety of multiple and cumulative factors.

I'll go even further. I am not trying to revive Freud's original trauma theory, and I have no intention of basing my views only on the general idea of childhood traumas as specific events or as a deficiency of primary relationships. All this exists and of course can have a powerful influence on the life of the individual. What I want to do is highlight the trauma in an adult age, to observe it as such, before reducing it, taking it back, extrapolating it, attempting to interpret it in the light of theories matured in child observation, although this has enriched my perspectives and the breadth of my interpretations.

Through its psychopathological correlates migration clearly becomes a traumatic event, especially when it takes place in extreme situations, calamity, forced exile, poverty, flight or other dramatic circumstances: unfortunately generally the case today in migration episodes that involve the public psychiatric services. My experience in supervising teams that work with political and humanitarian refugees and some direct interventions with individuals, families and small groups has refined my perception of the pertinent psychological aspects. Degrees in quantity and quality make a big difference, and the appropriate modalities of reception and cure are learnt through experience, free from stereotypes and idealized visions (unless one were to believe that all migrants could be classified, *ante litteram*, as persons who were already psychologically "at risk").

Those who maintain that migration in itself is not traumatic, but that it becomes traumatic because it reactivates preceding emotional experiences, end up by sanctioning a clear difference among the individuals involved. If the subject is psychologically healthy, he will overcome the crisis and open the way for the rebirth of his creative capacities. Otherwise the crisis will reveal his illness. There is something tautological in affirmations of this kind: he who succeeds, succeeds. Or an optimistic vision which refers to mental health consisting in "not having had preceding traumas." But who is in such a fortunate condition, and where? It is practically impossible to be psychologically healthy and well balanced when faced with certain challenges of life. By taking the extreme into consideration it becomes clear that external events and conditions, in different measure, will always play a part in determining psychological health.

Re-evaluating the traumatic aspect of the migratory event, at whatever age it took place, is useful as a way to reconnect soul and earth. If leaving a land is a trauma and putting down roots in another is a long and complex process, then that means that the land – and everything it means – is vitally important.

I therefore fully agree with Nathan's vision: the fruit of the encounter between cultural anthropology, George Devereux's ethnopsychiatry and the more open psychoanalysis, a fruit based on the fundamental contribution of the migratory phenomenon in France. In his *Principi di etnopsicoanalisi*, Nathan maintains:

> Long and intense clinical experience has shown me that work of a psychoanalytical type with patients from Black Africa, the Maghreb, the French-speaking islands of the Indian Ocean, from the Asiatic Southeast is possible only if the original theory of the clinician is modified. An attitude among psychoanalysts has always been that, at least from a psychological point of view, the only thing that distinguishes these patients from others is a thin superficial layer; in fact for our colleagues culture is like a garment. It is therefore not necessary to modify either one's conceptual picture or the therapeutic technique. Affirming universality *a priori* has long imprisoned us in ignorance on one of the principal dimensions of human psychism. This is why the word that means race often means "human being": Inuit means "man" for the Inuit Eskimos; yanoman means "man" for the Brazilian Yanoami and so on . . . In no case does this mean a shutting out of the world or a primary xenophobia of the traditional societies, but it is a recognition, by each of these cultures, of a paradoxical reality: one is not human if one is not at the same time Inuit, Yanoman, Guayaki, Douala. In other terms: no one has ever met that hypothetical universal human shown us by psychoanalytical thought.
>
> (Nathan 1996:99; translated from the Italian by transl.)

There can be no doubt but that it is easier to work in psychotherapy with a single theoretical model and that developing a more complex approach, in which there are no superdetermining theories, implies a capacity to stay completely with the patient, with his internal world, his culture, his trauma. It also implies a psychotherapeutic preparation with leeway for doubt, criticism, comparison, collateral disciplines, and with field research, which have meanwhile led to a relativization of some of the certainties of classic psychoanalysis.

At this point continuing with the usual false alternative – whether in the end foreign patients should or should not be treated like all the others – seems useless. In psychotherapy one works with individuals, couples or small groups, persons who come bringing themselves and their burdens to be shared for a while with the therapist. Every patient is particular, special, unique. If a foreigner, he will have something more: a world, a land, traditions, which will speak to the psychotherapist who knows how to listen to these voices and dreams.

The epistemological approach closest to what this group of patients requires, in addition to that inspired by ethnopsychoanalysis, is the phenomenological–existential approach, within which the various psychoanalyses and psychotherapies can each maintain their own particularities.

In the analyst's room: words and images

In this concluding chapter, space does not permit me to discuss in detail the case studies I followed for many years. Nor do I choose to. A general summary is sufficient. This is not meant to be a technical manual, but I invite my colleagues who work with foreign patients, occasionally or regularly, to consider the specific aspects of their situation and not forget to take account of the fact that their experiences have left their mark.

An exclusive use of the traditional theoretical model of attachment–separation, which at first sight might seem the most appropriate, would not let the psychodynamic complexity surrounding the experience of migration emerge. This includes at one and the same time a reconstruction of the life of the patient (where I come from), an investigation of his identity (who I am), the prospects of adaptation now and in the future (where I am and where I am going). In synthesis, attachment and separation seem to come to the fore more forcibly (or just as forcibly) with regard to the places and the spatial dimension – more affected by the event of detachment – than with regard to the persons and the temporal dimension, as is the case in the development of non-migrant individuals.

Around the end of the 1980s, after working for years with foreign patients in therapy and as psychological counselor with foreign students and teachers, I felt the need to compare my experiences with those of other colleagues who had had the same personal and professional development. The subject that interested us, as we discovered together, was not specifically dealt with in our psychoanalytical training, even of different theoretical orientation, nor had much light been thrown on it during our respective personal analysis. We had to make do on our own, working out the details of our condition, hidden under a good linguistic, cultural and professional adaptation that we ourselves had never dealt with, thanks to the unconscious attitude the migrant sets in motion in adapting himself to the new environment, toning down the differences. But patients also take us back to our personal problems, and therefore in speaking of them we also went on with our personal investigation. We formed a discussion group that had as object the theme of the cultural roots of identity (Antonieta Cervini, Paola Carducci, Maria Paternò, Ursula Prameshuber and, occasionally, other colleagues).

As our studies got under way, we found it odd that the theoretical–clinical attention of the psychoanalysts was not comparable to the growing number of immigrants. After all, the psychoanalysts themselves had been involved in migration. To begin with there was Freud, exiled towards the end of his life to London, and then Mahler, Spitz, Benedek, Bloss, Ekstein, the Grinbergs, the Fromms, Rank, Adler, the Deutsches, Alexander, Sachs, Erikson, Simmel, Rado, Fenichel, Hartmann, Horney, Reich, Kris and many others of the first generation, who emigrated to the United States, South America, or other European countries, such as Balint. The Jungian school in Italy owes its creation to a foreigner, Ernst Bernhard, a German Jew expatriate who fled to Rome during the Second World War. Bion and Masud Khan were born in India and in Pakistan, Matte Blanco in Chile. The list is long. In subsequent generations, many analysts changed countries for study, work, family, other interests, personally experiencing and entering in contact, in their work, with patients who were linguistically, ethnically and culturally different.

With time not only have the foreign patients increased, but in the past 30 years the foreign analysts and the literature on the subject have also finally been notably enriched. In 1992 I presented a paper at a National Congress of Analytical Psychology, in the name of our work group, at a round table called *The Ambivalence of the Therapeutic Field*. The title of the paper was "The foreigner in analysis: a metaphor of distance," from which some of the contents of this chapter have been taken. At the time I mentioned the Grinbergs' work, the book by J. Amati Mehler, S. Argentieri and J. Canestri, and J. Kristeva' s *Strangers to ourselves*, where the author maintained the non-translatability of the pre-verbal into the verbal, and therefore the presence of a factor of a perhaps irreducible discontinuity that produces the condition of foreigner, in a broad and metaphoric sense as well. I spoke of Merleau-Ponty and the "*Logos* of the stranger", of Camus, of Ulysses, of nostalgia and other themes developed in this book.

I maintained that having a foreign patient in psychotherapy introduced a discontinuity into the therapeutic field analogous, on a minor scale, to what immigration is creating in the political and economic setups in the world. In both cases it is a question of making room for the diverse. In the philosophical and anthropological contexts talk was then of xenology – from the Greek *ksénos*, foreigner – as the branch of philosophical knowledge whose object is the foreigner, in the sense however of being extraneous, i.e. diverse.

With the passage of time, this specific point has undoubtedly gained space and strength, mainly due to a more widespread counteractant education aimed at respecting all types of diversity, not only ethnic. Then time itself gradually worked in favor of integration, despite the difficulties and conflicts lying in wait. Then came the fashions, the music, art in general: all vehicles for mutual encounter, communication and knowledge.

These philosophical approaches, seen in the light of more recent developments, still considered the foreign patient in a metaphorical sense. This may be because in the cultural atmosphere of that period the illusion of creating a more receptive mentality was the mark of a more highly educated vision, which included metaphor and symbol as well as the thing in itself.

It may also be because getting down to the basics – I have the picture of the illegal immigrants in Italy who survived their journey, of the children sent to beg, the puzzled eyes of the women of color and the fierce eyes of the Slavic women – strikes a certain fear or sense of shame, and because psychoanalysis will always take refuge behind some code, some kind of hermeneutics that keeps it at a distance. The right distance, it is said, to understand better.

An intellectual approach to psychoanalysis is extremely risky for psychotherapy, for it tends to keep emotions at bay. The absolute priority that verbal communication assumes in analysis – specifically its primary and defining character of a "talking cure" – and the creation of a setting that in principle precludes types of exchange that are not mediated by the word, may erroneously authorize this drift.

In a session, what does not become word – not only because it is unconscious, but because it cannot be said or listened to – will remain cut off, above all if, as in the case of the foreign patient, the analyst is not contextually sensitized.

Imagine then a patient who is forced to use a language he does not know well, which is not in keeping with his communication needs, or another language in which he can express himself well but which is not his own, that has no emotional undertones or echoes, that has no roots in his memory.

A profound and special sensitivity to the relationship between mother tongue and foreign language in psychoanalysis is at the basis of the above-mentioned study by the Freudian colleagues (Amati Mehler et al. 1993), *The Babel of the Unconscious*, which opens with the question, today rather common, of whether being bilingual or plurilingual is a problem or an opportunity, a defect or a treasure. The book analyzes the way in which experience, affects, memory and word interact within the possibilities presented by plurilinguism, for both patient and analyst, and observes to what extent the alternation of languages plays a part in the structuring of subjectivity.

It would be long and complicated to extrapolate and interconnect many of the interesting observations in the book with my discussion. At the time they showed themselves to be extremely useful for me and for my patients.

But since I have chosen to deal particularly with the relationship between earth, places and the soul, submitted to the trauma of migration and expressed above all in literary, poetical, oneiric and fantastic images, the linguistic problem, though important, has been relegated to second place. Besides which, the abovementioned book says it all anyway.

The priority Jung gives to the imaginary level and my clinical experience with sandplay focused my attention on the "language of images," observed in its "universal and archetypal" form, as well as in its "cultural" and "personal" components. I could see the "cultural unconscious" in action.

For a multicultural psychotherapy

The scientific knowledge of the external world owes its progress to the development of the spatial conception . . . The lagging behind of our conceptions about mental phenomena would be linked to the rejection of space in their study.

Everyday and scientific language makes constant and inevitable use of space when referring to mental phenomena . . .

We may take at random some of the innumerable examples that could be given. For thinking processes: *transparent, sharp, obtuse, nebulous, deep, superficial, tangled, tortuous, obscure, confused* thinking.

We may conclude with certainty that *our conceptions of the mind are completely permeated with spatial comparison* . . . The only reasonable attitude, therefore, is taking seriously the concept of space in the study of mental phenomena.

(Matte Blanco 1975/1988:403–407)

Ignacio Matte Blanco subsequently developed the intent expressed in this quote in *Thinking, Feeling and Being* (1988), devoting more than one chapter to space, always on the level of the logic that structures the unconscious.

Space, the subject of the fourth chapter in this book, is a multiple and inexhaustible dimension. A foreign patient is a patient like all the others, but he finds himself in a space that is different from his usual space. For the foreigner who stays longer, this space at a certain point becomes familiar, but his relationship with his original space will never be cancelled. On a different level, this happens to everyone and everywhere, in view of the different spaces where one lived throughout one's life, reconstructing one's own story of places known.

But what about the role of the psychotherapist, who offers another new space for the soul of the patient? It would be easy at this point to maintain that in order to understand and treat the migratory experience one would have to have lived in some way or the other the same event, and therefore be a "foreign psychotherapist." One could also recommend that the analysis be conducted by an analyst who speaks the patient's language, even if he does not come from the same country. Moreover, whether one works with patients whose origins are the same, in one's own country or elsewhere, or, thanks to linguistic skills, patients from other nationalities are accepted, it is obvious that being acquainted with the difficulties and experiences of uprooting and integration in a new country will make it easier for both.

Even so, the mother tongue of the patients may not be one of the most commonly used languages, or there may be no psychotherapists who speak that language where they live, or they may already feel competent enough to undertake a complicated dialogue, such as that of psychology, in the new language. In any case, although the situation may not be ideal – as if they were at home, in their own country – a good therapist will still be able to go on with the treatment and provide the patients with a starting point for individuative processes.

When there is sufficient verbal comprehension the analyst can simply tap similar experiences of his own to create the necessary empathy and under-standing. These may include having to move as a child, a family decision where the child has no say, or an unhappy few weeks in a summer camp, or a visit abroad where the language was not understood and orientation in a different culture was difficult. Or, more simply, he can refer to inverse clinical situations: patients of the same nationality and language who narrate their past migratory experiences or travels, who find themselves having to deal with foreigners, in various circumstances, such as having a partner of another nationality. There is no dearth of occasions, they just have to be identified and arranged around the theme.

If the analyst speaks the same language and belongs to or knows the culture of the patient thoroughly – as in my case and in that of my colleagues in the abovementioned study group – the analyst's room can become a sort of *psychological embassy*, a safe and welcoming place that will protect the interests of the patient and where he can continue the inner development that was shattered in some other geographical place. In a sense it becomes "a transplanting greenhouse," where the plant can put down roots while coming to grips, in the external space, with diversity and occasionally exclusion.

In analysis, close-up observation of the patient's migratory experience makes the therapist observe his own personal reactions, the dynamics known technically as "countertransference." A general countertransference towards the foreign patients project an unconscious aura upon their provenience. Knowing that a person comes from one place or another and following their individual stories will activate an additional unconscious imaginary level that can sometimes be stereotyped in the attempt to fill in the distance with preconstituted knowledge. On the contrary, if the patient comes from our own parts, there is a risk that his particular situation may seem to be less out of the ordinary, in view of a reception that is taken for granted or experiences that are too close to ours. Other features of the relationship created will vary depending on the cultural combinations between analyst and patient. One might rightly say that this happens with all patients, but countertransference is not normally considered in the light of geographical provenience, elements of a cultural, linguistic nature, and the like, unless they become salient aspects, conflictually or otherwise. In the case of the foreign patient, however, all this is already in the foreground.

The fact that I too had experiences similar to those of my patients or that I spoke their language in the course of analysis did not necessarily lessen rather marked cultural differences. I was not familiar with all the cultures nor did I have a specific knowledge of them, and I had not visited all the countries from which my patients came.

Furthermore, always with regard to my sampling, the patients came from an environment that had already been mediated, that international world which embraces persons of countries far from each other and at times also at war. However, what they did have in common was the English language, the style of life, similar educational and working backgrounds, shared acquaintances and places. The original cultural identities in these cases are less evident and not as obviously flaunted.

It is more difficult to capture the differences, and therefore respect them, when on the surface they all appear alike and part of the same model of life.

Having mentioned the reductive risks of Freudian psychoanalysis, a similar danger exists in Jungian analysis.

The Jungian analyst, while not ignoring the Freudian model – in particular the post-Freudian with its wealth of technical and theoretical suggestions – bases himself on the central pilasters of Jung's work: the collective unconscious, the archetypes, the process of individuation, the objective and complex psyche, the Self, and so on, which may seem to be more pervious to multicultural aspects and more open to what is new and different. This freedom, theoretically and clinically inferred, is also evident in the aperture to other channels of communication besides the verbal – such as the techniques of imagination or the use of expressive and creative modalities and materials in general that can help solve the language problem in the case of foreign patients. But even then there is a risk of over-simplification. The interpretation of such materials may stress the universality of the archetypes and end up by obscuring the variety of cultural experiences. What appears as an initial relief to someone who feels he is a foreigner – "basically we are all the same and psychologically rotate around a limited number of archetypes" – ends up by mortifying the uniqueness of the expression of that archetype in the life of every individual. This uniqueness is always defined, and at the same time limited, by the earth and by time.

Aside from the theories of the founders of the schools, there is also a reductivism on a minor scale: the one set in motion in the analyst's room, especially if the presence of foreign/extraneous elements in the relational field produces an unconscious resistance in the therapist that leads him to use only a part of the theoretical background that we might call "the lowest common psychodynamic denominator." What does not correspond to this code of interpretation thus enters into a zone of indifference, as if the foreigner, with regard to the laws of analysis, did not exist at all. It is not a question of racism, or refusal, but the absence of a full mental reception.

If the purpose of a Jungian analysis is to help the process of individuation come to the fore and facilitate its development, the ethnic and cultural components must also be seen in the right light and their importance evaluated because, ignored or recognized, the patient's land of origin will in any case be there between himself and the analyst, stimulating fantasies, images, ideas, energies in the minds of both that risk remaining at an unconscious level.

This inner zone that I frequently refer to – the intermediate link between the collective unconscious in a broad sense and the personal unconscious, defined by other Jungians as the "cultural unconscious" – could also be qualified as the "geographic" or "environmental" unconscious, or with reference to the group to which the person belongs. It might also be considered a "social" or "group" unconscious, as is the case in some group therapy approaches.

Various interesting clinical experiences and related theoretical elaborations confirm Jung's hypothesis, enriched by the contribution of Bion. Among them are W.G. Lawrence's "social dreaming" and the "transpersonal" current of studies, which, inspired by Bion, connects the individual and the group, in the basic language and at the pre-verbal level.

Social dreaming is a discipline for discovering the social meaning and significance of dreams through sharing them with others. It starts from different assumptions than individual, therapeutic dreaming, because the systemic nature of dreaming was recognized and affirmed from the beginning. Not only do dreamers dream from their ecological niche, but also they dream themes that are systemically related.

This is done by the deliberate and sustained method of free association and amplification through the social dreaming TM matrix (Lawrence 2003, 2005, 2007).

Theoretically and clinically the most sensitive point is how to associate this collective, systemic unconscious with individual and group experiences of the community of one's origins and that of the new country.

In the case of Jungian psychology, the needs, stimulated by clinical experience, for a more in-depth-theoretical approach concerning the connections between archetypes, archetypal images and the cultural unconscious, and other cultural aspects of identity and their relationship with the concepts worked out by Jung of *Persona, Shadow, Animus/Anima* and *Self*, come to the fore.

Freud, Jung and the *genius loci*

A few more words about the human side of the therapeutic professions, with regard to the fathers of psychoanalysis.

Psychoanalysts of course are also vulnerable. They are people who may be afflicted by the same problems they are trying to cure, to the point of having been defined as "wounded healers." Both Freud and Jung had particular conflictual experiences with regard to soul and earth, with strong reactions to a few particular places: Freud had what he defined as a "disturbance of memory" on the Acropolis in Athens (Freud 1936) and Jung had a long and difficult relationship with the city of Rome, which he never succeeded in visiting.

Freud, who loved to travel, also suffered anxiety with regard to traveling by train. In 1904 he was subject to a "feeling of extraneousness" and mental confusion when he visited the Acropolis in Athens. Faced with a place so full of history and fame, suddenly he felt himself split between fantasy, recollection and reality, between his youthful expectations and the overwhelming impact of the experience. He interpreted this imbalance, to which he returned frequently over the years, in the light of the processes of depersonalization, unusual states of consciousness in which the personality splits to defend itself, during which the mind asks itself, incredulous and anxious: "But is it real? Am I really here? It's too beautiful to be real." The core of the disturbance, for Freud, was the repression of his past as a "poor gymnasium student" compared to the subsequent "having covered so much ground." The discourse was broadened to the general sense of his traveling, which he discovered was to satisfy the unsatisfied youthful desires of his family of origin. The experiences included a strong "sense of guilt" with regard to the satisfaction, guilt with regard to his father, since "success meant going further than the father." In this case the place "Acropolis" disappears behind the father figure.

But what had really happened to Freud?

The various experiences described by Graziella Magherini in her book *La Sindrome di Stendhal* (1989) are more dramatic and concern states of anxiety, crises of panic, depressive anxiety, somatic malaise with exhaustion and excitation, that bring the tourist to seek medical aid. The text, in addition to being a general treatment of the journey from the historical–cultural point of view, and of Freud's travels in particular, contains a psychoanalytical interpretation of what is now known as the Stendhal syndrome – inspired by the title dedicated to Stendhal and the psychological narration of his travels to Italy – accompanied by the results of a study on patients in the Hospital of S. Maria Novella in Florence.

The power of the esthetic experience in the cities of art seems to be at the origin of the syndrome, in the sense of triggering profound unconscious dynamics, which once they have surfaced and been treated lead to creative developments of the personality. Magherini, who also takes up the story told by Freud and interprets the phenomenon and its causes in general, goes further than the Freudian version of the feeling of guilt with regard to his father. She draws from D.W. Winnicott the theories on the true and false Self and the transitional area where the esthetic experience takes place. She turns to Meltzer for his theories on beauty, and to Bion for the "emotional thinking" and the "catastrophic change" implied in the experience of knowledge.

This is not the place to linger over these concepts, but their authors certainly offer different keys, within psychoanalytical thought, useful in understanding the psychological impact of the migratory phenomenon and, as in part already noted, the general relationship between soul and earth.

With Jung, just as impassioned a traveler as Freud, things become more mysterious. There was one place – the city of Rome, particularly desired – that had a powerful emotional charge. But this man who went just about everywhere in the world, and was ready to face places that were equally fraught with psychological meaning, never succeeded in visiting Rome. During his travels Jung had also had a number of episodes of the Stendhal syndrome: overwhelming emotions, phenomena of synchronicity and everything else that corresponded to his personality and his vision of life. This interdiction with regards to Rome is mentioned by Jung in terms that vary in the course of his life but in a sense remain incomprehensible to the analytical psychologist. They included fear he would not live up to the impression the city would have made, feeling he had secret obligations to Rome with regard to his unconscious that prohibited him from making a short visit to the city: he looked at it only from afar, on a ship going to Naples, and felt the power of its historical stratifications, marveling at the ease with which people went, as if it were just one among the other important cities in the world. None of these seem sufficient justifications to an analyst.

In my old age – in 1949 – I wished to repair this omission, but was stricken with a faint while I was buying tickets. After that the plans for a trip to Rome were once and for all laid aside.

(Jung 1963:319)

Psychoanalysts too have their dark zones. A Freudian interpretation of Jung's resistance might have invoked a sense of guilt towards his father, a Protestant pastor, with respect to Catholic Rome, or recalling the "mystical participation" so often mentioned by Jung. Yet other places and circumstances, such as Africa, which he visited, would seem more likely to trigger a preventive anxiety with regard to the idea of losing oneself or being overcome.

I rather think that if not Rome, it would have been some other place: a concept that I believe corresponds to Jung's spirit. He needed a place where he should not or could not go, a "taboo place." For that is what the human psyche requires, because myth, ritual, sacrifice, archetypes and the collective unconscious are important parts of Jung's analytical psychology, with which this prohibition is fully in keeping.

His gradual withdrawal into the Tower of Bollingen is rather like his renunciation of the broadest and most collective thing imaginable, the *caput mundi* city that synthesized the entire history of the West. It is a loss, a giving up, a sacrifice of the age-old, worldly, collective place in favor of an experience of the place that can be assimilated to the temple, the atrium, the "enclosed empty space" as a dwelling of the individuated Self, soul and body.

Moreover, whatever Jung had to say, it seems to me that there is little of the "Roman" in the spirit of his analytical psychology, and that Jung had absorbed everything that Rome could offer without going there, via his erudite culture.

I don't know if Jung would agree with this interpretation of mine, but sometimes putting together the contents of the work of an author, his biography, his personality and hindsight, one can succeed in glimpsing a different interpretative thread.

The patients

After these historical and theoretical observations, I will now describe my experiences with foreign patients from a clinical point of view.

First of all, the language I mostly used was English and not Spanish, the language of my early childhood together with Italian, my family's mother tongue. But English had already entered my life in childhood, for it was the only language spoken by Mildred, a colored woman from Trinidad who lived with us in Caracas.

Rome, where I lived and worked for many years, with its many public and private international institutions of a political, military, religious, cultural, commercial and other nature, is full of foreigners and English is the language used by the population of this community of persons of all ages, proveniences and professions. I practiced psychotherapy with English, Irish, American, Canadian, Australian, New Zealand, and South African patients in their language but also with continental Europeans, Slavs, North Africans, and with Asians, Indians, Japanese and others, always in English. Those who came to me most often were young students in a psychological or psychiatric crisis, various professionals and artists in unlimited sojourns, teachers, journalists, travelers who had fallen under the spell of Italy or were in search of their origins, diplomats and employees of foreign institutions, medium- or long-term residents.

The language of each psychotherapy was a peculiar mixture: for example, with some South Americans, who spoke English as well as Spanish, we used both languages and some Italian that sooner or later almost all introduce in line with their gradual integration and spontaneous needs of communication. In speaking I also adapted unconsciously to the accent of each patient.

The wanderings and difficulties of some of my patients and the stories of their families echoed mine, so that I was able to empathize fully with their experiences, and understand the specific difficulties that, despite the difference in time and place, and even in the more favorable conditions, afflicted all the migrants.

Voluntary exile – leaving the land of your origins for a better life elsewhere, or staying where one initially went to study or work or as a tourist – is a choice with psychological motivations, often unconscious, which mature with time, emerging further on in life and putting things into turmoil. This is why, aside from the success of the migration and the attachment for the new country, there are so many returns, even only temporary, to the country of origin.

The most frequent reason for the presence of my patients in Italy was work or study. Often the problems for which they came to me involved work, career, or symptomatologies for which they were already being treated in their country, difficulties in relating to others, and various themes where aspects regarding migration or cultural identity were not apparent. The working situation, as a reason for the therapy, concerned men and women equally. In general, and compared with Italian patients, I had a higher percentage of men among the foreign patients. And also of gay patients, both men and women.

In the second place, in this personal classification of mine, were family reasons, mixed marriages of an Italian with a foreign woman – more frequent than the Italian woman with a foreigner – or Italian family backgrounds with the "return to the origins" journey of later generations.

In the third place was a tourist stay which ended up, often in the case of artists or scholars, in choosing to stay longer, find a job or living more or less frugally on an annuity.

Whatever the case, aside from those of the military or diplomats who generally bring their families to the country they are assigned to, in most of the situations I observed there was a voluntary choice of transfer, which had set off expectations with regard to Italy, and Rome in particular, and naturally to its inhabitants, often with rather stereotyped images, both positive and negative. The strata of the cultural and geographical unconscious, the presence of the lands of origin, of nostalgia, together with the revisitation of the path undertaken, of the motivations for departure, of why they were in Italy, emerged in all these psychotherapies – some short and centered on the crisis; most of the others lasting at least three years, with some turning into real psychoanalyses lasting between six and eight years. All these elements, in various cases of apparently successful adaptation, were manifested initially by imperceptible signals, which I succeeded in identifying and codifying only as my clinical experience matured.

Probably in many successful migrations, with happy landings in places that are loved more than those of one's origins, where space and nourishment are found for development in society as well as for psychological individuation – all cases that rarely require the support of a psychotherapist – the life and context preceding migration remain, so to speak, defused: not necessarily repressed, but set in the past and free from psychopathogenic cores.

The community of foreigners

A subject that I have not yet seen treated in literature relative to the theme we are dealing with is that of "the community of foreigners," those who live comfortably integrated in the capitals of the advanced society of today. In the course of my work I have gradually drawn up a map of this community, its places, institutions and traditions, its rituals, based also on the interconnections that emerged from what my patients told me. It can be compared to living in a town within a large city.

My reflections on this collective aspect are not however limited to the analyst's room. I taught psychology for several years and have served as

Paola Maestroni, *Tobacco Road*, 2004.

specialized advisor in various foreign universities and schools. I also attended other foreign institutions, and have spoken and exchanged ideas with experts in the field of international policies, with foreign colleagues abroad and with others who work in the public health structures, thus bringing other points of view to my clinical experience. In addition, more recently, I devoted part of my practice to the problems of refugees, which provided me with a point of view that contrasted with that furnished by the group of fortunate migrants and gave me a more complete overall panorama.

On the whole the general picture echoes international public opinion, and the figure of the foreigner is still saddled with stereotypes and unilateralism, similar to the idea the migrant has of the country that receives him. Contradictions remain. On one hand, the foreigner is seen as a good worker who succeeds in integrating while maintaining his traditions more or less jealously, reconstituting his community in specific areas of the city, to which the various Chinatowns, or the Italian, Irish, Arabian, Turkish districts scattered throughout the various metropolises of the world bear witness. This is the foreigner, a poor migrant, whose children will go to the university, perhaps with a scholarship, will be successful in life and become valid citizens of the new country.

On the other hand the immigrant is seen as a dangerous element, an occasional delinquent or a member of organized crime in a mafia of some kind. There is a core of reality in both points of view, magnified by the aura of the cinema, one of the most important mass media sources of sociocultural conditioning today. This dangerous foreigner is, however, no longer recognizable. Just as the cultural, linguistic and folkloristic features are gradually fading in a globalized society, organized crime is becoming harder to identify and is more subtly threatening. Traffic of organs, pedophilia, the new forms of slavery, in addition to traditional crimes, are creating a disturbing shadow of the system where the foreigner collaborates with the local citizen, both dependent on mafia summits situated who knows where, thanks to the help of the new communication technologies. They all exploit those they can, everywhere.

In the collective unconscious of the advanced society, the mythical "divine foreigner" is being transformed into the bearer of potential threats for its inhabitants. He is, if nothing else, a foreigner who takes what little work there is from the locals, a man who could be a criminal and who, moreover, is in some cases also privileged by the institutions. In Italy there have been complaints because public services have guaranteed free diapers to the infants of immigrant and indigent mothers.

These are general observations, for individuals of the same geographic and cultural provenience coexist with others from different social groups in the country of immigration itself. There is the poor migrant and there is the affluent student, the embassy employee, the artist, etc. It is striking that, today as in the past, the differences and discriminations to be found in any society are reproduced abroad in the microcommunities that are reconstructed there. In these cases the interests of the social class predominate over those of a common geographic origin.

The new transversal land, ever more densely populated, is the far-flung territory designed by the international corporations whose privileged members communicate in English, work with a computer, use extremely refined technologies, travel by air and by car, go here and there where everything stays the same except the landscape, which hovers between virtual, photographic, and film reality and where it is hard to say what is what.

In this new context, one's countryman, who speaks the same mother tongue and whose traditions one knows, but who is poor, uncultured and needy, who dresses in an old-fashioned way or is not sufficiently deodorized, is more of a foreigner than those who come from elsewhere but with whom one shares common interests. The non-European Union migrants or the clandestine are often ignored, looked down upon, kept at arm's length by their more fortunate fellow countrymen, all the more so if both belong to cultures that are weak in the overall international picture. It is like being ashamed of poor relatives.

The differences between the country of origin and that of migration, when connected to childhood, to the sensorial and bodily levels, to identification with family and ancestors, remain powerfully present, even in the attempt to deny or overcome them in order to be more swiftly integrated into the hosting society. One example among many is that of a young African musician who insisted on his American origins, although he was not born in and had never been to the United States, counting on a distant relative who lived there. He thought he would be more easily accepted as a Black American than as an African. Yet, in the wake of what Jung says in *Mind and Earth*, his African compared to his American nature was intuitively clear from the way he walked, with a slower and more flexuous gait, how he occupied space, how he gesticulated and smiled.

This ensemble of differences and the need to put them into some kind of harmonious relationship produce mediations that are sometimes eccentric, sometimes authentically creative, like genetic encounters and hybridizations, somewhat mysterious and with a great potential for development. This also appears in the unconscious of patients, creating original solutions, ranging from neologisms to behavior, to resolve their new position. In the course of psychotherapy, all this comes through in dreams, fantasies, sandplay images. A virtual place frequently appears at a certain point, created from nothing, which in the best of cases represents the right balance for that particular individual between his continuity and the discontinuity brought about by migration. It is a dynamic and vital balance, instead of a simple and flat adhesion or maintenance of a defensive distance. Something similar to what is called the Mid-Atlantic accent, acceptable on both sides of the Atlantic Ocean.

Moving on to another aspect, living abroad in general tends to weaken not only the national identity but also the habits, traditions, and the moral canons, the sense of the law, including social rules of a religious origin, with the emergence of a tendency that is transgressive although not necessarily delinquent. Persons feel that their original country no longer has any control over them, and not knowing the rules and laws of the new country, they do things they could never do in their community of origin. This was the case with some young people I was treating for drug abuse, who came from rather rigid cultures.

In addition to the distinction between the wealthy and the poor that also characterizes the homeland, the mechanism we analysts call "repression" is accentuated and generalized abroad, be they persons of culture, profiteers, or scions of influential families. Repression of one's country, of its aspects of poverty, weakness, or crudeness, vulgarity and whatever else might be unpleasant or distressing, at times turns into scapegoat mechanisms with unexpected and not always evident forms. Especially in the younger, as with the musician of African provenience, there is the denial of one's land, language and traditions and the desire to integrate as quickly as possible in the contemporary lifestyle where what is looked down upon in one's own country is appreciated, such as folklore. That of the other person always looks more interesting. The phenomena of devaluation and overestimation are particularly frequent both with regard to one's self-esteem and in social relations with others.

In my clinical experience I never witnessed strongly discriminating dynamics, although there were a few rare episodes of racism to which the colored patients had been subjected and which they told me about. Yet in a session these same persons who had been discriminated against because of the color of their skin complained, albeit very subtly, that cultured and affluent as they were, they had been put in the same category as their less fortunate immigrant countrymen: in other words, demeaning and discriminating against their own.

These processes can all be found in a relatively recent past, including migrations from the rural districts to the large cities, whether within the same country or from the south to the north of the same continent, with the relative disparagement of the farmer's life. Thanks to a renewed interest in the environment, this has now entered a stage of reversal. Meanwhile, however, the countryside has been abandoned, family farming practically no longer exists, the myth of the city has led to the megalopolis with its shantytown in the suburbs, while this see-saw of devaluation strikes the identity of entire generations, on both sides.

The repressed essence of the origins of one's family and culture continues to exist in a latent form in the psyche of the foreigner, where it can subsequently produce effects that are difficult to predict, as well as weakening the individual and making him easy prey to new types of conditioning. If he has not been conditioned by his land, his family, the community – his natural point of reference – he will be conditioned by something different and extraneous, such as the new country and its social system based on a money economy. And this is what happens to immigrants in the "rest of the world."

I have dealt at length with the community of foreigners because it exists and is always the background against which the patient must be observed: a sort of third psychological container, in addition to that of the land of origin and that of immigration.

A special situation: the mixed couple

Or more precisely the couple where the woman is a foreigner, partner of an Italian man. I have chosen this from any number of possible examples – at the risk of generalizing and banalizing a highly varied situation – because the life of the couple represents a highly significant field of observation for the dynamics that interests us. If love can't succeed in overcoming discrimination and intercultural differences, what else could ever succeed?

Naturally here I am dealing with women and couples who had problems. I know many mixed couples that are successful and would never renege on their original choice.

Many foreign women I have had in psychotherapy – in addition to those living alone, or together with partners of the same nationality or other nationalities – were partners of Italian men whom they had met abroad and with whom they then came to live in Italy. Other men had kept them in Italy after successfully courting them, rather like the cinema of the fifties and sixties where the object of male desire was the foreign woman, who was considered fair prey in the streets of Rome.

If marriage and the life of the couple are a challenge even for those who come from the same country, the complexity of the variables that come into play between a man and a woman from different countries, and speaking different languages, can easily be imagined.

The pattern of the problems encountered is fairly manifest, even in its most subterranean aspects. The title I would give the script is: "choosing what is different to eventually find oneself with what is the same" – that is, the same as the past with respect to one's own problematic psychological core. Or: "choosing the unfamiliar in order to avoid previous familiar traumas." Obviously these self-deceits are mixed with love and a real interest in the person and do not always lead to the termination of the relationship, neither more nor less than in the relationships between persons whose origins are the same.

Clinical experience has shown me that when a greater awareness of the unconscious dynamics came to the fore during psychotherapy, individual or in a couple, the temporary difficulties were always overcome. As far as I could see, and what others told me, mixed marriages did not seem to be weaker than traditional ones.

The origins of the appeal of the foreigner – in this case an Italian for a woman of another nationality – can unquestionably be found in part in the primary affective relations, but there is more to it than that. A free and healthy desire for something new plays a role in the initial unconscious part that contributes to the choice of a foreign partner. It might be described as a youthful, vital aspect of the *puer*, a psychological leaving of the family of origin, a confrontation with the unknown, with a certain physical aspect that sometimes contrasts strongly with that of the family, with more immediate and emotional ways of communication, in view of the linguistic difficulties almost always present. It is a sense of beginning all over in a new place, freed from the definition of oneself by the previous community, an opportunity that is felt to be exceptional, in the sense of outside of the norm. There is, indeed, also an element of transgression, of betrayal of the clan, of betrayal of the mother – or the father – even more accentuated than in normal situations.

In recent years, for example, the increasing presence of women from the Eastern European countries, and from Brazil and other South and Central American countries, has resulted in couples apparently based on an ideal simplification of the relationship that contrasts with the complexity that, for some men, makes relationships with Italian women difficult. I hope the Italian men won't object to what I have to say, but the male point of view is still focused on the nurturing, possessive Mediterranean mother, incomparable and inimitable. The personality traits of the foreign woman, not as demanding and less dominant because of her cultural conditioning, or because she comes from a socially inferior world, or simply because she is intimidated by the new context, provide the man with a possible escape from the equivocal primary affect, and at the same time a guarantee that the maternal figure will not be corroded by inadmissible comparisons.

Speaking of stereotypes (which often correspond to reality), the Anglo-Saxon or Nordic woman is, for example, quite different from the Italian mother/mother-in-law. Often of few words, austere, used to another way of managing the house and children, she tends to put up with the women of her husband's family, without being able to rebel. The one who is unhappy is, in fact, almost always the foreigner.

Most of the foreign women with whom I worked in psychotherapy had psychological and psychosomatic symptoms of a neurotic type, brought about by the stress of adapting to the new country, undertaken alone, without any other support outside of her husband's family, which was also the manifest cause of her symptoms. The arrival of one or more children often represented a still further emotional charge, leading to a reactivation of bonds with her country of origin and nostalgia, as well as a motive of conflict concerning ways of taking care of and educating the children.

When the mixed couple requested the initial consultation, it was generally followed by a few sessions of couples therapy. It then came about naturally, and with full agreement of both parties, that I continue to see only the woman for an individual, more in-depth study.

In the first meeting, individual or as a couple, the woman almost always expressed her alarm at her anxious–depressive state, with or without other symptoms, the presence of quarrels and difficulties with her husband and preoccupation for the children. Always present in this state was nostalgia for her country, her language, her family of origin, even when it was a family explicitly defined as problematical. As in all couples, time and living together had eclipsed the initial enthusiasm, and brought to the surface, in each of the partners, the precedent psychological dynamics, comparing them with the reality of the present. There were regrets, dreams regarding the past, images of partners belonging to the woman's own culture or other figures of mediation, desires for future trips.

Various studies on the migratory phenomena have shown that after around three/four years of absence from one's country, even if interrupted by brief visits, the expatriate's need to return became ever stronger, and that a couple of times a year, for longer periods, seemed to be enough to satisfy this need. Preventive measures of this sort are not always possible, especially if the woman works, the children go to school and family finances are insufficient. This leads to a sense of being captive, of segregation, of a suffered exile, in which the place from which she escaped becomes the object of idealization.

Even so, and this is what interests us, it is almost never their relatives they say they miss, or at least not only. I have often heard "I miss my country, the air, the places, the climate, the colors, the customs, speaking my language with friends, going to special places to eat a certain food," and not "I miss my mother, my father, my relatives." On the contrary, visits from relatives, even if desired at the moment, often become ambivalent and fatiguing experiences.

The general sensation these women left me with was that of a state of subtle and perpetual bewilderment. This inner state, often rather blurred, was somehow also a source of shame: ashamed that they were not able to adapt quickly and successfully to the expectations of their new environment. They said they felt themselves outside their shell, exposed, helpless, sometimes angry, dependent and impotent despite themselves, hoping for a definitive return that perhaps would never take place, internally split between the past, and its places, and the future represented by the children who belonged, halfway and forever, to another culture. When these women did not work, the feeling of this constant loss was even sharper. Their husbands were often away. In daily life they faced difficulties in their contacts with the social and bureaucratic mechanisms and in adapting to the communicative habits of a culture as different and complex as the Italian. In the best of cases their isolation led them to turn to groups and associations in an attempt to find other women in the same situation, possibly of their own country, and their own language. In the worst of cases they turned to alcohol or drugs. All in all they had problems integrating, at times outright refusing integration, reopening old emotional wounds and producing new ones.

This was the starting point, if analysis was chosen, for a journey that could be individuative or in any case therapeutic.

In keeping with the theme of this book, I will limit my discussion here to a few aspects that struck me because of their recurrence and that concern not so much the previous psychological situation of my patients, but the way in which they chose to correct or compensate for it. Respect for privacy forbids discussion of the single elements that characterize each clinical case. The dreams, the tales and personal stories that emerged in the sessions and also appeared in non-migrant therapeutic sessions put them on an even footing with the universal aspect of individual psychology and are therefore irrelevant here.

Often the foreign women who came for analysis had wounds regarding the parental couple, involving losses, separations, inadequacies. Physical distance and interior distance were painfully familiar dimensions, unconsciously reactivated in relations that were complicated from the logistical point of view, such as one with a man of another nationality who also lived far away. The stereotype of the Italian man, seen as a Don Giovanni who was however attached to his family and protective of the woman, in addition to being passionate, jealous and possessive, has always had a certain effect on the female imaginary, assuming a compensatory role for their emotional deficiencies. But what can a foreign woman know about the power the Great Mediterranean Mother exerts on the Italian man? Distances, affects and stereotypes come together in a mixture favorable to an illusory amorous projection and the subsequent disillusion.

In the case of analogous phenomena observed from the other side – for example an Italian woman who falls in love with a foreigner – the male figure of the foreigner can assume different aspects depending on the specific projection of the cultural stereotype.

I was struck, for example, by the women who had Italian ancestors in their family history, even distant – a great-great-grandfather or a great-grandfather, for example – whom they had never known. This search for a stable point in their origins, for a revisitation in the search of something that had evidently been lost, had assumed a surprising force in the lives of some who unconsciously had felt themselves drawn to Italy and who only afterwards, after beginning a relationship with an Italian man, had become aware of the resemblance or identity, for example, in their names, in the physical type, profession or other characteristics, between the man of the family past and the man of the present. In some cases episodes or particular dynamics of relationships, unconsciously absorbed during childhood in the family stories, were reproduced: that of the mother's Italian fiancé, of the father who came to Italy during the war, books or photographs found at home, the unrealized desires of the parents to return to Italy, at least for a visit if not for ever. In many cases these peculiar connections emerged during analysis, consciously forgotten or undervalued, that threw light on the choice of the foreign partner.

Summarizing, in the love relationships in question I found:

- an emotional and affective quality that depended only partially on the story of the attachment/separation of childhood, which in the presence of a foreign partner can be either reproduced or avoided;
- an initial positive projection on the new places and cultural aspects, seen as redeeming with respect to one's own or atoning for deficiencies; the emergence of new resources and the activation of previously latent parts of the personality;
- the subsequent re-emergence of elements of the culture and places of origin and the need for a new synthesis; marital crises in the representation, through the partners, of the two cultures involved.

The most delicate and complex aspect of the psychological treatment now comes to a head, for the crisis can take the form of an antagonism between the two worlds, each partner considering their own as the best. This leads to a further development: a reinforcing, in comparison with the diverse, of the original cultural identity, even in those who were never aware of it. It is a discovery of the extent to which one is Italian or American or something else, forgetting often that one went away because one's own culture was too limiting. The end result can be the separation of the couple and the return home, or the working out of a choice that corresponds more to reality, where love was the initial channel but not the only underlying reason. In the long run love alone is not enough to guarantee happiness in a place. This too shows us how important the environment and the context are in a person's life.

Memories and spatial and temporal references to places and other components of the country of origin played an important role in the purely psychodynamic and relational aspects of these treatments, including overwhelming emotions and periods, even of considerable length, of mourning for their loss. I have already discussed nostalgia and how places are experienced in exile and in a possible return.

Final notes on the psychological condition of the foreigner

As this part of the book draws to a close, I would like once more to broach the question I asked at the beginning of the chapter on journeys, now seen in the light of my clinical experience. Are there differences in the personality characteristics or psychological dynamics between "those who go away" and become foreigners, and "those who stay"?

Speaking of the journey, I had divided people into two broad categories:

those who felt the need to move – or who did not tolerate staying – and those who would never go anywhere, for any reason in the world. I simply substantiated and respected this state of affairs, certainly better than shutting oneself off in a spurious alternative. A psychoanalyst, however, can unquestionably do more, such as exploring the influence of the type of personality on the phenomena involved. There are various theories on personality. Jung uses the parameters of extraversion and introversion. The Balints' Freudian theory defines it – in line with space, movement and the thrill-situations – as "the philobate," that is the individual who is attracted by risk, who plunges in, leaving safety behind, as opposed to the "ochnophile," that is the person who hangs on for dear life, who hesitates, afraid of the void and of loss (Balint and Balint 1959).

Both descriptions also refer to the relationship with what is external, the object in a broad sense, which implicates space, movement and the perception of one's self in the field, offering an interpretation of psychopathologies and their symptoms, such as agoraphobia, claustrophobia, panic attacks. Unquestionably foreign patients and travelers have a perception and experience of space that differs from those who choose the sedentary life. It is also true that the above-named symptoms have something to do with space and movement. How all this is interpreted in psychotherapy is something else.

Whether interpretations are based on Freudian, Jungian or other theories, in the case of the foreign patient an element of suspension and mystery to be respected remains. It involves an uncontrollable unpredictability, as in the behavior of any other patient, something that, in the face of the conceptualization and symbolization, refers to the body, to the concrete, to real space and movement. It is something that has to do with impulsiveness, the plunge into the void of Balint's philobate but also with the holding tight of the ochnophile. In being as psychoanalytical as one can get, "he who leaves and goes away" would be undertaking "a macroscopic acting-out." But since one cannot over-extend certain psychoanalytical concepts without exposing oneself to ridicule – for then all of life would be transformed into acting-out – the psychoanalyst would always find himself forced to tolerate, and accept, with all patients, the fact that words may not be enough to express the inner turmoil that sometimes explodes in impulsive behavior. This is particularly true of the foreign patient.

Belonging to one type of personality or another offers no protection from unconscious choices. Life, at times, runs swiftly, and the mind, even of the most mindful, is not always able to keep up with it. Things happen, there are encounters, opportunities are seized, situations are put up with that do not depend only on the individual, and then itineraries are begun that can lead one far, into a new country. Nothing strange or exceptional about it, above all today.

Then the time of life and age also play a role. When one is young and life is less structured, the impulse of the moment is more likely to dominate the scene, leading to doing and undoing, going and coming, before really having to choose.

Most of the foreigners answer the question "how come you are here?" with a rational answer that can satisfy the curiosity of the questioner.

But from the point of view of depth psychology things are different. I have often had to ask the question "how come you are here?" more than once to get the patients to understand that I believed there were other reasons they were here, not only in my studio, but in this country. Only after defenses of a paranoiac nature had been dropped could possible problematical, painful cores emerge, and the feeling of deficiency for which the foreigner, the true "culprit," was to blame. For they were the ones who left, who abandoned.

The feeling of blame for having left is present, in a milder form than with the exile, in all foreigners. As the proverb says, he who is absent is always the one at fault. Those who leave, I would add, take with them something for which they must be forgiven. They had dared to leave and the community will let them know, in one way or another. The threat of loss of consensus can induce behavior that is not always spontaneous in the foreigner, in a sort of obligation to placate those who remained at home, for fear of a second abandonment, of retaliation on their part. At the same time behavior designed to bring about acceptance by the new community is not completely spontaneous either. These dynamics also occur in migrations in the same country.

Most foreigners when asked "how are you getting along?" will tend to answer "fine," stressing the elements of encounter and integration in the new country. Then going more into depth, things are not always that way. Efforts to keep up with integration and confrontation with the new are constant. Disturbing feelings and experiences are repressed, as much as possible, because they would call on energy necessary on other fronts.

Most of the persons who remain in the new country, with time – by which I mean a few years – continue integrating and begin to look back and reflect on what has happened, aware that their relationship with "the before" – the places and persons – and with "the after" changes every year. With the "here" and the "there."

There will be moments when they are afraid of losing all contacts with a world that is gradually receding, within them. There will be fantasies of returning, doubts, and other factors, depending on what has happened in the meantime, of new bonds that have been formed, depending on how well one has adapted: a house of one's own, work with the possibilities of career, possibly children in school who already speak only the new language, a new network of friends.

When asked "but would you go back to live in your country?" these persons, no longer pure foreigners, answer with a sort of nod, a sort of "oh well!," maybe a sort of resigned half-smile that says "I'm doing fine here, sure I miss some things, but what can one do, that's how life is, you can't have everything . . ."

As the years pass, life will be more and more that of the new country. The places and story of the past will end up in photographs and memories and at a certain point the process will have become irreversible. Even if they returned, they would no longer speak the original language, but a mixture with the subsequent language, and the same with habits and all the rest. Old friends, except those closest, have been lost, the places have changed, continuity has been completely interrupted.

In the latter part of their lives many persons who have emigrated return to their original country. They have maintained contacts of some kind and, as Mellina (1992) reveals, they build a house there. It is the house for their retirement, a home for the family, for their children, who meanwhile are elsewhere and will probably never live there, and may not even go there on vacation.

This is truly what I would call "the dwelling of the soul," of that part connected to place, to the land that remained within them even though they did not live there, and to which they owe something: a sign of love. These houses are often empty for most of the year, or at least until an heir decides to sell them, because no one in the family ever goes there and maintenance is costly.

This rather dismal but realistic profile, with all the variations and limits imaginable, shapes a different, specific kind of psychology, consisting of things unsaid – very much within, at times completely secret – in which the sense of loss, unlike mourning for a dear one or the natural passing of life, always remains present. No matter how much it has changed, the place is always there, often including the persons, customs, traditions and language. It is another aspect of ineluctable concreteness.

It is there, testifying to the abandonment, and is the essence of the recurrent question "who knows what things would be like if I had stayed there?"

An experience of marginality that often continues to be present even in a successful integration is also a constituent part of the diversity of the foreigner.

For his adopted community, he will always be "the foreigner," and even after decades he will still be someone who comes "from elsewhere;" sometimes he will be identified by the city or country from where he comes. As time passes he will be considered more trustworthy, but only up to a certain point. He will never have the privileges in full of those who have belonged to the same community for generations.

With this as my point of departure I will now attempt to put the picture back into focus.

The choice

While the foreigner, by definition, will never have the status of native in another country, neither will he have all the duties and burdens. In many situations there are advantages to having one foot in and one out, and it may turn out to be the right thing for an individual who has in any case already chosen to leave his group of belonging. A foreigner would find it difficult to fit into family structures of a patriarchal type or other forms of close community. Inordinate responsibilities and traditional bonds would be intolerable to someone previously formed by others from which he was seeking to distance himself.

The mental aperture, often attributed to those who leave home, travel and have experiences abroad, is not simply something gained with time. It is already present, albeit obscurely, in the initial departure, whether or not it is flight; in the ability to leave and support the break and then face the unknown.

In addition to this basic capacity I want to cite another salient point that I believe defines a successful migration. It is being aware of the freedom to choose, knowing what it involves and its effect on one's identity. This means realizing just what had unconsciously been projected onto the new country – as with people – withdrawing it and therefore subsequently being freer to choose one's position.

Indeed, in the course of this book I have discussed forced migration and chosen migration, but I had not spoken of the fact that the choice is not always a conscious choice, or at least not as much as it appears to be.

Initially things were not actually of our choosing. The place of origin, the land said to be one's own, our name, the parents we happened to have – none of them were a matter of choice. We found we were part of an ethnic and social group, speaking a certain language and all the rest whether we liked it or not.

As an adult, however, one discovers that one can choose: choose to leave or to remain. Choose where and with whom to live. One can also make mistakes, correct oneself and change, choose again until one achieves what best corresponds to ourselves, to where we want to be, aware each time of what the possibilities are.

If with time those who remain are equally aware of their choice, the two truly correspond to each other.

Dreams and images from the world

A few brief examples in conclusion should make it easier to understand some of the affirmations made in this chapter.

My general picture of the psychological condition of the foreign patient in psychotherapy is that of a prolonged "rite of passage," played out in a multiple scenario: the collective place of the new country, the place of origin and the intimate space of the analyst's room. The place of psychotherapy often appeared, in different forms, in the dreams and fantasies of the patients.

All the components dealt with in the various chapters of this book have

Paola Maestroni, *Consider the Source*, 2004.

appeared, to a greater or lesser extent, in the stories of my patients. They described themselves and their emotional life through images that gradually emerged from the unconscious, at times adding verbal comments. Let me begin with these.

It is like living two dreams. If I wake up mentally with respect to my country, Italy becomes a dream. When I visit my country I can't think of anything that concerns Italy, it is all distant and I don't even want to speak the language – which I liked to do before, because it was like a game. As soon as I arrive in Italy, everything concerning my country becomes a dream, as if I hadn't really gone. Days and days of being tired, a fetal withdrawal. There in my country my feelings are more spontaneous, more vivid and stronger. Here I have a thousand problems. I can't conceive of the two worlds communicating with each other, except for when things go wrong and I listen to the music of my country. To remind me that I have another place in my life. I'm afraid of suffering, there and here.

Outside my country it is like crossing a desert, like Moses going to the Promised Land. Now the desert has become my central part and has made my country unreal.

Returning home would in reality be for me discovering a home, my new real home, a home that is outside and within, one only, united (about a dream in which the words "United" States appear).

I'm here because nobody visits my country, while as they say all roads lead to Rome. Here I feel at the center, less excluded.

Dream. The analyst returns from Stockholm after visiting some of my friends. She brings me a present from that city. (Stockholm is a reassuring place, even though it is not where the patient originally came from. It is a place where the patient, of Italian origin, lived more serenely and autonomously than in Italy, where he thought he would "find himself.")

Dream. From Germany I receive a package full of characteristic Italian things (dream of an American patient who was abandoned by his German fiancée).

Dream. An Italian man wears a straw hat, which at a certain point flies away. I catch it saying it belonged to his mother. The scene takes place near the sea. Regarding this dream the patient, of distant Italian origins, observes: It doesn't matter if one is integrated, I wasn't in my country either. Here on the other hand I feel it is my nationality, in Italy it is not a question of integrating, the relationship is with other things. My spirit has been here a long time, I found it and leaving now becomes a sacrifice.

Dream. I live on a ship, as if it were a house, with a precarious sense of life, always traveling, like a sailor.

Dream. There are two parts of two continents that are approaching each other, like a map in which the forms are moving. Then a detail becomes clear, it is the Bering Strait.

Dream. A Caribbean island with ancient ruins, perhaps monuments, a temple, or something else. I try to start up a windmill with a large wheel and to my surprise succeed in moving it, but it takes time before it turns properly, in the meantime with delicate, pastel-colored paint I paint the edges of the ruins, which stand out in the vegetation, but not too much, like an act of restoration, but artistic.

For those who use it, the dreams and the scenes of the sandplay are expressed, one might say, in counterpoint. They alternate, complete and stimulate each other. The fullness that they provide, in the cases of foreign patients, is highly useful for both them and the psychoanalyst.

In the sandplay, the geographic and naturalistic aspect becomes even more evident. Some patients of mixed origins, with up to four grandparents all belonging to different countries, and with parents born in still other countries, none of them connected to Italy, put representations of all these places in the sandtray and then they gradually had them interact until they found a satisfying harmony, while they dreamed and told the story of their own lives.

Others, as mentioned here and there, traced back their origins together with those of their ethnic group, reproducing places, personages, paths, introducing numerous objects that represent forms of connection (such as bridges, roads, paths) or boundaries (such as fences, walls, mountains) – spaces and places to cross or go over. One patient, suffering from acute nostalgia, had the plane crash into the sea. Places to which to return were represented by various houses in different styles, of which one, the most commonly chosen, of a European type, had a red roof, solid and welcoming.

The figurines representing the Native Americans were the ones chosen most by all foreigners, in particular a small child, an infant, and an Indian in a canoe, followed by ET, with his finger pointing homewards.

Nature was constantly reproduced, more or less in contrast with civilization and urbanization, depending on the point reached in the analysis. Completely urban scenes were rare, while nature scenes were very frequent.

In both, dream and play, there were numerous examples of the "third geographic place" which Jung would define as the achievement of the "transcendent function" and the appearance of the symbol that unifies opposites. Or as an alchemic crucible, container for the transformation.

The immediacy and function of synthesis of these images would become evident once the story, and especially the origin, of the patients was known. This would however make it too easy to identify them. A few comments on the scenes created in the sandtray:

I am in Africa and it is like returning home, to the origins of the life of man;
I am on a promontory in Ireland, together with a man. A poetic place, less closed than England, between this and Italy.
I am in Canada, I feel it is a halfway point between Italy and Germany.
I am in India, like a bridge between Japan and Italy.
Mexico is closer, as culture, to Italy than the United States, etc.
I returned to Poland, but my town has moved further south, next to Italy, where Yugoslavia is.
My husband, it is him, identical, but he speaks another language (that of a grandfather).

All this traveling of the psyche took place while the patients were in Italy, a country that for some had connections with their own real past, while for others it was an attempt at mediation, further bypassed by the unconscious, in these maneuvers of adjusting that took place during analysis. It was as if symbolic passages of the individuation processes needed to self-represent themselves with images of unusual, original places.

The patients often attributed explicit meanings to the objects in the play: this is the house of . . . the place is . . . this figure belongs to this country . . . or references to the earth–sand material, my land, the land of my country, my ocean, my desert . . . the space of my garden, of my room . . . Other times they presented objects put in upside down, confusion, syncretism, creations of forms by addition, contiguity, adhesion; they asked for inexistent objects so they could construct, leaving in the sandtray a structure to be deciphered awaiting further developments.

The inner changes of these patients, or at least the part taking place during analysis, emerged clearly and without words in the sequence of their sands, documented on slides and, looked at all together some time after the end of the treatment. In some cases the patients had left, returning to their country or going to some other country, and the revision took place several years later when they happened to come to Italy.

Some foreign patients who left initially wanted to keep in touch, but gradually it was limited to communicating important moments in their life. I still get Christmas greetings from a few patients I haven't seen for twenty years.

Perhaps a bit of nostalgia still keeps them tied to the "country of the soul."

Lastly, I used the sandplay also in non-therapeutic situations, with groups of persons in the educational and training field, but always of a psychological nature: university students, teachers, educators of early childhood, parents, women, psychologists, never more than twelve each time. I won't go into the specific rules of the play, but I simply want to highlight the sense of immediate aggregation and the exposure of the group dynamics that emerged through the play.

The first time I used this method with a group it was with students, all foreigners, in my psychology course at an American university in which I taught and also had my office for psychological counseling. I would never have expected the final coherence of the scene from these rather impetuous young people who played like children in the park, throwing objects that they seemed to have chosen by chance into the sandtray, without observing the scene, without pausing, chatting away. Some unconscious organizing principle must have been at work, that mystery that makes the whole more significant than the sum of its parts. The scene was crowded but it wasn't chaotic. The sandtray had contained the group together, rooted the individuals in a context, created a community that, like young people in some of the primitive tribes, had come to terms with its rite of passage.

In a sense close to the discourse of this book, here too the earth of the sandplay assimilated the soul of the group, creating a setting, a symbolic place of cohesion.

The story interpreted was the archetype of the hero myth, departure, a direction, the journey – by sea for a young man on a dolphin – ships and other means of transportation, monsters and other challenges to face, houses to be reached.

With some of my colleagues whose contributions appear in the last part of the book, I have also experimented, on the occasion of the seminar that had the same title as this book, with an initial sensitization and aggregation of the group using the sandplay. The sandtray was presented as "land" on which to meet as strangers, to "make soul" together, as an unsaturated space for a form and a desire.

In two days we built two pictures, one at the beginning and one at the end of the meeting. The context was not obviously psychotherapeutic and there were persons of different professions and proveniences among the participants.

A first encounter is always a delicate moment, of exposure and circumspection. Our encounter in Pari, a small hamlet in Tuscany – a neutral place for all the participants, "foreigners" from different places – could resemble that between migrants, pilgrims or vagabonds, searching for something not clearly or completely defined.

What might the expectations, illusions, and tensions underlying the manifest task, i.e. a "cultural seminar" with the title "Soul and Earth," be? In introducing the meeting, my questions as group leader were: are there special places or are the places in any case always animated by people and their goals? Why do certain people find themselves in certain places, and how is the place reflected within the group? What are the places: the obscure, disturbing places (an argument that Massimo Buttarini then dealt with) and the welcoming places, the archetypal places, such as the garden (of which Flavia D'Andreamatteo wrote)? What is the confrontation between the places of the soul and the earth in daily life, in urban, contemporary life? Elena Angelini, architect, took on this complex theme. What might the journey be, interpreted in its dimensions of soul and earth? Massimiliano Scarpelli discussed this in relation to the aboriginal Australian culture and the "songlines." Nostalgia was declaimed by Marcella Fragapane. The earth, then, is also matter and body; what is the relation between this dimension and the interior, spiritual dimension of the Self? Silvia Tomasi provided a few important indications.

The group, including others who are not represented here in writing, expressed its first form in the sandtray, showing a collection of places. Each individual silently constructed his own, shaping it and enclosing it in the common space, in fair equilibrium with the places of the others. Possession of the space was taken; they were present together but not yet in relation to each other.

In the second sandplay, the common scenario was immediately articulated in a story in a place within the place. A banquet appeared. No one consciously thought of or referred to Eranos, the "cultural banquets" of international Jungian tradition, the interdisciplinary encounters that still take place in Ascona in Switzerland, with scholars of different nationalities and disciplines. Like Chinese boxes, different places opened with their meanings, to symbolize that shared moment of study.

Natural groups of adults have very complex dynamics because of the interweaving of preoccupations and shadows regarding the common space, the urgency to establish boundaries "of mine and yours" as defense from intrusion, control of movements of spreading out and taking over, for everything that in a macroscopic form is part of geopolitics. Everywhere no one seems to be content with their own space and the resources it holds; everyone seems to want the space of the other and what it contains. Or even to dominate all the existing space. Yet children, who often inspire me, offer significant examples of the spontaneous human capacity for balance and measure. Contrary to what is commonly believed, in the first three years of their life children are already able to dwell in a space sharing it with other children and adults, to respect some limits and rules, to cross conflicting and empathetic dynamics in forming a group that has its affective bonds and a shared destiny.

It is hard to understand how this rich potentiality gets lost: it is hard to believe that conditioning by adults and the example they set has nothing to do with it.

Conclusions

> Our Mother Earth, the trees and all of nature,
> bear witness to our thoughts
> and our actions.
>
> (Winnebago)

Hopefully the reader will by now have become aware of my love for the earth, and the soul, and that my psychological discourse constantly takes the contemporary social and political scene into consideration.

If the uncompromising identity and historical affiliations that have engendered so many conflicts among peoples – and what the earth represents for them – could only be put aside, perhaps a more openminded approach could put human beings back in touch with earth–nature, earth–environment, earth–planet, the only possible globalization for survival. Everywhere, with the same love, the same respect and the same care.

No sustainable society or culture can exist without a land of that kind. There can be no soul, no psyche in harmony with a body that does not live a sustainable everyday life. Nowadays attention is no longer solely on sustainability but on "decrescence" as well as new forms of "localism."

Discovering the inventive power of the mind has put the technologically advanced societies in a state of permanent intoxication, their feet no longer on the ground. The intellectual culture and the mass media seem at times to ignore and underestimate the common reality shared by most, in favor of a reality that is increasingly self-referential, in which words and images become inconsistent, volatile, lacking foundations and roots.

The place–non-place fascinates and prospers in the jargon of virtuality and what is fashionable, while people live in ugly uncomfortable places full of useless objects. They drag themselves from one place to another unaware of the effect produced on man by the artificial environment – even though all are subject to malaise – and the disastrous effects on that environment for which human beings are to blame. Persons turn to the computer and traveling on the Internet, impatiently perched on a chair. It's worse than being in prison.

There is a limit to sacrifices, to losses, to the adaptation that an individual can make in the course of a life. The unconscious expresses these limits through the body and its symptoms, even when the mind, in its state of maniacal exaltation, feels no fatigue nor pain nor depression.

The psychotherapist listens, observes, sometimes speaks, for he also lives in the same environment, at times without realizing how much the psyche depends on the earth, and thinking he can heal the psyche using nothing but the language of the psyche.

Life breathes with a name and a story in the bodies of each and every one of us. One cannot live without body and without earth.

The myth or the collective fantasy of Gaia, Mother Earth, in distress also tells us that a certain sensitivity still exists and echoes throughout the world, not as the suffering of the individual but as a tension shared by all of Earth's inhabitants, a single forced breath gasping for air. The idea of the *Anima mundi* reappears here and there, with nostalgia for a time when microcosmos and macrocosmos reflected each other. This "psychological reality" must mean something, even if only a collective fantasy of redress or "repair" with regard to the ever-greater ecological damage to our natural resources. It is at least a beginning.

In an interview in 1950 Jung expressed himself as follows:

> Decentralization, on the other hand, allows for small social units. Every man should have his own plot of land so that the instincts can come to life again . . . We keep forgetting that we are primates and that we have to make allowances for these primitive layers in our psyche. The farmer is still closer to these layers . . . We all need nourishment for our psyche. It is impossible to find such nourishment in urban tenements without a patch of green or a blossoming tree. We need a relationship with nature . . . Individuation is not only an upward but also a downward process. Without any body, there is no mind and therefore no individuation. Our

"Image Parade," street performance by Teatro Potlach at Puerto Alegre, Brazil. Photo © Francesco Galli, 1993.

civilizing potential has led us down the wrong path ... I am fully committed to the idea that human existence should be rooted in the earth.

(McGuire and Hull, 1980:200–1)

Almost another 60 years have passed, hopefully making us wiser, so let me add that this earth does not have to be "mine." Just let us live and enjoy it, and above all commit ourselves to handing it over intact to our children.

Bibliography

Abbott, E.A. (1882/1991) *Flatland: A Romance of Many Dimensions*. Princeton, NJ: Princeton University Press.

Adams, M.V. (1996) *The Multicultural Imagination: Race, Color and the Unconscious*. London: Routledge.

Aite, P. (2003) *Paesaggi della psiche*. Turin, Italy: Bollati Boringhieri.

Algini, M.L. and Lugones, M. (eds) (1999) *Emigrazione e sofferenze di identità*. Rome: Borla.

Amati Mehler, J., Argentieri, S. and Canestri, J. (1993) *The Babel of the Unconscious: Mother Tongue and Foreign Tongues in the Analytic Dimension*. Madison, CT: International Universities Press.

American Psychiatric Association (2000) *Diagnostic and Statistical Manual of Mental Disorders*, 4th edn. Washington, DC: American Psychiatric Association.

Ammann, R. (1991) *Healing and Transformation in Sandplay*. Chicago: Open Court.

Ancis, J.R. (ed.) (2004) *Culturally Responsive Interventions*. Hove, UK: Brunner-Routledge.

Arena, L.V. (ed.) (1995) *Haiku*. Milan: Rizzoli-Bur.

Augé, M. (1995) *Non-Places: Introduction to an Anthropology of Supermodernity*. London: Verso.

Bachelard, G. (2002) *Earth and Reveries of Will: An Essay on the Imagination of Matter*. Dallas, TX: Dallas Institute of Humanities and Culture.

—— (1969) *The Poetics of Space*. Boston: Beacon Press.

Bakan, D. (1969) *Sigmund Freud and the Jewish Mystical Tradition*. New York: Schocken.

Balint, M. and Balint, E. (1959) *Thrills and Regressions*. New York: International Universities Press.

Bascetta, M. (ed.) (1992) *Radici e nazioni*. Rome: manifestolibri.

Basho (2002) *The Complete Basho Poems*. Northfield, MN: Black Willow.

Bateson, G. (1979) *Mind and Nature: A Necessary Unit*. New York: E. P. Dutton.

Bauman, Z. (2003) *Cities of Fear, Cities of Hope*, London: Goldsmith's College.

Benzi, M. (1998) *Wirárika. Gli sciamani della Sierra Madre*. Celleno, Italy: La Piccola Editrice.

Bernhard, E. (1977) *Mitobiografia*. Milan: Bompiani.

Berthoz, A. (1997) *The Brain's Sense of Movement*. Cambridge, MA: Harvard University Press.

Bettelheim, B. (1982) *Freud and Man's Soul: An Important Re-interpretation of Freudian Theory*. New York: Knopf.

Bion, W. (1984) *Learning from Experience*. London: Karnac Books.

—— (1966) *Catastrophic Change*, Bulletin 5, British Psycho-Analytical Society, London.

—— (1984) *Transformations*. London: Maresfield Reprints.

—— (1991) *A Memoir of the Future*. London: Karnac Books.

Blake, W. (1971) *Songs of Innocence*. New York: Dover.

Bowlby, J. (1969) *Attachment and Loss*. London: Hogarth Press.

Bronfenbrenner, U. (1979) *The Ecology of Human Development: Experiments by Nature and Design*. Cambridge, MA: Harvard University Press.

Burgio, A. (2001) *La guerra delle razze*. Rome: manifestolibri.

Byington, C. (1986) "The pathological shadow of the Western cultural self", in *Proceedings of the 10th IAAP Congress*, Berlin.

Calabrese, O., Giovannoli, R. and Pezzini, I. (eds) (1983) *Hic sunt lexones. Geografia fantastica e viaggi immaginari*. Milan: Electa.

Calvino, I. (1972) *Invisible Cities*. San Francisco: Arion Press.

Campolieti, G. (1987) *Nostalgia*. Naples, Italy: T. Pironti Editore.

Carotenuto, A. (1988) *La nostalgia della memoria*. Milan: Bompiani.

Casey, E.S. (1993) "Anima loci", *Sphinx*, vol. 5. London: The London Convivium of Archetypal Studies.

Cassirer, E. (1929/1996) *The Philosophy of Symbolic Forms*. New Haven, CT: Yale University Press.

Chatwin, B. (1988) *The Songlines*. London: Pan Books.

—— (1989) *What am I doing here?*, New York: Viking.

Chatwin, B. and Ryle, J. (1996) *Anatomy of Restlessness*. New York: Viking.

Chevalier, J. and Gheerbrant, A. (1986) *Dizionario dei simboli*. Milan: Rizzoli.

Chomsky, N. (1998) *The Common Good*. Monroe, ME: Odonian Press.

Christopher, E. and McFarland Solomon, H. (eds) (1999) *Jungian Thought in the Modern World*. London: Free Association Books.

Clayton, S. and Opotow, S. (eds) (2003) *Identity and the Natural Environment: The Psychological Significance of Nature*. Cambridge, MA: MIT Press.

Coppola Pignatelli, P. (1977) *I luoghi dell'abitare*. Rome: Officina.

—— (1982) *Spazio e immaginario. Maschile e femminile in architettura*. Rome: Officina.

—— (2004) *Emozioni di pietra*. Rome: Edizioni Magi.

Corbin, H. (1973) *Storia della filosofia islamica*. Milan: Adelphi.

—— (1983) *L'immagine del tempio*. Turin, Italy: Boringhieri.

—— (1989) *Spiritual Body & Celestial Earth*. Princeton, NJ: Princeton University Press, Bollingen Series XCI.

Dahmash, W., Di Francesco, T. and Blasone, P. (eds) (2002) *La terra più amata. Voci della letteratura palestinese*. Rome: manifestolibri.

Dalal, F. (2004) *Race, Colour and the Process of Racialization*. Hove, UK: Brunner-Routledge.

Daniels, E.B. (1985) "Nostalgia and hidden meaning", *American Imago*, 42, 371–383.

Del Re McWeeny, V. (2004) *Persya mistica*. Pisa, Italy: Edizioni ETS.

Derrida, J. (2000) *Sull'ospitalità*. Milan: Baldini & Castoldi.

Devereux, G. (1969) *Reality and Dream: The Psychotherapy of a Plains Indian*. New York: International Universities Press.

—— (1978) *Saggi di etnopsichiatria generale*. Rome: Armando.

Diamond, J. (1997) *Guns, Germs and Steel: The Fates of Human Societies*. New York: W.W. Norton.

Di Micco, V. and Martelli, P. (1993) *Passaggi di confine, etnopsichiatria e migrazioni*. Naples, Italy: Liguori.

Di Paolo, N. (2001) *Emigrazione: Da Ellis Island ai giorni nostri*. Salerno, Italy: Edizioni del Paguro.

Durand, G. (1972) *Le strutture antropologiche dell'immaginario*. Bari, Italy: Dedalo.

Eliade, M. (1954) *Myth of the Eternal Return or Cosmos and History*. Princeton, NJ: Princeton University Press.

—— (1972) *La nostalgia delle origini. Storia e significato nella religione*. Brescia, Italy: Morcelliana.

—— (1988) *Spezzare il tetto della casa*. Milan: Jaca Book.

Ellenberger, H. (1970) *The Discovery of the Unconscious*. New York: Basic Books.

Enzensberger, H.M. (1989) *Ah, Europa*. Milan: Garzanti.

—— (1992) *The Great Migration*. London: Granta.

Fachinelli, E. (1983) *Claustrofilia*. Milan: Adelphi.

Feldenkrais, M. (1972) *Awareness through Movement*. New York: Harper & Row.

Fernando, S. (ed.) (2004) *Cultural Diversity, Mental Health and Psychiatry: The Struggle against Racism*, Hove, UK: Brunner-Routledge.

Fordham, M. (1969) *Children as Individuals*. London: Hodder and Stoughton.

Fossi, G. and Tanzella, M. (1986) *Le storie degli inizi*. Rome: Borla.

Freud, S. (1953–74) *The Standard Edition of the Complete Works of Sigmund Freud*, 24 volumes, ed. by James Strachey et al. London: The Hogarth Press and the Institute of Psychoanalysis.

—— (1936) *A Disturbance of Memory on the Acropolis*. Standard Edition, 22.

Frigessi Castelnuovo, D. and Risso, M. (1982) *A mezza parete, Emigrazione, nostalgia, malattia mentale*. Turin, Italy: Einaudi.

Galimberti, U. (1983) *Il corpo, antropologia, psicoanalisi, fenomenologia*. Milan: Feltrinelli.

—— (1999) *Psiche e techne*. Milan: Feltrinelli.

Gallard, M. (1993) "Tentativo di comprensione dell'atteggiamento di Jung durante la seconda guerra mondiale, alla luce del contesto storico e professionale", *Psicoanalisi e metodo, 1*. Rome: Borla.

Gay, P. (1987) *A Godless Jew: Freud, Atheism and the Making of Psychoanalysis*. New Haven, CT: Yale University Press.

Gerbi, D. (2003) *Costruttori di pace. Storia di un ebreo profugo dalla Libia*. Rome: Edizioni Appunti di Viaggio.

Gibney, M.J. (ed.) (2003) *Globalizing Rights: The Oxford Amnesty Lectures*. Oxford: Oxford University Press.

Gibran, K. (1945) *The Wanderer*. New York: A.A. Knopf.

Giuliani, A. (2002) *Il mito di Caino e altri saggi*. Manziana, Italy: Vecchiarelli Editore.

Goitein, S.D. (1999) *A Mediterranean Society*. Berkeley, CA: University of California Press.

Grinberg, L. and Grinberg, R. (1989) *Psychoanalytic Perspectives on Migration and Exile*. New Haven, CT: Yale University Press.

Hacking, I. (1998) *Mad Travelers: Reflections on the Reality of Transient Mental Illnesses*. Charlottesville, VA: University Press of Virginia.

Hall, E.T. (1966) *The Hidden Dimension*. Garden City, NY: Doubleday.

Hammad, R. (2002) *Palestina nel cuore*. Rome: Sinnos.

Happold, F.C. (1975) *Mysticism: A Study and an Anthology*. Harmondsworth, UK: Penguin.

Harper, R. (1966) *Nostalgia: An Existential Exploration of Longing and Fulfilment in the Modern Age*. Cleveland, OH: Press of Western Reserve University.

Hauke, C. (2000) *Jung and the Postmodern*. London: Routledge.

Henderson, J.L. (1984) *Cultural Attitudes in Psychological Perspective*. Toronto, Canada: Inner City Books.

—— (1990) *Shadow and Self: Selected Papers in Analytical Psychology*, Wilmette, IL: Chiron.

Hillman, J. (1978) *City and Soul*. University of Dallas, Dallas, TX. Also in *Uniform Edition of the Writings of James Hillman*, Vol. 2: *City and Soul* (R. Leaver, ed.). Putnam, CT: Spring Publications, 2005.

—— (1979) *The Dream and the Underworld*. New York: Harper & Row.

—— (1994) *Kinds of Power*. New York: Doubleday Currency.

—— (1999) *Politica della bellezza*. Bergamo, Italy: Moretti & Vitali.

—— (2004) *L'anima dei luoghi. Conversazione con Carlo Truppi*. Milan: Rizzoli.

Huxley, A. (1954) *The Doors of Perception*. London: Chatto & Windus.

Illich, I. (1973) *Tools for Conviviality*. New York: Harper & Row.

—— (1982) *Il Potere di abitare*. Collettivo per un abitare autogestito/ricerca & azione. Florence: Libreria editrice fiorentina.

Illich, I. and Cayley, D. (2005) *The Rivers North of the Future: The Testament of Ivan Illich*. Toronto, Canada: House of Anansi Press.

Illich, I. and Sanders, B. (1988) *ABC: The Alphabetization of the Popular Mind*. San Francisco: North Point Press.

Irigaray, L. (1997) *Tra Oriente e Occidente, dalla singolarità alla comunità*. Rome: Manifestolibri.

—— (2004) *Key Writings*. London: Continuum.

Jabès, E. (1991) *Il libro dell'ospitalità*. Milan: Raffaello Cortina. French edition: *Le livre de l'Hospitalité*. Paris: Gallimard, 1991.

John of the Cross (1991) *The Collected Works of Saint John of the Cross*. Washington, DC: ICS Publications.

Jung, C.G. (1953–1979) *The Collected Works*, 20 vols. London: Routledge.

—— (1921/1971) *Psychological Types, Collected Works*, 6.

—— (1927) "Mind and Earth", *Collected Works*, 10.

—— (1928) "The Swiss Line in the European Spectrum", *Collected Works*, 10.

—— (1930a) "The Complications of American Psychology", *Collected Works*, 10.

—— (1930b) "The Stages of Life", *Collected Works*, 8.

—— (1930c) "The Rise of a New World", review, *Collected Works*, 10.

—— (1934a) "The Soul and Death", *Collected Works*, 8.

—— (1934b) "La Révolution mondiale", review, *Collected Works*, 10.

—— (1939) "The Dreamlike World of India", *Collected Works*, 10.

—— (1942), "Psychotherapy Today", *Collected Works*, 16.

—— (1945) "After the Catastrophe", *Collected Works*, 10.

—— (1946) *The Psychology of Transference, Collected Works*, 16.

—— (1952) *Symbols of Transformation, Collected Works*, 5.

—— (1957) *The Undiscovered Self (Present and Future), Collected Works*, 10.

—— (1958) *Flying Saucers: A Modern Myth of Things Seen in the Skies, Collected Works*, 10.
—— (1963) *Memories, Dreams, Reflections* (3rd edn). London: Random House.
—— (1983) *C.G. Jung: Word and Image* (ed.) A. Jaffé. Princeton, NJ: Princeton University Press, Bollingen Series.
Kabat-Zinn, J. (1997) *Wherever You Go, There You Are*. New York: Hyperion.
Kaès, R., Fainberg, H., Enriques, M. and Baranes, J.J. (1995) *La trasmissione della vita psichica tra le generazioni*. Rome: Borla.
Kalff, D. (1980) *Sandplay*. Boston: Sigo Press.
Kalsched, D. (1996) *The Inner World of Trauma*. London: Routledge.
Keene, S. (1995) *Anthology of Japanese Literature*. New York: Grove Press.
Khalidi, R. (2003) *Identità palestinese*. Turin, Italy: Bollati Boringhieri.
Khan, M. (1993) *In Solitudine e nostalgia*. Turin, Italy: Bollati Boringhieri.
Kottler, J.A., Carlson, J. and Keeney, B. (2004) *American Shaman: An Odyssey of Global Healing Traditions*. New York: Brunner-Routledge.
Kozakai, T. (2002) *Lo straniero, l'identità. Saggio sull'integrazione culturale*. Rome: Borla.
Kristeva, J. (1991) *Strangers to Ourselves*. New York: Columbia University Press.
Laing, R.D. (1977) *The Facts of Life*. Harmondsworth, UK: Penguin.
Lao Tzu (1989) *The Complete Tao Te Ching* (transl. Gia-fu-Feng and Jane English). New York: Vintage.
Latouche, S. (2007) *La Scommessa della Decrescita*. Milan: Feltrinelli.
Laungani, P. (2004) *Asian Perspectives in Counselling and Psychotherapy*. Hove, UK: Brunner-Routledge.
Lawrence, W.G. (2003) *Experiences in Social Dreaming*. London: Karnac Books.
—— (2005) *Introduction to Social Dreaming*. London: Karnac Books.
—— (2007) *Infinite Possibilities of Social Dreaming*. London: Karnac Books.
Leed, E.J. (1991) *The Mind of the Traveler: From Gilgamesh to Global Tourism*. New York: Basic Books.
Leff, J. (1988) *Psychiatry Around the Globe: A Transcultural View*. London: Gaskell.
Liotta, E. (1993) "Caos, frattali e Gioco della sabbia. Mente/corpo e geometria dell'individuazione", *Rivista di Psicologia Analitica, 47*.
—— (1994) "Spazio, Forma e creatività nel Gioco della sabbia", *Rivista di Psicologia Analitica, 50*.
—— (1998a) "Dinamiche della tras-formazione", in *Quaderni di Filosofia naturale Informazione e complessità. Physis, vita, mente, intorno e oltre, 5*, I. Licata (ed.). Bologna, Italy: Andromeda.
—— (1998b) "Scienza, psicoanalisi e identità dell'analista", *Rivista di Psicologia Analitica, 58*.
—— (2001) *Educare al Sé*. Rome: Edizioni Magi.
—— (2003) *Le solitudini nella società globale*. Celleno, Italy: La Piccola Editrice.
—— (2006) *La maschera trasparente. Apparire o Essere?* Celleno, Italy: La Piccola Editrice.
—— (2007) *A modo mio. Donne tra creatività e potere*. Rome: Edizioni Magi.
Liotta, E., Turno, M. and Orsucci F. (eds) (1996) *Fra ordine e caos*. Bologna, Italy: Cosmopoli.
Lorenzi, P. (2000) "Nel segno della lontananza", *Anima: Un oscuro impulso interiore*. Bergamo, Italy: Moretti & Vitali.

Magherini, G. (1992) *La sindrome di Stendhal*. Milan: Feltrinelli.
Magli, I. (1997) *Contro l'Europa*. Milan: Bompiani.
Maidenbaum, A. and Berwick, M.E. (2002) *Jung and the Shadow of Anti-Semitism*. York Beach, ME : Nicolas-Hays.
Maidenbaum, A. and Martin, S.A. (eds) (1991) *Lingering Shadows: Jungian, Freudians and Anti-Semitism*. Boston: Shambala.
Maistre, X. de (1908) *A Journey Round My Room*. London: Sisley's.
Mancini, M. (ed.) (2004) *Esilio, pellegrinaggio e altri viaggi*. Viterbo, Italy: Settecittà.
Matte Blanco, I. (1975/1988) *The Unconscious as Infinite Sets*. London: Karnac Books.
—— (1988) *Thinking, Feeling and Being*. London: Routledge.
Maturana, H. and Varela, F. (1980) *Autopoiesis and Cognition: The Realization of Living*. Boston: D. Riedl.
—— (1992) *The Tree of Knowledge: The Biological Roots of Human Understanding*. Boston: Shambala.
McGuire, W. and Hull, R.F.C. (eds.), (1980) *C. G. Jung Speaking: Interviews and Encounters*. London: Pan Books.
Meghnagi, D. (1993) *Freud and Judaism*. London: Karnac Books.
Mellina, S. (1987) *La nostalgia nella valigia*. Padua, Italy: Marsilio.
—— (1992) *Psicopatologia dei migranti*. Rome: G. Lombardo.
—— (1997) *Medici e sciamani, fratelli separati*. Rome: G. Lombardo.
Mengheri, M. (1991) *Il Gioco della sabbia. Dal comportamentismo alla psicologia analitica attraverso la psicologia ambientale*. Pisa, Italy: ETS.
Merleau-Ponty, M. (1962) *Phenomenology of Perception*. London: Routledge.
Mernissi, F. (2001) *Scheherazade goes West*. New York: Washington Square.
Merton, T. (1970) *The Wisdom of the Desert: Sayings from the Desert Fathers of the Fourth Century*. New York: New Directions.
Mio, J.S. and Iwamasa, G.Y. (2004) *Culturally Diverse Mental Health*. Hove, UK: Brunner-Routledge.
Montessori, M. (1972) *Education and Peace*. Chicago: Regnery.
Moore, T. (1992) *Care of the Soul*. New York: Harper Collins.
Morgan, H. (2002) "Exploring Racism", *Journal of Analytical Psychology*, 47.
Nathan, T. (1990) *La follia degli altri. Trattato di Etnopsichiatria clinica*. Florence, Italy: Ponte alle Grazie.
—— (1996) *Etnopsicoanalisi*. Turin, Italy: Bollati Boringhieri.
Natoli, S. (1986) *L'esperienza del dolore*. Milan: Feltrinelli.
Neumann, E. (1949/1989) *The Origins and History of Consciousness*. London: Maresfield.
—— (1955/1974) *The Great Mother*. Princeton, NJ: Princeton University Press.
Orango, O. (ed.) (1991) *Le migrazioni internazionali*. Castrovillari, Italy: Teda Edizioni.
Oury, J. (1992) *Creazione e schizofrenia*. Milan: Spirali/Vel. French edition: *Creation et Schizophrenie* (Collection Debats) Paris: Editions Galilee, 1989.
Panepucci, A. and Piacentini Corsi, T. (eds) (1997) *Individuo e società nel pensiero filosofico e psicoanalitico contemporaneo*. Milan: Franco Angeli.
Papadopoulos, R.K. (2002) *Therapeutic Care for Refugees: No Place like Home*. London: Karnac Books.
Pavese, C. (2002) *The Moon and the Bonfires*. New York: New York Review of Books.

Peat, D. (1987) *Synchronicity*. New York: Bantam Books.
—— (1994) *Lighting the Seventh Fire: The Spiritual Ways, Healing and Science of the Native Americans*. Birch Lane Press.
—— (2005) *Pathways of Change*. Grosseto, Italy: Pari Publishing.
Peat, D. and Briggs, J. (1990) *Turbulent Mirror*. New York: Harper & Row.
Pedrotti, W. (ed.) (1995) *Dal popolo degli uomini. Canti, miti, narrazioni, preghiere degli Indiani del Nordamerica*. Verona, Italy: Demetra.
Perec, G. (1997) *Species of Spaces and Other Pieces*. London: Penguin.
Perez, L. (2001) "Geografie e topografie reali, immaginarie e immaginali." Paper presented at Seminari di Psicologia e Cultura, Catania, Italy, 21 April.
—— (2003) "Homo viator e pellegrinaggio", in *Anima. Figure della devozione*. Bergamo, Italy: Moretti & Vitali.
—— (2004) "Viaggi estatici dell'anima." Paper presented at Amici della Collina conference, Catania, Italy.
Piaget, J. and Inhelder, B. (1967) *The Child's Conception of Space*. New York: W.W. Norton.
Pierantoni, R. (1986) *Forma Fluens. Il movimento e la sua rappresentazione nella scienza, nell'arte e nella tecnica*. Turin, Italy: Boringhieri.
Pignatelli, M. (ed) (1978) *Rivista di Psicologia Analitica: Per una simbolica dell'ambiente, 18*. Venice, Italy: Marsilio.
Plaut, A. (1966) "Reflections about Not Being Able to Imagine", *Journal of Analytical Psychology, 11*, 113–133.
Pompeo, F. (ed.) (1998) *Altri orizzonti. Viaggi, scoperte, tradimenti. Un atlante interculturale*. Rome: Il Mondo 3 Edizioni.
Prete, A. (ed.) (1992) *Nostalgia. Storia di un sentimento*. Milan: Raffaello Cortina Editore.
Puech, H.C. (1985) *Sulle tracce della gnosi*. Milan: Adelphi.
Radin, P. and Blowsnake, S. (1963) *The Autobiography of a Winnebago Indian*. New York: Dover Publications.
Ramorino, F. (1988) *Mitologia classica illustrata*. Milan: Hoepli.
Rank, O. (1952) *The Trauma of Birth*. New York: R. Brunner.
Reagan, T. (2000) *Non-Western Educational Traditions*. London: Lawrence Erlbaum Associates.
Rendell, J., Penner, B. and Borden, I. (eds) (2000) *Gender, Space and Architecture*. London: Routledge.
Roheim, G. (1967) *Psicoanalisi e antropologia*. Paris: Gallimard.
Roland, A. (1988) *In Search of Self in India and Japan: Toward a Cross-Cultural Psychology*. Princeton, NJ: Princeton University Press.
—— (2000) *Cultural Pluralism and Psychoanalysis: The Asian and North American Experience*. Hove, UK: Brunner-Routledge.
Rolf, I. (1978) *Rolfing and Physical Reality*. Rochester, VT: Healing Arts Press.
Rubenstein, R.L. (1985) *The Religious Imagination: A Study in Psychoanalysis and Jewish Theology*. Lanham, MD: University Press of America.
Rucker, R. (1985) *The Fourth Dimension and How to Get There*. London: Rider.
Ryce-Menuhin, J. (ed) (1993) *Jung and the Monotheisms: Judaism, Christianity and Islam*. Hove, UK: Brunner-Routledge.
Samuels, A. (1989) "Fred Plaut in Conversation with Andrew Samuels", *Journal of Analytical Psychology, 34*, 159–183.

—— (1993a) *The Political Psyche*. London: Routledge.
—— (2001) *Politics on the Couch*. London: Profile Books.
—— (1993b) "New Material concerning Jung, Anti-semitism and the Nazis", *Journal of Analytical Psychology*, *38*, 463–470.
Sardello, R. (1988–1989) "Luoghi dell'anima", *Anima*, *1–2*.
—— (1995) *Love and the Soul: Creating a Future for Earth*. New York: Harper Collins.
Saul, J.R. (1999) *The Unconscious Civilization*. New York: Free Press.
—— (2004) *On Equilibrium: Six Qualities of the New Humanism*. New York: Four Walls Eight Windows.
—— (2005) *The Collapse of Globalism and the Reinvention of the World*. New York: Overlook Press.
Sayigh, T. (2002) in W. Dahmash, T. Di Francesco, and P. Blasone (eds) *La terra più amata. Voci della letteratura palestinese*. Rome: Manifestolibri.
Scarpi, P. (1992) *La fuga e il ritorno. Storia e mitologia del viaggio*. Venice, Italy: Marsilio.
Schmitt, C. (1991) *Il nomos della terra*. Milan: Adelphi.
Schumacher, E.F. (1973) *Small Is Beautiful: Economics as if People Mattered*. New York: Harper & Row.
Sheng-yen (ed.) (2001) *La poesia dell'illuminazione*. Rome: Astrolabio.
Sherry, J. (1986) "Jung, the Jews, and Hitler", *Spring*, *46*, 163–175.
Shiva, V. (2005), *Earth Democracy*. Cambridge, MA: South End Press.
Singer, T. (ed.) (2000) *The Vision Thing: Myth, Politics and Psyche in the World*. London: Routledge.
Singer, T. and Kimbles, S.L. (eds) (2004) *The Cultural Complex*. Hove, UK: Brunner-Routledge.
S.I.P.A.G. (1997) *Quaderni di psicoterapia di gruppo: Transpersonale e sogno*. Rome: Borla.
Stern, D.N. (1977) *The First Relationship: Infant and Mother*. Cambridge, MA: Harvard University Press.
—— (1985) *The Interpersonal World of the Infant*. New York: Basic Books.
Stern, D.N. and Bruschweiler-Stern N. (1998) *The Birth of a Mother*. New York: Basic Books.
Symington, J. and Symington, N. (1996) *The Clinical Thinking of Wilfred Bion*. London: Routledge.
Tacey, D. (1993) "Jung's ambivalence toward the World-Soul", *Sphinx*, *5*. London: The London Convivium of Archetypal Studies.
—— (2004) *The Spirituality Revolution*. Hove, UK: Brunner-Routledge.
Thomson, J. (1993) "But where do you really come from?", *Journal of Analytical Psychology*, *38*, 65–76.
Tescione, E. (2003) *Architettura della mente. Brani scelti di letteratura psicoanalitica*. Turin, Italy: Testo & Immagine.
Thoreau, H.D. (1957) *Walden, The Portable Thoreau*. New York: Viking Press.
Tiezzi, E. (1998) *La bellezza e la scienza*. Milan: Raffaello Cortina.
—— (1999) *Che cos'è lo sviluppo sostenibile*. Rome: Donzelli.
Tobin, J.J., Wu, D.Y.H. and Davidson, D.H. (1989) *Preschool in Three Cultures*. New Haven, CT: Yale University Press.
Tolja, J. and Speciani, F. (2000) *Pensare col corpo*. Milan: Zelig editore.
Tomatis, A. (1991) *The Conscious Ear*. Barrytown, NY: Station Hill Press.

—— (2001) *Come nasce e si sviluppa l'ascolto umano*. Como, Italy: Red.
—— (2003) *Siamo tutti nati poliglotti*. Como-Pavia, Italy: Ibis.
Tonucci, F. (1996) *La città dei bambini*. Bari, Italy: Laterza.
Tribe, R. and Raval, H. (2004) *Working with Interpreters in Mental Health*. Hove, UK: Brunner-Routledge.
Trombetta, C. (ed.) (1989) *Psicologia analitica contemporanea*. Milan: Bompiani.
Vacc, N.A., Devaney, S.B. and Brendel, J.M. (2004) *Counseling Multicultural and Diverse Populations*. Hove, UK: Brunner-Routledge.
Vecchio, S. (ed) (1989) *Nostalgia. Scritti psicoanalitici*. Bergamo, Italy: P. Lubrina Editore.
Vianello, M. and Caramazza, E. (2005) *Gender, Space, Power*. London: Free Associates.
Virilio, P. (1986) *Speed and Politics*. New York: Columbia University Press.
—— (1998) *The Virilio Reader*. Malden, MA: Blackwell Press.
—— (2004) *Città panico*. Milan: Raffaello Cortina.
Vitale, E. (2004) *Jus migrandi. Figure di erranti al di qua della cosmopoli*. Turin, Italy: Bollati Boringhieri.
Vitolo, A. (1990) *Un esilio impossibile*. Rome: Borla.
—— (1997) *Le radici della cultura laica*. Rome: Borla.
Weinrib, E. (1983) *Images of the Self*. Boston: Sigo Press.
Widmann, C. (ed.) (1999) *Il viaggio come metafora dell'esistenza*. Rome: Edizioni Magi.
Wiernicki, K. (1997) *Storia degli zingari*. Milan: Rusconi.
Winnicott, D.W. (1985) *Playing and Reality*. London: Pelican Books.
—— (1986) *Home Is Where We Start from*. London: Penguin.
—— (1988) *Human Nature*. London: Free Association Books.
Winston, A.S. (2004) *Defining Difference. Race and Racism in the History of Psychology*. Washington, DC: APA Books.
Yates, F. (1969) *The Art of Memory*. Harmondsworth, UK: Penguin.
Zambrano, M. (1999) *Delirium and Destiny*. Albany, NY: State of New York University Press.
Zayyad, T. (2002) "The Plain of Bani Amer", in W. Dahmash, T. Di Francesco and P. Blasone (eds) *La terra più amata. Voci della letteratura palestinese*. Rome: Manifestolibri.
Zoja, L. (2004) *Storia dell'arroganza. Psicologia e limiti dello sviluppo*. Bergamo, Italy: Moretti & Vitali.
Zolla, E. (1969) *I letterati e lo sciamano. Il pellerossa come cattiva coscienza del bianco*. Milan: Bompiani.

Chapter 9

"Animated" places

Rooting and impermanence

Elena Angelini

I believe that everyone – the people who use space as well as city planners – is aware of the profound malaise to be found in the "meaning" and "form" of the city in this particular historical moment. It is increasingly evident that for architects and city planners the approach to the project has become a long, complex and contradictory process and that it is increasingly difficult for those who work in this sphere to contribute to the creation of spaces in a clear and qualitatively relevant way: especially in the current "anonymous" mode of production.

The difficult "livability" of the city spaces – a clear expression of an equally difficult modality of social experiences – therefore clearly comes to the fore, with questions that are not always easy to answer.

A partial, occasional, but above all detached relationship of those directly involved in the structuring, the study of the spaces, education to the project (architects, town planners or teachers) seems to characterize this malaise. All things considered, interaction with minds, texts or studies from different ambiences turns out to be more useful and worthwhile.

For quite some time the human sciences, philosophy, psychology and anthropology have been proposing reflections on the "meaning of places," more profound and less "distracted" than those proposed by specialists in the field. These ideas, however, are often ignored in the name of a "profession" considered to be of a more "realistic" nature.

Actually for some time now the world of architecture has put a more humanistic approach on the back burner in favor of a more technical approach which, while necessary, ends up by being tuned more to the requirements of the market than to those of the configuration of space.

The hypothesis on which this reflection is based is that two professions as apparently different as architecture and psychoanalysis have their points of encounter. Both are committed to building and supporting something pertaining to man, something that accompanies him throughout his life, in a constant equilibrium between concrete and spiritual facts, body and mind: in other words, between "soul and earth."

As noted by Ruth Ammann (2001), if an encounter between two professions that look at the world is feasible, with a convergence of the architectural and the psychological visions, the principal element that could be treated and discussed is that common and continuous work of union between the internal and the external eye that should characterize both professions.

In C.G. Jung's analytical psychology, the bond between soul and earth dwells in and is expressed by the archetypes. In their contents they symbolize the attachment to nature of the soul and how it continuously influences us. For Jung, however, the soul includes both conscious and unconscious psychic phenomena. This becomes the nodal aspect of his essay, and perhaps also the most equivocal, for us as architects.

In introducing the problems regarding this theme, I have tried to sum up some of the critical aspects I consider to be characteristic of contemporary space, derived from the radical changes in society in recent years. This chapter is therefore organized in a few sub-themes:

- the problems of "form" and "meaning" of space, where I will attempt to list synthetically the principal changes in the sense of collective space in the city and in that of the private space of the home in passing from premodern to modern times (by "premodern" I mean the period that precedes the 17th century, and by "modern" the period that begins around the 17th century)
- the problems of "form" and "measurement" of space, in which I will try to pinpoint the consequences of the excessive size of the contemporary city
- the problems deriving from the use of an imposed rather than a spontaneous form of space, where I will identify the critical aspects resulting from the creation of the figure of the "space technician."

Problems of form and significance of space

The problems connected with the changes that have taken place in the relationship between the form and meaning of a space provide an initial point of departure. The importance and contents of these problems have varied since the advent of modernity.

The pre-industrial city

For example, if we think of the space of the city, we can begin with the fact, I believe indisputable, that the idea of a continuous city no longer exists. The well-defined, limited city has always been considered an ideal image: the city of pre-industrial space, characterized by a continuity of type and morphology, as in most of the lesser Italian historical centers that have become "museums" thanks to conservation aimed at maintaining in time the image rather than the sense of these spaces. This spatiality, expression of cultural continuity, is impossible to create now for it was produced by social forms that have disappeared. Moreover, pre-industrial spatiality cannot be compared with contemporary spatiality, for they come from different social syntheses (Sohn-Rethel 1977). One is a social synthesis based on production (in which there is no social separation of hand and mind in work), and the other a social synthesis based on appropriation, in which hand and mind are socially distinct and, therefore, there is appropriation of the products of work (including intellectual) by those who do not work.

Pre-industrial spatiality was characterized by formal solutions that took shape in time and were collectively formulated. This is no longer possible, for the city today is no longer a homogeneous and continuous ensemble characterized by homogeneous materials, features and techniques.

From the point of view of shape, the pre-industrial city was loosely defined by empty and full spaces, organically connected to the morphology of the land, almost never subject to regular geometrical patterns. This implied a freedom in composition, also connected to rules (such as the statutes), which were however interpreted by the collectivity, leaving a margin of freedom.

With this type of society and this projectual modality we have lost a "qualitative spatiality" (Decandia 2000), the possibility of perfecting spaces with a wealth of possibilities based principally on a first-hand immediate experience rather than on visual perception.

In the pre-industrial city the body played an important part as a means of knowing. There was a relationship of trust, of accessibility, that was established with the physical and natural world as a result of the determined appropriation of everyday use, in a time that passed slowly, marked by the cycles of the seasons, the passing of the years and the rhythm of natural events.

The body moved in and "felt" space, its qualities, the differences, the sounds, the odors, etc. This did not mean that we have now inevitably lost these human characteristics and these ways of appropriation of spaces, but only that we have drastically reduced their value with respect to others. Actually we are faced with the loss of a knowledge of a poietic type, knowing that in premodern times the entire community was involved in actively structuring the spaces, which created a non-separation between knowledge and praxis.

The interaction with the territory ultimately established by the pre-industrial community included symbolic (Cassirer 1961), existential, social, ecological, esthetic, economic and productive valences, organizing an "artificial" structuring of space that was strongly permeated with nature.

The modern city

What, on the other hand, has fundamentally changed with the advent of modernity? After the passage to modern science in the 17th century and the advent of so-called modernity, a new reformulation of the concept of nature and knowledge was introduced, which led to important changes in the organization of space and time.

Knowledge, first of all, became objectifiable. The ordered cosmos, structured and comprehensible, of which man understood the meaning and that provided his life with order, was replaced by the idea of an inanimate mechanism, completely detached from the knowledgeable subject, lacking all spiritual essence and all expressive dimension, that functions autonomously in a self-sufficient manner according to a universal law and order.

The idea that time could be thought of as separate from matter and not incorporated in the creation of phenomena but seen as a system of measure external to matter was connected to this concept. Time then was transformed into a question of distances, in a dimension without a story, without memory.

Reason became the self-sufficient criterion by which human activities were explained, and the beautiful was identified with the order of the world.

Reality is no longer the place for events and qualities but an extension outside of the knowing individual. Territorial space, in precedence perceived and described by means of a qualitative intuition aimed at capturing an indefinite variety of aspects and circumstances, begins theoretically to be reduced to a geometric parameter, to an absolute scheme of reference and measure.

There is a progressive disenchantment of the territory, an increasingly pronounced separation of man-made objects, natural elements and monuments from any spiritual and expressive contents.

The city becomes a background to contemplate, something that relegates the affective memory and the social value of that collectivity to second place. At the same time, contemplative esthetic pleasure becomes the only way to compensate for the loss of transcendence and heal the wound caused by the disenchantment of the world (Bodei 1995).

Pleasure in the beautiful, which depended on experience, was replaced definitively by the detached and contemplative eye.

With the creation of the expert and the need for method, the role of the community in designing the city is increasingly curtailed. This process affects the right and capacity of each of us to structure our environment, alienating the wealth of knowledge involved in the common practice of living and construction.

But from the first, problems began to appear with the modern city, orderly and "sanitized." As early as 1940 the writings of Anna Freud and John Bowlby demonstrated that mental health did not coincide with physical health, while what remained irreplaceable was a certain affective climate (Choay 1965). The progressive city planners indeed did not take account of the fact that rational urban spaces, laid out hygienically, were not enough for a successful environment. Integration of human behavior into the urban environment depends above all on the presence of a certain existential climate (Choay 1965).

The most stimulating postwar studies are those resulting from the advent of phenomenology, calling attention to the subjectivizing of space and the American studies of the 1960s connected with the study of urban perception. The latter turned their attention anew to the inhabitants, changing them from passive subjects to interlocutors of the planners (Kepes 1961, Lynch 1969).

The city was no longer simply a picture for the users of the city but was thought of as a function of other aspects (existential, practical, affective, etc.). What is to be studied therefore, as Choay pointed out, is the irreconcilable difference between the esthetic perception and the much more specific perception of the city.

The scientific aspect of town planning still seems to be a myth of the industrial society, and the models applied remain nothing more than rationalized projections of collective and individual images.

The city therefore has to function, but it must also be the bearer of meanings. And the real problem is none other than a lack of meanings.

As Choay maintains, the city not only is an object or an instrument to carry out certain vital functions, but is equally a chart of mental relationships, the locus of an activity that uses more complex sign systems.

The contemporary city

Every day we are all aware of, or at least we all experience (those of us who live in cities), the recent changes in the contemporary city. At this point it is natural to ask if the form of the dwelling today (and with it the city) is still a graph of the contents of the life of the individuals and their way of living together (Coppola Pignatelli 1982).

What can be deduced from the current way of "space making?" From the feeling provided by the spaces in our cities? From the total absence of spontaneity in the organization of the apartment, the last scrap of place still at our disposal?

The answer is relatively banal. Our current situation is that of someone who has had something important expropriated, and this has deprived us of a part of ourselves.

Today spaces are designed by the groups in power that characterize our society and who have developed a specific jargon of their own – a logotechnique. The users of the spaces do not participate either in the creation of this jargon or in the other constituent semiological systems. But this logotechnique has not achieved the completeness of a language.

The fact that the structuring of space is not due to the simple satisfaction of human needs cannot be denied. In the past this functionalism, including architecture, tried to have the structuring of space correspond to a "good answer," connected to a series of needs, but this interpretation circumvented the complex relationship that exists between forms and social order.

The great differences between the many spatial structures existing today that apparently satisfy the same needs demonstrate how limited this interpretation is (Mumford 1961, Rapaport 1972).

As Signorelli (1982) reminds us, it is the social relations that give form to the infinitely ductile human needs or instincts, and not vice versa. Therefore it is still the relations of power that determine the constitution of the social system and the structuring of the city. To have space (in the sense of a resource) therefore means having power; and therefore more space, more power; less space, less power.

But then if the person–space relationship coincides with the relationship between persons in space and with the cultural conscience of this relationship, we must, in speaking of spaces, turn to a situation historically defined and manipulated on a cultural level.

The rule that defines our individual cities is that of individualism, producing fragmentation and solitude.

The house/home

The home, the private dwelling space, is one of the most representative aspects of a resistance to change (Coppola Pignatelli 1982). The home and the social group (the family) that has been structuring this space for centuries has been stabilized in a model that guarantees its continuity throughout the years. Together "family–home" is, and has been, society's controlling instrument (Angelini 2002).

Today, however, the family is undergoing profound changes. Its role is characterized by other tasks with respect to the preceding model. While every economic–social system produces its own type of family (or of non-family), it is also true that a type of family corresponds to a type of dwelling that perpetuates its life.

In contemporary society the family is no longer the productive nucleus. It is still a primary place of socialization (when possible) but above all it is a compensatory place where individual frustrations and insecurities are healed.

A change in the definition of space–house corresponds to this aspect. The house today is a space that has been diminished in the sense that its functions have been reduced (a place to eat, sleep, but one meets people elsewhere . . .), a place where the predominating law is consumption (goods, information, etc.) as a passive acceptance of the current values imposed by mass production. Consumption massifies the family in producing socialization and in discharging tensions, with a consequent leveling of behavior and consensus that is also expressed in the structuring of the spaces.

Even though their lifestyles in the many living quarters for singles are different (no longer bound to the rigid image of the woman as angel of the hearth or the man as head of the house), in the definition of their new space they simply perpetuate the stereotypes proposed by the market (often even inverting the roles: "playboy" houses for the women, "angel of the hearth" houses for the men).

The result, in other words, is that the contemporary city has chosen to replace the complex fabric of private and collective spaces with an expansion and super-evaluation of the private space. Today the individual space, the space of an apartment or of a one-family house, is what characterizes the city: no longer something shared by all. The exterior is often perceived as hostile and the home increasingly becomes (in particular in Italy) a refuge and guarantee for the future. Search for (and the ownership of) a house that is "in tune" (Augé 1994) with one's personal role (real or imagined) is becoming increasingly spasmodic and significant.

While on one hand the search for a concordance of the house with the idea one has of oneself is seen as natural and necessary – one cannot help but think of the home as an individual extension, as the expression of one's personal growth – on the other hand, the importance of the individual space–house seems disturbing, above all if compared to the almost absent sense of the city and collectivity.

The organization of private space has always revealed "profound bonds with the biological and psychological requirements of the individuals and groups that use it." As interpreted by Heidegger (1958), this type of constructing or giving form has been definitively replaced by the pre-packaged market version of a space-form, proposed by illustrated periodicals (reflections of the dominant culture) that tell us what our way of living should be.

The lack of life and of appropriation expressed by most of the domestic interiors to be found at all social levels is extraordinary and at the same time indicative. Also to be noted is the standardization, with improbable houses suggested by the media or the more or less specialized magazines to be found everywhere: "minimalist" bare and empty houses, without objects, in a time when the object rules everyday life, or "theater" houses, "ethnic" houses, "peasant" houses, high-tech houses, filled with super-efficient objects, "humble" houses, "museum" houses overflowing with useless objects, fake family "souvenirs," mementos from other cultures or more real identities (where the objects are still really used). And all this in an epoch where it is increasingly difficult to find even a fragmentary identity.

Our homes then appear as any number of models of human relationship, but they remain an unreal and imaginary catalogue of possibilities since they bear witness to the renouncing of the experience of doing in favor of the juxtaposition of a "sign": a sign that is condemned to a sterile solitude, lacking any real comparison with life and human relations.

Problems of form and measurement of space

I have been nurturing a dream ever since I was small and lived in what were called, disparagingly, *borgate romane* or "Roman outer suburbs." I wanted to live in a house that had the "right relationship with the land," in other words that had a small green space round the house, a space where I could dream and see a few small plants grow. Today this is "the" dream (real or imagined), bordering on the neurotic, of many persons. The house surrounded by a lawn and a garden, no matter how large or small, is the leitmotiv present in the minds of almost all those who buy a house, an approach that is anything but insignificant.

Kinds of cities

The contemporary city is no longer something that can be completely known. It is enormous, stretching out beyond the humanly conceivable. The advent of industrialization and the possibilities connected to mobility have had strong repercussions on its current design and have produced a variety of spatial forms and ways of use that have changed the livability of the city itself.

The introduction of delocalized functions with the advent of capitalism, and therefore the fact that home and work were no longer in the same place, imposed a model of life that involves traveling daily over considerable distances. Added to these were the new technological possibilities that allowed increasingly daring, but also less human, forms and proportions of spaces.

There are many types currently identified by architects and city planners as the new kinds of cities. The best known among these are the "diffused city," the "global city," the "city region," the "market city," etc. But the extraordinary variety highlights the difficulty in recognizing forms that are homogeneous and subject to repetition, with a complete breakdown of the form into many and more complex types and groups.

Today the widespread illusion regarding the infinite possibilities of mobility that we believe we can realize has led to the creation of what Chiara Merlini has identified as unifamily territories (Merlini 1998). These extensive residential areas are composed of one-family dwellings, characterized by the absence of places for social relations and based solely on the celebration of the private environment. The myth of green areas here merges with the indifference to the place.

The problem is not, however, moralistic. These more dispersed "kinds of cities" are not new, nor are they to be censured. What is perplexing is the difficulty (or, better, the intrinsic impossibility) of living in these spatial forms with simplicity and spontaneity, especially regarding relationships and sense of identity with the place. It is as if in forming these new aggregation models we had ignored the identifying aspects, the body, its needs and characteristics, dissociating them from the real desires and uses that take place on different levels.

Other real or presumed phenomena are connected to these attitudes of individualism, such as the widespread "fear" of the condominium (joint ownership), the strong desire for a return to nature (generally seen as a moment of isolation from the collectivity, from the city and the urban environment), the recent fashions of cocooning and nesting, and lastly the increasing influence of various disciplines that call attention and care to space, such as bioregionalism (of American inspiration) or the *feng-shui* (of oriental stamp) also translated into a banal Western-style space clearing (Lambert 2002).

Ecology and the sacred

But what do these improvements and these more or less realistic requirements tell us?

If the spreading fear of condominium can on the whole be connected to the powerful sense of individuality expressed by the current aggregational forms of space, the call of bioregionalism and nature goes deeper.

The aspiration to a new (or old) contact with nature seems to me on the whole to be due to a growing need for a new morality of life, of simplicity, of distance from the masses and consumption; a sort of atonement for all our more or less capitalistic forms of life. Added to these are the various political overtones regarding the social commitment with reference to ecology and a (perhaps less imaginable) search for a sense of the ecological sacred (Bateson 1979, Todd and Todd 1989).

The mechanistic view of the universe that interprets the various systems of life as inert instruments of an imagined model is gradually being countered (although with difficulty) by the idea of scientific development no longer based on the Cartesian separation of body and soul, but an idea of progress based on the search for a synthesis of nature and culture, in which the sanctity of every living being is honored.

It is this new recoupling of sacred and profane that therefore pervades most of the movements involved in biological planning.

In other words, a corresponding need for fusion between natural and artificial seems to be emerging concurrently with the phenomenon of individualistic isolation, apparently "ignoring" the aspect connected to human relations and the fundamental rapport between place and community.

Non-places

In 1995 a booklet by Marc Augé made a great flurry in the world of architects, anthropologists and those who had anything to do with space. The title was *Non-Places: Introduction to an Anthropology of Supermodernity*. Augé tackled the definition of "anthropologic place" (inherited from M. Mauss) as opposed to "non-place," a typical expression of the current situation of super-modernity whose principal characteristic was excess.

Non-places are not defined by the classical anthropological features of place connected to geographical, historical and national identities or to conventional relational functions. The non-place does not integrate the original place; it is a mute place of solitary individuality, a place of provisory passage. He who uses space and frequents the non-places returns by way of contrast to a place rooted in the territory. But if the non-places are the complete expression of supermodernity, they also constitute a paradoxical attraction, an experience that, according to Augé, in its anonymity will make us feel the communion of human destinies in solitude.

In the 1990s Augé's text unleashed a fierce, albeit "academic" diatribe with a variety of definitions (cities without places, cities of places, of crossing, etc.), polemics that have left their mark but that basically alienated the main theme under discussion: the space of the city and its relationship with those who live there.

Space, people, relations

Much earlier a text outdated, but classic, titled in Italian *Il feticcio urbano* by the psychologist Alexander Mitscherlich (1965) had identified various fundamental aspects: space is people and their relationships.

Mitscherlich identified some of the banes of the contemporary city in a few basic elements, such as private property and the limits of town planning. Anticipating the more recent concepts of a metropolis characterized by conflict and dis-identity, he pointed out how the relationship with the place and its values of possession were fundamental to man and his relationships, all without sentimentalism and regrets for the "lost city."

What he did was to broach a fundamental idea: return to the capacity to develop preliminary intuits, ideas, concepts and everything that was not produced unilaterally in a planning office. What is required is a public opinion that is able to define itself not only in commercial but also in spiritual terms.

Problems of imposed, non-spontaneous form

[. . .] there is a Greek word, as commonly used now as in antiquity, and which we could recover for that which is the inverse of architecture: *oikodomia* . . . the art of building the house, *oikodomesthai oikema*, making oneself a home.
(Ivan Illich 1980; translated from the Italian by transl.)

In a recent piece on the strategic plan of Turin, I find this definition of a city:

The city must be seen as a saleable product, whose clients are the citizens; as such the city must be competitive and must be able to vary its products in line with the diversification of the demand.

This note and in particular the term "saleable product" reveal one of the fundamental problems involved in designing a city. The meaning of the project has been lost, the city and its spaces are drawing ever closer to a market product. There is no longer a direct relationship between needs, cultural models and spaces, within which the architect interprets and expresses the collective needs.

The contemporary project thought up by technicians, by experts, is no longer collective or participated in, but imposed. It reveals its contradictions when the spotlight falls on the spaces of the unexpected city (Cottino 2003), provisory and fragmentary spaces that fall outside the "norm" and are therefore subject to planning that is an alternative to the traditional.

The relationship with place is no longer fundamental and the technician can plan a space where we can live and grow old apart from the relationships we have with it. One can therefore use a territory without really knowing it, without appropriative relationships based on values. It seems to have been forgotten that the differences depend in part on the communities and the appropriative values they attribute to places.

Paradoxically today, however, an interest in context and other spaces corresponds to this widespread detachment from place and identity. The elimination of spatial barriers, the diffusion of the media, communication via Internet and the spread of economic forms based on the free flow of capital have ended up by making the image of the differences spectacular and outclassing reality (Harvey 1988).

The differences, the local aspects, are not images to which attention is given for the formal components, without considering the meaning, but community constructions. Identity is not only a matter of forms, but also the outcome of an interactive constructive process between society and environment.

The point then is that if we are looking for an "authentic" architecture (Coppola Pignatelli 1982) – where, in other words, there is a fusion of project and natural and cultural environment – it can spring spontaneously from the relationship between need, spaces and culture, or it can be carried out. But when there is no direct relationship between needs, cultural models and spaces that provides guidelines to be used by the architect in interpreting and expressing the collective needs, the spaces are no longer an authentic spontaneous production but are only the result of an ongoing conceptual experimentation.

The task of the architect has therefore become complex and contradictory. It is no longer aimed at expressing a common search for cultural models of reference, but is concerned with interpreting needs and values expressed by communities that have been broken up in a state of unwitting confusion.

Architect

The architect cannot of course renounce his role of "interpreter" without dramatically contradicting, and dissociating himself from, his profession. But neither can he renounce a more profound contact with the value, the wealth and the complexity that making space represents.

Moreover, in current production the instruments used often shift the balance of the work of planning in the direction of a geometric, rational type of spatiality, connected to mathematics. On the other hand, the spatial aspects most directly connected to the experience of the senses and kinesthetics (which can now be studied by means of complicated virtual technologies) must be considered anew, although often in the profession they are neglected by virtue of the banalization required in reducing inhabiting to the production of merchandise that repeats stereotyped models. This widespread diseducation in terms of the space of the senses that has currently played in favor of a greater enrichment of signs of another type (cultural . . .) must after all be coped with in the planning.

The *house* itself, as previously mentioned, cannot today be considered solely merchandise or social service. How then can the distance that still divides the user and the planner be dealt with and remedied? How can the capacity of the user to produce his own image of space and his personal way of appropriation resurface?

Appropriation of space

As Carotenuto (1982) reminds us, space, the surroundings, and the territory can be considered "transitional objects," as defined by Winnicott, that serve as mediators between ourselves and the external world. But space nowadays no longer belongs to us, nor does it console us as the transitional object would in the absence of the mother.

The relative lack of meaning of the project mortifies the message. The space planned receives very little from outside and talks to itself in a melancholy monologue understood only by specialists and academic schools or, alternatively, presents itself as a product navigating between fashionable references. Thus this spatial distance between subject and space is one of the elements that must be attended to and studied more in the future, since it is the privileged place of communication. Indeed the project, so far, is seen as an untouchable product to which modifications or adaptations cannot be made, the creative work of an individual.

When the role of the community is of an interpretative, adaptive type, it is a sign that the capacity for the conservation of the essential cultural heritage, no matter how humble and reduced to minimum terms it may be, persists.

It is not a matter of turning to "cosmetic practices" such as the "spurious" projects of a participative nature (between architects, users and institutions) that fall within the great market operations. Major consideration must once more be given to the role of the community, as well as an awareness on the part of the planner, in an attempt to identify a system through which the capacity of the community to transform and manage the physical space will not be wasted (Paolella 2003).

The speculative character it has today has not always defined housing by people, but in the past was also a qualified expression of autonomous municipalities who succeeded in consciously sharing objectives and techniques.

Participation

The contents of participation can be renewed if its aim is that of overcoming the separation between citizens and place. It is clear that if places are lived in without creating a community, participation will not happen simply because it is considered good, but it must be specifically focalized and constructed coherently and with method.

While this is apparently a paradox – how can a community be formed if there is no preceding sharing? – it is actually one of the few feasible avenues, since re-establishing a general conscious commitment to creating a more human space in the future that is actually sustainable is a priority. The desires expressed today by the community are often imposed by trends and cultural fashions and are continuously changing. For a real change of values and ideas, the only possible instrument will be the chance to experience things directly.

Experience

People change when they actively discover that another way of doing things, of living, or of being, is more pleasant or satisfying than the old way.

Our commitment as planners must then be directed towards a recovery of the relationship and the participation of the community in the transformation and management of space, possibly with the help of more convivial techniques such as those mentioned by Ivan Illich. This renewed relationship will serve not only to increase an ephemeral consensus, but will attempt to connect the creativity of the planners to that of the settled community (Paolella 2003).

Creativity

The point of departure must be the creativity that is so important to the profession, attempting to bring it to the schools and to briefings on the project (and in education), so that each of us will once more be aware of its value.

It will be aimed at an architecture that is not only something outside us, to look at in a detached way, but space endowed with a meaning that is perceptive – in relationship with sensations – as well as psychological, communicating with our varied cultural references. The current challenge is that of working in this perspective. Until architecture recovers its role of being a stimulating space, a welcoming place, taken care of, cared for (above all by those who create and design it), consisting of relationships, persons and feelings (in addition to more or less beautified physical materials), it will not be able to trigger and maintain emotional susceptibility, or restore the wealth and complexity of our souls.

References

Ammann, R. (2001) *Gli spazi che abitiamo. Architettura e psicoanalisi*, "Anima". Bergamo, Italy: Moretti & Vitali.

Angelini, E. (2002) "Firenze, tipologia e rappresentatività sociale. L'esperimento dell'Isolotto", in *Edilizia popolare*, no. 273–274.

Augé, M. (1994) *Ville e tenute. Etnologia della casa di campagna*. Milan: Elèuthera.

—— (1995) *Non-Places: Introduction to an Anthropology of Supermodernity*. London: Verso.

Bateson, G. (1979) *Mind and Nature: A Necessary Unit*. New York: E. P. Dutton.

Bodei, R. (1995) *Le forme del bello*. Bologna, Italy: Il Mulino.

Carotenuto, A. (1982) "Territorialità, distanza, spazio esistenziale, corporalità: elementi di psicologia dello spazio ad uso dell'architetto", in P. Coppola Pignatelli (ed.), *I luoghi dell'abitare. Note di progettazione*. Rome: Officina Edizioni.

Cassirer, E. (1961) *Filosofia delle forme simboliche*, vol. II, *Il pensiero mitico*. Florence, Italy: La Nuova Italia.

Choay, F. (1965) *L'Urbanisme: utopie et réalités*. Paris: Ed. du Seuil.

Coppola Pignatelli, P. (ed.) (1982) *I luoghi dell'abitare. Note di progettazione*. Rome: Officina Edizioni.

Cottino, P. (2003) *La città imprevista. Il dissenso nell'uso dello spazio urbano*. Milan: Elèuthera.

Decandia, L. (2000) *Dell'identità. Saggio sui luoghi: per una critica della razionalità urbanistica*. Soveria Mannelli, Italy: Rubbettino.

Harvey, D. (1988) "I luoghi urbani all'interno del 'villaggio globale': reflections on the urban condition in late twentieth century capitalism", in L. Mazza (ed.), *Le città e il futuro delle metropoli*. Milan: Electa.

Heidegger, M. (1958) "Bâtir Habiter Penser", in *Essais et Conférences*. Paris: Gallimard.

Illich, I. (1980) (ed. Collettivo per un Abitare autogestito) *Autcostruzione e tecnologie conviviali per uso delle tecnologie alternative nel costruire-abitare*. Bologna: CLUEB.

Kepes, G. (1961) *The Language of Vision*. Chicago: Theobald.

Lambert, M. (2002) *Ogni cosa al suo posto e un posto per ogni cosa*. Milan: Corbaccio.

Lynch, K. (1969) *L'immagine della città*. Venice, Italy: Marsilio.

Merlini, C. (1998) "Territori unifamiliari", in *Metamorfosi Quaderni di architettura*, no. 38.

Mitscherlich, A. (1965) *Die Unwirtlichkeit unserer Städte. Anstiftung zum Unfrieden*. Frankfurt am Main, Germany: Suhrkamp Verlag.

Mumford, L. (1961) *The City in History*. New York: Harcourt Brace and World.

Paolella, A. (2003) *Progettare er abitare. Dalla percezione delle richieste alle soluzioni tecnologiche*. Milan: Elèuthera.

Rapaport, A. (1972) *Pour une anthropologie de la maison*. Paris: Dunod.

Signorelli, A. (1982) "Integrazione, consenso, dominio: spazio e alloggio in una prospettiva antropologica", in P. Coppola Pignatelli (ed.), *I luoghi dell'abitare. Note di progettazione*. Rome: Officina Edizioni.

Sohn-Rethel, A. (1977) *Lavoro intellettuale e lavoro manuale. Per la teoria della sintesi sociale*. Milan: Feltrinelli.

Todd, N.J. and Todd, J. (1989) *Progettare secondo natura*. Milan: Elèuthera.

Turner, J.F.C. (1972) *Freedom to Build: Dweller Control of the Housing Process*. New York: Macmillan.

—— (1976) *Housing by People: Towards Autonomy in Building Environments*, London: Marion Boyars.

Chapter 10

The garden, psychic landscape

Flavia D'Andreamatteo

In the imaginary, the idea of "garden" is not limited to architecture and botany but gravitates towards an ideal and mythical world. It is therefore an ideal subject to use in describing the connection between soul and earth.

Not infrequently I have worked in institutions for children, centers for the disabled or for those with schizophrenic disorders that were surrounded by trees and plants. The approach often led through parks or gardens, some beautiful, others less so. These short walks marked the beginning of interior journeys and generated psychological repercussions.

The garden was thus transformed into a body that was alive within, which became to my eyes an effective metaphor for psychic dynamism.

This chapter, with countless possible ramifications, consists of various thoughts on the garden, integrating my experience with some of my favorite excerpts from Jung. I intend to pause along the way as I confront various themes, as if they were flowerbeds, where the inner psychic life and the objective reality of the garden interpenetrate. I will then move on into the main body of the garden with four parts devoted to suffering, anger, sacrifice, and care. Other considerations will conclude this map of the symbolism of the garden.

Introduction

In Western tradition the first image of the garden is that of paradise: "And the Lord God planted a garden eastward in Eden and there he put the man whom he had formed" (Genesis). Humans, expelled from Eden, in all times and in many places, attempted to recreate that lost paradise, constructing gardens. The history of gardens shows us that human beings have always considered the garden as something special, a font of nostalgia, infused with profound aspirations.

> Every garden, indeed, bears witness to the inner life of a community and becomes a cultural container, a place for interpreting the world. Man is

the maker of his gardens, whether ideal or real, and they are an integral part of the transfiguration of the landscape in which he lives.

(Venturi Ferraiolo 1987)

The development of the art of the garden through the centuries also provides a clue to how the relationship between psyche and earth was transformed.

The first garden is a tree in an enclosure, the original boundary between culture and nature. The first temple also consisted of stones arranged around a tree, confirming the relation between garden and the desire for transcendence. The gardens that have more than others represented this desire are the *hortus conclusus* and the Zen gardens, dating to the same period but far removed geographically. The *hortus conclusus* reflects above all the soul of the monks in their attempts at being reunited with God in the freedom of solitude. The wall of the *hortus conclusus* marks the boundary between an inner world of prayer and work and an external world seen as vain and violent. The garden is virginal, not like wild nature but like Mary from whom Christ was born; it is the new Eden for the new Adam. The functionality of the garden (permitting the monks to grow flowers, fruits, vegetables, and medicinal herbs in distinct spaces) did not overshadow its symbolic valence. Its structure was the reproduction of paradise. The model for the monastic cloister, even if no longer seen as symbol, is still to be found in modern European gardens.

The Zen garden based on rocks and the way in which they are arranged comes from the Japanese Buddhist tradition and its goal is an essential beauty in minimum size. Rather than religious images, the Zen monks prefer gardens as a means of expression of forms that, as they change, reflect the constantly changing universe. The succession of immobile landscapes gives the mind the peace it needs to permit expansion.

In the Greek garden the gods often appear among amber trees and ponds surrounded by roses. The Arabs protected their ideal private paradises of plants and flowers and couches with canals and high walls. For the Romans the garden became a place of leisure and reflection: the dwelling of the tutelary gods of the house where refuge and council were to be found. As previously mentioned, the medieval garden developed in inner protected spaces where monks cultivated the hope of defeating sickness and the devil.

Nature became matter for the man of the Renaissance. The Italian garden, halfway between equilibrium and play, is an authentic explosion of geometrical patterns and splendor. The landscape gardeners of the 18th century created natural pictures framed by gardens: nature was the protagonist, illuminated by man's reason. With the 19th century the feeling for nature exploded and the Romantic garden is emotion and the search for reflections of the soul. The peaceful garden was transformed into a visionary place where nature displayed its disturbing superiority. In the 20th century the garden became smaller, the place where the evils of the city could be healed and cured. Garden cities were invented. In designing interior spaces, architects were interested in a mutual interpenetration of nature and progress.

From the 1960s on, in creating gardens artists working with Land Art have been looking for a way to connect art and environment, moved by the ethical desire to reconstruct a harmonious relationship between nature and the industrial society. Contemporary landscape gardeners cannot ignore the ecological aspect. Today creating a garden is also a way in which to take care of the earth, restoring the space and care that is its due.

Suffering and loss

There is a basic contradiction in man's ambition to create transcendental places on the earth, for man and nature can never be separated. There is no garden, from the most essential to the most ecstatic, that does not depend on its subterranean life. The yearning for paradise is based, and sometimes, sinks, on the most elementary need for earthly certainty. James Hillman ("Betrayal," in *Senex et puer*) says that the image of the garden as the beginning of the human condition is the representation of what we might call primary faith. It is the absolute conviction, beyond any anxiety, fear or doubt, that the earth under our feet is solid and will not fail. The desire for a life of blessed abandon without responsibility can be clipped but probably never completely truncated.

Every time we create privileged relationships we return to the divine garden and let ourselves be lulled in the illusion of an indestructible union. Looking elsewhere, however, we realize that we are still on earth. Our relationship, precious as it may be, is not perfect and, like every terrestrial garden, it has its visible vegetation and invisible roots, sun and shadows. The risk of abandonment becomes a suffering with which to live; weeds, nettles and darnel grow among the innocent flowers, aside from any reclamation.

We are no longer in paradise but on the earth, and at night the place where we walked with joy in the light of day becomes a theater for atrocious crimes. The person we wholeheartedly trusted betrays us and no longer wants us by his side, and everything around us seems to reflect the duplicity of life. Nature does not explain its actions but leaves those whose task is creative to figure out why (Hillman, 1973). Nature's indifference means we have to deal with our judgment alone.

Reflection, so in keeping with the atmosphere of the garden, produces an awareness of one's condition and the sorrow of exile (Starobinski, 1990). When the illusion that someone will carry the weight of reality for us has vanished, we find ourselves face to face with the sensation of a life that is provisional, like the flowers.

When we enter a garden, we can establish a relationship with nature, feel we are within a greater vital cycle, participating in the various forms of life around us. We can overcome our narcissism and feel we are physically in direct relation, like the plants, to the sun and the wind. This can help us to assimilate, without sinking, the awareness of impermanence, partiality and incompleteness. For the garden is also an evocation of mortality, of the loss of the paradise in the making. Recognizing our limits brings us close both to life and its mysterious becoming and to the awareness that our psychic and corporeal innerness is made of the same substance as the earth.

In Jung's concept the body of the garden is the earth and the dependence of mind on the earth is a question that concerns the very beginnings and foundations of the mind – things that from time immemorial have lain buried in the darkness. Jung is referring to a bond that is both immediate and inscrutable, and that envelops us but does not reveal itself. It is a mystery that might possibly be more tangible in a garden (Jung 1927).

Anger

Eden is a place for contemplation and a place for nourishment. Adam, without effort and in the fullest sense, enjoys a beautiful benevolent nature but, once outside of paradise, he experiences the fatigue of work. Human hands and the mind learn and make progress, but regret and nostalgia linger on. The memory of the original garden must, therefore, be eliminated. Nature must be exploited and used. Places for cultivation, for producing, for living are separated from places for the observation and enjoyment of nature, creating a split between what is useful and what is beautiful. The greater the functionality, the less is the space devoted to the garden, eliminated from land to be used for growing food and eliminated from the cities, where at the most a few "playgrounds" can be tolerated. The countryside, increasingly less contemplative but highly productive, welcomes the advent of industrial agriculture which forces monocultures on the earth and also deprives it of animal life.

In this fierce exploitation one cannot help but discern the type of cynicism developed by the person who feels betrayed. The relationship with the earth reflects the symptoms of physical fear of an unelaborated psychical fear. Landscapes are created, ironclad defenses against the unexpected and betrayal. The result is a paranoid universe characterized not by trust but by the force of a power that wants to exclude every unknown. The risk of another devastating fall from Eden must be kept in check. What in nature cannot be regulated – its shadows and its disorder – are kept at arm's length, denied or considered useless.

Surrounding nature with ironclad defenses, outside and within us, can lock the soul inside a preordained plan of development that, at times, is the same as betrayal of ourselves. Not only unproductive nature or the person who might abandon us are thought of as the enemy. The enemy is something that devours us in the shadow within us that we pretend not to feel.

The inability to merge with the incompleteness of external nature and the poverty of the other, and recognize them in oneself, makes man unintentionally inconsistent, narrow-minded and avaricious. The production, exchange and consumption of the earth or the relationship with others, perpetuated with anger and a sense of egoistic retaliation, does not satisfy but triggers new desires, new needs. "Need can be seen as a sign that an object is lacking, whether in the exterior world of the senses or the interior experience. The inextinguishable thirst aroused is the effect of the impossibility of saturation, of its dynamics aspiring to the infinite" (Màdera and Tarca 2003).

There seems to be no end to the way we are using our resources to destroy our species, animals, the land. In seeking to keep real privation at arm's length, we are developing an ethics of profit that overrides the "ethics of contemplation," a defensive system that deprives us of the experience of participation in the beautiful. This partial relationship with nature creates an artificial and falsified esthetics, profoundly anesthetic because it helps us not to feel the pain. In contrast, "the esthetic experience presupposes the inseparability of the contemplation of a landscape from living in it . . . the content and living in what we contemplate are inseparable" (Assunto 1973:174). Respecting and preserving a superior natural order possibly brings us too close to the sense of abandonment and fragility, too close to the experience of the mystery of the earth.

The sacrifice

In the myth of the Garden of Eden, the earth on which Adam and Eve fall is the place of punishment. In the story of the expulsion from paradise, nature appears corrupt and this myth corrupts the whole world, with nature perceived as something defiled (Campbell and Moyers 1988). Campbell's words reinforce the hypothesis that the relationship with nature reflects a fixation on the trauma of abandonment. The unsuccessful elaboration of the loss of a paradisiacal existence makes it difficult to simply pause in contemplation of what the world of nature is. This would probably require strenuous efforts on the part of human consciousness. Looking at the earth as a useful consumer product, an area for business speculation, or transforming the vitality of a lovely landscape or the charm of a garden into settings for publicity seems to be a rapid and productive way of eliminating a problem. For Jung, production and usefulness were ideals that seemed to want to indicate a way to flee from problematic complications, with the consequent development of the physical existence, but not of civilization (Jung 1931–33). The difficulty of renouncing weakens our awareness that nature and the sacrifice of her resources are what our complex social systems depend on for their survival.

On the other hand, in the myths of the origins of agriculture it is the hero who sacrifices himself, transforming himself into food for his grateful community. The plant growing from the dismembered body parts of a divinity or a hero is a motif that recurs frequently in various parts of the world. For the

Algonquin Indians corn grows where a beautiful girl with green feathers on her head is buried. In Polynesia the coconut takes life from a young man who asks his beloved to kill him and bury his head from which a tree will grow. Obviously there is also an analogy with the Christian rite of communion in which Christ, with his sacrifice, becomes food for the human spirit. The relationship with the plant world is characterized by the sacrificial cycle. One tends a plant that will be eaten; what increases life is a death. The individual is not an entity completely separated from the nature around him, but is like the branch of the plant that nourishes it.

The loss of the sense of belonging that man and nature once had has reached pathological levels in the organization of Western society today, and the ecological emergency reveals its limits.

In the cities, parks and gardens are the only nature that accompanies us every day, but while they are intact in our imagination or in garden theories, they are not so in practice. The public parks are often misused and their "living beauty" humiliated. But we are unable to consider this a personal problem. In the complex scenario of modernity and the contradictory relationships with nature, the garden presents itself as a metaphor for the creation of a new synthesis. The capacity to suspend the desire for personal gratification and, at the same time, to contemplate what has been lost, is the sacrifice the garden asks of us. Pausing in its dark side we can support the weight of our consciousness, in contact with and not against nature, imagining new landscapes in which to exist.

The sacrifice of the divine garden brings forth the consciousness that generates culture, which, in turn, conforming to the cycles of the plant world, recreates a terrestrial garden. The culture, characteristic of the cultured man, is first of all the art of cultivating the land (Venturi Ferraiolo 1987).

Nature and human wisdom work together in the art of the garden. As he works, a good gardener uses his creative and organizational capacities but he also knows how to give things up, adjusting to and confronting the nature on which he depends. He is wise and accepts the death of his loveliest flowers, drastically prunes and, during the most cruel seasons, does not curse the earth but nourishes her with the vision of the new flowering.

The beauty of the garden, as with some human lives, is therefore the fruit of works that consciously sacrifice nature, model it, limit its form, impose criteria of growth unknown to nature herself, make her less innocent and full of lights, shadows and depth.

Care

Caring for a terrestrial garden as if it were an interior dimension or, conversely, devoting oneself to the psyche with the attention of the gardener, trying to balance forms and colors, without ambitions of eternity and perfection, might help us raise our eyes to heaven and keep our feet on the ground.

Just as in imagining a terrain to be transformed one organizes the variety of plants provided by nature, so the instincts are adapted by awareness, synthesizing conscious and unconscious contents: a process that for Jung is the highest result of the psychic drive.

The image of the garden becomes an evocation of instinct in another form, a place where the soul can be reconciled with what has been lost.

Etymologically the word "garden," from the Indo-Germanic *ghordho* (enclosure), can be traced back to the idea of a contained and protected terrain, a space that echoes the field of therapeutic relationship. It has been suggested that the expression "therapeutic field" be replaced by "therapeutic garden" to give more depth to a word that is overly two-dimensional. But *kepos*, the term used by the Greeks, means circular enclosure connected to the female pubes: place of fertility in which the life force must take form, providing a glimpse not only of the lost paradise but of a paradise still to construct, which seems to coincide with the dynamic becoming of the therapeutic process.

When a garden appears in the dreams of patients, I try to imagine it and sometimes it is as if I were one of those children who peer through the garden gates, sure there is some adventure on the other side. In one of his writings Luciano Perez states that he believes that landscape has a soul or could be the expression thereof. This holds above all for works of art and for dreams. The landscape, that is, is not a sort of indifferent theater, a neutral setting. On the contrary, often it communicates something very significant and profound. The imaginary landscape of the dream or the work of art, whether figurative or literary, assumes imaginal characteristics, becomes the bearer of meaning.

Recently a patient, with whom we had made a good beginning, permitting her to transform a condition of severe stress, repeatedly dreamed of her beloved garden. A sequence of three dreams was as follows: in the first the garden is as it really is; in the second the garden is flooded; in the third the water is very high and an animal is drowning. My patient was in a period of relative tranquility and had decided to continue because she wanted to go into more depth, although she was afraid she might not have enough themes for an analytical confrontation. By taking me into her garden the sense of our future work seemed to be indicated with great precision.

The discordant feelings that inhabit, but do not destroy, the garden and the analyst's room help create new correlations between the external and the internal worlds. Both are intermediate spaces between two worlds, between the conscious house-structure and the unconscious wild nature. The capacity to contain conscious and unconscious, plant and roots, suffering and its possible transformation, uprooting and new grafting, the memory of what was and the vision of what one could become, seed and flowering, makes depth analysis resemble a gardening technique. In creating a garden, as in therapy, patient and constant work is required and the result will be the fruit of a number of factors.

Suffering, anger, sacrifice find meaning in the garden and the possibility of transformation in its care. The space of psychotherapy presents itself as a terrain that is able to support the weight of disturbing and uncultivated interior aspects (Widmann 1997). Sometimes the analyst is asked for help because the ground under our feet has given way. Our moods are winds that blow us away like leaves. We are impatient to leave suffering behind, we want to be strong and autonomous, but we feel like a small plant set out to fill a wilderness. For that slender twig that needs attention, the garden is probably the most suitable place to construct more solid and deeper roots.

From this perspective, the construction of one's own interior garden will initially be in the hands of the analytical couple, and will subsequently be entrusted to the individual. A tree or a bush, once it has taken hold, tends to follow its own course. Thus our interior garden is also a place of autonomous life that requires an introspective aptitude: the primary source, according to Jung's teaching, of knowledge and discovery. One can draw from what it has to offer, provided it is constantly nurtured. For Jung the great problems of life are never definitively solved, and if they seem to be it is always to our detriment (Jung 1931–33).

Botany has shown that plants have a character of their own, that they are capable of passions and experience amorous idylls and profound hate. They are connected to their land of origin. Unless their shape, history and character are respected the plants will not grow, the flowers will not blossom and they will take their revenge on man and his regulations. A vital garden, external or interior, respects every plant, as with every psychic factor. Biodiversity or individual differences need to evolve with natural systems rather than being forced, manipulated, assimilated by overweening botanical or existential colonialisms, in a continuous equilibrium between belonging to everything and faithfulness to their own original uniqueness: between the land of the world and the land of the soul.

Refuge

Psychological life has passages in which nothing is defined outside or inside us – phases in which the only necessity is a refuge – and the garden is like that too. In the garden or park the human norm exists together with portions of wild soil. Lovers and vagabonds share the same bench because the earth belongs to everyone. Nature regenerates, giving new identities when, encouraged by the movement of the soul, we are looking for new frontiers in which to find refuge. The garden offers itself as a shelter, as a place where one can discover anew a sense of belonging: not a city or a nation, but that highly personal land of the soul that is reflected in the garden. Woods or gardens are places of passage, of suspension, of new beginnings in our daily life as well as in stories. They are spaces for children and senior citizens, who confront the acquisition and the loss of physical and psychological confines every day.

Tourists, who have deliberately left their social persona at home, often rest in parks. Migrants, who do not yet have a new identity, gather together in gardens or parks. The travelers and the homeless who have renounced an identity, either temporarily or definitively, often sleep on the benches and lawns of historical villas.

The garden is not only splendor but also a no-man's-land that receives the rejects, the excluded, those driven out. A frontier that dilates: not only a line of separation but also a time and a place to stop in, to begin to hope again; and, as Zanini (1997) says, it is a space for dialogue, requiring the use of all our senses, taken to their extreme in the attempt to perceive what may be there but that cannot yet be seen.

Not infrequently psychiatric patients work in parks on special projects. They sometimes make me think of those myriad refugees who are born, live and sometimes die in no-man's-land. In tending to places everyone can enjoy, I believe that momentarily their feeling of separation is overcome, not in a real sense but on a more intimate level, and that these green spaces can be areas of soul sharing (*anima mundi*).

> Looking around me
> I see something new
> perhaps a new era
> This one,
> disrupted by landslides and earthquakes
> will soon be a garden.
> (R.L., participant in an expressive workshop;
> translated from the Italian by transl.)

The tree

Speaking of gardens means speaking of trees. Trees are what join the garden to the sky, matter reaching out for the spirit of air from below the ground. After all, the first garden and the first temple were spaces that enclosed a tree.

In all cultures this plant symbol outranks all others, beginning with the tree of life and the tree of good and evil that God planted in the Garden of Eden. There are philosophic trees, genealogical trees, cosmic trees. The tree consoles and favors profound mediation. Buddha was enlightened under a tree, and Jesus sought protection among the olives. The tree dispenses wisdom, for it is wise in its imperturbable immobility and never-ending change.

From a psychological point of view the tree is the source of many and profound points of departure. For Jung it was the image of psychic growth which is never rectilinear but grows slowly and in the shape of a spiral; a profound synthesis in which the symbols of death and resurrection merge (see also Perez).

Among the many myths involving divinities and trees, that of Inanna seems to be particularly pertinent here with regard specifically to the theme of sacrifice. In the hymn known as *The Tree of Huluppu*, the great Sumerian Goddess "queen of heaven and hearth" must choose maturity.

Inanna picked up and tended the Huluppu tree which was dying. She planted it in her private garden with the intent of making it her throne and nuptial bed, symbols of maturity, knowledge and sexuality. Yet she was unable to separate herself from the desires and fears of adolescence evoked by the tree in its state of pure nature. For three creatures dominated by instinct had found refuge in its trunk: the bird Anzu, the serpent and Lilith.

To fulfill the sacrifice of growth, the goddess asked her brother, the mortal hero Gilgamesh, for help. With his axe he cut down the tree and the weakness that oppressed Inanna. The transformation of the tree of Huluppu is a new beginning, for when the goddess governs from her throne and when she sleeps in her bed she takes with her the knowledge of life and death.

Water, melancholy, Echo and Narcissus

The bond between garden and water is powerful and eternal, a biological pact and a legendary union. The former cannot exist without the latter; water brings movement to the illusionary static condition of plants, and the mythology of the garden is amplified if the fount dispenses life or eternal youth. The famous gardens of Babylon, one of the Seven Wonders of the World, had a sophisticated irrigation system built by the Arabs. The Roman garden was organized so that the baths could also use the water, garden and water both serving for beauty and health. The combination of buildings, plants and water found in Hadrian's villa (118–138 AD) is the prelude to the gardens of the future. Not by chance was Villa d'Este (1550–1580), perhaps the most complete water garden ever built, inspired by the neighboring imperial villa. Mention must also be made of the monumental garden of Versailles, with the Grand Canal and not a fountain at its center.

The water in our gardens is that of the fountains, but the sound of jets of water rising in the air possibly keeps at bay the sense of melancholy shared by the garden and its waters.

Melancholy requires reflection, and this is mirrored by the water of the garden. It sets it into a broader and perennially mobile scenario. A setting of beauty and harmony accompanies the image of the person who languishes or feels himself dying within. Suspended, like the garden, between subterranean obscurity and high aspirations, the melancholy individual is set apart from, although in, the world, and finds comfort in the crepuscular light of the garden and among the paths where he slowly, without illusions, walks.

On the other hand, if a desire for what we do not have prevents us from seeing the movement of the water – if we continue to look only at our image – what we see is a reflection of self.

Halfway between creative reflection and pathological fixation, melancholy is the land of poetry but also of illness. "The melancholic person is one who better than any other can raise himself to the highest thoughts; but if the black bile, from glowing as it was, ends up by consuming itself and cools it becomes glacial and will turn to black poison" (Starobinski 1990). The loss of a broad context in which to reflect transforms the sentiment into a black mood, and the person withdraws into an unyielding time and space. He is forced into a closed place where there is no flow of inner movement; a room of mirrors where only the image of the person who enters is reflected. The walls of petrified material give back an innerness that immobilizes oneself.

A brief reference to Echo and Narcissus is in line with the theme. It deals with only one of the aspects of the complexity of the myth, but refers to an experience of mine.

Sometimes I observe seriously ill patients in the setting of a garden. In silence they seem to want to say: "I can't think or feel because I cannot abandon my image that I see reflected everywhere." As in the story of Narcissus and Echo the impossibility of communication petrifies the myth. This fixation becomes contagious, and the diagnosis is like a stone behind which to hide the frustration of not being able to establish a relationship.

But changing the point of observation and observing how the water observes Narcissus, how the forest listens to Echo, I realize that the "need . . . to see others for what they are has been buried by our culture, that the cult of well-being and of belonging has separated the reflection of the image from the body to which it belongs. In remaining inert, in their being "patient" with their fixation, they too are like the bush next to which they sit, immobile but alive. Melancholy never goes away but it opens my eyes.

> [. . .] the plant is rooted in the earth, helpless victim of nature or in absolute harmony with it.
>
> (L. Perez, citing Jung, in Chapter 16, this volume)

References

Adorisio, A. (1997) "Going toward complexity: the myth of Echo and Narcissus", in P. Pallaro (ed.) (2007), *Authentic Movement: Moving the Body, Moving the Self* (vol. 2, pp. 80–96). London: Jessica Kingsley.
Assunto, R. (1973) *Il paesaggio e l'estetica*. Palermo, Italy: Novecento.
Campbell, J. and Moyers, B. (1988) *The Power of Myth*, New York: Doubleday.
Detienne, H. (1972) *I giardini di Adone*. Turin, Italy: Einaudi.
Hillman, J. (1973) *Senex et puer*. Padua, Italy: Marsilio.
Jung, C.G. (1927) "Mind and Earth", *Collected Works* 10, London: Routledge.
—— (1931–33) "The Stages of Life", *Collected Works* 8, Princeton, NJ: Princeton University Press.
Màdera, R. and Tarca, L.V. (2007) *Philosophy as Life Path: An Introduction to Philosophical Practice*. Milan: Ipocpress.

Perez, L. *Geografie e topografie reali, immaginarie e immaginali.* Material kindly made available to the author.

Starobinski, J. (1990) *La malinconia allo specchio.* Milan: Garzanti.

Starobinski, J. and Kemp, W.S. (1966) "The Idea of Nostalgia", *Diogenes*, *54*, 81–103.

Venturi Ferraiolo, M. (1987) *Il giardino idea natura realtà, paesaggio.* Milan: Guerini.

Widmann, C. (ed.) (1997) *Ecologica-mente.* Ravenna, Italy: Longo.

Zanini, P. (1997) *Significati del confine.* Milan: Mondadori.

Chapter 11

The dark places, or on the evil of innocence

Massimo Buttarini

> Midway upon the journey of our life
> I found myself within a forest dark,
> For the straightforward pathway had been lost.
>
> Dante Alighieri, *Divine Comedy*

The marvelous image with which Dante begins his *Divine Comedy* has become the archetypal symbol par excellence of a dark place in the collective imaginary: the disturbing mirror of the inner world, where one can authentically find oneself only by agreeing to lose oneself in the intricate labyrinths of the soul.

In the introduction to *Luoghi della letteratura italiana* the editors write:

> Places are important as places, but often they are just as important as mirrors of the inner world. Another qualifying element therefore is the external-internal relationship that every place communicates in its own way. We go into and come out of places, carrying with us the inner experience and enriching it with the one acquired in the external world. There is continuous transmission between the exterior of place and the interior of man.
>
> (translated from the Italian by the transl.)

The entire discipline of psychology, and not only depth psychology, upholds this idea: some further studies and hypotheses appear in the present volume.

James Hillman in particular – a point of reference for the specific current of depth psychology known as imaginal psychology – has dealt with the soul of places. In speaking of architecture, Hillman (2004) points out that it has too often been considered only construction, design, concept, while in reality it is also and above all imagination: an idea that is fundamental, next to that of the soul, in the thought of this American psychologist. Hillman maintains that a second fundamental point in dealing with the soul of places is the recovery of the sense of individuality of the place, lost when rationalist thought took over. Every place has a precise specific nature, just as, I would add, every person has his preeminent and individual differences. With his reflections Hillman takes us back in time:

> In ancient Greece, places such as crossings, springs, wells, woods and the like had specific qualities and specific personifications: gods, demons, nymphs, *daimones*, and if one was unaware of all this, if one was inattentive to the figures that lived in a crossing or in a woods, if one was insensitive to the places, one was in serious danger. One could be possessed. Consider, for example, nympholepsy: the nymphs or Pan could seize the traveler. Therefore one had to be aware of what was happening, of what spirit, of what sensitivity, what imagination presided over a particular place, or like the psyche, the soul, corresponded to the place in which one was. Some places were avoided, while others were beneficial and healing.
>
> (Hillman 2004; translated from the Italian by transl.)

Hillman goes on to say that with his manipulatory activities man has perverted the original character of certain places and that it is therefore important to recover the intimate and specific quality of a particular place, which manifests itself to one's body through the senses. The specific atmosphere of a place, inherent and part of its characteristics, which Hillman believes we are unable to recognize, will be discussed further on.

> We are unable to recognize the soul of place. This is due to the culture in which we live. We have lost our answer to the esthetic. The an-esthetic anesthetizes us. Sounds are so loud that the ears are deadened. A phenomenon called "psychic racket (pandemonium)." One can buy any anesthetic in the pharmacy. But what is anesthesia? What does the word mean? It means being without sensitivity, including the esthetic sensitivity. It means being aesthetically incompetent: in a state of stupor, stupid. "Stupid" is more precise than "ignorant." It is an idea conterminous to that of stupor – no sensation, no esthetic sense. This, I believe, is the most important aspect in the training of an architect: the awakening to the esthetic response, the awakening from anesthesia. Return to animism, to paganism. One becomes pagan like the Celts, the Indians, because one realizes that everything is alive. Everything begins to "speak" a bit. One is no longer anesthetized. This is the last fundamental point. I believe that this analgesia, or anesthesia, dominates our culture not only to avoid pain, but in many other subtle ways. If instead the senses remain alive, acute, not anesthetized, suffering, nourished by contemporary living, cannot suffocate them, cannot extinguish them.
>
> (Hillman 2004; translated from the Italian by transl.)

My working hypothesis, specifically, is that there are particularly dark places, like Dante's woods, which evoke and activate the darker part of the human soul that can be possessed by the archetypal images with their spellbinding powers instigated by the place itself.

In defining the phrase *mystic participation* in his *Psychological Types*, Jung traces the term back to Lévy-Bruhl, in the sense of a particular type of psychological bond with the object. It is a mystic participation because the subject has a direct relationship with the object, a sort of partial identity based on the original unity of subject and object. Mystic participation is therefore a residue of the primordial state and does not touch on all relationships between subject and object, but only some. It is naturally a phenomenon best seen among the primitives although it is also frequent among civilized people, to varying degrees of intensity, and generally involves people: rarely a person and a thing. In the first case it is a so-called relation of transference, in which the object has an almost magical influence on the subject. In the second case it is either an analogous action exercised by a thing or a sort of identification with a thing or the idea of the thing.

The term *dark places* as used in this chapter implies identification with places or with the idea of places that have a magical or malign influence and atmosphere, casting a spell over the individual.

A whole current in literature and the cinema is centered on the bewitched cursed house, inhabited by restless ghosts who are unable to find peace. The place that should represent shelter, safety and peace is transformed in these contexts into a dark place where monstrous crimes take place and the house has a life of its own.

Unfortunately, reality often far outdoes the most fervid imagination, and thus in the history of crime the spotlight has fallen on many houses where heinous homicides have taken place. The dark place *par excellence* of the house is the cellar, and it is there that serial killers have tried to conceal the remains of their unwitting victims, drawn into the trap like flies in the spider's web. In dreams too the house has a highly important symbolic value and among its various places the cellar, as Bachelard reminds us in *The Poetics of Space*, represents the dark being of the house, the being that participates in subterranean powers.

The cellar is the symbolic representation of the unconscious and of all the ghosts that live there: if man can't find the courage to face his interior cellar, taking shelter in the reassuring rationalization of the attic, he risks being overcome. If he does not face the ghosts that live there and does not consciously integrate them, they will possess him like evil spirits. Since serial killers are pathologically incapable of symbolizing, their fantasies of sex and death take over; they identify completely with the obscurity that becomes the realm of their destruction. Their sins are buried in the cellar and the cadavers become the humus that nourishes the shades of the unconscious, in an inarrestable compulsion to repeat their acts.

Often the protagonists in the horror films mentioned above are adolescents, victims of Satanic sects who sacrifice them to their chthonic divinities.

In this case too, I wish I could say that it is only cinematographic make-believe, but we know that the phenomenon of Satanism is still alive. Examples would be the crimes of the so-called monster of Florence, and more recently the crimes and presumed suicides in Northern Italy, which concealed much more disturbing facts connected to the Satanic sect known as "the beasts of Satan."

The darkness that envelops their world emerges upon observation of the places where the victims are found, the moment in which the ritual murders take place, the places chosen by the Satanists for their diabolic ceremonies. The ceremonies take place at night. Like that of the serial killer theirs is a realm enveloped in darkness; the participants are masked and therefore their identity is also enveloped in obscurity. When the places are outside, those located at crossings are almost always hidden, secret places, immersed in nature and not easy for non-initiates to come to. Often they are cemeteries and deconsecrated churches. In addition to animals, the preferred sacrificial victims are children and adolescents whose innocence is offered to Satan to obtain his favors. The victims can be exploited for Satanic orgies characterized by pedophile sadism. In many cases, the executioners are the parents themselves, adherents to the sect for money or because they themselves believe that sacrificing their children will give them money and power. Often adolescents approach Satanism as a way of expressing their anger and their rebellious and apparently anti-conformist spirit.

In his book *Delitti rituali*, Angelo Zappalà, psychologist and specialist in clinical criminology, refers to a study carried out on 143 adolescents involved in Satanism, which showed that embracing this creed was the expression of malaise. It represented a form of rebellion and an attempt to belong to a group enabling the members to overcome the difficulties encountered with their peers and their solitude. Satanism, continues the author, furnishes them with feelings of power that compensate for their lack of self-esteem:

> The male members of this group in particular satisfy their need for power and display attitudes of revenge with regard to the world. The females, more than the males, show nihilistic feelings. Generally they have dietary problems and practice self-mutilation. These adolescents live in problematic families with intense family conflicts, and not infrequently the girls were sexually abused.
>
> (Zappalà 2004; translated from the Italian by trans.)

Sects, whether Satanic or otherwise, target the psychic fragility of the individual who lacks points of reference and finds an answer to his disorientation in the sect. Yet paradoxically, by falling into the mystificational and manipulative network of the sect the individual ends up by completely losing himself and is transformed into an automaton in the hands of individuals without scruples.

There are many ways in which one can lose oneself, under the illusion of having found a stable and sure landfall. I would like to refer here to the film *The Family Man* (directed by Brett Ratner, 2000), in which losing and finding oneself are represented by different and opposing places. The protagonist played by Nicholas Cage, a successful man apparently gratified by his work and social position, wakes up one morning in a humble unknown house and finds himself married to a woman whom he had left long ago to pursue money and power, and in the role of father; all this disorients and terrorizes him. He tries to return to his luxurious apartment but is driven away, and is not recognized by his former high-society colleagues and friends. Slowly he resigns himself to this less elevated social level and, as time passes begins to appreciate the values, the genuineness of small daily things. He finds he is in love with the woman who initially represented only an obstacle, and that he loves his children. But when the miracle seems to have taken place, one morning he wakes up again in his first life, and with anguish sees how false and empty, without warmth, it is. This reference is sufficient, even if the film doesn't end there, to note that sometimes in chasing after the ephemeral one loses contact, in the best of cases temporarily, with the authentic parts of one's identity.

There is something both tangible and intangible about the atmosphere that characterizes a place, whether real or invented, in a dream or in the imagination. It is unique, like a fingerprint. In thinking about dark places, it is their particular tone that transmits specific perceptions, sensations, feelings, evoking particular thoughts on the place itself or our life and ourselves, and capable of influencing us profoundly.

The atmosphere of a place is something that can invite us to enter or can make us flee. If it is an interior this can depend also on the design or setup of the space. A space that is too empty can determine a feeling of anguish even though there is plenty of space; an excessively full space can transmit oppression and a sense of claustrophobia.

Our emotive reaction to a particular place and its atmosphere can also be determined by smell. People never speak of the unpleasant smells, such as the odor of mold characteristic of houses that have been closed for a long time, the strong smells of the countryside such as those that surrounded me when I was a child, the characteristic smells of the ocean, the disturbing smells of certain sections of the hospital and retirement homes, the strong smell of disinfectant and urine that characterize, in their squalor, railroad stations and public toilets; the obscure odors of putrefaction. Sight too can capture the characteristic atmosphere of certain places and condition us: neon lights, strobe lights in the discos that are overwhelmingly psychedelic compared with the muted colors of dawn or the evocative and inspiring reflective half-shadows of sunset. Then there are sounds: some places are too noisy to live in. Certainly the sounds we hear as we walk along the beach or in the midst of the woods are quite different: a completely different music and atmosphere that could suddenly change if, in the middle of the night, we heard a piercing scream and cries for help.

The disturbing atmosphere of certain places is beautifully captured in cinema. The classic example, containing everything I have tried to say here concerning the darkness of certain places, their disturbing atmosphere and the psychodynamics of the protagonists who move in these spaces, is Jonathan Demme's *The Silence of the Lambs*. Aside from the admirable representation of the maximum security prison and the Gothic atmosphere of the serial killer's house, the theme of dangerous relations appears. In the film the young FBI agent, Clarice Starling, confronts the monster Hannibal Lecter, psychiatrist and murderer, cannibal and skilful manipulator of the minds of those who are unlucky enough to cross his path. The predominant colors in this film are red and black: red like the blood of the lambs and black like the blood-curdling silence of their death. In the film the young Clarice is magnetically attracted by the disturbing and fascinating personage who in turn is attracted by the innocence of the woman. In order to finish her work she must remain lucid and cautiously move among the countless psychological traps he sets. All this tells us of the dark sides of relationships characterized by the need for control or dominion, such as a sadomasochistic relationship, and the dangerous mechanisms of projected identification where the dark and unintegrated sides imprison and make partners of the victim and the executioner.

Another aspect that determines the atmosphere of a place is the appearance of the unexpected: an encounter that disorients us and triggers anxiety, a landscape that appears and fills us with magical astonishment. The unexpected, surprising us, almost always finds us unprepared for good and for evil, putting us face to face with our insecurity, desires we didn't know we had, sensations we never dreamt of feeling. The unexpected destabilizes and can be dangerous in certain cases, above all when life is based on certainties and leaves little space for uncertainty and doubt, because it can reveal our inner dark places, our shadow side. In turn we find ourselves involved in delicate balancing acts that at the same time let us test our potentialities and our most authentic nature. The unexpected also puts us face to face with inevitable ethical responsibilities, forcing us to look at the guilt, fragility and ambivalence of human nature, both noble and wretched.

Often patients who bring a dream say "I had a dream," signifying a conscious intentionality that has little to do with the dream. We might say instead that the dream with its paradoxical and irrational aspects represents the unexpected that crowds out consciousness, introducing it to that subterranean, infernal, obscure dimension, so well described by Hillman:

When we use the word underworld, we are referring to a wholly psychic perspective, where one's entire mode of being has been desubstantialized, killed of natural life, and yet is in every shape and sense and size the exact replica of natural life. The underworld of Ba of Egypt and the underworld psyche of Homeric Greece was the whole person as in life but devoid of life. This means that the underworld perspective radically alters our experience of life. It no longer matters on its own terms but only in terms of the psyche. To know the psyche at its basic depths, for a true depth psychology, one must go to the underworld.

(Hillman 1979: 46)

We mentioned dark places as evocations of the inner world. We referred to the dark places present in the interior world and to the dark places of violent crimes, to the places of literature and the cinema and to the natural or artificial places collectively endowed with a strong archetypal value.

The following is a true-to-life version of the fable of Little Red Riding Hood. When one gets lost because one ignores the signals or warnings, the woods or the garden become obscure for lack of lucidity or because the serpent/wolf in disguise makes its appearance: innocence and/or the unconscious do the rest. In this case the place is more than anything a frame – a context, not the main thing – represented by the relationship of undue influence, power and abuse.

It must be said, however, that the place is not always dark: that something dark can manifest itself in a place that is connected with an interior obscure aspect. In this case the serpent of the dream/rapist who attacks the young woman in a wood makes the concrete place dark, but the crime could take place elsewhere. Or perhaps more simply, the place becomes dark in the mind of the criminal, identified with the wolf/serpent, but not yet in the unwitting victim who, like the little girl in the fairy tale, walks innocently through the woods.

Neil Russack in his *Animal Guides in Life, Myth and Dreams* (2002) writes of the symbolism of the serpent in relation to a patient of his. The instinctual power of the serpent, as in the mythic Eden, can explode in the most familiar of gardens.

He maintains that the symbol of the serpent gives us the ability to enter into contact with our deepest instincts, with animal life, and in this sense it could be said that it comes to our aid. He then recounts the dream of a woman who grew up in a rigidly patriarchal family, in which everyone's behavior had to conform to the strict conventions of a fundamentalist Christianity. She dreamed she was at a party with a friend; as they were walking in the garden they saw a man, an army general, being transformed into a serpent. The dreamer then grabs hold of the general and he recognizes her but she can't understand the meaning of his expression. His head is the last thing to be transformed and he seems to be aware that she will have to live with what she saw, and that if she says anything no one will believer her. The dreamer isn't frightened but wonders if it is against the rules, if civilization is in danger. When she informs her companion and says she should tell someone, he too says no one would believe her. But she knows she is telling the truth, and truth should be believed. He repeats, however, that no one would believe her.

An episode in the patient's adolescence is then also cited. After school the dreamer, who was fifteen at the time, had missed the bus. A pleasant man drew up in a car and asked if he could drive her home. She immediately felt there was something about the man that didn't convince her and that it would be better not to accept a ride from someone she didn't know, but he seemed so nice that in the end she accepted. At first he went in the right direction, but then he turned towards the country and the woods. The girl became frightened. The man stopped in an isolated place and tried to rape her, but she managed to escape. She was too ashamed to tell anyone about her experience. She felt that it might be the rapist who had killed various girls her age. After this, the man killed one more before being caught. Russack again explains that this is basically a story of how our relationship with the serpent can be spoiled. By not trusting her instincts and by following the false rationality of her parents, being clean, good and pleasant, she became vulnerable to someone else's instinct. Both victim and criminal receive the evil energy of the serpent, ignored by the victim, but with which the criminal identifies. He has lost his human values and has been changed into a serpent – has been eaten by the serpent.

Maturing psychologically means leaving the paradisiacal garden of childhood, that naïve innocence with which we want to look at others and ourselves and see only the good. Evil exists, and so do extremely dangerous individuals who are fascinated by it.

The evil of innocence and the innocence of evil. The archetypes as models of human behavior always have two polarities, and to consider only one leads to a dissociated and partial vision of the world and the things in it. In his complex and imagined vision of the psyche, Hillman constantly invites us to embrace the archetype in its entirety so as not to lose sight of the totality.

Thomas Moore, another Hillmanian analyst, explores the dark side of Eros in Sade's work, discussing the archetype of innocence personified by Justine:

> One sees the mask of Justine worn by people who use innocence to avoid the harsh realities that life presents or that well up from the heart.
>
> (Moore 1990:34)

The author invites us to embrace both innocence and corruption because "the virgin and the dirty old man go together as a tandem. One elicits the other."

> (Moore 1990:36)

Tempted to take sides in this Sadeian tandem of innocence and cruelty, we would rather identify with Justine and project the libertine. In that act we get rid of guilt and bask in innocence. Then the innocent one only "feels guilty," which is different from appropriating one's actual guilt. "The wise man," Jung says, "learns only from his own guilt." He looks into his own heart, a phrase that echoes Sade's intentions as a novelist – to ask why this should happen to me. This is not exactly loss of innocence; it is more finding the tandem to innocence. Feelings of guilt invite us to complete innocence with a look at our own cruelty. As a symptom, feeling guilty sustains innocence, but it also invites responsibility. Following through on feelings of guilt might eventually lead to an effective realization of guilt.

(Moore 1990:41–42)

In dark places guilt and innocence are diabolically bound together. The assassin and the victim are connected by a common destiny that will lead them to their destruction. This happens in both the external and the interior world, where the murderer as an intrapsychic aspect can kill the possibility of the Ego to integrate and channel the destructive energies creatively. The girl who goes into the woods can become the victim of her adolescent innocence, if this makes her unaware. This is where a bad wolf can lurk, perhaps in the guise of a kind gentleman, and it is this that fatally attracts her.

With reference to the title and the quote with which I opened this chapter, going into the woods with Dante's image means opening oneself to the challenge of maturity, confronting the dark side of life and risking losing oneself when, face to face with the other, the inner projections and the destructive dynamics prevail.

Places become dark when they house an initiation drama that does not always end with rebirth and when they remain in the collective memory charged with a universal psychological value that is at the same time a warning and an invitation to exploration: as is the case with all bipolar archetypes of the human psyche in Jung's vision.

References

Anselmi, G.M. and Ruozzi, G. (eds) (2003) *Luoghi della letteratura italiana*. Milan: Bruno Mondadori.
Bachelard, G. (1969) *The Poetics of Space*. Boston: Beacon Press.
Hillman, J. (1979) *The Dream and the Underworld*. New York: Harper & Row.
—— (2004) *L'anima dei luoghi, Conversazione con Carlo Truppi*. Milan: Rizzoli.
Jung, C.G. (1921) *Psychological Types, The Collected Works*, 6. London: Routledge.
Moore, T. (1990) *Dark Eros: The Imagination of Sadism*. Dallas, TX: Spring Publications.
Russack, N. (2002) *Animal Guides in Life, Myth and Dreams*. Toronto, Canada: Inner City Books.
Zappalà, A. (2004) *Delitti rituali*. Turin, Italy: Centro Scientifico editore.

Chapter 12

The earth, the song, the symbol

Massimiliano Scarpelli

"Exploring" the symbolic universe evoked by earth and its images means entering into contact with the most archaic forms of thought. Age-old metaphors connect human events to the cycle of natural events and the rhythms of matter. The typically human way of giving a symbolic sense to what is first experienced as foreign and dangerous has its roots in the great Mother Earth, or "grandmother earth" as the Native Americans called her.

"Understanding" the bond that has come to characterize the relationship of women and men with the earth means, as Italo Calvino (1988) says, overcoming the heaviness and flying in other spaces, like Perseus. New space is such insofar as it consists of the symbolic universe that provides the human experience with sense and meaning. The place of origin of images and imaginative tales is the womb of the earth, from which poetic thought springs. The creative potentialities of the psyche are rooted in the age-old rites of agriculture and plant life whose powerful echo reaches us in mysterious ways. The fecundating act of poetry infuses daily life with vigor and provides sweeping breadth to the individual capacity for design.

"Feeling" the chthonic images opens up the possibility of entering one's "inner land," in other words the poetical capacity of the psyche for transformation. This must not however be interpreted as a "flight into dreams or the irrational" (Calvino, 1988), for the language of the symbol permits, if integrated, a concreteness that is fuller and packed with meaning.

A better understanding can be had of how the relationship with the earth stimulates and fuses the human tendency for symbolic creation by approaching the world of myths and rituals. The Australian myth of the origins of the world is particularly significant, narrated in an exemplary manner by an English author for whom traveling was synonymous with life.

Bruce Chatwin's *The Songlines* is a travelogue that describes the author's journey in Australia. Chatwin, theoretician of human unrest, wanted to discover what the Aborigines meant when they said that their earth was born with song.

The story begins in the time of the dream that is the moment of genesis. The ancestors create themselves with clay and thousands of them become the founders of the various clans and their totems. Chatwin says: "when an aboriginal tells you, 'I have a Wallaby Dreaming,' he means, 'My totem is Wallaby. I am a member of the Wallaby Clan'" (Chatwin 1987:14).

Every ancestor is the original father of a clan, and all the members of the clan descend from his "dream," or his creative act.

In the time of the dream the ancestor gives origin to his race and at the same time creates the earth. As he walks the ancestor gives life to the world by scattering a wake of words and musical notes, melodies that compose the *songlines*. These roads, the paths of the dream, remained on the earth as communication routes between the various tribes scattered through the vast territory of the Australian lands.

At the time of creation the country did not exist until the ancestors had sung it, and thus the Aborigines believe in the existence of the earth only if they recognize the song.

The melodies that compose and describe the songlines act as a geographic map that makes the paths visible and existent. Sometimes the Aborigines undertake journeys where they move over the songlines so that the various totems of numerous ethnic groups cross over into a complex network of dreams.

It is a ritual journey in which the mystery of creation is renewed. Moving over the song of the ancestor means finding the way and re-creating it. The earth cannot exist without its song, just as it is impossible to orient oneself without following the notes of the origins.

In the grip of the irresistible call of a mysterious *daimon*, the Aborigines sometimes leave whatever they are doing to undertake a journey of thousands of kilometers on the tracks of the dream.

In narrating these events Chatwin describes the amazement of Anglo-Saxon employers as they are suddenly abandoned by their Aborigine workers, who wander off into the outback without any apparent reason. The whites have no word to describe these incomprehensible crossings, and call them "walkabouts."

The word closes the circle of the meanings, containing in itself a judgment that is derived from a precise mentality: walking around with an apparently concrete and productive goal does not merit other semantic space and can be explained by the backwardness of the primitive. "Walkabout" liquidates the mystery and elusiveness of the symbolic experience, but also eliminates the unease such an act produces. Western man, used to linear thought, fosters the illusion of being protected from the feeling of restlessness generated by contact with something profound, age-old, human, but at the same time foreign.

It is the sensation that Freud called *unheimlich*, "disconcerting." It is a reaction of fear and dismay when faced with something unknown and frightening. But Freud notes that the term also contains the opposite meaning – familiar, known.

Freud deduced that what is disturbing is so because it recalls something that is not unknown but, on the contrary, was once familiar and of which we have an obscure and partial awareness.

Western language keeps the obscure intimation of its limits at bay, labeling as useless anything that is not immediately productive.

Yet the ritual walks through the songlines were not only a way of celebrating the ancestors but also a peculiar way of survival.

The Australian territory is extremely unpredictable in dispensing its fruits, and a single year of plenty can be followed by years of dearth. Moving meant surviving and remaining put might mean perishing. Exchanging products and information was vital for the various clans. Moreover, the songlines that guaranteed the exchanges also became places of cult and witnesses of the "dream" of the ancestor who through the melody had created and left various pieces of land as legacy.

Chatwin recounts how the Aborigines ensured ownership and transmission in a way that was incomprehensible for the whites because it was based on a radically different concept: "no one in Australia was landless, since everyone inherited, as his or her private property, a stretch of the Ancestor's song and the stretch of country over which the song passed" (Chatwin 1987:64). Selling the land or getting rid of it was inconceivable, although it could be lent, receiving in exchange other loans.

The concept of property was connected to myth and creation, and property had no political boundaries as it does in the West.

The image of the songlines is a highly effective way of expressing a relationship with the land that alludes to something connected to the origins, a bond that calls forth each time the place of genesis.

The earth exists if it is sung, and the melody connects what otherwise would appear as separate and foreign. This refined form of estheticizing measurement of the Aborigines allows us to speak of the soul and its relationship with the earth.

The bridge that reunites man to the "foreign" external environment is a symbolic creation that discloses and invents a meaning, a destiny, a project. The soul is seen as a function of the relationship between everyday thought and the archaic forms of thought rooted in the primordial relationship with the environment.

Says Jung:

> Archetypes are systems of readiness for action, and at the same time images and emotions . . . They represent, on the one hand, a very strong instinctive conservatism, while on the other hand they are the most effective means conceivable of instinctive adaptation. They are thus, essentially, the chthonic portion of the psyche, if we may use such an expression – that portion through which the psyche is attached to nature, or in which its links with the earth and the world appears at its most

tangible. The psychic influence of the earth and its laws is seen most clearly in these primordial images.

(Jung 1927:30)

Tracing the map of a songline means recomposing that original fracture born from the emergence of thought, which breaks the symbolic unity, making man a stranger on the earth.

In his *La terra senza il male*, Umberto Galimberti, philosopher and Jungian analyst, expresses the sense of laceration that results from the birth of consciousness. In his words:

> This e-merging, this e-xisting, is the beginning of that remaining outside of the symbolic composition, which no longer culminates in the integration of the human being into the totality of being: on the contrary, it marks that insurmountable abyss that separates man from everything. His consciousness makes him feel a foreigner and his extraneousness can be felt in every act of reflection.
>
> (Galimberti 1984:14; translated from the Italian by transl.)

The function of the symbol is that of reuniting consciousness with the depths of the psyche, creating images that lend space and meaning to the psychic tension generated between such diverse components of the personality.

For Jung the unifying element is the symbol, for it expresses the end of a conflict between opposing tendencies, which achieve a dialectic supersession in a perspective that harmonizes rational and irrational aspects. In this way the psyche is protected from violent ruptures that would keep instincts at a distance from consciousness, repressing and making them dangerous.

The symbol is mysterious not because it contains an enigma to be deciphered and to adapt to known languages, but because it reveals the word still to be accomplished and suggests the sense of creation and the design.

As Mario Trevi, Jungian analyst and researcher particularly interested in the symbolic function, says:

> If by project we mean the anticipation of the possibilities of the individual to make himself such and we recognize the possible unconscious nature of the project, then the symbol stands as the most adequate expression of that not yet contained in the project – allusive representation, as vivacious as it is necessarily obscure – of a condition not yet admitted by the conscience.
>
> (Trevi 1987:76; translated from the Italian by transl.)

In Western culture the roots of the symbol are never to be found in the earth, and this deprives them of the chthonic dimension from which the creation of the thought springs. But, as Jung notes, the most archaic forms of thought are based on natural events and on the terrestrial events that become metaphors for the fecundating energy of the unconscious.

The Australian man binds himself to the land with his song and in this way redefines the unwelcoming aspects and creates a relationship with his surroundings, projecting his "being in the world" empathetically with the environment. The songline is an invention full of meaning; it is a third element that comes from the relationship with the archaic foundations of human existence, in other words the earth and its mystery. With the song that feeling of hostility and extraneousness in which thought and the natural rhythm of things are confronted is in part recomposed.

The song is the "tertium" that is created to survive in an environment that is often hostile, but also to express the mythopoietic capacity of the psyche rooted in the metaphors of the earth.

The Aborigine creates the songline that permits him to reach more fertile areas. With time this assumes a sense that transcends the mere material fact and emerges as a mode of transformation and renewal. The creation of the song inaugurates the birth of something that presents itself as an imaginal element of the relationship with what the earth metaphors represent in the psyche.

It is what Jung means in *Symbols of Transformation* when he says that it is through imaginative thought that a connection is established between directed thinking and the oldest strata of the human spirit. For the Swiss psychiatrist, imaginative thought expressed in songs, in myths and in artistic forms takes on essentially different valences.

Jung does not share the depreciation of archaic forms of expression that characterized all of positivist thought. He is interested in the totality of the psyche and not only the directed and linear thought considered as most useful for the progress of civilization in Western culture.

Even though he considers the *logos* and reason as a way of adaptation, for Jung psychological science must essentially indicate the way to express the potentialities inherent in the global psyche. Thanks to the use of mythical material, conscious fantasies represent determined tendencies of the personality not yet or no longer recognized. Imaginative thinking is not, in this sense, residual and is not connected only to the infancy of the human race. It constitutes one of the ways in which the psyche functions.

These considerations were then also taken up in Freudian circles. The psychoanalyst Wilfred Bion was well aware of the importance of daydreaming. He felt that every person had to be able to dream an experience while it was happening, whether in a dream or awake. The capacity to produce images and therefore to translate chaotic moods is, according to Bion, fundamental for a healthy relationship with the environment and with one's inner self.

To be able to concede imaginal space to one's psychic events means recovering and containing one's own interior song, which can indicate new and unknown existential boundaries.

With regard to dreams, Jung says that they have a compensatory function: in other words, they can indicate the need to enlarge a conscious horizon that is becoming narrow and turning into a sterile and desolate land. Speaking and singing one's innermost being then makes it possible to keep those irrational contents, foreign to and banished from Western lands, from causing illness and disadaptation. On the contrary, the creation of the symbol protects against the destructive outbreak of the inner images.

Chatwin explains that for the Aborigines the *tjuringa* is an ancient "map" that illustrates the pathway of the songs and the itineraries of the melodies of the earth: "it is both musical score and mythological guide to the Ancestor's travels. It is the actual body of the Ancestor (*pars pro toto*). It is a man's *alter ego*; his soul; his obol to Charon; his title-deed to country; his passport and his ticket 'back in'" (Chatwin 1987:318).

When the Aborigine elders discover that a cache of *tjuringa* has been destroyed and plundered by white men, the end is approaching. The world enters into chaos since the principle that supports the meaning of everything is no more.

The magical quality of the object then "holds together" the world and is presented as a "unifying symbol" of opposites that enter into a relationship with each other and that emerge from the laceration of an apparent *non sense*.

The *tjuringa* guards identity and equilibrium and makes it possible to create but also to turn back: to turn back after having gone "within."

Jung stresses the dynamic and energetic character of the *tjuringa* as a sacred symbol that receives and provides the psychic energy of the individual and of the group and gives it perspective meaning. It is analogous to the Polynesian *mana* and the *wakanda* of the North American Dakota Indians. These symbolic forms express the almost universal diffusion of the primitive concept of energy.

As Gaston Bachelard affirms, the journey towards the interior reveals that any awareness of the intimacy of things is immediately a poem. According to the French philosopher, the path towards the earth permits a *rêverie materiale* and leads towards a dialectic of the imagination.

> Let's think of the spectator who comes from the outer world where he saw flowers, trees and lights. He enters the dark closed world and finds efflorescences, tree-like forms, luminescences. All these vague forms make him dream: an oneiric sign rests in these vague forms that are waiting to be achieved, liberated.
>
> (Bachelard 1994:20; translated from the Italian by transl.)

The thread of Ariadne that makes the dark world of the caverns intelligible is the imaginal language that creates and recreates reality working on the intimate echo that the forms of the world call forth in the soul.

Contact with the earth then appears as a source of continuous creation, and the symbol is the new reality that is placed in what in analytical psychology is called the "third" or imaginal area. A complex emotional exchange between patient and therapist, recalling ancient healing rituals, can also come to pass in the place of analytical therapy.

In tracing the history of dynamic psychiatry, Ellenberger notes how some shaman procedures are based on establishing an intense relationship between the ill person and the "witch doctor," and establishes an analogy between magical practices and the work of the modern psychotherapist. He cites a study on the Quechua Indian shamans who were curing an illness that consisted of various symptoms including irritability, sleep disturbances and a depressive state called *michko*. The Indians believed that the illness was caused essentially by the loss of the soul, torn away by obscure forces, but that among the evil forces that can cause the loss of the soul, the influence of the earth is considered supreme. He notes that the Quechua are in particular awe of certain rocks and certain caverns, in particular of the ancient Inca ruins (Ellenberger 1970).

In this case the earth is considered in its destructive aspect, the cavern a starving throat that takes back what is vital and with which it has been unable to establish a fertile relationship.

The healing ritual is complex and consists of preparing the sick person to receive his soul anew. He is sprinkled with a mixture of grains and leaves, and the mixture itself, wrapped in the sick man's clothing, is offered to the earth. The sacrificial gift takes place near a cave or a particularly feared tomb.

For Erich Neumann the cave is a vital space as well as a dwelling of death. The character of the vessel of the archetype of the female not only hides what is not yet born in the vessel of the body and what is born in the vessel of the world, but also takes back what is dead in the vessel of death, in the cave or in the coffin of the tomb or in the urn (Neumann 1955).

In line with Neumann's concept, then, the dark cavity is the unconscious that becomes desolate earth unless a dialectic relationship is established. But according to Ellenberger, it can be said that the psychotherapist traces the path of the old shamans as they attempt to retrieve the soul from the earth, offering a tribute of love and gratitude to the ancient mother.

The analytical space can generate a transitional area where the intense communication of each of the two participants merges and generates something that goes beyond the individualities. A new language is created from the images of the place of healing that, by allowing an intimate reverie, leads to the recreation of the images and a profound revision of one's own story.

In this sense, the fantasy of a patient I had in therapy not long ago is of interest here. This person, a 34-year-old woman, has been in analysis for about a year and asked for help because she had problems in relating with the outside world, and in particular with the male sphere. One day she says "I have an uncontrollable desire to take pieces of earth and eat them, to swallow them." She stays silent for a couple of minutes and asks me why she feels this strange desire. I say nothing and she begins to bring forth a series of images: "you know I remember that years ago when I went to the sea I used to take mouthfuls of sand and I liked the taste . . . my parents scolded me but I loved eating the beach." The story becomes more intense and, following painful associations, her tender feeling for her attentive and caring father comes to the fore between words and tears. Up to not long before, this father had been described as rigid and inaccessible, cold and authoritarian.

The intensity of the fantasy of eating earth creates an imaginal and emotional echo that leads to the creation of new metaphors and new stories.

Some African tribes have a custom of eating the earth, symbol of participation and identification. The "one who sacrifices" tastes the earth, the pregnant woman eats it. Fire springs from the earth that is eaten. It is then said that the *womb catches fire*. Bachelard says that what eats the earth in the imaginary is also the root. In the subsoil it draws force and is nourished, draws lymph and energy from the profound cavities. The image of the root that eats the earth is basic to the dream of being nourished, and generates the dynamism of material intimacy. But the root leads us to the image of the tree that according to Neumann is solidly planted in the nourishing earth. It rises in the aerial space and develops there. In its protective shade living matter takes refuge, which it nourishes with its fruits, capable of placating hunger and thirst.

The tree whose branches are stretching skywards represents a cosmic axis, for it is rooted deep down and eating the earth can *set fire to its womb*, creating new horizons. From the depth of the unconscious rise solar directions that are vital if anchored to the nocturnal nourishment of the terrestrial mysteries.

Back once more to the patient, we can hypothesize that her return to the earth has something to do with ancient ritual memories, recovered in the therapeutic space, a space that becomes a place for the construction of a new song.

Something happens in the new dimension of the therapeutic story that, to paraphrase James Hillman, can be defined as the "healing song."

In contact with the womb of death that has stolen the soul, patient and analyst agree to go back over the pathways of genesis, as the Australian Aborigines did. The new story thus exists from the moment in which it is sung and that is the moment in which the earth, generous lover, gives back the stolen soul. The paths where the past is dark and without memories become image dreams, vague recollections. But this is possible only if one agrees to follow an unknown path or to undertake the feared walkabout, which leads to the cavern, to the roots, and the dark womb of ancient ruins. Moving along a path created in the journey itself means giving up something, a sacrifice.

In speaking of the sacrificial act Jung stresses the importance of choosing a direction that abandons ways that do not permit the flow of interior events. The vital direction is the one that takes account of the emerging fantasies, one's own dream thoughts.

In the course of analysis, renouncing the acting out as a fulfillment of immediate satisfaction also means attuning oneself to the rhythms of the earth, of sowing and harvesting. The suffering of exposure to one's inner self creates the premise for fertilizing the field that is gradually being created by the modern medicine man and the person requesting help.

The new silence makes it possible to invent something that could not come forth in solitude, in the deafening explosion of incessant lights and sounds. Contact with suffering, if it can be supported, creates a dimension of authenticity that unfolds (gradually manifests itself) in the ambit of an intense and affective relationship. Contact with the other allows for communication with oneself, but at the same time exploring one's otherness also means understanding the external world better.

The Australian Aborigines sang the earth to give meaning to their own pathway but also to communicate, traveling, with the other inhabitants of the territory, and thus the creation of the earth also revealed the prospect of relationships with their fellows.

In following Jung when he says that "individuation includes the world," we think of our work as the Aborigines do when they sing their song: that we are creating a continuous and fertile place, face to face with our unconscious and with the environment.

The song in this sense appears as a function that incessantly creates and recreates the earth, indicating a dynamic pathway that appears as the fruit of continuous invention and coincides with life itself.

References

Bachelard, G. (1948) *La Terre et les revêries du repos*. Paris: Corti
—— (1994) La terra e il riposo (ed. M. Citterio and A.C. Peduzzi). Como, Italy: Red edizioni.
Bion, W.R. (1962) *Learning from Experience*. London: William Heinemann.
—— (1972) *Apprendere dall'esperienza*. Rome: Armando.
Calvino, I. (1988) *Lezioni americane*. Milan: Garzanti.
Chatwin, B. (1987) *The Songlines*. London: Pan Books.
Ellenberger, H.F. (1970) *Discovery of the Unconscious: The history and evolution of dynamic psychiatry*. New York: Basic Books.
Freud, S. (1919) "The Uncanny", *Standard Edition of Collected Works*, 9. London: Hogarth Press.
Galimberti, U. (1984) *La terra senza il male*. Milan: Feltrinelli.
Jung, C.G. (1921) *Psychological Types. Collected Works*, 6. London: Routledge.
Neumann, E. (1955) *The Great Mother*. Princeton, NJ: Princeton University Press.
Trevi, M. (1987) *Per uno junghismo critico*. Milan: Bompiani.

Chapter 13

Exile

An impossible return?

Ursula Prameshuber

In ancient Rome the word "exile," from the Latin *exsilium*, originally indicated a voluntary absence from the city. It was a right of Roman citizens, the so-called *ius exsilii*, and only later did it lose its voluntary characteristic and become punishment. It was such a drastic type of punishment that at times it even replaced the death sentence. Today, those banished from their country for political or religious reasons still go into exile. But this is not the type of exile I wish to discuss here.

What I want to deal with here is a less explored form: that of the voluntary exile of persons who choose to live far from their native country because of work or love. In these cases, what at first sight appears to be a choice often reveals an inner constriction, a particular psychological node. It is an interior and not a political court that sentences the individual "to exile." The result is that often those exiled end up in the studios of analysts whose culture and language are the same, who are likewise foreigners and exiled, and the studio becomes a sort of "psychic embassy" within which those exiled can attempt to work out the psychic problems at the root of their exile.

The "puer" aspect in exile

Feelings closely connected with the experiences of those who live in exile are extraneousness, solitude, uprooting and nostalgia. Nostalgia or the suffering of return that torments anyone far from home takes on its extreme form in exile, for it is without hope of return, or *nostos*. The exile belongs "to no place, neither of departure nor arrival," is without "protection or direction" (Prete 1988:27) and suffers from an "invisibility of destination and of origins." It is an eternal nostalgia that only death can extinguish, for the exile can hope to return to his homeland only after death.

But let's listen to the words of one of the most famous exiles, Ovid, in his *Poems of Exile*:

> Since if the deathless spirit flies on high in the empty air,
> and old Pythagoras of Samos's words are true,

a Roman will wander among Sarmatian shades,
a stranger forever among the savage dead.
But make sure my bones are brought back in a little urn:
so I'll not be an exile still in death.
(From Book III, translated by A.S. Kline, 2003)

The desire to return home, the lost paradise, an unbridgeable restlessness, wandering, a sense of extraneousness and uprooting, as well as a profound nostalgia: all these feelings and experiences connected to the experience of exile take us back to Jung's concept of *puer*.

The *puer* individual feels suffocated and oppressed by all the values that belong to the world of the *senex*: the family, work, marriage, children, career, economic security, homeland, order, limits, continuity, time, history. "The horizontal world, the space-time continuum which we call 'reality', is not its world" (Hillman 1967:326).

The concept of *puer*, developed by Jung in *Symbols of Transformation*, has been elaborated in particular by Marie-Louise von Franz and James Hillman. A dual aspect characterizes the *puer*: he can be seen as trapped in the maternal complex or in relationship with the paternal complex and the interior search. We will try to show how this dual aspect of the *puer* corresponds also to a different way of living the experience of exile.

When speaking of Attis, Adonis and Tammuz in his *Symbols of Transformation*, Jung describes the figure of the *puer* as follows: "he only lives on and through the mother and can strike no roots in the world" (Jung 1952:258, para. 392). In this concept, what the *puer* is looking for in his wanderings is the lost mother. He lives only in relation to the mother. He "is the dream of the mother in matriarchal times, when there was as yet no father to stand by the side of the son" (Jung 1952:259, para. 392).

In her book *Puer Aeternus*, M.-L. von Franz (1970) deals with the overwhelming dependence of the *puer* on the mother. His psychology is that of an adolescent and he leads an interim life where nothing is definite, nothing is established. Everything is still possible; he is in continuous expectation of something that will happen in the future, refusing to live in the here and now. He is dominated by a sense of impermanence, fleetingness and a nostalgic desire of death.

This aspect of the *puer*, trapped in the maternal, is characterized by the arrest of psychic development. How is it expressed in the concrete case of an exile?

Frequently exiles do not succeed in putting down roots in their new homeland. They live a provisional life, suspended between suffering for the past and hope for the future, refusing to accept their present as exiles. In this sense the cause of the exile's suffering is his desire for the return to the personal or symbolic mother, the mother-country left behind. All his psychic energies are engaged there, all his thoughts are turned to the past, while the present is experienced as a condition of privation, of absence, of suffering.

These individuals do not establish significant relationships with others in their new cultural ambience, fraternizing mainly with their fellow exiles. Often they refuse to learn the language of the new country and are marked by an attachment to the mother tongue that represents the only thing they have been able to save from their old mother-country. Authors who have chosen to write their works in the language of their new country are few and far between. Among the exceptions are Joseph Conrad, Elias Canetti and Milan Kundera. Sometimes the geographic exile also becomes a linguistic exile, whereby the mother tongue acts as the mother-country left behind. This seems to be the case with the Austrian writer, Ingeborg Bachmann, born in 1926 in Klagenfurt, Austria. She died in tragic circumstances in 1973 in Rome, where she had been living for years "in exile" and which is expressed so well in her poem *Exile*.

Until the exiled person succeeds in moving forward in his development, until he succeeds in separating and freeing himself from his psychically incestuous bond with the mother figure, he will be unable to take advantage of what is to be learned from his experience as exile and evolve.

In his subsequent writings, Jung sees the *puer* more in relation to the paternal sphere and the world of the spirit. In *Psychology of the Child Archetype* of 1940 as well as in *The Spirit Mercury* of 1943, Jung describes the *puer* aspect as the representation of the drive to self-realization, the evolution towards autonomy and separation from the origins. The archetype of the child appears in the human psyche in the processes of individuation and the development of the Self.

James Hillman follows and amplifies the aspect of the *puer* connected to the paternal problem and spiritual development:

> the focus is upon the Puer necessity: redeeming the father . . . the Puer represents the necessity of seeking the fathering spirit, the capacity to father.
>
> (Hillman 1973:167)

In his article *Pothos* (1974), Hillman speaks of the three components of Eros: *himeros*, physical desire; *anteros*, love returned; and finally *pothos*. In Greek *pothos* means desire, for a person or thing lost; lack, regret and mourning. It is the desire for the unattainable, for the unobtainable, for impossible love, that can never be completely satisfied and that therefore continuously pushes us ahead, always beyond the boundaries, always searching. It leads us to melancholy wandering. The desire can never be satisfied and becomes the aim in itself. The desired object almost loses importance. It is the force of *pothos* that drives the *puer* in so many of his adventurous undertakings, in his nostalgic desire to move. He is a restless spirit who, as Hillman says, is without a dwelling on earth, and always arriving from somewhere and leaving for somewhere, but always passing through.

The *puer*'s disposition to failure takes him into impossible situations and undertakings, the source of which is always *pothos*, which leads to shipwreck: a psychic shipwreck.

Another feature of the *puer* is that he lives outside of time. He believes, as the name *puer aeternus* indicates, that he will live in eternity, that he will not be subject to the transformation and limitations brought by time. For him time is not gradual, linear, chronological. His time is the *kairos*, the right moment, the opportunity he can catch on the wing with his infallible instinct for what is new, unknown, not yet tested and affirmed, always possible.

The *puer*'s search is an inner, spiritual search. He needs an acknowledgment of the spirit by the spirit, that in the end leads to the paternity of the *puer* himself (Hillman 1979). It is this spiritual search that represents the positive side of the *puer* structure, which, with its follies and fragility, sets every new beginning going, lies behind everything in the *status nascendi*. His is an authentic spirit always associated with uncertainty, risk, possible failure.

The *puer*'s wandering "is as the spirit wanders, without attachment and not as an odyssey of experience. It wanders to spend or to capture . . . to try its luck, but not with the aim of going home" (Hillman 1967:326).

How does the spiritual aspect of the *puer* manifest itself in the experience of exile?

We were saying that there are two different ways of experiencing exile – either as regret for the lost mother and the incapacity to live as exile in the present or as a spiritual search.

In the second case, there is often a *kairos* moment at the beginning of the exile, an opportunity to go away captured on the wing, such as a love story or a study grant. There is no premeditated aspect, no long and linear preparation for exile.

In many clinical stories of exiled foreign patients the idea of leaving the homeland seemed to appear out of the blue and had never been concretely considered before. In the course of therapy one discovers however that, at home, in their native land, these persons had always felt out of place, not in tune with a cultural and family ambience that was too limited. They had always been restless and finally found an answer in exile. These patients also suffer from nostalgia, but at the same time they face the challenge of integrating into a new country, learning the language, trying to understand the people and the culture. How many new things to discover and learn! And this is just what the *puer* wants: novelty, risk, possible failure. The difficulty and the concreteness of life in exile force the *puer* into a confrontation with the *senex* aspect. Often the experience of exile helps the *puer* to accept the fact that the past is irreversible, that roots have to be set somewhere, to commit to reality.

The *puer*'s spiritual search, the search for a father – or in the concrete case of an exile, for a new "fatherland" – can then take place.

The history of psychoanalysis and literature is full of examples of exiles who managed to continue on their road and go on with their spiritual search notwithstanding difficult conditions of life. One example among many is a citation from Hermann Broch's autobiography. Broch, author of *The Death of Virgil*, was born in Vienna in 1886 and at the age of 54 chose to become an exile in America, where he continued his artistic activity and where he died in 1951. He writes that he always felt that from the beginning his emigration was an enormous existential enrichment, a gift, so to speak, that destiny had given him for the last part of his life, to the point where he ardently desired to collect as many experiences as possible, information on new human constellations, environments, quality and structure (Broch 2002:51).

The temporal dimension of exile

At first sight exile seems to be purely a problem of space. If only the exile could return to his homeland, his feelings of isolation, uprooting, of being far away, would cease and he would no longer be tormented by the suffering of return: in other words, nostalgia. To recover, all one has to do is return home.

Paradoxically, this is not at all the case. One can talk about a "nostalgic space" whose principal characteristic is that it cannot be interchanged with any other place. Jankélévitch (1988) talks about a sort of "pathetic geography" and a "mystical topography" where all that is needed to set off memories and the interconnected images is the name of the native city. Sometimes nostalgia for one's country of origin is objectively difficult to understand. Think for instance of a person who comes from the North and who is in exile in Capri, missing his gray skies. Or the Jew who escaped the Holocaust and who feels nostalgia for Germany. Everyone has a place or site of their own on this "passionate world globe," to which his desire is directed.

Kant in "The Irreversible" spoke of persons who, afflicted by nostalgia, return to their place of origin, are disappointed and attribute this to the fact that everything has changed there. But in reality what these persons long for and can no longer find is their youth, their lost childhood (Kant 2006). See Jankélévitch's (1974) meditation on this in *L'Irreversible et la nostalgie*.

What is truly irreversible is time and the changes it brings about. Even if the exile or the traveler returns to the point of departure, in the meantime he himself has grown older. While in his idealized vision the lost homeland and himself are always the same, returning he must take account of the years that have passed, not only for himself but also for the dearly desired place that will really have changed, or that no longer corresponds to what it represented in his imagination.

For Jankélévitch the real object of nostalgia is not absence opposed to presence, but the past in relationship to the present. Since the present time of "exile" is a provisional life – a necessary and painful intermezzo – it is never accepted as definitive, is never experienced completely. The exile oscillates between the past, idealizing his native place, and the future seen as his only hope and the illusion that it can alleviate what is unsupportable: the present time of exile. As Jankélévitch puts it, the real remedy of nostalgia is not going back in space but moving back towards the past in time.

The passing of time, aging, accepting the idea that time imposes limits and that it is no longer possible to realize all we dreamed of, create enormous difficulties for the *puer* who lives in a sort of atemporality, in a state of continuous waiting and transitoriness that makes it difficult or even impossible to live in the present, consider reality, accept the inevitable changes or the end of all things. The suffering of the past and the hope for the future create the lack of a present. The *puer* who always seems to be on the move from one place to another, from one undertaking to another, one project to another, basically uses these activities to conceal his difficulty in accepting change. He is, actually, marked by a great immobility. The nostalgia of the exile has its roots in the lack of the capacity to live in the present that implies the acceptance of the past with all its transformations.

What is irremediable about this type of exile is not simply that of having left the homeland, but of having left it so many years ago. While what the exile hopes to find again is his place of birth, the place he left behind, what he is really looking for is "the young man he was when he lived there."

Puer personalities, so skilful in constructing a way of life where the space– time dimension, the continuity, order and limits are criteria that seem to be foreign to their world, do everything they can to avoid returning to their nostalgic space. The entire purpose of their life is to wander, to be without roots and a home that would give them cause for their insatiable nostalgia, for the suffering of return. Returning would put them face to face with the world of the *senex*, too close to temporality.

The feared contact with temporality, confrontation with the "elusive flow of time," also brings them face to face with the "infinite otherness of every being," because every being and every thing in every moment becomes another by itself, changes, like the homeland and them themselves.

Thus the illusion of a "spatialization of time" that then shows itself to be a "temporalization of space" (Jankélévitch 1988) forces confrontation with suffering and disappointment, but at the same time offers the possibility of an encounter with reality and with themselves.

In conclusion, let me return to the question in the title: exile: an impossible return? As I have tried to show, there are two different psychological ways to live the experience of exile connected to the two different faces of the *puer*.

If exile is connected to the aspect of the *puer* that desires only to return to the mother, concrete or symbolic insofar as mother-country, then the return is impossible because of the irreversibility of time.

If on the other hand exile is lived as the aspect of the *puer*'s spiritual search then the problem of return is different. It is a return to one's roots to find one's own Self, anew. This search is possible in exile, and in many cases it is the condition of exile that favors the search for one's Self.

References

Broch, H. (2002) *Autobiografia psichica* (R. Rizzo, ed.). Bologna, Italy: Il Capitello del Sole.

Hillman, J. (1967) "Senex and Puer", in *Eranos Jahrbuch*. Zurich, Switzerland: Rhein Verlage.

—— (1973), "The Great Mother, her son, her hero and the Puer" in Berry, P. (ed) *Fathers and Mothers*. Zurich: Spring Publications.

—— (1974) "Pothos: the nostalgia of the Puer Aeternus", *Loose Ends*, Zurich: Spring Publications.

—— (1979) "Puer wounds and Ulysses' scar," *Puer Papers*. Dallas: Spring Publications.

Jankélévitch, V. (1974) *L'Irreversible et la nostalgie*. Paris: Flammarion.

Jung, C.G. (1952) *Symbols of Transformation. Collected Works*, 5. London: Routledge.

Kant, I. (1789) "The irreversible", in *Anthropology from a Pragmatic Point of View*. Cambridge: Cambridge University Press, 2006.

Prete, A. (1988) "Nostalgia. Storia di un sentimento", in A. Prete (ed.), *Nostalgia*. Milan: Raffaello Cortina Editore.

Von Franz, M.-L. (1970) *Puer Aeternus*. New York: Spring Publications.

Chapter 14

Places of healing

Riccardo Mondo

From the beginning I felt the Tower as in some way a place of maturation –
a maternal womb or a maternal figure in which I could become what I was,
what I am and will be.

(Jung 1961:252)

In the early 1990s I entered a psychiatric hospital, my first as a psychologist.
It was a theatrical vision: men and women walked aimlessly up and down in
a narrow courtyard framed by four tall walls, occupying all the available
space. Others, seated at the sides in white smocks, were camped there waiting
for their turn; curiously, a gate opening onto a garden seemed permanently
closed.

This place was a non-place, a deposit for cast-offs and fragmentations
that I found particularly upsetting, not so much for the psychiatric illnesses
it contained, nor for the suffering of those men. At the time I wasn't able to
define what was happening to me in any other way; I only wanted to go away
from a place I later learned to love. My first rehabilitation intervention was
to convince the community to leave that gate open. Beyond the gate one
could see a dense wood, and this marked the beginning of the transformation
of the "place."

An experience in an institutional psychiatric facility set off an analogous
reflection on places of healing. It was a place full of *pothos*, of lack, where the
furniture was uncared for and insufficient – it was hard to find a chair – and
the faces of the workers seemed to be transformed when they checked in; they
somehow had to share this decadent fate and conform to their surroundings.
Yet individually they were sometimes endowed with true compassion and
top-class professionalism.

In analytical spheres as well, particular attention has been given to places
of healing. More than once I noted that excellent colleagues in the field who
were skilled in penetrating the meanderings of the unconscious psyche paid
scant attention to what their analytical studios looked like, yet this material is
of prime importance in the development of their patients. As the years passed

I realized that this was not a sporadic or marginal aspect but reflected an unconscious area in psychological training, rehabilitation and therapy. It is evident in the lack of attention paid to the psychic quality of the environment in which the therapeutic exchange takes place, to the bio-psychosocial identity where healing is done, to an awareness of the "soul of the place."

The tower

In ancient Greece it was customary to dedicate steep cliffs, unapproachable springs or woods and crossings to gods, demons or nymphs. These personifications and the stories they inspired were related to the specific qualities of the place. The wanderer who passed by had to honor the powers present, be sensitive to the soul of the place and what characterized it, making it suitable for one purpose rather than another. In the same way, the Romans would choose a place where a fort was to be built, around which they then traced a circle with a plow. At the center of this circle they dug a hole – *fundus* – in which to make sacrifices to the gods before building the fortress. We know that some places had to be avoided; others were beneficial and at times healing. It is of interest that there were often places for representation and collective catharsis near the places of healing. These are just a few examples of what happened everywhere on the earth. For thousands of years mankind lived in profound harmony with mother earth, on which he depended in every moment of life. In every place there are traces of the story of this process, gratitude expressed in various forms and tales in which horror is mixed with amazement. It is the story of mankind, its accomplishments and its hazards, from the growing importance of our species to the progressive differentiation, and the consequent *opus contra naturam* that has made our life on this planet as we now live and know it.

In a conversation with the architect Carlo Truppi, James Hillman traced the consequences of this process for Western man. He noted that Newton and Descartes contributed to the loss of the soul of place in the unlimited uniformity of the *res extensa*. This leads to an absolute and progressive psychic blindness to anything considered external to the subject: the roads, the metropolitan environments, the cities, the houses. Today man tends to dominate the environment, exploiting it without ever asking what has no voice: *do you agree to the use I want to make of you?* A plant, an animal, an inanimate object on the other hand cannot answer, nor defend itself from our abuses.

A small digression in this direction is that of calling attention to that unhappy cohabitation with other living beings grouped together in the generic term of "animal." Jacques Derrida discusses it, reproposing after Adorno a critical and deconstructive ecology that reconsiders the dominion of man over nature that has become *man against nature*. After Kant, Derrida notes, there is no longer compassion between man and animal, no affinity or contact. "The Kantian feels only hate for man's anomalies. More precisely this is his taboo." There is not enough space to analyze the consequences for the cohabitation among living beings on the planet, but one cannot gloss over the importance of re-educating ourselves to the fact that we belong to the *Anima Mundi*. In this sense psychoanalysis appears to pay little attention to systemic and environmental affiliations and their consequences.

Carl Gustav Jung was beyond the pale in structurally reconnecting the individual psyche to the collective system of affiliation, as proposed in his theories on archetypes and the collective unconscious. The extent to which Jung's existential vision separated him from his Viennese colleague Sigmund Freud comes to the fore when one reads Jung's autobiography – *Memories, Dreams, Reflections*.

The lifestyle of the two founding fathers was different: the souls of the Seestrasse in Kusnacht-Zurich and even more of Bollingen were completely different from that of the Berggasse in Vienna where Freud lived and had his practice. The two masters, for the development of their psychological thought, drew intellectual energy from different environmental substrates.

The problem of the point at which the author's psychobiography merges with his theories has been long debated, especially in psychological theory.

In "The environment: our mother earth" Jean Pearson (in Christopher and Solomon, 1999) affirms that the time is ripe on a collective level for the use of the individuative metaphor proposed by Jung. Remember that for Jung individuation marks a process by which to heal the fracture – necessary in differentiating man from mother earth – between the male sphere of the conscious and the female sphere of the unconscious. I agree with the author that we are not suggesting a romantic return to Nature, but rather a conscious integration of the opposites present within each of us.

In Jung's proposal the therapist's individuative search takes on pivotal importance: in the objective psyche of which man is part, the ego can or cannot harmonize with a transpersonal Self, but an ego not in tune with transpersonal needs remains insufficient.

To counter the criticism frequently raised of the presumed intellectualism of Jung's theory, based on his indisputable erudition, reference can be made to his search for the essential in daily life, to how attentive he was to the material. In this sense, the Tower Jung built seems to express factually the tension of his individuative search.

Attention to the symbolic power of place is also present in his oneiric odyssey, becoming an element that inspired his theoretical construction:

I was in a house I did not know which had two stories. It was "my house."
I found myself in the upper story, where there was a kind of salon furnished with fine old pieces in rococo style . . . But then it occurred to me that I did not know what the lower floor looked like. Descending the stairs I reached the ground floor. There everything was much older . . . I

came upon a heavy door, and opened it. Beyond it, I discovered a stone stairway that led down into the cellar. Descending again, I found myself in a beautifully vaulted room which looked exceedingly ancient. Examining the walls, I discovered layers of brick among the ordinary stone blocks, and chips of brick in the mortar. As soon as I saw this I knew that the walls dated from Roman times ... I discovered a ring [in the floor]. When I pulled it, the stone slab lifted, and again I saw a stairway of narrow stone steps leading down into the depths ... I descended ... in the dust were scattered bones and broken pottery, like remains of a primitive culture. I discovered two human skulls.

(Bennet 1985)

Jung had this dream while he was visiting Freud at Clark University and, as he confessed to Bennet over forty years later, "it was then, in that moment, that I had the idea of the collective unconscious."

Reading the chapter "The Tower" in his autobiography *Memories, Dreams, Reflections*, in which Jung tells us of his personal adventure of building a place-other, symbolically connected to the Self, what strikes one is the active search for environmental harmony. The construction of the Tower represented for Jung a material condensation of his scientific research, "a confession of faith in stone." He was to write that "without my earth my work would not have been born," and he defines the place that guarantees him that esthetic and natural harmony to become "what I was, what I am and will be. It gave me a feeling as if I were being reborn in the stone ... In Bollingen I am in the midst of my true life, I am most deeply myself. Here I am, as it were, the 'age-old son of the mother.'" It is interesting to observe how Jung "the architect" developed the construction of the work in conformity with his psychic becoming and the fundamental moments in his life. He built the first round building in 1923, two months after the death of his mother, and he completed his "work in stone" in 1955, a year after his wife died. "Earlier, I would not have been able to do this; I would have regarded it as presumptuous self-emphasis. Now it signified an extension of consciousness achieved in old age" (Jung 1961:251–252).

Jung seems to propose a psychological model that looks for harmonies and resonance within himself, and between himself and the environment, as a condition of therapeutic intervention.

In this sense, Jung's Tower appears as the place from which to begin for a reflection on the places of healing and their fate.

Promoting health

Today there is much talk of promoting health, a term that in recent years has been used increasingly, replacing the obsolete term of "prevention." Talking about it has served to shift the axis of the intervention to a search for "well-being" as a daily positive practice of life rather than focusing on prevention of the illness. It can be affirmed, briefly, that satisfying the needs for adaptation and individuation, this search for well-being, as a profound matrix, should orient any type of intervention, whether therapeutic or rehabilitative.

But in speaking with those who should be promoting this, working in hospital, rehabilitative or educational institutions – in other words, moving around in the places of healing in which this promotion of health should be practiced – a profound perception of psychological disharmony and anesthesia often takes over. Can well-being be promoted in these places?

In these conditions, what existential nourishment can we offer those who hand over to us the wounded in soul? And if this condition is so obvious, why are these facts so ignored?

On the other hand, the World Health Organization (WHO) definition of health is "a state of physical, mental and social well being and not only the absence of illness or infirmity." Therapeutic and/or rehabilitative intervention is therefore allocated to the individual who suffers from any type of illness and is meant to restore or put him in a condition to regain a proportion of normal well-being.

In this case, promotion of health is oriented to situational mechanisms of adaptation of the subject and on how they can possibly be improved, by broadening and modifying them.

This first element in promoting health aimed at helping the subject overcome the existential crisis determined by the illness is certainly fundamental. It is however incomplete and insufficient unless it is set into a holistic perspective which has its rhizome in Greek culture.

The Platonic dialogue on Beauty, in *Phaedrus*, teaches us the foundations of a holistic paradigm, in particular in this dialogue:

Socrates: And do you think that you can know the nature of the soul intelligently without knowing the nature of the whole?
Phaedrus: Hippocrates the Asclepiad says that the nature even of the body can only be understood as a whole.

Therefore Plato is an initial advocate of the holistic method, reproposed throughout the centuries in any number of variations, and he reminds us that one can attempt the cure only by looking for the totality of the being. This cure of the totality was sought in the temple of Asclepius, a place considered sacred, where the healing of the soul was practiced together with the healing of the body, and where various methods of psychological incubation and catharsis prepared the individual for the healing experience. Therefore today, with the elements of magical thinking that nourished the age-old holistic vision erased from our aims, one can in effect speak of its cultural reinterpretation.

The well-being of the operator

If we succeed in imagining that the rehabilitative event between an operator and a patient is a field of intersubjective interaction – determining a continuous constructing of identity – the logic of rehabilitation is put in a different perspective in which seeking the well-being of the operator–patient relationship, and not only of the patient, becomes essential.

This means a radical and systematic approach to the well-being of the operator, no longer seen as an accessory to the rehabilitation project; it means facing problems such as "burn out" and "mobbing."

The great number of professional pathologies of this sort to be found in all kinds of institutional contexts and in all the caring professions is unquestionably a sign that focusing attention on the operator's rehabilitative activity with regard to the patient, a residue of the 19th-century "acting on the other," has been a complete failure. Even so, attention to well-being in the therapeutic relationship is still seen as a sort of deluxe accessory.

We must therefore set ourselves the crucial question of how someone who is not oriented to a constant search for a state of personal well-being can help those afflicted with an identity malaise to achieve or rediscover "a state of physical, mental, social well-being" – as defined by the WHO.

How can operators of this sort "promote health"? The communications systems existing in many work groups are there for all to see. How can the psyche of a man who is suffering be supported if the relational context itself is suffering?

This problem is important and concerns everyone. It cannot be solved simply with the aid of new rehabilitative techniques.

With regard to promoting health, the well-being of the patient and the well-being of the operator must be looked after. Above all, though, it is necessary to think of working for the well-being of the operator–patient relationship.

I wish to say a few more words on this concept of searching for the well-being of the operator to avoid any narcissistic interpretations. How can the search for the individual well-being of the operator be reconciled with his constant contact with suffering, with pain and with mutilation, not to mention the likelihood of the patient's death?

Imagining the most disparate pathologies rooted in the body, the attempt to flee from suffering is absolutely human and understandable. It is only in embracing a metamorphic perspective in the relationship of assistance, and in overcoming the inner scission between "ill" and "healthy," that the suffering of others can be accepted without jeopardizing the well-being of the operator. Hillman says, "If you drive out the devil you also drive out the angel. From here the sacrality of the incurable ward, for hell is also part of the vision of God." Here is the metamorphic element: in the anomaly, in the disorder that suffering entails and provokes, "the mission is changed into a transformation, not of the disorder, but of my norms of order" (Hillman 1985; translated from the Italian by transl.).

In establishing a relationship with the illness, it is not a matter of instituting schools of suffering, but of creating spaces that that do not inhibit the symbolic, imaginary and linguistic powers of the patient.

Brunella Antomarini (2001) has written an interesting article on the philosophy of medicine. Culturally a phobic attitude towards the communication of suffering predominates, despite the fact that "the sick person is hoping to meet someone with whom to share the pleasure of a knowledge of self, the healthy aspect of meeting another person who can tell him what to do if and when he finds himself fighting pain or a threat of death from illness" (Antomarini 2001:75; translated from the Italian by transl.).

What struck me particularly in this excerpt from Antomarini was the way in which she spoke of knowledge of self through the illness. "In the same way," she continues, "a psychic and linguistic and intersubjective place can be imagined in which with time a complex of complicated emotions and feelings connected to the illness is formed, so that one can comprehend the transformation of one's personality from that tradition" (Antomarini 2001:76; translated from the Italian by transl.).

Here, incidentally, I ask myself how we can work concretely to create this place in which emotions of this sort can be made manifest. Not a relationship, but a place!

The community aspect of the place of healing

Another essential point concerns the capacity to re-evaluate the collective dimensions of the place of healing, so that the therapeutic act favors the well-being of every social actor involved. The re-evaluation of the collective dimension is particularly necessary in psychotherapeutic workshops, where, as it is often a person-to-person relationship, there is a tendency to consider the place of healing a sort of "free zone" not subject to the social regulations in force in the outside world. The place of healing in this sense would become overly private, ignoring the fact that the principal aim of every psychotherapy is to overcome the subject's rigidly narcissistic perspective opening a window on the world. Aristotle said that man was by nature a political animal, instinctively part of the multitude that formed the polis, but the current cultural direction of mass individualism produces individuals who behave according to the following convictions: everyone has their own values and they cannot be contested by others; the moral ideal is allegiance to oneself and self-realization, without taking account of a super-individual horizon. We have a new "technological prehistoric" collectivity with an extremely low level of social participation and a search for immediate satisfaction of driving needs, as if there were no historical memory and consequently no future to realize. Members of the current society do not dream of merging into the arms of mother earth, like their ancestors. In a postmodern manner they live completely separated from nature, losing the natural human impulses towards all forms of parenthood, always less desired, in a new condition in which technology hypertrophies the ego, expanding it still further.

I therefore ask myself: what can professionals do who have not been educated by the institution, and in the institution, to adequately use the parental function in communicating with their users? It is obvious that "educating the health operator to parenthood" must become the primary objective in promoting health (Hillman: 1988).

In *Psiche e Techne*, Umberto Galimberti (1999) affirms that in our technological era, identity is dissolved in professionalism, and therefore character becomes a manifestation of capabilities. Identification with one's capacity as an efficient individual is what mainly determines our individual subjectivity.

Giuseppe Ruvolo (2000) goes deeper into the theme. He notes that in social institutions individuals are reduced to their "curricula," and in an impersonal relationship of this type the Other – the one who cures or rehabilitates – can be manipulated at pleasure. The author observes that "the diffusion of this cultural model generates the process of progressively turning the social institutions into business firms . . . that lose their character of anthropological community." The consequences of this development are there for all to see, and the rampant dehumanization of the social institutions comes to the fore, in which the fact that the healing project cannot be submitted to a "rehabilitation assembly line logic" is often ignored. When this ideology becomes all-absorbing in the rehabilitation spaces, it is actually deleterious with regard to the human aspect of the treatment. In the therapeutic project the element of relationship must become real and spontaneous: a central element, integrated with the shared and renewable meaning of the project as a whole.

> Attention to the collective dimension of living together makes the world a livable place for man, and stops it from being transformed into a despairing "inferno."
>
> (Ruvolo 2000; translated from the Italian by transl.)

This is why the place of healing that is blind to the collective dimension creates unnecessary hardships for the operators without achieving its objectives.

Participating in the *Anima Mundi*

A promotion of health that is truly holistic requires a definition by the community that goes beyond the perception of the community space as exclusively relative to a group of persons who share ideas, projects, objectives of rehabilitation. What has to be done, as mentioned in the first part of this chapter, is to hypothesize a community vision that re-evaluates the environmental element, educating us to participate in the *Anima Mundi*.

> Now, becoming aware does not mean only becoming aware of our feelings and our memories, but above all reawakening our personal responses to the beautiful and the ugly. We have become unaware of the impact of the world: with regard to the world our souls seem to have been walled in.
>
> (Hillman, 1999:10; translated from the Italian by transl.)

The way in which places of healing are imagined, how their purposes and values are planned, including the sense of esthetic perception, contribute to redefining the identity of all those involved, patient and/or operator.

What is really wrong with our rehabilitative spaces is that we have, unconsciously, lost our sense of esthetic participation in the environment, have forgotten that the external world must be perceived with all our senses. Paying attention to the esthetical aspect has nothing to do with a superficial interest in the esthetic qualities of the institutional reality. The question concerns the relationship between esthetics and ethics and a unification of the two, in the wake of the classic tradition, in the sense of *kosmos*: an "orderly harmonious system."

In his most recent work, Hillman states that:

> When we pay particular attention to what the other person, place or thing needs and wants, we are carefully observing and perceiving with (esthetic) precision and we are also making concessions to the requirements of the other (ethics).
>
> (Hillman 2004:53; translated from the Italian by transl.)

Therefore in a search for this orderly harmonious system, does participating in meetings or seeing patients in spaces and ways that are inadequate, and with little attention given to sounds, smells and the habitability of the rehabilitation rooms, mean very much?

Entering a rehabilitation or educational room trying to "identify the space," to feel how it was built, furnished, experienced, will provide us with a great deal of information as to how the rehabilitation project was planned, or what points the project missed out on.

Often the esthetic care devoted to the space prepared to receive a guest is a measure of his importance. With what care do we prepare our therapeutic room? Does the way in which we create our places of healing, planning them with a view to feasible objectives, help in redefining the identity of every individual – patient and/or operator – involved?

Considering the world as foreign to the therapy, and the individual as the only possible site for therapeutic work, is a mistaken concept. We are fine-tuning the instruments we use in working with the individual who suffers from malaise, we are improving them, we are hyperspecializing, but we run the risk of remaining indifferent to the environment in which all this takes place.

References

Antomarini, Brunella (2001) *Per una bioestetica. Note sull'arte della medicina.* Rome: Manifestolibri.

Bennet, E.A. (1985) *Meetings with Jung: Conversations Recorded during the Years 1946–1961.* Einsiedeln, Switzerland: Daimon.

Christopher, E. and Solomon, H. (eds) (1999) *Jungian Thought in the Modern World.* London: Free Association Books.

Derrida, J. (2003) *Il sogno di Benjamin.* Milan: Bompiani.

Galimberti, U. (1999) *Psiche e techne.* Milan: Feltrinelli.

Hillman, J. (1985) "Disturbi cronici e cultura", in *Trame perdute.* Milan: Raffaello Cortina Editore.

—— (1988) "Dallo specchio alla finestra: curare il narcisismo della psicoanalisi", in P. Aite and A. Carotenuto (eds), *Itinerari del pensiero junghiano.* Milan: Raffaello Cortina Editore.

—— (1999) *Politica della Bellezza*, Donfrancesco, F. (ed), Bergamo: Moretti & Vitali.

Jung, C.G. (1961) *Memories, Dreams, Reflections.* London: Random House.

Mondo, R. (2003) *L'arco e la freccia. Prospettive per una genitorialità consapevole.* Rome: Edizioni Magi.

Ruvolo, G. (2000), in R. Mondo (ed.), *Atti del convegno Identità e Lavoro*, Progetto Multiregionale Horizon Self-Prop sud. Catania, Italy: Cooperativa Il Girasole.

Chapter 15

Body and psyche
Compenetration of opposites

Silvia Tomasi

In his essay "Mind and Earth," Jung commences by explaining that, in the Chinese animistic doctrine, there is a *shen*-soul of the sky and a *kwei*-soul of the earth. Since, Jung continues, we Westerners know nothing of the substance of the soul, we must content ourselves with speaking of only two of its apparent aspects.

In the place of a *shen*-soul we might speak of a first principle without cause, and instead of a *kwei*-soul we might consider it the result of a system of cause and effect.

It is this second aspect that Jung uses as his point of departure in this essay. He considers the soul (mind) a reality resulting from a cause-and-effect system, and in particular "a system of adaptation determined by the conditions of an earthly environment." Moreover, in order to really understand "the dependency of the soul on the earth," he explains how it is necessary to probe more deeply the problem of the structure of the unconscious, since this is a fundamental part of the soul even if it cannot be directly observed like the phenomena of consciousness.

The contents of the unconscious are the archetypes, which in turn constitute the foundations of the conscious soul, i.e. its roots in the earth and the world. The archetypes as such are not represented by contents since an original image can be determined by a content only when it is conscious. The archetype is rather the form of a content, or better, as Jung explains in other writings, a *facultas praeformandi*, an *a priori* possibility of representation. On one hand the archetype predisposes for a strong instinctive prejudice, and on the other it is one of the most effective aids for instinctive adaptation.

> They are thus, essentially, the cthonic portion of the psyche . . . that portion through which the psyche is attached to nature, or in which its link with the earth and the world appears at its most tangible. The psychic influence of the earth and its laws is seen most clearly in those primordial images.
>
> (Jung 1927:31)

The archetype, then, is to be seen as a fragment of non-rational prehistoric psychology.

Jung continues in his explanation, but what I wish to focus on here is this inseparable bond between the soul as a tangible non-material part of us and the earth seen as matter and body, i.e. between our energetic aspect and our material aspect and our relationship with the world. Matter and energy, in fact, have a relationship of dynamic interdependence and are called by different names depending on the spheres in which they are taken into consideration.

Many at this point agree that the body is more than just a container and the soul is not just something "contained," but that these two entities are in a condition of mutual interdependence and that the existence of the one is conditioned by the existence of the other. The body can be the origin but also the epiphenomenon of what is happening in the soul. In like manner, what happens at the level of our psyche, conscious and unconscious, produces effects on the body that can be directly observed to varying degrees.

Western culture has accustomed us to think of the mind and the body as two distinct and separate entitities, with autonomous lives which, in rare cases, can cross over.

Traditional medicine is one of the clearest symptoms of this sharp scission between mind and body or, as Jung says, between soul and earth. In medicine, the concept of illness is connected to the demonstration that a multitude of signs and symptoms, objectively observed and referred by the patient, are significantly correlated to objectively demonstrated anatomical–pathological lesions or biological alterations. It is a system based on "scission": the illness is dissociated from the sick person, the psyche is dissociated from the body and, lastly, all the organs are dissociated from the body with each considered a system to itself. This makes it difficult to see the person as a totality or to consider body and psyche as dependent on each other in a mutual relationship of dynamic interdependence. In this context, however, practical experiences more sensitive to integration, in orthodox as well as in so-called alternative medicine, are not lacking.

I would like to cite as example the case of Anna, a little girl eight years old, whom I got to know well.

Anna, a lively, sociable child, had been in analysis for several years on account of emotional problems resulting from the separation of her parents. When I first met Anna she had an allergy and her hands itched terribly, with lesions that often bled or produced serum. This was discouraging for the child because she had to wear cotton gloves when the allergy was most acute, with contingent problems, primarily of a social nature. Although the analysis was going well, as the therapist confirmed, and despite the untold number of dermatologists consulted, the allergy showed no signs of abating. At a certain point Anna's mother decided to take her to a so-called "alternative doctor" who specialized in nutritional and homeopathic therapy. The new doctor immediately put Anna on a strict diet for around a month and a half and prescribed a few homeopathic medicines to relieve the peak moments. With the new cure Anna was healed and she felt reborn; her social problems disappeared as well as the emotional tension that stopped her from serenely facing the psychological conflicts expressed in the allergy. In therapy too she is now taking big steps forward.

This example not only illustrates how our body and our soul are inseparable, but is also an invitation not to consider introspection and analysis as the only key to the solution of all problems, underestimating other ways of integration.

In Chinese traditional medicine based on the ancient Tao tradition, health is not simply the absence of illness, as in Western medicine, but is a dynamic equilibrium: an objective not always easy to achieve. Every organ has an energetic meridian of its own that runs throughout the body and "communicates" with the other meridians. The illness is therefore interpreted as a striking symptom of a pre-existing energetic imbalance. Prevention is an extremely important aspect in the search for and the maintenance of the energetic equilibrium, both within the individual and in his relationship with the universe. Energetic imbalance can subsequently take concrete form in symptoms we call psychological or physical. For example, a depressed or anxious mood can be interpreted as the consequence of an energetic stasis at the level of some of the organs or meridians. In particular I would like to mention the therapeutic *qigong*, a Taoist discipline that is part of traditional Chinese medicine. There were already experts in the practice of this discipline between 800 and 400 BC, such as Laotze, whose writings revealed the bases and fundamental principles of this discipline, as well as some of the specific techniques. With these as a point of departure many people in Chinese society have helped this discipline to develop enormously in the past 2000 years.

There are two broad categories in traditional Chinese medicine, by now well known also in the West: the *yin* and the *yang*, interconnected. Since the two are in close relationship, a deficiency or lack of *yin* always implies an excess of *yang*. The two categories are inevitably joined in the body, where they support each other. The principle regulating the activity of the *yin* and *yang* is that of the complementarity of opposites which attract and penetrate each other, transforming themselves mutually in time. The *yin* represents what is tender, female, soft, obscure, passive, etc.; the *yang* what is hard, male, rigid, luminous, active, etc. The *Taiji tu* symbol indicates the union of *yin* and *yang*: the white part is the *yang* and the black the *yin*. The black and white dots indicate that the *yin* and *yang* do not exist as absolutes but as relatives, since when the *yin* achieves its maximum manifestation it always contains the seed of the *yang* potentialities and vice versa.

Upon observing this representation closely we discover that the two principles are always present in every part. If we decided to cut the *yin/yang* circle like a pie, we would discover that every slice contained an always variable proportion of *yin* and *yang*. *Yin* and *yang*, therefore, are to each other as day is to night: two inevitable aspects that form a *unicum*. Everyone can distinguish day from night, but no one can perceive the exact moment in which day passes into night.

The following example will make the discourse more concrete on a medical level.

Let's take hypertension: traditional Chinese medicine describes it as a deficiency of *yin* and an excess of *yang*. In particular the blood, controlled by the liver, has a deficiency of *yin* activity, therefore its *yang* activity is in excess and moves upwards. This rising causes a series of specific manifestations, among which emotional tension stands out and which, in turn, can aggravate the conditions of deficiency of *yin* and excess of *yang*.

In other words, in this type of analysis the psychological aspect as well as the physical aspect of *yin* is taken into consideration. There are manifestations of a psychological type, therefore of *yang*, that lead to pathology, and traditional Chinese medicine tries to regulate both aspects to create an equilibrium. Thus if the imbalance of the physical aspect has been redressed, the same must be done for the psychological aspect (*yang*), guaranteeing a more successful therapy.

In particular there are *qigong* exercises that serve to cure both aspects of the disease and, therefore, are particularly effective. Pharmacological therapy in treating prolonged cases of hypertension does not bring the two aspects back into balance and its effects are therefore limited.

Jung, in his studies of numerous aspects of Eastern thought, had intuited the profound bond between body and psyche. His seminar in the autumn of 1932 on the reawakening of the *kundalini* is of particular interest here. In these lectures Jung thoroughly analyzed the symbolic valence of the *kundalini* and its progressive reawakening through the *chakra* which, from the lowest to the highest, represented a progression towards individuation.

The *chakra*s are the "energetic vortexes" that attract universal energy to nourish the various levels of the energetic field, and to connect them with the physical body. Their proper functioning is of fundamental importance because they influence both the psyche and the body: an unbalanced flow of energy can cause disturbances or alterations of a psychological nature and, consequently, the onset of various pathologies on a physical level.

Jung points out that in tantric teaching there is a stimulus to "produce a personality": something that, in Western terms, could be explained as a "stimulus or instinct towards individuation." The *chakra*s are therefore new worlds of awareness, of natural growth, one above another, rooted in the body. Each of them has a precise physical location and is associated with an element.

The first chakra is the *muladhara*, located in the perineum; it is associated with the earth and represents our being rooted in the world, our roots, our consciousness. The second chakra, *svadhistana*, is associated with the sea and represents the unconscious. The symbolism associated with this chakra is that of baptism through water: after having been under water, one comes out regenerated or destroyed. Its color is flame red. Once the danger of being destroyed has been overcome, one attains the third chakra, *manipura*, which means "the fullness of the jewels" (lustrous gem): it is the center of fire, the place where the sun is born, and is localized in the solar plexus, the center of the abdomen.

According to Jung, this site is highly important because it is the first psychic site of which we are aware. There was a time in which awareness was so obscure that men only noted things that disturbed their intestinal functions; anything that did not affect them was inexistent.

With the passage to the fourth chakra, the *anahata*, located in the heart and associated with air, the real process of individuation begins because we no longer identify with our emotions but start to establish a difference between ourselves and the exploding of our passions. It is the beginning of the discovery of the Self. From *manipura* we cross the threshold and pass from the visible and tangible things under the diaphragm to those almost invisible and intangible above the diaphragm – the psychic facts that are in the *anahata*. The *anahata* then is the region of feeling and thought. The heart is characteristic of feeling, the air of thought. One can learn something with the head but one does not remember it unless one takes it to the heart. Curiously, in English too when one memorizes, one "learns by heart."

In the *visuddha*, the fifth chakra, we reach the heart of the ether, and go beyond the effective vision of the world – the *visuddha* is the world of ideas and abstract values. This chakra represents a recognition of the essences or psychic substances as the fundamental essences of the world in virtue not of mere speculation, but of a real experience.

Jung attempts to describe the sixth chakra, *ajna*, through symbols. It resembles a winged seed, but is in any case completely outside our grasp. In this chakra one is nothing but psyche: a psyche that contains us and in which the ego disappears completely.

Lastly Jung mentions the seventh chakra, *sahasrara*, the lotus of a thousand petals, of which however it is impossible to speak because it is a purely philosophical concept that has no substance for us and that is far beyond any possible experience. While in the *ajna* there is still the experience of the self that is apparently unlike the object, the God, in the *sahasrara* there is no experience because it is one, without a second: it is *nirvana*.

In these lectures Jung compared the process of the reawakening of the kundalini to the process of analysis. In the same way in which through the practice of kundalini yoga the mind must be purified, so in analysis the patient must succeed in admitting that there is a possibility that something is moving in his mind independently of his will. Only through the knowledge of one's dark parts and one's passions can one achieve a superior level of awareness and integration. It is interesting to note that for Jung, awareness of one's emotions and the unconscious begins, in the story of man, above all from physical sensations and, thanks to them, acquires a particular force and concreteness.

Returning to Western culture, the psychiatrist Ludwig Binswanger, in line with the teachings of philosophers such as Husserl and Heidegger, demonstrated the dual heritage of a Cartesian matrix on which the scientific approach of many 20th-century psychiatrists and psychologists is based. The psyche is thus reduced to the level of things in the world and stripped of its uniqueness.

Binswanger incorporated Husserl's phenomenological method and Heidegger's philosophy so that the peculiarity of human existence was no longer seen as an abstract subject or a natural object, but as a concrete man within the world, in which to orient and plan one's life.

Just as Husserl had affirmed that consciousness is intentional, Heidegger affirms that man is his world. Heidegger identifies an awareness of his being as the specific trait of man. To be human means, then, to be in the world, to express globally one's presence in a worldly project and set oneself in relation to the things and the other existences. Man therefore is not a thing of the world, but he for whom a world is disclosed. For Binswanger, presence is above all human totality that includes in itself soul and body, consciousness and unconsciousness, thought and action, emotivity, affectivity and instinct. It is the facticity of existence as it is disclosed in its here and now, opening itself to the world, but also projecting it as its own.

The world in which a presence lives is, in some way, the expression of what it is. At this point studying the body and the soul in relation to time and geometric space no longer makes sense: in fact the body is no longer only the material body described by anatomist pathologists, but "the body *I* mean it to be." My space becomes the space where *I transcend myself*; my body is there as far as my presence, my intentionality, extends.

> Every act of mine in fact reveals that my presence is corporeal and that the body is the modality of my appearance.
>
> (Galimberti 2002; translated from the Italian by transl.)

In his book *Il Corpo*, Galimberti explains how in archaic society the body was expressed in its ambivalence as "fluctuating significance." In fact the body was a symbol – *sym-bállein* in Greek means to compose – and therefore contained in itself those ambivalences, those discordant meanings such as good and evil, true and false, beautiful and ugly, that later, through the various historical periods and the different cultural codes, separated. In the course of Western history the body has been submerged by the signs with which science, economy, religion, psychoanalysis, etc. have described it. The ambivalence of the body and all that it signifies and involves cannot be salvaged until this dual Cartesian attitude that separates the *res cogitans* from the *res extensa* is overcome, the psyche of the body, the soul of the earth. The body described by the anatomist-pathologists is the body reduced to only one of its multiple aspects.

Galimberti, as Binswanger had already done, invites us to rediscover the meaning of true psychology meant to study man in his oneness and uniqueness, and stop dividing him.

In this sense the error that psychology is still facing is that of attempting to place itself on the same level as the natural sciences, destroying its specificity: in other words, the significance that every phenomenon has for the individual who feels, thinks and perceives. In this sense, Jung's call to recognize the interdependence of soul and earth is also a warning to keep in mind the delicacy of the equilibriums that connect the individual to his environment. And this holds true not only for psychology.

References

Binswanger, L. (1945) *Il caso Ellen West e altri saggi*. Milan: Bompiani, 1973 (Italian transl., ed. C. Mainoldi; original title: *Der Fall Ellen West*).
—— (1978) *Being-In-The-World: Selected Papers of Ludwig Binswanger*. East Longmeadow, MA: Condor Books.
Ellenberger, H.F. (1970) *La scoperta dell'inconscio*. Turin, Italy: Bollati Boringhieri 1976 (Italian transl. by W. Bertola, A. Cinato, F. Mazzone and R. Valla; original title: *The Discovery of the Unconscious*).
Galimberti, U. (2002) *Il corpo* (p. 15). Milan: Feltrinelli.
Jung C.G. (1964) "Mind and Earth" in *Collected Works* 10. London: Routledge & Kegan Paul.
—— (1967) "Commentary on the Secret of the Golden Flower", in *Collected Works*, 13. London: Routledge & Kegan Paul.
—— (1996) *The Psychology of Kundalini Yoga: Notes on the Seminar Given in 1932* (ed. by S. Shamdasani). Princeton, NJ: Princeton University Press.
Li Xiaoming (1997) *I Stage di qi gong medico*. Bologna, Italy: Compositori.
Li Xiaoming et al. (1998) *Medicina cinese e biocibernetica*. Bologna, Italy: Compositori.

Chapter 16

"Every rose is telling of the secrets of the universal"

Symbols and the natural world

Luciano Perez

In his *Dream Analysis*, Jung tells of a conversation he had in Africa with his Somali caravan driver:

> He belonged to a Mohammedan sect, and I asked him about Khidr, the god of that particular cult, and the ways in which he appeared. He said: "He can appear as a common man, like me or that man over there, but you know it is Khidr, and then you have to go immediately to him, take both his hands, hold them tight and say: 'Peace be with you' and he will say: 'Peace be with you' and all your wishes will be granted. Or he can appear as a light, but not the light of a candle or a fire, but like a pure white light, and from this you recognize that it is Khidr." Then, bending over, he picked a blade of grass and said: "Or he can appear like this."
>
> (Jung 1984)

Jung repeats this story other times – both in *Visions* and in the essay "Concerning Rebirth," where he fully examines the figure of Khidr – which demonstrates how strongly the affirmation of the Sufi caravan driver struck him. Khidr, affirms Jung, is an image of the Self, and therefore the Self can also appear in a humble blade of grass, as green as Khidr himself: "the green one," as his name says.

The concept is treated less simply, although much more elegantly, by the great mystic and supreme Persian poet, Rumi, in his *Mathnawi*, from which I borrowed the line for my title:

> Every rose that is sweet-scented within, that rose is telling of the secrets of the Universal.
>
> *Mathnawi*, I, verse 2022

A few lines above, we find:

> These trees are like the interred ones: they have lifted up their hands from the bosom of the earth.

They are making a hundred signs to the people and speaking plainly to
   him who has ears [to hear].
With green tongue and with long hand [fingers] they are telling secrets
   from the earth's conscience [inmost heart].
[Sunk in earth] like ducks that have plunged their heads in water, they
   have become [gay as] peacocks, though [in winter] they were [dark and
   bare] as crows.
If during the winter He imprisoned them [in ice and snow], God made
   those "crows" like "peacocks" [in spring].
Although He put them to death in winter, He revived them by means
   of spring and gave [them] leaves.
   . . .
God, in spite of them, caused [spiritual] gardens and plots of sweet
   flowers to grow in the hearts of His friends.

Ibid. verses 2015–2121

Further poetical testimony to the divine presence in nature appears in
the writings (1861) of Gustav Theodor Fechner, the father of scientific
psychology:

I was walking outside one lovely spring morning. The fields were green,
the birds were singing, the dew sparkled, mists were rising; a light settled
over all things, transfiguring them; it was nothing but a small fragment of
the earth . . . yet it did not seem to me only so beautiful, but so real and
evident that it was an Angel, and such a gorgeous Angel, so fresh, so like
a flower, and at the same time so concrete and undisturbed moving in the
sky . . . that I asked myself how men could be so blind as to see in the
Earth nothing but an arid mass and to look for the Angels above or next
to the void of the sky, and not find them anywhere. Yet an idea like this
will be thought of as a fancy. The Earth is a globe, and whatever else it is,
is to be looked for in the natural history cabinets.

(Fechner as cited in Corbin 1986:265; translated from the
Italian by transl.)

These affirmations make one reflect on the natural order of things, in particular on the theme that I wish to deal with: symbols and the natural
world. With its reference to the angel, the celestial messenger, the quote from
Fechner can be seen in relation to the dream: the message *par excellence* that
reaches us from the unconscious.

The plant world

I believe that when a symbol that has to do with the world of nature – plant,
animal or mineral – appears in a dream, it often has a specific profound

meaning and should be considered with special attention. Explanations might be poetical, or mythical and therefore archetypal, as exemplified in this delightful passage from the *Mathnawi*:

> First he [Man] came into the clime [world] of inorganic things, and from the state of inorganic things he passed into the vegetable state.
> [Many] years he lived in the vegetable state and did not remember the inorganic state because of the opposition [between them];
> And when he passed from the vegetable into the animal state, the vegetable state was not remembered by him at all,
> Save only for the inclination which he has towards that [state] especially in the season of spring and sweet herbs.
> Like the inclination of babes toward their mothers: it [the babe] does not know the secret of its desire for being suckled.
>
> *Mathnawi*, IV, verses 3637 ff.

The plant symbol here does seem to have a sort of particular status. More than once in his *Collected Works*, in particular in the essay "The Philosophical Tree," and in the seminars, Jung insists on the singularity of the plant symbol and in particular on how it differs significantly from the animal symbol. While the reproductive cycle of the animal is connected to the seasons and is therefore natural – it can run and move from one place to another – the plant is rooted in the earth, a helpless victim or in absolute harmony with nature.

The animal is literally less attached to the laws of the earth. The life of man is even more detached since we have built ourselves an artificial world far from the laws of nature and with a completely different rhythm. The life principle of the plant is much closer to the laws of the earth than even the animal (Jung 1997, vol. 1).

This is why Jung compares the tree when it appears in a symbolic form, as in a dream, to spiritual growth, whether it is the tree of yoga or of life, the tree turned upside down, the cosmic tree or whatever. Another interesting aspect is the spiral-shaped form of the plant's growth, typical of the psychological growth and maturation of the human being, which is not rectilinear but in the form of a spiral or a labyrinth, as in the coming closer to the Self. Another important characteristic of this type of growth is that when an insurmountable obstacle is encountered, we can grow above it, and, if dealing with it directly is an impossible undertaking at that time, we can calmly wait until an interior growth overcomes it.

When a natural element of a symbolic nature appears in a dream, it brings to mind the craving or urgent need to take a walk in the woods or in the country, to go to the mountains, to take a swim in the ocean, felt by those who are too immersed in that artificial world, far from the laws of nature and with a completely different rhythm, of which Jung speaks. Getting away from it all means getting back to nature, a ritual and life-giving immersion, a lustral bath that puts us back in touch with ways of life and laws older than our very young civilized world. It is a getting back in touch with the ever new and fresh sap of ancient roots, a sort of psychotherapeutic session that, unfortunately, often costs us dearly, the high price once more imposed by our civilization, with the interminable and inevitable traffic jams that those fleeing or returning to the large cities get caught in, or the piles of trash encountered on our beaches or in our woods.

Despite all this, however, if people became aware of the profoundly symbolic nature of these "escapes" and their implicit ritual character, things might change. They might feel themselves less "weekend convicts" forced into doing things they would gladly avoid, giving that liberating and sacral character – now praised to the skies in a degenerated form by a flood of illustrated glossy brochures – a chance to develop.

Obviously in dreams the natural world can present itself in any number of ways, but there are also magical moments in daily life in which one can "see" and in which the natural element reveals its hidden symbolic meaning. There is no need to seek out majestic landscapes, an impressive mountain, a breathtaking waterfall or an age-old venerable tree, imbued with a sense of the numinous for everyone. The humblest of things can also put us into contact with that eternal world of symbols. I would like to give you a personal example.

The vision of the portulacas

There are many flowers and decorative bushes in the inner courtyard of the house where I spend most of my summer vacations. Among them is a large terracotta bowl full of brightly colored portulacas – yellow, red, white, purple, orange – that sometimes mysteriously mix together in the sense that the flowers on the same plant have different colors. Portulacas are humble plants, once used to border the cement sidewalk between the farmhouse and the farmyard. One fine day – or rather, one terrible day – on getting up after a sleepless night due to the death of a dear friend, I went into the courtyard. I somehow felt a need for a contact with nature. I was gloomy and pensive; my thoughts were black and vague regarding, obviously, death, pain, loss and mourning. Suddenly the first rays of sun struck the bowl of portulacas. These flowers close at night and as soon as they are touched by the sun they open so fast one can actually see them opening. The plant that had seemed to be dead with its unopened flowers was transformed into a mass of brilliant colors, a true hymn to the sun and life, sung by a plant with the vibrations the blossoms transmit to the air as they open. It was what the neo-Platonist Proclus Diadochus described with regard to the prayer of the heliotrope in his treatise on the hieratic art of the Greeks, when he noted that the heliotrope moved in accordance with the sun and the moonflower with the moon, with all things singing, as only a plant can sing, a hymn to their king.

The power of the symbolic aspect of this natural and common event made an extraordinary impression on me. It had taken me back to those roots and those eternal laws thanks to which we recover the deepest meaning of events, that sense that transcends the pain of the ego or that, at least, sets it in a cosmic context that gives it a different meaning. Even if the ego continues to suffer, in me, so to speak, the *Tao* – that elusive concept to be captured using only intuition and sentiment – has been re-established: "the Mystery, the supreme Mystery, the doorway of all prodigies," as the *Tao Te Ching* so marvelously says (Duyvendak 1953). The opening of those modest brightly colored little flowers opened "the doorway of all prodigies" for me, where all my gloomy intellectual ruminations on "understanding why" had done nothing but add darkness to darkness, pain to pain, gloom to gloom.

The capacity of capturing the symbolic aspect of natural elements has to be cultivated, just as one educates oneself to so many other things. When a lady told Picasso that she didn't understand his art at all, that for her it was like something written in Chinese, the painter ironically but wisely answered: "you'll just have to learn to do it!" This obviously means cultivating the function of intuition, the function that lets us see "beyond" an object – its potentialities – or to see "through" it. By using a suitable faculty of perception, it is a process that takes the forms back to their archetypal core.

It is this use [of a suitable faculty of perception] that is designated [in Persian] with the technical term *ta'wil*, that etymologically means "to return or revert" the data to their source, to their donor. In order to do this they must be retrieved [on the level of] each fact of the being or level through which they had to "descend" to reach the way of being that corresponds to the level where our ordinary consciousness becomes evident. These levels must be made to symbolize each other.

Therefore the *ta'wil* is *par excellence* the hermeneutics of the symbols, the *exēgēsis*, the acquisition of the hidden spiritual meanings . . . without the world of Hūrqalyā . . . that is, without the *mundus imaginalis*, the world of the imaginal Forms, where the imaginative perception is active, able to penetrate the hidden meaning because it transforms into symbols the material data of the external story; in other words, without the "imaginal story," whose happenings take place in Hūrqalyā, a *ta'wil* would not be possible. The *ta'wil* presupposes the superposition of worlds and interworlds, as the correlative foundation of the plurality of meanings of one selfsame text.

(Corbin 1979; translated from the Italian by transl.)

The animal world

Nature is *naturally* boundless (the pun is intended), and perhaps, within the limits of human knowledge, infinite. A naturalist could spend his whole life examining, identifying and classifying the individual elements of just one small lawn and it might not be enough. It is staggering to think of the extremely small, the sub-atomic particles, the wavelengths, etc. or the extremely large, the galaxies, interstellar spaces . . . Even keeping to a much more "human" dimension, the variety of natural elements that can appear in a dream is endless. Take, for example, the animals. Particular attention must be paid to every animal that appears in a dream since, as Jung warns us:

> Any animal, taken psychologically, represents instinct in man. In as much as we are automatic and instinctive we are nothing but animals, because our behaviour is then in no way different from that of an animal. We can say it is an instinct whenever an animal occurs in a dream, but, mind you, it is always a very particular instinct, by no means *the* instinct. A lion or a huge snake would mean something quite different.
>
> (Jung 1984:513)

There can be more varieties of animals in dreams than in any real zoo, or fantastic and bizarre equestrian circus. Yet each time what needs to be reflected on is the specific animal that appears in the specific dream of that specific patient. While this is common knowledge, at times indolence or the feeling that he is wasting time keeps the analyst from examining more in depth elements that could be invaluable, on the basis of a supposed "knowledge" that in fact is at times more paltry than an abridged version of the most banal dictionary of symbols. I'm not saying that, no matter what, one must undertake a frantic "search for the archetype," which would risk being misleading, as shown by a humorous anecdote in Charles Baudoin's book *Introduction à l'analyse des rêves.* If I remember rightly it was the story of a patient who had dreamed that he was eating fish, and a fishbone got stuck in his throat. He couldn't swallow or spit it out. The "archetype hunter" therapist gave the patient a long, learned and elaborate interpretation of the fact that he had not succeeded, as he should have, in accepting the Christian message (the fish is a common Christian symbol indicating Christ himself, since the letters ιχθύς, fish in Greek, are an acronym for Jesus Christ, Son of God the Savior). Actually, as was later discovered, perhaps by another therapist, the dream alluded to a much more prosaic problem: the patient had not succeeded in "swallowing" his humble origins; his mother was a fishmonger in a local market.

Difficulties can arise when, as happens all too often, the patient is unable to provide associations regarding the animal that appeared in his dream. Here too Jung comes to our help:

> When we are interpreting with no regard to the patient's associations, we must be careful to be as naïve as possible, to have no prejudices in connection with the associations. Take the thing literally, concretely.
>
> (Jung 1984:513)

Taking things literally, concretely, is a priceless rule, but it is not always easy to follow. The analyst – and in this case the more cultured person is handicapped – may very well project an unconscious amplification of his own on a specific dream image. It seems almost superfluous to stress the importance of being acquainted with the social context (as in the case of the fish) and the cultural context of the patient. I remember a delightful case my friend and colleague Neil Russack mentions in his particularly enjoyable and invaluable book, *Animal Guides*, concerning a dragon. The lady in question was quite old and depressed, but despite this there was something spring-like about her. She had dreamed of a small, very elegant dragon who was sleeping curled up inside her ear. When he woke up, she would die. To our Western minds, used to seeing the dragon as a great devouring enemy to be killed in a face-to-face encounter or, if we are swallowed, from the inside as in the hero myths or Campbell's monomyth, it sounds like an extremely threatening dream. Actually this old lady was drenched in Oriental culture. She lived in San Francisco and her parents had collected Oriental art, of which she too was particularly fond. For her the dragon therefore meant something completely different.

The fact that the little dragon chose to reside in her ear was very reassuring. It felt safe there and comforted her. She said that her ear represented her connection to others. "All myths spring right there in my ear. It's very ancient. The dragon represents fire and gold associated with meditation. It's part of my personal mythology." When she was younger she had been in Jungian analysis, and knew that the Chinese dragon was a life symbol and its undulating movement and firepower invested all things with dynamic energy. Safely tucked in her ear, it supplied her with a vital relationship to her psychic life (Russack 2002).

The mineral world

With regard to the mineral world, one of the natural elements that often appear in dreams is the precious stone. The symbolic relationship of the precious stone or jewel with the Self is too well known to discuss at length here. A few specific examples are, however, of particular interest. One of my patients dreamed that she was wearing a round pendant, with emeralds at the center and a single diamond on the outer edge, therefore eccentrically placed. The dream seemed to indicate a particular psychological situation: the center of the pendant was teeming with precious green stones, the color of growth as well as hope. It is the color of nature that wakens in spring, of renewal, of a new birth after the dark and cold of winter. The diamond perplexed me. As the most precious stone, it should be at the center, representing the center itself, the heart, the organizer of the vital forces represented by the green stones. Did not being – or not yet being – in that position imply a center paradoxically peripheral, that had not found its right place? This interpretation, though, raised doubts: was I perhaps unconsciously being influenced by a sort of fascination with symmetry and therefore a static and fixed vision? Might the unconscious, with this image, perhaps be transmitting the paradoxical idea that the center "had" to be in the periphery, where it could circulate, providing a more dynamic image, or that the center had to be in a mediating position between the living internal forces, the green stones, and the world? It is clear that only subsequent dreams could solve my doubts, putting it all in the right light.

What I said above still holds in the case of other mineral elements. Humble stones as well as jewels can convey invaluable information. The great lesson of alchemy, *Psalm* 118, verse 22, tells us that "The stone the builders discarded became the corner stone." Moreover, simple pebbles from the lake where what allowed Jung to get back in touch with his own internal creativity, which in turn permitted him to undertake his *nekyia*: the radical, and fundamental, confrontation with the unconscious.

Jung tells us that it was for him a decisive moment in his destiny, but he gave in only after much opposition: it was a painful and humiliating experience to feel forced to play like a child. Even so, he began to pile up suitable stones, picking them up from the lake, both on the shore and under the water, and began to build.

How many stone quarries, deserts of sand or rock are encountered in dreams, and how many hidden corners that need to come to the light they show us! I remember the dream of a deeply depressed patient that represented the beginning of a dramatic and sincerely unexpected improvement. After a limited number of vague dreams, which however seemed to represent her inner situation – dark, gloomy, with an absolutely indeterminate subterranean space in which she remembered only that there were spider webs, bones and trash, and which were monotonously repeated, making me feel, like the patient, desperate and impotent – suddenly a vivid image: a desert, or better a desert zone in full sunlight with a column standing upright. The image left a strong impression on the patient and, obviously, also on me. Finally a sign: someone had been there and had left that sign, unquestionably human. A center? An *axis mundi*? A point of departure or of arrival? A milestone? The indication of a sacred or at least important place? Right then it didn't matter much. In that "mineral" dream a spatial organizer had appeared; an organizer of that inner and indefinite space, without form. It was an image in which both I and, much more importantly, the patient became powerfully aware of the numinous aspect. It was a moment of creation, as when in a South American myth the bird Icanchu found a piece of charcoal in a world destroyed by an unimaginable fire and began beating it, dancing to the rhythm. Then, as Sullivan says, "at the dawn of the New Day, a green shoot sprang from the charcoal drum and rapidly flowered like the Primigenial Tree, the Tree of the initiatic trials at the Center of the World. From its branches blossomed the forms of life that flourish in the New World."

Two examples

As I approach the conclusion of this chapter I should like to propose two more examples of how a natural symbol, or better a natural element raised to the status of symbol, can appear in dreams. In a certain sense we are going back to the beginning, because in both cases they are plants and moreover because, in searching for the title and subject matter for this chapter I was inspired – perhaps on account of that "mysterious inclination for plants" that takes place "above all in springtime and with its flowers" – by the sight of wisteria in bloom. This in turn called to mind the dream of one of my patients, of many years ago. It is the "wisteria dream."

The dreamer was a man of around 35, highly intelligent, whose serious pathology had however held him back from developing as he could have. He was tortured by what came close to being a delusion, of being poisoned. He lived in a tiny apartment. Although he owned other much more comfortable apartments in the same building, he had chosen this tiny one because he could more easily seal off with tape and other much more complicated expedients (he had a brilliant technical degree) all cracks through which, at night, miasma, radiations, gas or any other invisible impalpable elements might enter and which, once asleep, he could not control.

The situation was tragic and serious. He did have a social and working life, but it was extremely limited. As for a love life, it was absolutely zero. Sexually there were sporadic mercenary relationships leaving intense and absurd aftermaths of guilt.

I have to say, without boasting, that the analysis was successful. He moved, and his delusional fears disappeared with the exception of antennas (radio and television; luckily those for cell phones didn't exist yet): fears the patient justified scientifically, and which proved later to have a scientific basis. He even had a girlfriend, with whom he established an excellent affective and sexual relationship.

At this point the drama: the girl left him. He returned to me fearing a relapse, and I must say I agreed with him. And then the laconic wisteria dream: "I was looking at a wisteria plant in a large vase." Despite the fact that he was well acquainted with nature, although it was more of an agricultural type, he considered the wisteria a flowering plant like any other and was therefore greatly surprised when I told him that the wisteria blossomed twice, in spring and in summer. Even though he wasn't aware of it, his observant mind, so attentive to natural phenomena, had probably unconsciously noted and registered this.

His unconscious had therefore proposed an extremely significant therapeutic image. The wisteria with its flowers, and his feelings to which their extraordinary delicacy probably also referred – the type of flower, color and fragrance – could blossom again. The interpreted dream resolved his fears of a relapse, and even if the wisteria suggested, at least to me, that he still needed support like the plant, he went away happy and content. "I feel healed," he said, and I never saw him again.

The second example concerns a dream of mine, of many years ago in August 1977. It was the first time I took part in the Eranos meetings, which I already knew thanks to their yearbooks. I recall it in the words I have already used on another occasion.

The meetings of that year had a title that for me was emblematic: "the sense of imperfection." One night, after one of the talks – by James Hillman – I had a dream in which I saw a stretch of the hill road I took every day to go to the meeting, with a sharp curve, a real turn, over which a majestic plane tree loomed. It was a cross between an American plane and an Oriental plane, the dwelling of a *genius loci* – the same *genius loci ignotus*, I suppose, to which Olga Fröbe-Kapteyn, the founder of Eranos, erected a cippus – that presided over and "ruled" that curve. The air was humid and fresh, renewed as after a thunderstorm – a common event in that season.

It was a truly emblematic dream of the impression those encounters left with me. Since then I have continued attending those meetings, which represented an enormous cultural and psychic enrichment, in addition to being the place where I made deep, lasting friendships.

A real turn presided over by a tree – a tree that, as I mentioned at the beginning, represented the image of psychic growth for Jung, slow and spiral-shaped – joining in itself East and West, not only in the concrete aspect of the comparison between Eastern and Western symbolism, the initial purpose of the Eranos conferences, but also as an image that anticipated a deeper synthesis, a real *coniunctio oppositorum*. A plane tree, moreover, like a serpent that changes its skin every year – and as such a symbol of death and resurrection – visibly recreates its bark.

Conclusion

I hope I have succeeded in demonstrating that symbols drawn from the natural world, in a world increasingly devoted to appearance, to pretence and psychic manipulation, and in which the sphere of the ether no longer permits us to see the crust of the earth and its angelic qualities, represent a powerful call to those natural truths, rooted and profound, that are "the Mystery, the Supreme Mystery, the doorway of all prodigies."

References

Baudoin, C. (1950) *Introduction à l'analyse des rêves*. Paris: L'Arche.
Campbell, J. (1949) *The Hero with a Thousand Faces*. Princeton, NJ: Princeton University Press.
Corbin, H. (1979) *Terre céleste et corps de résurrection*. Paris: Buchet/Chastel.
—— (1986) *Corpo spirituale e terra celeste*. Milan: Adelphi.

—— (1989) *Spiritual Body and Celestial Earth*, Bollingen Series XCI. Princeton, NJ: Princeton University Press.

—— (1998) *Alone with the Alone: Creative Imagination in the Sufism of Ibn 'Arabi*, (trans. R. Manheim). Princeton, NJ: Princeton University Press.

Duyvendak, J.-J.-L. (ed. and trans.) (1953) *Tao Te Ching*. Paris: A. Maisonneuve.

Fechner, G.T. (1861) *Über die Seelenfrage, ein Gang durch die sichtbare Welt, um die unsichtbare zu finden*. Leipzig, Germany: Amelong.

Jung, C.G. (1940) "Concerning Rebirth", in *Collected Works*, 9i. London: Routledge & Kegan Paul.

—— (1984) *Dream Analysis: Notes of the Seminar Given in 1928–1930* (ed. W. McGuire). London: Routledge & Kegan Paul.

—— (1997) *Visions, Notes of the Seminar Given in 1930–1934* (ed. C. Douglas). Princeton, NJ: Princeton University Press.

Rumi, Jalalu'Ddin (1982) *The Mathnawi* (trans. R.A. Nicholson). London: Gibb Memorial Trust.

Russack, N. (2002) *Animal Guides in Life, Myths and Dreams*. Toronto, Canada: Inner City.

Sullivan, E.S. (1988) *Icanchu's Drum: An Orientation to Meaning in South American Religions*. New York: Macmillan.

Chapter 17

"Gentle Action"

Environmental sustainability in soul and earth

David Peat

My journey to the Italian village of Pari has been a strange one, not so much guided by logical decisions and careful planning, but rather pushed along by quirks of fate and intuitive promptings. I was born in Liverpool, England where I developed a passion for science, or more exactly for experiments carried out in a shed behind my home. In retrospect, what I was doing was closer to alchemy than to any formal scientific endeavor. I was experiencing the way matter changes; its essential mutability as metals dissolved in acids, solutions crystallized, solids transformed into gases and gases condensed into liquids.

Later, science became more formal, first at university and then as a theoretical physicist with the National Research Council of Canada in Ottawa. I don't think I was ever a "good scientist," in the professional sense of someone who finds a problem to work on and then pursues it relentlessly while publishing a series of research papers with an eye on promotion. Once I realized what lay at the bottom of a problem, or how to solve something, I lost interest. What was more fascinating to me was the question that lies beneath the question, and then the question that lies beyond that.

Later, my meeting and friendship with David Bohm, who had been a student of Oppenheimer and a friend of Einstein, made me even more sensitive to the claustrophobic atmosphere that exists in universities and institutions where people are rewarded for working on small problems and fragmentary pieces of knowledge. In the end I left the world of institutions because I needed to pursue ideas on my own. I wanted to investigate ideas from quantum theory to Carl Jung, from chaos theory to contemporary art.

It is said that if you want to learn something there are only two ways: one is to give a course; the other is to write a book. And so I began to write books, in part as a way of investigating new questions in depth, in part to address that younger self who had spent hours in the local public library learning about the world.

Freedom from the restraints of an institution certainly brought economic anxiety – an anxiety that remains to this day – but it also brought great freedom. To begin with I could pursue immensely satisfying dialogues with artists, writers and actors. In so many ways the artist and the scientist complement each other in the different visions they have of the world and the inner nature of matter.

Thanks to a friendship with Leroy Little Bear, a Blackfoot lawyer, there was another series of conversations. Because of this and other contacts I made trips to the Blackfoot reservation in Alberta and attended the ceremony of the Sun Dance. A series of meetings led to more formal roundtable dialogues that Leroy and I organized between Western scientists and Native American elders. Deep exchanges became possible as we explored each other's worldview and sense of culture.

To the Blackfoot, and others who speak the Algonquin family of languages, the world is flux and change. Nothing is permanent; a person's name can change during their life, as do the names of animals in various seasons. The ancestors had made compacts with the energies and spirits of the land, and with the keepers of the animals. And, since all is flux and change, these compacts have to be kept alive through ceremonies of renewal – the pipe smoked each dawn, the Sun Dance, the opening of sacred bundles and constant prayer.

One of these prayers is to "all my relations" and expresses the relationship of each person to the group, to the birds and animals, to the rocks and trees, to the beings who live under the earth and in the sky. In all things relationship is the key.

If there is flux there is also the circle of time in which the seasons return. Individuals are not trapped in the linear time of progress but can move more freely. This worldview is reflected in the verb-based Blackfoot language, one that does not use our familiar subject–predicate structure in which the world is constructed out of nouns ("things with names") that are connected via verbs ("interactions"). It is no wonder that Newtonian physics proved so powerful in the West, for its description of a world in terms of objects in interaction fits perfectly into most Indo-European language forms.

An example of another way of speaking about the world is found in a dictionary that had been translated by Jesuits in the 18th century. It gave the meaning of a long Blackfoot word as "the sorcerer sings to the sick man" – "sorcerer" being the way Jesuits perceived traditional medicine people. In fact the world was a verb that expressed the act of singing and included, as modifiers, one who sang and one who received the song. But this latter description is again to fall into our trap of reifying the world into objects in interaction. More properly it would say, "singing is going on" or "the song is singing itself." Ironically, this notion of a world of connections and relationships, a world in constant transformation and flux, has been rediscovered at the leading edge of modern physics.

While I could never enter the world of the Blackfoot – I could not speak their language and, as they say, "our science IS our language" – at least I could begin to see my world through their eyes. Our Western minds are hard, they say, and I could see how our ways of thinking so often do violence to the world around us. Many of us have lost a deep relationship to the sacred nature of the land. I also contrasted our hierarchical organizations with the way decisions can be made spontaneously when each person knows when "the time is right" and "the place is right." I saw how this emerged out of constant contact within the group through what we would call gossip, the way decisions were reached by people sitting in the traditional circles around the fire, and how deep feelings could be expressed in the circle, yet did not appear to be held at an individual level but experienced in depth by the whole group; not held onto, but constantly arising and dying away.

All this caused me to wonder about what we could call the "Western" or "European" mind. Had it always been this way? Or are we at root, as the Native Americans say, all indigenous people? These thoughts were in my mind when I left Canada and moved to the medieval hilltop village of Pari.

Canada in many ways had been an ideal country. It is clean and relatively free from crime. It has a fine record in international relations and peacekeeping. It is strong on civil rights and education, and had a health system the world could envy. On the other hand North America, of which Canada is a part, is a center of consumerisms. Many families have two or more cars. On the street where we lived every house had its little patch of grass at the front and every family owned an electric or gasoline powered lawn mower (and a snow blower in the winter) that could be brought out for ten minutes once a week. But why was this necessary: why not cooperate, why not share? Canada is a vast and clean country, yet we knew that the meat we ate and the milk we drank was filled with hormones and antibiotics.

So much of this is connected with the goal of endless progress and profit, and with the desire to control the world around us. But the more affluent we became, the less a sense of community, of people who greeted each other by name, existed. We were all moving too fast; we had no time to reflect on where we were going, or the enormity of the decisions that society, science and technology were taking in our name.

There were other issues that concerned me, such as the way modern society has specialized and fragmented. In modern universities knowledge is pre-packed in neat, watertight compartments. To think widely or hold conversations across disciplines is taken as a mark of the intellectual dilettante. In so many ways the universities are failing to be the preservers of culture, to inspire young minds to a deeper vision of the world and to encourage wisdom.

Would Pari be any different? For the first two months in the village I did nothing, not even read a book, but simply sat in the sun or did the daily tour. I suppose I was beginning to sense something about the roots of European mind – roots that were much closer to the ground – and of time that was governed by the seasons and the rising and setting of the sun, of the heat in midday that forced people to leave the fields and go to their homes until the late afternoon.

I began to see that Pari was like an extended family with complex inter-relationships of cousins between various families that went back for generations. Like any family, there was a sense of closeness, but also of friction – people who would not speak to each other or who recalled slights and incidents from the past. At times it almost seemed to me that there was no need to adhere to a persona – the mask we sometimes wear in public – in such a community, for people were simply who they were. After all, so many had gone to school together and watched each other grow up, adopt a nickname and have families of their own. And speaking of families, how refreshing it was that our grandchildren could simply go out of the front door and play with others without having to worry where they could be or what harm could come to them – for everyone knew everyone else and would look out for children at play or old people who had become confused as to where they were.

The way we see the world influences the way we act and how we behave to those around us. And the way we see the world is influenced by what we have been taught – in explicit ways via schools, television and newspapers, and in more subtle ways via the whole underlying culture, sets of relationships and the particular way we use the language we speak.

As time went on I began to see that this field of knowing and seeing was subtly different in Pari than in a city like Ottawa, New York or London. Pari had been around since medieval times and there had probably been Etruscan settlements over two thousand years ago. For centuries the village had been self-sufficient for its food, clothing from wool and ginestra (broom – a shrub used for weaving), fuel from the surrounding woods, rocks for building, clay for bricks and even iron and copper from local mines. For centuries the land had provided everything. There was little need for money and economics could be based on barter. But then in the late 1950s and 1960s a migration to cities began, and Pari's population fell from around one thousand to two hundred. Shops and bars closed; the population aged. Working the land from dawn to dusk no longer looked so attractive. With the coming of running water, electricity, television and automobiles people needed money and the community could no longer function on a barter system. In such a world, what future would there be for young people?

When we arrived in 1994 one way of life was ending and another, filled with uncertainty, was beginning. What path would villages like Pari take as they entered the 21st century? We could see the final members of countless generations working in the olive groves, vineyards and gardens. Who would take their place? Who wanted to continue such hard labor – a city dweller from Los Angeles, perhaps, who wanted to give up the rat race and turn to the land for a deeper sense of connectedness? Would the community die a slow death like many other small villages across Europe? Would it turn into a vacation village, a Disneyland parody of itself, a village filled with life for one or two months of the year and then given over to security patrols and an electronic concierge? Or was a new mixed economy possible – a combination of farming, crafts and electronic work?

At first these were no more than speculations. We were outsiders and had no business interfering in the life of a village where family names went back for centuries. Yet fate stepped in and took a hand. In 1999 I ran a weekend encounter of artists and scientists in the October Gallery, London. It was so successful that it led to an Internet-based discussion forum that asked why the universities and other institutions were not supporting such dialogues, and why so much fragmentation of knowledge continued to persist. Someone offered to support a second meeting on "The Future of the Academy," to be held in London or New York. But why not Pari, I began to think? After all, the Palazzo, formerly a school, had recently been refurbished and was vacant. And so I spoke to Tommaso Minnaci, president of Pari's Pro Loco "Ass.ne Sette Colli," and asked if they would arrange the infrastructure for the meeting – housing, drivers, food, and so on.

And so our first conference took place in October 2000. On the final day all the participants spoke of the deep need they had felt for a meeting such as that. It was important to come together in a safe and congenial place, to be totally free to speak openly, to be made to feel so welcome by the local people and not to have some pressing agenda hanging over them. This fostering of dialogue must continue, they said, and it should take place in Pari. And so the Pari Center for New Learning was born. What is more, the people of Pari told me that they had so much enjoyed having visitors from all over the world that they wanted more conferences.

From that point we have gone from strength to strength, beginning with international conferences and courses. What was totally unexpected was the number of visitors that simply dropped in from all over the world – some quite literally arriving at our doorstep unannounced. They had heard about Pari through a friend, or read about the Center on the Internet, and now they wanted to see what was going on at first hand. Some came for a day or two but many were here for weeks or even several months. As so there was always a stimulating group around our dinner table in the evening. Without ever planning it, we had become an ongoing academy in which new voices were being added to a continuing debate.

We adopted as our motto Carlo Levi's remark that "the future has an ancient heart." Our focus would be "Art, Science, Community and Spirit." We also saw ourselves as occupying the unique position of being both global and local. We are global since each month thousands of virtual visitors come to the Pari Center web site from all over the world. Our physical visitors come from Europe, North America, Japan, Taiwan, Africa, and the Middle East.

These visitors are bringing new faces, new ideas and new attitudes to Pari. Cultural exchange transcends language, as when two Mexican ladies made and cooked tortillas on a Hibachi outdoors, watched by other women in the village. Another Mexican made a traditional Piñata for the children of the village. A man from Jordan sat in the village square smoking a mixture of tobacco, honey and apple in a hookah and offered the pipe around. Probably the most significant cultural exchange comes in the form of music. We have had music from many countries sung and played in the village. From songs on the medieval harp, though Jewish and Arabic songs from Spain, pop and folk music from North America, England and Spain, and on to Bach cello suites.

Exchange is by no means one-way. We are also local because each person is made welcome and feels part of a village whose culture is so strong that it can have a great influence on the way people re-vision the world. As people enter the life of the village, wander the streets, drop into the bar, watch the groups who congregate in the piazza of an evening or the children playing, they slow down, spend more time over their meals and learn how to take things easy.

In this way Pari and the Center can have a profound effect on people. Most enjoy being welcomed and cushioned; just a very few become claustrophic to the point where they must leave. Then there are those special ones who have a life-changing experience in Pari. Maybe it is the spirit of the place with its ancient energy, maybe it is the excitement of the ideas that are discussed round the table, maybe it is simply being able to slow down and stop. Whatever it is, we have had visitors who have decided on a major life change, for example leaving a well-paying job and comfortable lifestyle for something that will bring more meaning to their lives. And people do return to Pari – for weeks, months or even years. Others are inspired to return home and make some positive change within their community.

And what of the influence of our visitors on Pari itself? Certainly it has an impact on the local economy, although for a non-economist like myself this is difficult to quantify. Food is purchased at the local shop, people use the bar and the two local restaurants, empty houses are rented out for weeks or months at a time. During courses and conferences local people are employed as cooks and helpers and a percentage of the money is donated to the village association. But while economics can be important, I believe that more valuable things are taking place. New faces open up new doors; they suggest different possibilities for work, different ways of thinking.

Indeed, the question of social change had also been on my mind when I came to Pari. Back in Canada I had been acting as a consultant for a policy group and, as a citizen, I had followed debates about a host of topics from the "greening of the planet," to the provision of aid overseas. In so many cases it seemed that projects begun with the best of intentions foundered or, worse still, ended up producing unforeseen and undesirable side-effects. Native Americans joke that the very worst words they might hear are "We are from the government. We're here to help you."

It may at first sight seem to be advantageous to "green the planet" and increase food yields in developing countries. But what if the result is a total disruption of social and economic structure? What if that Third World country becomes dependent on the industrialized world for seeds, pesticides, herbicides, fertilizers, and ripeners? It may be a wonderful thing to ship food to poor areas of the world, but what if that food is not part of their normal diet or, in the case of milk, if it is given to children who do not possess the enzymes necessary for its digestion?

Nevertheless policies and programs run blindly on, sometimes doing more harm than good. The root, I believe, lies in the paradigm that, bolstered by science, has persisted for the past few hundred years. It is based on notions of unlimited progress, prediction and control. Organizations make action plans that are supposed to improve or control some system external to them. When things do not turn out as predicted this is considered to be a fault or failing within the system. Something has gone wrong. It must be put right. We must exert control. We must interfere. And if that does not work, then we must exert even more control.

Such a deeply ingrained way of seeing the world can do enormous damage. History has shown the way it has affected environments and ecosystems, societies and traditional ways of living, economics and education, health services and other infrastructures. In this rather mechanistic way of looking at the world, policies and organizations are often more rigid than the very systems they are suppose to help and control.

Thankfully, science has taught us a very important lesson in the form of chaos theory. Natural systems, economies and the complex interactions of businesses and societies tell us that, in principle, we can never have complete information about any system. We must be prepared to tolerate missing information. We may spot a trend or pattern in the fluctuation of the stock market but we will never know the precise value of one stock in 24 hours' time.

Chaos theory tells us that neither can we exercise absolute control. A society, an ecosystem, an economy or a business resides within a complex landscape of flat plains, valleys, mountain peaks, and swamps. There may be regions of this landscape when a system will respond to a corrective push. There will be others in which it is remarkably resistant to all change, and yet others where an intervention will send it into chaos. Then there are those special regions known as bifurcation points where the slightest breath of wind will tip a system into a radically new form of behavior – the so-called butterfly effect.

The role of an effective leader, policy-maker, organization – or even a village like Pari – is not to aim for some preconceived goal, or obey a preset mission statement, irrespective of the terrain it encounters. Rather it is to navigate within this fluctuating landscape and find the place where one is supposed to be – the right place at the right time. This means being open and highly creative. It means operating with sensitivity and courage. I coined a term for this – Gentle Action. It expresses an action that is not imposed from outside but emerges out of the system itself in a gentle and highly intelligent way. Gentle Action is, I believe, the wave of the future, but in the words of

Levy this future has "an ancient heart," for ideas of "right action" go back to ancient India and the wisdom traditions of other cultures.

I said earlier that Pari can have a profound effect on visitors. Let me take one example of this in terms of "Gentle Action." Clare and Gordon Shippey visited Pari to take a course. Their home was a North of England city that was a haven for drug dealers, petty crime and burnt-out cars. By contrast, Pari was a place where people didn't bother to lock their cars, left the keys in the front door and greeted everyone by name. One evening, after watching a video of Pari's September Sagra, Gordon and Clare asked themselves why their own community was so dysfunctional.

On returning home, Gordon did a very simple thing. He knocked on the doors of the houses in his street and introduced himself by name. Soon a neighbor joined him and they went down the street together. The next step was the formation of a local association and a making of a video designed to show the mayor the terrible state of their area. The end result was that a deserted factory, used for drug deals, was boarded up, access roads into the area were blocked to traffic and the immigrant Asian community now worked hand in hand with "white" families. The burnt-out cars have gone, petty crime has almost been eliminated, children are playing on the streets and it is the ordinary people of the area and not the politicians who are running things. In transforming their community the Shippeys also observed an interesting vicious circle: when crime is perceived to be on the streets then ordinary people stay indoors. And when ordinary people stay indoors, crime and drug-dealing flourish on the streets. Yet all of this was transformed by the simple act of knocking on doors and addressing people by their names.

Inevitably things in Pari are also changing – that began with the first car to be seen in the village, with running water in the 1950s, with radio and television. There is a certain irony in a story that appeared a few years ago in the village newspaper. It told of the arduous journey to Grosseto to bring back a gramophone for dancing on St Biagio's Day (the patron saint of the village). It did not mention that at that time there was a flourishing Pari band and today all those instruments are stored away, unused, in cellars.

One visitor noticed that the metal seats on the outskirts of Pari do not, in fact, look outwards to the views of hills, but inwards towards the village. Maybe Pari has always felt itself to be isolated. But now the wider world has entered. It came with radio and television, and now comes through the Internet. Already a group in Pari is exploring the idea of 24-hour broadband via a satellite dish. This opens the possibility for new forms of work and, with a camera mounted in the Piazza, people all over the world could watch the village Sagra. But would this be a cultural exchange of a high order, or simply turning Pari into a village like that of the film *The Truman Show*?

How Pari will change is hard to know. Only time will tell. New faces are seen throughout the year. These are not tourists or sightseers but serious people who have chosen to come to Pari to study and think, and who have a deep appreciation for the village in which they are living. In 2003 the village opened a library of novels and non-fiction – or rather it reopened something that was closed for many years. There has also been talk of creating a museum of photography – a museum of memory – or a museum of artifacts that would tell how people lived a generation or two ago. On Sundays the Palazzo is being used to run groups for the children of the village – stories, crafts, dance and music.

The overall question is whether Pari will be forced to change as a result of outside forces, or whether it can take those forces into consideration and remain master of its own destiny. Change is going to come, and of its very nature some of this will be unpredictable and uncontrollable. And, just as a business must learn to steer its way though a fluctuating economic landscape, so too Pari will learn to survive, preserving what is best and cautiously accepting that which is new and which fits. Maybe there are many places in the world where one could say, "this is a good place in which to live." But with children and grandchildren in Pari it is also comforting to be able to say, "this is a good place in which to live and to die."

Index

Note: *italic* page numbers denote reference to illustrations/photographs.